Develop East 1

MW01169330

Developments in Central and East European Politics 3

Edited by

Stephen White
Judy Batt
and
Paul G. Lewis

Duke University Press
Durham 2003

Individual chapters (in order) © Judy Batt; Frances Millard;
Kieran Williams; Mark Pittaway; Tom Gallagher; Andrew Wilson; Ray Taras;
Petr Kopecky; Paul G. Lewis; Krzysztof Jasiewicz; Klaus von Beyme;
George Blazyca; Terry Cox; Heather Grabbe; Geoffrey Pridham 2003

Published in the United States by Duke University Press, Durham,
NC 27708–0660
and in the United Kingdom by
PALGRAVE MACMILLAN
Houndmills, Basingstoke, Hampshire RG21 6XS and
175 Fifth Avenue, New York, N.Y. 10010

This book is printed on paper suitable for recycling and made from fully
managed and sustained forest sources.

A catalogue record for this book is available from the British Library.

Library of Congress Cataloging-in-Publication Data

Developments in Central and East European politics 3 / edited by
Stephen White, Judy Batt, and Paul G. Lewis.
    p. cm.
Includes bibliographical references and index.
   ISBN 0–8223–3082–2 (pbk) – ISBN 0–8223–3094–6 (cloth)
1. Democracy–Europe, Eastern. 2. Europe, Eastern–Politics and
government–1989. I. White, Stephen, 1945– II. Batt, Judy.
III. Lewis, Paul G., 1945–
JN96 .A58D48 2003
320.94′09171′7–dc21   2003005953

Printed and bound in Great Britain by
Creative Print & Design (Wales) Ebbw Vale

This book is a direct replacement for Developments in Central and
East European Politics 2, published 1998, reprinted four times.

Contents

List of Tables and Figures

ix

Preface

It used to be easy to define 'Eastern Europe'. Broadly speaking, it was a group of states on the far side of what was for many years an Iron Curtain. Many of them bordered on the Soviet Union, and most of them were bound to it by economic and military alliances as well as by a close interconnection at the level of their communist party leaderships. Their fate, it appeared, had been largely determined at the end of World War II, when Europe had been divided – however provisionally – into rival spheres of influence. Yugoslavia had successfully separated itself from the Soviet alliance in the late 1940s, and from the 1960s Albania and Romania were increasingly independent. All the states in the region nonetheless remained under communist leadership, state ownership was dominant, and public life was framed by the requirements of Marxism-Leninism.

The dramatic changes of the late 1980s and early 1990s shattered these earlier patterns, and brought an end to the division of Europe and – at least in its original form – to communist rule. The changes that began in 1989 took a variety of forms and governments changed more quickly than forms of ownership, let alone the habits and practices that had developed over the forty years of communist rule – and in some cases over a much longer period. By the late 1980s, nonetheless, the Central and East European countries were facing a very similar set of challenges. Could they develop forms of rule, including party systems and structures of participation, that could replace the authoritarianism of the communist years? Could they find a balance between effective leadership, often expressed in a presidency, and accountability, typically to an elected parliament? Could they reverse the economic decline of the late communist years, and could they best do so through 'shock therapy' or by a more gradual process? Could they, in any case, carry out programmes of change that had popular support, notwithstanding the sacrifices that were involved and the increasingly difficult position of the elderly, the unemployed and the marginal?

These are just some of the issues that are addressed in this volume of specially commissioned chapters, which (like its predecessors in 1993 and 1998) brings together contributions from leading specialists from both sides of the Atlantic. We begin with a chapter that seeks to define this elusive half-continent, and then in further chapters we consider the patterns of change that have taken place in individual countries or groups of countries. We turn, in the second part of the book, to the framework of contemporary politics: constitutions, leaderships, parliaments, political parties and electoral behaviour. The third part of the book explores the policy process in more detail, looking at the forms it has taken in the economy and in social relations. We examine the complex effects of a growing 'Europeanization' centred around the widening membership of the European Union, and then in a final part we place the pattern of political change across the region within a broader comparative perspective.

Developments in Central and East European Politics 3 is intended, like its predecessors, as a guide to the common patterns as well as individual variety of a group of states that were formerly modelled on the Soviet Union but which are now a distinctive and varied presence within a continent that has been redefining its own boundaries and values. We hope not only our students, but also our colleagues and readers in other walks of life, will find something of value in the result.

Stephen White
Judy Batt
Paul G. Lewis

Notes on the Contributors

Judy Batt is Jean Monnet Chair in the European Integration of South East Europe at the Centre for Russian and East European Studies/European Research Institute, the University of Birmingham, where she teaches Central and East European politics. In 1992–3 she worked on secondment to the UK Foreign and Commonwealth Office. Her main publications include *Economic Reform and Political Change in Eastern Europe* (1988); *East Central Europe from Reform to Transformation* (1991); with Giuliano Amato, *The Long-Term Implications of EU Enlargement: The Nature of the New Border* (1999); and co-edited with Kataryna Wolczuk, *Region, State and Identity in Central and Eastern Europe* (2002).

Klaus von Beyme is Professor Emeritus at the University of Heidelberg, and from 1982 to 1985 was president of the International Political Science Association. His major fields of work are comparative politics (Eastern and Western Europe), and political theory. His recent books include *Transition to Democracy in Eastern Europe* (edited, 1996) and *Russland zwischen Anarchie und Autokratie* (2001).

George Blazyca is Professor of European Economic Studies at the Paisley Business School, University of Paisley, in Scotland. He is a specialist on Polish economic development, and director of the Paisley Centre for Contemporary European Studies. His recent publications include *Poland into the New Millennium* (co-edited, 2001) and *Restructuring Local Economies – Towards A Comparative Study of Scotland and Upper Silesia* (edited, 2003).

Terry Cox is Reader in the Department of Government at the University of Strathclyde in Glasgow. His interests include the sociology and politics of Russia and East Central Europe and he is currently working on a project on interest representation and policy-making in Hungary. Recent books include *From Perestroika to Privatization* (1996), *Hungary 1956 – Forty Years On* (edited, 1997) and *Social and Economic Transformation in East Central Europe* (with Bob Mason, 1999).

Tom Gallagher holds the Chair of Ethnic Conflict and Peace at Bradford University. He has published widely on the role of nationalism in a South-Eastern Europe experimenting with democracy and on individual countries, particularly Romania. *Outcast Europe: The Balkans from the Ottomans to Milosevic: 1789–1989* was published in 2001. His *Distrusting Democracy: Romania since 1989*, was published in 2003, and the same year saw the publication of his *From Tyranny to Tragedy: The Balkans since the Cold War*.

Heather Grabbe is Research Director at the Centre for European Reform, an independent think-tank based in London, and a nonstipendiary fellow of Wolfson College, Oxford University. Her publications include *Germany and Britain: An Alliance of Necessity* (written jointly with Wolfgang Münchau, 2002), *Profiting from EU Enlargement* (2001) and *Enlarging the EU Eastwards* (written jointly with Kirsty Hughes, 1998). She was previously Research Fellow at the Royal Institute of International Affairs and has been a visiting fellow at the European University Institute (Florence), the European Union Institute for Security Studies (Paris) and the Centre for International Relations (Warsaw).

Krzysztof Jasiewicz received his MA in Sociology at Warsaw University (1972) and his PhD at the Polish Academy of Sciences (1976, also in Sociology). He has taught and/or held fellowships at Warsaw University, Harvard, Oxford, and UCLA, among others. In the 1980s, he was a co-author of a series of political attitudes surveys in Poland. Currently, he is Professor of Sociology at Washington and Lee University in Lexington, Virginia, USA, and Research Fellow at the Institute of Political Studies of the Polish Academy of Sciences (ISP PAN) in Warsaw, Poland. He is currently working on a project on religiosity and political behaviour in contemporary Poland.

Petr Kopecky is Lecturer at the Department of Politics, University of Sheffield. He was Research Fellow at the European University Institute in Florence and is currently Research Fellow at Leiden University in the Netherlands. His main research interests include East European politics, political parties, civil society and democratization theory, and he has published widely in journals and edited volumes on these subjects. His books include *Parliaments in the Czech and Slovak Republics: Party Competition and Parliamentary Institutionalization* (2001) and *Uncivil Society? Contentious Politics in Eastern Europe* (co-edited, 2003).

Paul G. Lewis is Reader in Central and East European Politics at the Open University. His publications range over diverse aspects of comparative and East European politics. His books include _Central Europe since 1945_ (1994), _Political Parties in PostCommunist Eastern Europe_ (2000), and an edited work on _Party Development and Democratic Change in PostCommunist Europe_ (2001). His main research interests concern the continuing development of political parties in Central and Eastern Europe.

Frances Millard is Reader in the Department of Government at the University of Essex. Her books include _Embodying Democracy: Electoral System Design in Post-Communist Europe_ (with Sarah Birch, Marina Popescu and Kieran Williams, 2002); _Polish Politics and Society_ (1999); and _The Anatomy of the New Poland_ (1994). She has written widely on communist and postcommunist political and social developments, particularly in Poland.

Mark Pittaway is Lecturer in European Studies in the Department of History at the Open University. His research deals with the relationship between history, society and identity in postwar Hungary. He is currently completing a book that focuses on the creation of socialist regimes in industrial communities in that country between 1944 and 1958 and a general social history of Central and Eastern Europe in the postwar period.

Geoffrey Pridham is Professor of European Politics at the University of Bristol. He has worked extensively on democratization in Central and Eastern Europe; and is currently engaged, with a Leverhulme Fellowship, in a project on EU enlargement and democratization, and has a special interest in Slovak affairs. His recent book publications include _Experimenting with Democracy: Regime Change in the Balkans_, co-edited with Tom Gallagher (2000); _The Dynamics of Democratization: A Comparative Approach_ (2000); and _Prospects for Democratic Consolidation in East-Central Europe_, co-edited with Attila Agh (2001).

Ray Taras is Professor of Politics at Tulane University in New Orleans. He studied at the Université de Montreal in Canada, Universities of Sussex and Essex in Britain, and the University of Warsaw in Poland. His books include _Postcommunist Presidents_ (co-edited, 1998), _Democracy in Poland_ (with Marjorie Castle, 2002), and _Liberal and Illiberal Nationalisms_ (2002).

Stephen White is Professor of International Politics and a Senior Research Associate of the Institute of Central and East European studies at the University of Glasgow. He was President of the British Association for Slavonic and East European Studies in 1994–7, and is chief editor of the *Journal of Communist Studies and Transition Politics*. His recent publications include *Russia's New Politics* (2000), *The Soviet Elite from Lenin to Gorbachev* (with Evan Mawdsley, 2000), several studies of the implications of EU and NATO enlargement for Russia, Ukraine, Belarus and Moldova, and a forthcoming jointly authored study of *Postcommunist Belarus*.

Kieran Williams is Senior Lecturer in Politics at the School of Slavonic and East European Studies, University College London. He is the author of *The Prague Spring and its Aftermath: Czechoslovak Politics 1968–1970* (1997) and editor of *Slovakia after Communism and Meciarism* (2000). He is the co-author with Dennis Deletant of *Security Intelligence Services in New Democracies: The Czech Republic, Slovakia and Romania* (2001) and, with Sarah Birch, Frances Millard and Marina Popescu, of *Embodying Democracy: Electoral System Design in Post-Communist Europe* (2002).

Andrew Wilson is Senior Lecturer in Ukrainian Studies at the School of Slavonic and East European Studies, University College London. His recent publications include *Ukraine: Perestroika to Independence* (with Taras Kuzio, 1994), *Ukrainian Nationalism in the 1990s: A Minority Faith* (1997) and *The Ukrainians: Unexpected Nation* (2000, with a second paperback edition in 2002).

List of Abbreviations

ANO	Alliance of the New Citizen (Slovakia)
AWS	Solidarity Election Action (Poland)
AWSP	Solidarity Election Action – the Right (Poland)
BBWR	Non-Party Reform Bloc (Poland)
BSP	Bulgarian Socialist Party
CEE	Central and Eastern Europe
CIS	Commonwealth of Independent States
CPU	Communist Party of Ukraine
CSCE	Conference on Security and Cooperation in Europe
CSSD	Czech Social Democratic Party
EBRD	European Bank for Reconstruction and Development
EECR	*East European Constitutional Review*
EPP	European People's Party
EU	European Union
FDD	Foreign direct investment
FIDESZ	Alliance of Young Democrats (Hungary)
FKGP	Independent Smallholders' Party (Hungary)
FRY	Federal Republic of Yugoslavia
FSN	National Salvation Front (Romania)
FSU	Former Soviet Union
HDZ	Christian Democratic Union
HZDS	Movement for a Democratic Slovakia
IMF	International Monetary Fund
JUL	Yugoslav United Left
KDNP	Christian Democratic People's Party (Hungary)
KDU–CSL	Christian Democratic Union (Czech Republic)
KLD	Liberal Party (Poland)
KSCM	Communist Party of Bohemia and Moravia
LPR	League of Polish Families
MDF	Hungarian Democratic Forum
MDS	Movement for a Democratic Slovakia
MIEP	Hungarian Justice and Life Party
MMP	Hungarian Civic Party
MSZMP	Hungarian Socialist Workers' Party
MSZP	Hungarian Socialist Party

NATO	North Atlantic Treaty Organization
NLA	National Liberation Army (Albania)
NSF	National Salvation Front (Romania)
ODS	Civic Democratic Party (Czech Republic)
OSCE	Organization for Security and Cooperation in Europe (later CSCE)
PC	Centre Accord (Poland)
PiS	Law and Justice (Poland)
PO	Civic Platform (Poland)
PSD	Social Democratic Party (Romania)
PSL	Peasant Party (Poland)
PZPR	Polish United Workers' Party
ROAD	Civic Movement of Democratic Action (Poland)
RS	Social Movement (Poland)
SAA	Stabilization and Association Agreement
SDL	Party of the Democratic Left (Slovakia)
SIS	Security and Intelligence Services (Czech Republic)
SKL	Conservative People's Party (Poland)
SLD	Alliance of the Democratic Left (Poland)
SO	Self-Defence (Poland)
StB	Security Police (Czech Republic)
SZDSZ	Alliance of Free Democrats (Hungary)
UDF	Union of Democratic Forces (Bulgaria)
UP	Labour Union (Poland)
US	United States
UW	Freedom Union (Poland)
VMRO	International Macedonian Revolutionary Organization

Map of Europe

KEY:
Azer. Azerbaijan
BiH. Bosnia and Hercegovina
K. Kosovo
L. Liechtenstein
Ma. Macedonia
Mo. Montenegro
Rus. Fed. Russian Federation

PART ONE

Anatomy of a Diverse Region

1

Introduction: Defining Central and Eastern Europe

JUDY BATT

What is the justification for treating all together in one book the politics of the Central and Eastern European states? A region, as Kundera (1984) has put it, that is a 'condensed version of Europe in all its cultural variety', made up according to one rule: the greatest variety within the smallest space'? This amorphous region spans states as diverse as tiny Slovenia in the far south-west, a cohesive nation of just under two million, with a standard of living approaching that of the West European average, and a lifestyle that has much in common with its Alpine neighbours Austria and Italy; and, in the east, vast Ukraine sprawling across the steppes, with a population of 50 million, a state that, having emerged almost by accident in 1991 upon the collapse of the Soviet Union, has been struggling ever since with uncertainty as to its national identity and place in the world, profound economic decline and mass improvement, and poor government by a corrupt oligarchy of former communist apparatchiks.

The peoples of Central and Eastern Europe, their languages, religions and cultures, are extremely diverse (see Tables 1.1 and 1.2). Linguistic proximity, for example, among the largest, Slavonic language group, is cross-cut by the religious divide between the mainly Roman Catholic Poles, Czechs and Slovaks (the latter two also including Protestant minorities) and the Orthodox Russians, Belarusians and Ukrainians (the latter also including a significant minority of 'Greek' Catholics, combining Orthodox rites with recognition of the Pope in Rome as spiritual leader). Speakers of Serbo-Croat, long recognized as a single language within the South

3

TABLE 1.1   *Major languages spoken in Central and Eastern Europe*

Indo-European group	Non-Indo-European groups

Slavonic
West: Polish, Czech, Slovak
East: Russian, Ukrainian, Rusyn,
  Byelorussian
South: Serbo-Croat, Slovene,
  Bulgarian, Macedonian
	Uralic
	Finnic: Estonian
	Ugric: Hungarian
	Altaic
	Turkish
	Gagauz

Germanic German, Yiddish	
Baltic Latvian, Lithuanian	
Italic (Latin-based) Romanian (including Moldovan)	
Albanian	

Slavonic sub-group, comprise three separate and now tragically antagonistic nations – Serbs, Croats and Bosniaks – primarily identified by their respective Orthodox, Catholic and Muslim traditions. Romanians, who speak a Latin-based language, are by religion mainly Orthodox, with a sizeable Greek-Catholic minority; while Hungarians, whose language falls outside the Indo-European group, share with their Central European neighbours the western Catholic and protestant religious traditions.

Irrepressible Diversity

In fact, *diversity* is the hallmark of Central and Eastern Europe, within countries as much as between them, and this has often been a source of political tension. Although the region's history has also been marked by long periods of peaceful inter-ethnic coexistence, the prevailing Western perception is one of chronic fragmentation and conflict between states and peoples. When we come to look for a common identity, as the historian Timothy Garton Ash has written,

> we shall at once be lost in a forest of historical complexity – an endlessly intriguing forest to be sure, a territory where peoples, cultures, languages are fantastically intertwined, where every

TABLE 1.2 *Religious traditions in Central and Eastern Europe*

MAINLY ROMAN CATHOLIC: Poles Lithuanians Slovenes German 'Schwabs' in Hungary, Romania and former Yugoslavia Croats MAJORITY CATHOLIC WITH SIGNIFICANT PROTESTANT MINORITY: Czechs Slovaks Hungarians MAINLY PROTESTANT: Latvians Estonians German 'Saxons' in Romania (Transylvania) MAJORITY ORTHODOX WITH SIGNIFICANT UNIATE (GREEK-CATHOLIC) MINORITY: Ukrainians Rusyns Romanians JEWS: mainly urban dwellers throughout Central and Eastern Europe; much reduced by assimilation in the nineteenth century and the Holocaust in World War II.	MAINLY ORTHODOX: Russians Bulgarians Serbs Montenegrins Macedonians Moldovans Gagauzi MUSLIMS: Bosnian Muslims Turkish minorities Sandzhak Muslims in Serbia MAINLY MUSLIM WITH CATHOLIC AND ORTHODOX MINORITIES: Albanians NB: The Roma throughout Central and Eastern Europe tend to adopt the major religion of the locality in which they live; but many recently have joined various Christian sects and the Seventh Day Adventists.

place has several names and men change their citizenship as often as their shoes, an enchanted wood full of wizards and witches, but one which bears over its entrance the words: 'Abandon all hope, ye who enter here, of ever again seeing the wood for the trees.' (Garton Ash, 1989, p. 197)

A first stop in the search for commonalities would be the fact that all the states covered in this book experienced several decades of communist rule until the dramatic changes of 1989–91, since when they have all set about the 'transition to democracy'. The communist system was a unique form of dictatorship that was characterized not only by the monopoly of political power in the hands of a single party, but also by far-reaching expropriation of private property and the direct subordination of the economy and society to political control. Communist ideology was universalist, in the sense that it predicted a common destiny for all mankind, a utopia of equality and justice transcending class and national divisions. The communist politico-economic system, pioneered by the Soviet Union, was justified as a universally valid 'model' that all peoples would follow on the path to this utopia. Communism was thus an experiment in enforcing conformity to this model upon the highly diverse region of Central and Eastern Europe. When it failed, all these countries faced broadly similar challenges in unscrambling its legacies and building anew: establishing new multi-party systems; holding competitive elections for the first time in decades; transforming parliaments from puppet theatres in which the communists pulled all the strings into working arenas for debate and legislation; dismantling the pervasive networks of the political police; as well as re-privatizing their economies and establishing functioning market economies virtually from scratch.

However, when we dig deeper into the communist past, we discover that communism took on markedly different forms across the states of Central and Eastern Europe. As one historian put it, 'the entire history of Eastern Europe from 1945 to 1989 ... can be considered one spasmodic imposition of Stalinism followed by forty years of adjusting, accommodating, opposing, reinterpreting, and rejecting' (Stokes, 1997, p. 184). This started with Yugoslavia's breakaway in 1948 from the 'bloc' of countries under the control of the Soviet Union. The Yugoslav communists soon realized that in order to stabilize and consolidate their control without external help from the Soviet Union, they needed to develop their own 'road to socialism', more in conformity with their own conditions. They bolstered their independence by attacking the centralist form of communism imposed throughout the Soviet bloc as a 'bureaucratic deformation', and in its place they proposed a decentralized model of 'self-management'. The Yugoslav economic system was transformed into what became known as 'market socialism'. Central planning was abolished, enterprises were no longer controlled by the state but by their own employees, and market forces were allowed considerable latitude. The political system was federalized, and the six national republics and two autonomous provinces came to enjoy a large measure of political and economic autonomy. For many years the Yugoslav economy appeared to flourish, bolstered by growing ties with the West (including financial support), and by remittances sent home by large numbers of Yugoslavs allowed to work abroad in Western Europe.

Diversification also began among the countries remaining within the Soviet bloc after the death in 1953 of Joseph Stalin, who had brought communism to the region at the end of World War II. Revolts and attempted revolutions in East Berlin in 1953, Hungary and Poland in 1956, Czechoslovakia in 1968, and Poland in 1980–81 demonstrated the fragility of the centralized Soviet model, its lack of genuine roots in the societies and cultures of the region, and its inability to provide the promised superior economy and standard of living to that provided by Western capitalism. Although these revolts were all put down by force, and Soviet-style 'normalization' quickly reimposed, it was clear that some leeway had to be granted to the different countries to respond more flexibly to national conditions. In the cases of Poland and Hungary, local communist leaders experimented with economic reforms, some aspects of which (particularly in Poland and Hungary) were similar to the Yugoslav experiment. The aim was to make the economy more flexible and dynamic, and so to buy popularity for the communist system, without weakening the communist party's monopoly of power. Nevertheless, reforms did lead to a significantly less oppressive political atmosphere in these countries than, for example, in the German Democratic Republic (GDR, or East Germany) and Czechoslovakia (after 1968). The latter two regimes stuck to a rigid form of barely modified Stalinist centralism, as did Romania. But, in contrast to the GDR and Czechoslovakia, the Soviet Union's staunchest allies, Romania under Ceausescu pursued an independent foreign policy, cultivating ties with the Soviet Union's chief 'enemies', China, Israel and the West. This did not mean political relaxation at home: in fact the Ceausescu regime was the most repressive of all, culminating in a personalized dictatorship that recalled inter-war fascist glorification of the Leader, drawing heavily on Romanian nationalist symbols to appeal to the masses, backed up by all-pervading secret police intimidation. However, by the end of the communist period, all of the countries of Central and Eastern Europe faced profound economic crisis. So when in 1989 the then Soviet leader Gorbachev took the momentous decision to withdraw from Central and Eastern Europe, these communist regimes collapsed in rapid succession. This culminated in the Soviet Union in 1991 when the Baltic Republics, Ukraine and other former Soviet republics broke away to form new independent states.

Although all states faced challenges of postcommunist political and economic transformation, each did so in its own specific way. Precisely what had to be unscrambled when communism collapsed, and what material and human resources were available on which to build, varied widely. Hungary, Poland and Yugoslavia were all saddled with crippling debts and high inflation resulting from their failed reform experiments; but at least their elites contained political pragmatists and technocrats having some understanding of the market economy, and their peoples had had a chance over the previous decades to engage in small-scale private entrepreneurship. Travel to the West, or at least access to information about it, was quite widespread. Yugoslavia, however, squandered these initial advantages when its crisis-ridden federation broke down into more than a decade of inter-ethnic war. One of the Yugoslav republics, Slovenia, did manage to escape unscathed, and having established its independence, now stands alongside Hungary and Poland in the group of states that have forged ahead in political and economic transformation and are approaching accession to the European Union. Romania, by contrast, has lagged behind, its economic transformation burdened by the impoverishment inherited from Ceausescu's misrule, the ambiguities of its postcommunist elite about change, and the political weaknesses and inexperience of alternative non-communist elites.

The GDR disappeared altogether after unification with the Federal Republic in 1991, which ensured its radical economic and political transformation by a unique process of absorption into another state (and also its exclusion from this volume). Czechoslovakia too disappeared by 1993, fractured into two independent states as a result of long-submerged national differences between Czechs and Slovaks that resurfaced after 1989. Nearly seventy years of common statehood and forty years of communist centralism have not prevented the two new Czech and Slovak states from taking on quite different profiles. The same is even more obvious in the cases of former Soviet republics: the Baltic republics' experience of independent statehood in the inter-war period – albeit brief – seems to have given them a head-start over Ukraine, which has been teetering on the brink of an economic and political abyss for most of the period since independence.

Thus the diversity that was already becoming apparent in the communist period has further deepened since the end of communism, hence the question with which we started remains to be answered. What justifies treating together these highly disparate states? If we take a longer historical view, we can identify some broad, recurrent themes that have shaped – and continue to shape – the political development of the region and its interactions with the wider Europe.

The 'Lands in Between': A Geopolitical Predicament

Central and Eastern Europe often seems easier to define by what it is not, than by what it is. It is an area without clear geographical borders that stretches from the Baltic Sea in the north to the Adriatic in the south, and south-eastward to the Black Sea. In the north, it comprises part of the Great European Plain that extends to the west across northern Germany and the Low Countries and to the east deep into Russia. In the centre is the upland plateau of the Czech lands and the Danubian Basin spreading out between the Alps and the Carpathian mountains. Further south still is the mountainous, often remote and inaccessible region of the Balkans, and to the south-east the land stretches away into the steppes of Ukraine. These are sometimes called the 'Lands in Between', a broad frontier zone between Russia and Germany, Europe and Asia, East and West.

This indeterminate location has had a fundamental impact on the shaping of political identities throughout the region. The lack of natural borders exposed the region to successive waves of migration over the centuries, while inaccessibility and economic marginalization helped preserve distinctive local cultures, languages and dialects – hence the region's ethnic diversity. An enormous variety of peoples came to settle here, not for the most part (until the twentieth century) in consolidated and clearly defined territories, but intermingled in a complex ethnic patchwork. As a result of its geopolitical exposure, the region has been chronically vulnerable to invasion by larger and stronger powers to the west, east and south. Between the fifteenth and seventeenth centuries, when in Western Europe the foundations of modern nation-states were being laid, Central and Eastern Europe fell under the control of large multi-national empires. The Balkans and most of Hungary were conquered by the Ottoman Empire, and were thus isolated from the West in a formative period

(handwritten, right margin, vertical): IMPACT OF PHYSICAL GEOGRAPHY

when the cultural influences of the Renaissance and Reformation took hold. The Ottomans were finally driven out of Hungary by the early eighteenth century by the forces of the Habsburg Empire, after which Hungary fell under the rule of Vienna. Meanwhile, the Russian Empire in the seventeenth and eighteenth centuries expanded its might southwards to the Black Sea and, in the northwest, captured the southern shore of the Baltic from the Swedes. In the late eighteenth century, Poland was partitioned between Russia, Prussia and Habsburg Austria.

The establishment of the various empires promoted (or forced) further migrations of the peoples of the region as some groups fled before one imperial army to seek protection under another, others moved in to fill their place, and new ruling groups were brought from far-away imperial capitals to run the local administration. Along with ethnic diversity and intermingling, imperial rule promoted and entrenched complex patterns of ethnic stratification. Typically, the landowning nobility was of a different language and/or religion from the peasants who worked their estates, and different again from the administrative elites, commercial and professional classes in the towns. Thus, for example, in Hungary, Magyar nobles lorded it over Slovak or Romanian peasants; in Austrian Galicia, Polish nobles did the same over Ukrainians and Rusyns; in the Baltic, it was Germans and Swedes who dominated the Estonian and Latvian masses. Servicing the bureaucratic and military needs of empire brought fresh influxes of German-speakers to the eastern towns of the Habsburg Empire, to join long-settled communities of German craftsmen. Russians came to govern the cities of Ukraine, Moldavia and the part of Poland that had fallen under Russian control at the end of the eighteenth century. Greeks came from Constantinople in order to take on that role on behalf of the Ottomans in much of the Balkans. Throughout the region, Jews constituted a significant proportion of the urban population occupied in trade and commerce, petty crafts and the professions. Ethnic stratification was exploited by imperial rule, which favoured some ethnic groups over others, such as the Germans in imperial Russia's Baltic provinces, or Slavic converts to Islam in parts of the Balkans under Ottoman control. Challenges to the central imperial authorities were thus fended off by a strategy of 'divide and rule' whose consequences are still being felt in inter-ethnic relations in the region today.

The lack of defensible territorial borders had led, by the late eighteenth century, to the whole of Central and Eastern Europe being swallowed up between rival multinational empires that, in the course of the nineteenth century, began to look increasingly ramshackle. Autocratic rule and socio-economic stagnation blocked the development of dynamic modern civil societies. The intermingling of peoples did not lead to a 'multicultural' paradise or the emergence of an integrated, coherent 'body politic' capable of calling the state to account. The very absence of clear territorial bases for the exercise of political power led rather to the accentuation of language and religion as key markers of social group formation.

'Catching Up' with Europe: The Problem of Statehood

In the course of the nineteenth century, the challenge of cultural, political and economic modernization posed by the example of more developed and dynamic nation-states in Western Europe began to make itself felt among the peoples of the dynastic empires of Central and Eastern Europe. Defeat in war made the rulers of the region aware that the economic backwardness of their empires was a major source of military weakness. In the late nineteenth century, state-promoted industrialization drives were launched, but proceeded only unevenly, in fits and starts. 'Take-off' into sustained growth was held back by rigidly conservative political and social institutions, chief among which was the preservation of a feudal-type agricultural system in which peasants remained tied to the land as serfs. Despite, or rather, because of this social and economic backwardness, the ideas of individual liberty, social emancipation and national self-determination proclaimed by the French Revolution held enormous appeal for educated elites throughout the region, who came to see 'catching up' with the mainstream of Western Europe as the key goal for their societies. The ideal of the 'nation-state', a political order in which the state was held to be accountable to the 'people', furnished would-be reformers with the intellectual ammunition with which to attack autocracy, feudal privilege, ossified conservative traditions and social injustice in the name of the European liberal ideals of individual freedom, equal rights, the rule of law, and constitutional government.

But problems arose with the redefinition of the state as representative of the 'nation'. In the French context, the 'nation' had been conceived as the whole 'people' inhabiting the existing state's well-established historical territory, a free association of individual citizens with equal rights. Transformation of the Central and East European empires along the same lines was blocked not only by the entrenched resistance of the old regimes but also by lack of consensus on who precisely constituted 'the people' to whom the state was to be made accountable. By the early nineteenth century, under the influence of German Romanticism and especially of Johann von Herder (a native of the Baltic province of East Prussia), the idea of the 'nation' in the Central and East European context began to depart from the state-centred French concept, which defined 'citizens' in terms of residence on the state's territory, and moved towards a definition which drew political borders along cultural and linguistic lines. Thus the demand for 'national self-determination' was raised on behalf of ethnic communities, and implied the creation of new states for the respective ethnic communities on whatever territory they claimed as their homeland. Effectively this meant that the multinational Central and East European empires could only be transformed into 'nation-states' by redrawing territorial borders and breaking them up. But further, because most of the empires' constituent territories contained more than one ethnic nation, and because of the extensive intermingling of peoples that had in the meanwhile taken place, competing claims were laid by the various ethnic nations to the various parts of the imperial territories.

The collapse of the Ottoman, Russian and Habsburg empires, culminating at the end of World War I, left the victorious Western powers with the task of implementing the principle of 'national self-determination' as promised by the American President Woodrow Wilson (see Macmillan, 2001). The way seemed open for the peoples of the region finally to acquire their own sovereign nation-states and so to reach political modernity on the pattern already laid down by their neighbours in the West. The disintegration of the Russian Empire into the chaos of revolution in 1917 and civil war in the following years allowed the Estonians, Latvians and Lithuanians to break free and form their own states. The simultaneous demise of the Habsburg Empire and the defeat of Germany paved the way for a united independent Poland to reappear on the map of Europe. The Czechs and Slovaks formed a new common state of Czechoslovakia, while the South Slavs of Austria–Hungary united with Serbia in the Kingdom of Serbs, Croats and Slovenes, later Yugoslavia. Romania, which like Serbia had wrested independence from Ottoman control in the late nineteenth century, acquired from Hungary to its west and

Russia to its east extensive new territories where Romanians formed local majorities. Other nations were less successful, notably the Ukrainians, who remained divided between the Soviet Union in the east and Poland in the west; and the Hungarians, who gained independence from Austria only to lose two-thirds of their historic territory to Romania, Czechoslovakia and Yugoslavia. The new nation-states of Central and Eastern Europe faced enormous internal and external challenges in the inter-war period. The heritage of history and the endemic problem of geopolitical vulnerability did not melt away overnight. First of all, the new states did not, for the most part, inherit ready-made administrations and integrated political communities of citizens. These had to be built almost from scratch on the territories inherited from various former rulers. So, for example, the Polish leader Pilsudski faced a huge task in 1918:

Pilsudski had to weld together different economies, different laws and different bureaucracies. He had to rationalise nine separate legal systems. He had to reduce five currencies to one, and he did not even have the means to print banknotes. Railways were a nightmare, with 66 different kinds of rails, 165 types of locomotives and a patchwork of signalling systems. (Macmillan, 2001, p. 220)

Most important of all, most states were not 'nation-states' in the sense in which their new rulers had expected – states of and for a single, united 'nation' in ethnic terms, but contained sizeable minorities, more or less aggrieved at the changes in borders that had taken place over their heads. Thus Poland, reborn in its pre-partition borders, contained large minorities of Ukrainians and other east Slavic, Orthodox peoples who identified more closely with kinsfolk over the border in the Soviet Union than with their Polish fellow-citizens; Germans, who found it hard to accept their diminished status in a state dominated by Poles whom they tended to disdain; and Jews, who were regarded as alien by their devoutly Catholic Polish neighbours. Both Czechoslovakia and Yugoslavia posed unresolved questions of whether the aim was to construct a unified nation-state resting on a single composite political identity, or whether in fact they were multinational states that should give institutional recognition to their constituent national groups. The dismantling of historic Hungarian territory to the benefit of neighbouring Czechoslovakia, Romania and Yugoslavia transferred large minorities of Hungarians to rule by the peoples whom they had previously dominated, and who regarded them as 'foreigners' rather than fellow-citizens. Moreover, many individuals were of two (or more) minds as to their ethnic identity and how it related to the new political order, as the inter-war writer Odon von Horvath explained:

> If you ask me what is my native country, I answer: I was born in Fiume, I grew up in Belgrade, Budapest, Pressburg, Vienna and Munich, and I have a Hungarian passport: but I have no fatherland. I am a very typical mix of old Austria-Hungary: at once Magyar, Croatian, German and Czech; my country is Hungary, my mother tongue is German. (Quoted in Rupnik, 1990, p. 250)

The strategy adopted by state-builders across Central and Eastern Europe was to impose from above a centralized state apparatus in order to enforce maximum uniformity within tightly controlled borders. This accorded with their perception of the French republican model, and fitted well with their objectives of securing the sovereignty and hegemony of the majority nation in whose name the state had been founded. But it was to prove a recipe for internal instability and external conflict. Firstly, nationalistic policies of building up state strength by economic protectionism exacerbated the economic difficulties caused by the fragmentation of previously relatively open, large markets of the imperial territories, and made the whole region peculiarly vulnerable to the economic crisis of the late 1920s and 1930s. This was combined with the explosive fact that most states were multinational. On one side stood the 'nationalizing' elites, bent on entrenching the hegemony of the majority by means of centralized political and administrative structures, ostensibly in the name of modernization, efficiency and civic equality. On another side stood the national minorities, for whom this represented just another form of bureaucratic pressure for assimilation and subjection to the untrammelled 'tyranny of the majority'. Often too there was a third side, a neighbouring state aggrieved by the outcome of the post-World War I peace treaties, which took upon itself the role of 'protector' of minorities abroad where these were ethnic kinsfolk, and aimed at eventual revision of the new borders (see Brubaker, 1996).

Bearing the Brunt of European Power Politics

All of these tensions were exacerbated by the external threats posed in the inter-war period by the resurgence of Germany in the west and Soviet Russia in the east. By the early 1930s, these rival powers were set upon expansion into the Central and East European territories they had 'lost' at the end of the World War I, and promoted their aims in the name of the radically opposed and profoundly illiberal ideologies of fascism and communism. Most of the new states in Central and Eastern Europe, by contrast, were small in size, economically weak, and deficient in military organization and capacities. Moreover, mutual mistrust among them obstructed any move toward common defence against the looming threats. The peace settlement had failed to provide an overarching security framework and structures to promote regional cooperation, without which 'national self-determination' was to be precarious and short-lived. This point was not lost on more perceptive individuals in the region, such as the Hungarian Oszkar Jaszi, who early recognized the unsustainability of the situation:

The only possible cure for Europe's ills is a democratic confederation of democratic peoples, the extirpation of rigid and selfish national sovereignty, peaceful and rational cooperation between all countries for the good of all. The fundamentals of this system are to be found in two basic institutions: one, free trade between all parties to the confederation; the other, a system of honest national and cultural autonomy for all national minorities living within the boundaries of the confederation. Under such conditions political frontiers would slowly become mere demarcations of administrative divisions. (Jaszi, 1923, pp. 280–1)

Voices such as Jaszi's were not heeded at the time. Instead, Central and East Europe fell prey to a new round of imperial conquest, more brutal and oppressive than anything experienced before. After 1939, Nazi Germany and the Soviet Union redrew the map of Europe by carving up the lands in between them. Poland once again disappeared, partitioned between the rival powers. Poles became forced labourers for the Nazi war machine, their military elite massacred by the Soviet army advancing from the east, and their country reduced to the site of the major death camps into which Jews from the whole of Europe were herded and exterminated. The Baltic republics were invaded first by Germany then forcibly incorporated into the Soviet Union. Divisions among the Central and East Europeans themselves were ruthlessly exploited: Czechoslovakia and Yugoslavia were dismembered, and Nazi-backed puppet states were formed in breakaway Slovakia and Croatia. Axis ally Italy seized the Dalmatian coast and ran an enlarged Albania, while Hungary seized the opportunity to regain lost lands in southern Slovakia, north-western Romania and northern Serbia. As Great Power rivalry was being fought out over their heads, bitter ethnic wars meanwhile broke out on the ground between Poles and Ukrainians, Hungarians and Romanians, Serbs, Croats and Bosnian Muslims; and Jews and gypsies suffered at the hands not only of the Nazi invaders but also of their own neighbours.

The peace that eventually came to the region at the end of World War II was bought at an exceptionally heavy price with the advance westward of the Soviet Army, by now in alliance with the Western powers. 'Liberation' from Nazi control by Soviet forces was rapidly followed by the installation of temporary governments stacked with local communist recruits and fellow-travellers. For the Western allies, preoccupied with the final defeat of Germany and Japan, keeping Stalin on side in the last months of the war was the priority. By the time they turned their attention to the situation in Central and Eastern Europe at the end of the war, the Western allies' national capacities and their will to intervene to avert the consolidating Soviet grip over the region were exhausted. The main result of belated efforts on the part of the new US administration under Truman to 'roll back' communism in Europe was to prompt Stalin to seal off the Central and East European states that his troops had occupied behind an 'Iron Curtain'. Thereafter, all remaining non-communist parties and politicians were ousted from government, and the local communist parties were tightly bound into a communist international system that enforced uniformity and subordination to the dictates of Moscow.

The states of Central and Eastern Europe thereafter found themselves set on a new course of 'socialist construction' following the Soviet model. This was a project of 'catching up' with the West, but one explicitly designed in opposition to the capitalist path relaunched in Western Europe with US support in the 'Marshall Plan'. The continent was divided into two opposing blocs, and Central and Eastern Europe became once again the front line of East–West superpower rivalry. Although the project of 'catching up and overtaking' the West presented by communist rule held some attractions for the peoples of the region insofar as it promised rapid social and economic modernization, communist rule was regarded as politically alien, a new form of imperialism that suppressed their political freedom, their religions, and above all their national identity. For centuries, it had been Western Europe, not Russia, that they had regarded as the model to emulate and the centre of their cultural gravitational field. Although communist ideology was certainly a Western import into Russia, when it was forcibly imposed from the east onto Central and Eastern Europe, it was experienced as a form of 'Asiatic despotism' with which only a narrow minority could ever identify. The subsequent failure of communist regimes to deliver the promised economic and social progress only exposed the acute fragility of these regimes in the region, which explains why they all collapsed so quickly in 1989–91.

The 'Return to Europe'

The slogan that best encapsulated popular understanding of the meaning of the revolutions of 1989–91 in Central and Eastern Europe was the 'return to Europe'. Of course geographically they had never moved, but meanwhile Western Europe had surged ahead. Postwar recovery was followed by decades of economic growth and radical technological innovation; unprecedentedly prosperous societies enjoyed the additional security of extensive state welfare provision; and the problem of German power seemed to have been resolved by binding its larger western part, the Federal Republic, into political and economic integration within the European Community (later European Union) and military integration in NATO. Buoyed up by self-confidence and not a little complacency, the western side of the Iron Curtain had come to regard itself as 'Europe'. In 1989, it awoke to find long-forgotten neighbours clamouring to join in. For what the Central and East Europeans recognized in the 'Europe' represented by the EU and NATO was precisely that 'democratic confederation of democratic peoples' that Jaszi, among others, had envisioned: an overarching framework for the weak, small and divided peoples of the region to overcome their geopolitical predicament and achieve the security and prosperity without which the long-cherished goal of 'national self-determination' would remain unfulfilled. 'Returning to Europe' held the promise of replicating a tried-and-tested formula that would allow them finally to 'catch up' with the West.

Western observers have often remarked on the apparent contradiction in the revolutions of 1989, which simultaneously expressed aspirations to recover national independence and to join in West European processes of deepening political, economic and military integration that unquestionably affect key aspects of the traditional sovereignty of nation-states. The end of communist rule in Central and Eastern Europe saw an upsurge of nationalist rhetoric, leading not only to a revival of the sort of tensions between ethno-national majorities and minorities that had fatefully afflicted the stability of the region in the inter-war period, but also to the break-up of the three major multinational communist states – the Soviet Union, Yugoslavia and Czechoslovakia – to form a whole set of new nation-states. The temptation is to regard this as a symptom of some endemic, recurrent Central and East Europe disease that sets this part of the continent apart from the Western 'mainstream'. This in turn raises questions about whether history has so shaped this region as to preclude its ever being fully integrated into the mainstream of modern Europe. Enlargement of the EU and NATO, from the Western perspective, could thus seem a profoundly risky undertaking. It threatened to overwhelm these elaborately constructed and highly valued European institutions with an influx of states whose fragile new political and administrative structures seemed unready to play by the established Western 'rules of the game', whose ruined economies would be heavily dependent on Western support for decades to come, and who seemed more likely to consume than to contribute to common security.

For Central and East Europeans, the contradiction between 'national self-determination' and joining the EU and NATO is much less obvious, for reasons that this chapter has sought to make clear. The notion of 'returning to Europe' usefully captures an essential fact of life in this region: the inseparability of the internal and external dimensions of politics. Establishing and consolidating democracy and the rule of law, overcoming inter-ethnic tensions, nationalistic rivalries and mistrust, and creating flourishing and competitive economies all largely depend on a stable external environment, free of the threat of imperialist domination, in which borders can be freely crossed by people, products and capital. The EU, for all its shortcomings, has proved a markedly successful model in the West, where similar challenges were faced at the end of

World War II. The process of integration into pan-European structures can now provide practical support and incentives for Central
and East Europeans to stay the course of difficult, painful reforms
and get through the wrenching social upheavals they may bring.
Reciprocally, political stabilization and economic revival in Central
and Eastern Europe offers Western Europe its best guarantee of
security in a new era: 'Fortress Europe' ceased to be an option once
the Iron Curtain came down and the balance-of-terror system of the
Cold War collapsed. Security must be now rebuilt on the bases of
intense cooperation with neighbours, and of explicit recognition that
the benefits will be mutual and self-reinforcing. Arguments such as
these in favour of EU and NATO enlargement eventually won out
over Western scepticism. In 1993, the EU explicitly recognized
enlargement into Central and Eastern Europe as a goal, and accession negotiations with ten states of the region have been under way
since 1998. The first new members expect to be admitted in May
2004. NATO took the decision to expand in 1996. Three new members (Poland, Hungary and the Czech Republic) were admitted in
1999, and several more were invited to join in late 2002.

The process of EU and NATO enlargement, however, raises
new questions for the definition of our region insofar as it is taking
place in stages: not all the states of Central and Eastern Europe will
join at the same time, if at all. This is particularly relevant as far as
EU membership is concerned, because of the complex conditions
and far-reaching implications of membership. In the early 1990s,
the EU concluded 'Europe Agreements' (which carried, after
1993, the commitment to eventual membership) with ten states: the
three Baltic Republics, Poland, the Czech and Slovak Republics,
Hungary, Slovenia, Romania and Bulgaria. It started accession
negotiations with Estonia, Poland, the Czech Republic, Hungary
and Slovenia in 1998, and with the other five, deemed to be less far
advanced in economic and/or political reform, two years later.
Some of the latter group have caught up with the 'front runners'
and will join in 2004, but Bulgaria and Romania will not.
Meanwhile, countries of the former Yugoslavia and Albania have
been offered 'Stabilisation and Association Agreements' that, while
acknowledging eventual membership as a goal, assume that this
will only be achievable in the long term. So far, only Croatia and
Macedonia have concluded such Agreements. On the other hand,
Ukraine, which has expressed interest in eventual EU membership,
and Moldova, which remains ambivalent, are not yet recognized as

potential EU members at all. What is emerging are important sub-divisions within the region, with the term 'Central Europe' now being commonly used in official circles to encompass the candidate states with 'Europe Agreements', the 'Stability and Association' states being grouped together as 'the western Balkans' or 'eastern Adriatic', leaving Ukraine and Moldova as 'Eastern Europe' alongside Russia, Belarus and other states that are part of the Commonwealth of Independent States that was set up in 1991 to manage the dismantling of the former Soviet Union.

These distinctions have important consequences, because the new borders they set up between 'ins', 'pre-ins' and 'outs' cut across a region that is only just emerging from the damaging divisions imposed by communist rule to rediscover shared history and to identify strongly with the idea of a united Europe. The point was dramatically demonstrated in 1999, when, three weeks after taking in the new CEE members, NATO launched its bombardment of Serbia. For the Czechs, with strong historic sympathies for their fellow Slavs the Serbs, and for Hungary, with some 400,000 ethnic kin living over their southern border in Serbia, this proved an unexpected wrench of their loyalties. More generally, exclusion from enlargement has a demoralizing psychological impact. Because EU membership in particular has become equated with 'being European', and because, in Central and Eastern Europe, being 'European' has come to mean much the same as being 'civilized' and 'modern', exclusion from EU enlargement can be a national humiliation that may encourage a resentful backlash. Differentiation can also revive tensions and rivalries between states. For example, Romania has sometimes expressed the fear that if Hungary joins the EU before itself, Hungary might exploit its position on the 'inside' to secure concessions from Romania as regards treatment of the still large and somewhat restive Hungarian minority there, an old fear of Hungarian intervention kept alive by memories of the inter-war period. Another point is that those states that join the EU first will benefit from full access to the single market and to substantial transfers from the EU's structural funds, far exceeding what is delivered in the various EU assistance programmes for non-members. This could further accelerate the divergence in economic performance between states of the region.

Moreover, EU widening is taking place at the same time as accelerated deepening of integration in key fields. One result is that while nation-state borders are becoming less significant between member-states, the EU's external border is becoming ever more salient as a line demarcating the unified economic, monetary and trading space within from those on the outside. The EU border is also coming to perform external security and policing functions formerly in the hands of member-states, which the new EU entrants will be expected to take on once they become the outer limits of the EU's 'Area of Freedom, Security and Justice'. The EU now has a common visa regime, and is moving towards common policies on immigration and asylum. These have divisive implications for the Central and East European region. For example, once Poland and Hungary join, they will require visitors from Ukraine or Yugoslavia to obtain visas, which at present they do not need. It is hard to see how cultural and economic interchange between these states will not be severely affected as a result. Thus 'Europeanization' of the region, insofar as it takes place in stages, seems likely to become as much a factor for further diversification within the region as for its unification. In future editions of this book, therefore, it may make less sense than it does today to treat the countries of Central and Eastern Europe together.

In the chapters that follow we pursue the themes of divergence and convergence between the states of Central and Eastern Europe, and between them and Western Europe, through a set of country studies and comparative thematic chapters. Variations in national patterns of democratization are explained by reference to the histories of individual countries, to the specific legacies of communist rule, and to the external influences exerted by the West through the processes of EU and NATO enlargement. Even those furthest advanced in their 'return to Europe', such as the Central European states of Poland, Hungary, the Czech Republic and Slovakia, continue to face the challenge of underpinning their democratic institutions with popular confidence, efficient administrative practices and habitual respect for the rule of law. At the same time, even those fragile states in war-torn former Yugoslavia have made some progress in recent years towards national reconciliation and reconstruction. Western engagement, especially on the part of the EU, is now recognized as essential, yet here there is also room for concern. West European public opinion seems to have lost its enthusiasm for extending the benefits of integration too far to the east and south-east, instead focusing on concerns about illegal migration and the penetration of international organized crime into their societies. Western democracies themselves are undergoing challenges as political disaffection, social fragmentation and exposure to global economic pressures bring increased uncertainty. The 'Europe' to which the Central and East Europeans aspire to 'return' is itself in a state of flux, and this no doubt helps to explain why Western political leaders have not yet shown the courage and far-sightedness necessary for cooperation in concerted and sustained programmes of support for the postcommunist region. Yet support of this kind is in the interests of all Europeans as they confront the inescapable task of building a common future.

2

Poland

FRANCES MILLARD

Poland was the most persistently turbulent and the most trouble-some of the Soviet Union's communist allies in Europe. Poland also proved the 'trend-setter' for democratization (Lewis, 1999) as the first to install a non-communist prime minister committed to system transformation. Two major factors influenced Poland's development as a liberal democracy poised to join the European Union as the final stage of its 'return to Europe'. The first was the legacy of the Round Table Agreement of April 1989, including the emergence of a strong elite consensus supporting democratic change and ensuring a basic continuity of key policies, but also a set of institutional structures not designed for fully democratic processes. The second was the manner in which the two main pro-tagonists, the Communist Party (the PZPR, Polish United Workers' Party) and the opposition trade union Solidarity, adapted to new circumstances: while the PZPR successfully transformed itself into a credible social democratic left alternative, Solidarity failed to generate a successful major political party, and the fissiparous nature of the right continued to plague Polish politics.

Governments of differing persuasion maintained a basic policy continuity, but the new political class did not inspire the popula-tion's affection or confidence. Although economic growth was strong after 1992–3, it also created scope for a distinctive kind of 'political capitalism' based on insider linkages and outright cor-ruption, as well as generating marked social inequalities. The path to democracy was never smooth and it was punctuated by periods of shock, unease, and anger. Yet both NATO, with full membership for Poland in 1999, and the EU, confirming Poland's fulfilment of the democratic criteria for membership, provided the imprimatur of external legitimacy. Given the multiplicity of approaches to and definitions of democratic consolidation (Schedler, 1998) and indeed of democracy itself (Collier and Livitsky, 1997), Poland's democracy may be judged in very different lights; without doubt it remained flawed and imperfect. Clearly, however, by the start of the second decade, fundamental changes had taken place, providing a set of unchallenged democratic institutions. Issues had shifted from those of the fundamental restructuring of the system to piecemeal tinkering to improve the workings of institutions and the quality of the policy process.

The Transition to Postcommunism

Many distinctive features of communist Poland made themselves felt in the processes of postcommunist transformation. The communists faced a society with (i) a strong commitment to the Roman Catholic Church, (ii) a willingness to confront them with open protest, and (iii) a comparatively large private sector, especially in agriculture. The Communist Party itself was chronically divided and faction-ridden. From the first social upheavals in 1956 its periodic efforts to reform the system proved as fruitless as its measures to suppress discontent, culminating in martial law and the suppression of the Solidarity trade union in December 1981. Solidarity had mobilized the largest, most disciplined movement ever seen in Europe. Some ten million members challenged the regime's right to control society, while Solidarity reasserted the importance of the Church as a moral reference point and national symbol. Martial law drove Solidarity underground, where it maintained a precarious existence in the 1980s. However, when new strikes broke out in 1988, the regime turned to Solidarity's leaders in an attempt to break the cycle of protest.

Poland's transition is often described as a 'negotiated' one, arising from the agreement of government and opposition elites. Indeed, Solidarity gave the regime an interlocutor in the early months of 1989, though deep mutual suspicion persisted. The Round Table Agreement was certainly a 'pact', agreed after difficult negotiations; but it was not an agreement for an immediate transition to democracy. It was an attempt by the communists to provide a role for the opposition while themselves retaining the key levers of power (Hayden, 2001). The communists lost control of the process of change in the first phase of implementing the agreement – the election of June 1989. Nor was the Round Table agreement the 'top-down' imposition associated with elite pacts. Solidarity retained vast reserves of popular support that were rapidly reactivated as soon as a window of opportunity opened. To its own amazement and that of its opponents, in the election Solidarity won all but one of the freely contested seats.

The Round Table agreement resulted from a complex set of trade-offs leading to institutional changes that first facilitated (in the short term), then complicated (in the medium term) Poland's transition to democracy. The electoral process was the initial key to Solidarity's new role. The agreement provided for elections to the lower house (Sejm) on the basis of a complex semi-competitive system with the outcome determined in advance: 65 per cent of the seats for the communists and their allies, including 35 seats on an uncontested national list, and 35 per cent for the opposition. The composition of the new 100-member Senate was determined by a genuinely free contest (Lewis, 1990).

Solidarity's sweeping electoral success sounded the death knell of communism, but it was not immediately apparent that this was indeed transition-by-election. Five developments proved crucial in fostering the potential for consensual evolution rather than the politics of confrontation. First, 33 party leaders standing on the national list were defeated, and they were not permitted to stand in the second round of the election. This increased the presence of younger, reform-oriented deputies in the new Sejm. Secondly, it immediately became clear that Gorbachev's non-interventionist strategy was genuine and that there were no grounds for fearing intervention by the USSR. This further eroded the influence of communist hard-liners. Thirdly, parliament elected communist leader General Wojciech Jaruzelski to the new office of president. Jaruzelski's character was important, since the Round Table had given the president potentially strong powers. He had been scarred by the ignominy heaped on him as the architect of martial law, and he made no effort to obstruct the new reform agenda.

Fourthly, the regime's two satellite parties rapidly realized that they held the balance of power in the Sejm. They refused to support the communists, who thus lacked the majority of seats necessary to form a government. Protracted negotiations generated a compromise in which all parties would participate under a Solidarity prime minister – with the communists retaining the key ministries of Interior and Defence. From September 1989 Tadeusz

Mazowiecki's new government embarked on radical political and economic transformation supported by the 'contract Sejm'. Finally, in parallel with these developments the outcome of the June election led to a process of shocked re-evaluation and stocktaking within the Communist Party. This in turn saw the victory of the social democratic option, firmly committed to parliamentary democracy; with the dissolution of the PZPR in January 1990, reformist elements under Aleksander Kwasniewski led the new Social Democratic Party.

Mazowiecki's government initially enjoyed enormous public confidence, and in January 1990 finance minister Balcerowicz embarked on his controversial programme of economic 'shock therapy'. Constitutional amendments and new laws provided the basis for competitive politics, the removal of censorship, and stimulus to the further growth of the private sector. Despite its undemocratic origins, the Sejm proved a determined vehicle of reform. At the same time industrial recession hit harder than anticipated; the standard of living plummeted, with inflation and unemployment rising rapidly. Consensus frayed, social protest re-emerged, and leading politicians began to express reservations about Balcerowicz's unfettered market liberalism. By spring 1990 Solidarity was unravelling into a myriad of small quasi- and proto-parties, given further impetus by Solidarity leader Lech Walesa's determination to seek the presidency (Gortat, 1993). In July, Mazowiecki removed communist ministers from his government, and soon Jaruzelski resigned to permit a (now direct) presidential election, which Walesa won convincingly.

Elections and Governments

Successive elections provide convenient benchmarks for Poland's political development. The first free parliamentary election took place in October 1991, followed by an early election in September 1993 and routine elections in 1997 and 2001. In 1995 Walesa narrowly lost the presidency to Kwasniewski, who won again in 2000. All parliamentary elections witnessed an alternation in office: (i) a variety of Solidarity parties in 1991–3; (ii) the successor Social Democratic (united in the Alliance of the Democratic Left (SLD)) and Peasant (PSL) parties from 1993 to 1997; (iii) a coalition of Solidarity provenance, the Freedom Union (UW) and

Solidarity Election Action (AWS) from October 1997 until June 2001, when the UW withdrew leaving a minority AWS government; and (iv) the SLD and PSL after October 2001, with the Labour Union (UP) as a third coalition partner. Three presidents and ten prime ministers held office between 1989 and 2002 (see Table 2.1) under three sets of constitutional arrangements. Mazowiecki's third-place showing in the first round of the presidential election in 1990 led to his immediate resignation. Yet despite Walesa's promises to mitigate the impact of economic changes, Krzysztof Bielecki's new government followed the same trajectory of economic reform, still under Balcerowicz. Drafting a new constitution, however, needed the democratic legitimacy of a freely elected parliament. This gave the electoral system

TABLE 2.1   *Polish prime ministers, 1989–2002*

Prime Minister	Affiliation	Tenure	Reason for leaving office
Tadeusz Mazowiecki	Solidarity/ROAD*	September 1989– December 1990	Resigned after defeat in presidential election.
Jan Krzysztof Bielecki	Solidarity/Liberal	January 1991– October 1991	Parliamentary elections.
Jan Olszewski	Centre Accord	December 1991– June 1992	No confidence vote, June 1992.
Waldemar Pawlak	Polish Peasant Party	June–July 1992	Could not form government.
Hanna Suchocka	Democratic Union	July 1992– September 1993	No confidence vote, May 1993.
Waldemar Pawlak	Polish Peasant Party	October 1993– March 1995	Resigned under pressure from president.
Jozef Oleksy	Social Democrat	March 1995– February 1996	Constructive vote of no confidence.
Wlodzimerz Cimoszewicz	Alliance of the Democratic Left	February 1996– October 1997	Parliamentary elections.
Jerzy Buzek	Solidarity Election Action	November, 1997– October 2001	Parliamentary elections.
Leszek Miller	Alliance of the Democratic Left	October 2001–	

*ROAD subsequently became the nucleus of the Democratic Union (UD).

paramount importance, since the 1989 law was inherently undemocratic. The process of agreeing a new electoral law proved bitter and protracted (Birch *et al.*, 2002). From June 1990 to March
1991 the Sejm remained deeply divided over new electoral regulations. Then the president raised numerous objections and another
dispute ensued, with further delays and two presidential vetoes.
Finally the Sejm abandoned its complex earlier versions of a mixed
system and settled on proportional representation, which would at
least ensure a representative parliament. Walesa's (unconstitu-
tional) threats to dissolve parliament rallied the Sejm to override
his second veto; and the president backed down. The final result
was open-list PR with a 5 per cent threshold for 69 seats allocated
from national party lists.

1991
VOTING
PROCEDURE

The 1991 Election and Problems of Government Formation

More than two years had passed, accordingly, between the end of
communist rule and the first free parliamentary elections in
October 1991. The mood of optimism had eroded, but there were
few clear-cut prescriptions on offer from the myriad of self-styled
political parties that emerged. These 'parties' vied for election with
social organizations and local bodies: in all, 111 contenders stood
(see *http://www.essex.ac.uk/elections* for election results from
1991). Voters found it difficult to identify the contestants, let alone
to identify with them, and the turnout of 43 per cent was disap-
pointingly low. Solidarity deputies had enjoyed media exposure
after 1989 and their formations did best, but no dominant force
emerged. The new Sejm was notable above all for its divisions:
29 different entities won seats. With 12.3 per cent, Mazowiecki's
Democratic Union was in first place, and the Alliance of the
Democratic Left (SLD) ran it a close second.

MASSIVE DIVISION AND CHAOS IN THE SEJM

   The Sejm's extreme fragmentation complicated the process of
government formation, and only in late December did Jan
Olszewski succeed in establishing a minority government promising radical decommunization, a review of privatization, and an
overtly Catholic social agenda. Olszewski's relations with
President Walesa were poor, especially in regard to control of the
military and the orientation of defence policy. In June 1992
Olszewski fell on a vote of no confidence after the 'lustration
affair', centring on the circulation of a secret list of alleged
'collaborators' with the communist regime, including Walesa

OLSZEWSKI PM IN MINORITY 2 MNTHS LATER)
BUT FALLS DUE TO
LUSTRATION FIASCO

himself and other former anti-communist dissidents. Lustration, the 'cleansing' of the regime, was to remain on the political agenda; but both the Sejm and the president opposed the manner in which the list was compiled, its suspect nature, and the lack of safeguards for civil liberties. A new division emerged between the pro-presidential section of the Polish right and anti-presidential elements around Olszewski. The latter saw communists as deeply embedded in the system and a continuing threat to Poland's sovereignty. Walesa's designation as prime minister of Waldemar Pawlak, leader of the Polish Peasant Party (successor to the former communist satellite), only confirmed their doubts about the president's anti-communist credentials. However, Pawlak could not form a government, and the political crisis deepened.

The Solidarity trade union had done badly in the 1991 election, but it carried considerable authority among the Solidarity groupings within parliament. Solidarity brokered a deal for a seven-party government under Hanna Suchocka of the Democratic Union. Suchocka's government effectively renewed the reform strategies of Mazowiecki and Bielecki (who took charge of negotiations with the European Community), while promising to remain neutral on ideologically divisive issues that could threaten the coalition's unity. *PR a B/c it => chaos* Concerns over the workings of the institutions led to an interim Little Constitution, and work began on revising the electoral system, which was widely blamed for the fragmentation of the Sejm.

Moreover, a renewal of strikes and protests (Ekiert and Kubiak, *Dev of 3 partite bargaining* 1999) generated a conciliatory attitude to trades unions and the development of tripartite structures of consultation. This did not prevent renewed union anxieties, especially over the plight of workers paid from the state budget. Although Solidarity's motion of no confidence on 28 May 1993 was aimed at bringing pressure on the government, not at bringing it down, the vote unexpectedly succeeded. On the same day the Sejm completed the final stages of electoral reform. President Walesa signed the law immediately and called an election for 19 September. Suchocka continued in a caretaker capacity, though she departed from the convention of taking only uncontroversial decisions when she signed a Concordat with the Vatican in July.

1993 and the Victory of the Successor Parties

Important changes were made in the 1993 electoral law: the size of constituencies was reduced; new thresholds were introduced, of

5 per cent (parties), 8 per cent (coalitions), and 7 per cent (the national list); and the formula for translating votes into seats was altered to d'Hondt. The thresholds and the new formula were intended to give greater weight to larger parties and thus to encourage alliances and mergers of smaller ones. The law succeeded with a vengeance in the first and failed utterly in the second. Most smaller parties ignored the changes and chose to stand alone; their failure to reach the thresholds meant a high wasted vote of some 35 per cent. Only six parties entered the Sejm, along with the German Minority, which was exempt from thresholds. This meant a huge seat premium for the winners. The Alliance of the Democratic Left (20 per cent of the vote) and the Polish Peasant Party (15 per cent) gained 66 per cent of the seats. The Democratic Union won 11 per cent of the vote. The Labour Union (UP), an exceptional merger of two Solidarity parties with some former-communist social democrats, won 7 per cent. The populist Confederation of Independent Poland and an *ad hoc* pro-Walesa formation, the Non-Party Reform Bloc (BBWR), won seats but failed to qualify for national list allocations.

Despite fears that the successor parties would oversee stagnation or a reversal of previous achievements, the SLD–PSL coalition effectively continued the policies of its predecessors. The SLD, mindful of residual fears of its anti-democratic tendencies, yielded the premiership to Pawlak, while Kwasniewski led the SLD in parliament. However, Polish-style 'cohabitation' of president and government was not a success, as Walesa abandoned his earlier conciliatory approach and geared up to fight for the presidency on a renewed anti-communist platform. The Little Constitution had given the president a say in the allocation of three key ministries – foreign affairs, the interior, and defence. Rather surprisingly, Pawlak passively accepted Walesa's nominations, leading to the anomalous situation where three 'presidential' ministers of opposed political orientation sat in government councils. Yet if Walesa expected Pawlak to be equally pliable in other respects, he proved badly mistaken. In 1994 relations deteriorated in an atmosphere of mutual recrimination. Walesa harassed the government, exercised his veto power relentlessly, and referred numerous laws to the Constitutional Tribunal. This was not a discriminating use of presidential powers to strengthen the democratic order but a scatter-gun technique to cause maximum harm to the government (Millard, 2000). Pawlak finally resigned in March 1995, to be replaced by Jozef Oleksy of the SLD.

Kwasniewski's victory in the 1995 presidential contest removed one major source of friction, but Walesa's departure caused fresh upheaval when his outgoing interior minister accused Oleksy of being a Russian agent. The 'Oleksy affair' remained murky and unexplained despite successive investigations, but the prime minister could not survive allegations of such gravity. In February 1996 Justice Minister ('clean hands') Wlodzimierz Cimoszewicz succeeded him. Yet difficulties also remained within the coalition itself. The PSL became increasingly assertive following Pawlak's resignation. It bargained hard for the interests of its own agricultural constituency. It voted against the government on key issues such as lustration and abortion and effectively vetoed the reform of the country's administrative structures. The PSL's recalcitrance increased as the election approached, and it paid a high price.

[handwritten margin note: WALESA LOSES => OLESKY AFFAIR]

The Return of Solidarity

The September 1997 election saw the renewed triumph of Solidarity, whose fractious elements were united in Solidarity Election Action by Solidarity trade union leader Marian Krzaklewski following Kwasniewski's presidential victory. Consolidation of the centre was also apparent with the merger in April 1994 of the Democratic Union with Bielecki's Liberals (KLD) to form the Freedom Union under the leadership of Leszek Balcerowicz. AWS emerged as the clear victor with 34 per cent of the vote, while the UW gained 13 per cent. The SLD did well, increasing its vote to 27 per cent, but the Peasant Party's vote dropped by almost half. Olszewski's Movement for Rebuilding Poland scraped over the threshold, but the Labour Union did not (the BBWR and the Confederation for Independent Poland had virtually disappeared).

[handwritten margin note: 97 ELECTIONS SEE SOLIDARITY COMEBACK (AWS)]

Solidarity heirs AWS and UW formed a coalition under the unknown academic Jerzy Buzek, with Balcerowicz again at the Ministry of Finance. Balcerowicz was unloved by AWS, and the coalition was beset by tensions from the outset. Early battles over patronage – in central and provincial government and on boards of government, industry, and health care – brought the government into disrepute. Various segments of AWS carved out their own fiefdoms within government, and Buzek proved an ineffective leader seen largely as a front man for Solidarity's Krzaklewski. The 'four great reforms' of the administrative system, the health service, education, and pensions further undermined the government's credibility, whether because of inadequate preparation, poor implementation, or both. AWS deputies in particular proved an unruly lot, and even AWS ministers voted at times against the government. The UW left the coalition in June 2000.

Kwasniewski's victory on the first ballot of the 2000 presidential election (Szczerbiak, 2001b) proved a decisive blow to AWS. Krzaklewski came an ignominious third, after the independent candidate Andrzej Olechowski. Following the election, Olechowski wreaked havoc on the party system, with his new Civic Platform (PO) attracting elements from the Freedom Union and AWS. AWS splintered further, leaving Buzek leading a rump Solidarity Election Action – the Right (AWSP). Unemployment was rising again and the general economic outlook looked unfavourable as parliamentary elections approached. One survey recorded the lowest level of consumer confidence since June 1993, with fear of unemployment a crucial dimension of this new pessimism (*Rzeczpospolita*, 26–27 May 2001). Floods in the summer, revelations of the depth of crisis in the public finances, and new corruption scandals brought no respite to the rudderless government.

The Election of 2001

The SLD's victory in September 2001 thus came as no surprise. In alliance with the Labour Union it garnered over 40 per cent of the vote (see Table 2.2), as well as 75 per cent of Senate seats. Politics ceased to embody the historic division between the heirs of communism and the heirs of Solidarity that had dominated political life since 1989. The divide between the SLD and various emanations of the 1980s opposition movement was maintained in rhetoric, in programmatic differences, and in popular support throughout the 1990s. It remained crucial in 1997, with strong polarization of the two forces. But the 2000 presidential election and the 2001 parliamentary elections showed the now-feeble relevance of anti-communism and re-emphasized the democratic legitimacy of the SLD.

Moreover, neither Buzek's AWSP nor AWS's erstwhile partner, the Freedom Union, gained representation in the Sejm. Incumbents have often done badly in postcommunist elections, but this was a savage

(handwritten margin notes, left side:) SLD (ex-communists) win in 2001 151 ; SOLIDARITY CRUSHED in 2001

TABLE 2.2   *Results for national contenders for the Sejm, 23 September 2001*

Party/coalition*	Vote	% vote	Seats	% seats
SLD–UP	5,342,519	41.04	216	46.96
PO	1,651,099	12.68	65	14.13
SO	1,327,624	10.20	53	11.52
PiS	1,236,787	9.50	44	9.56
PSL	1,168,659	8.98	42	9.13
LPR	1,025,148	7.87	38	8.26
MN+	47,230	0.02	2	0.43
AWSP++	729,207	5.60	0	n/a
UW	404,074	3.10	0	n/a
Alternatywa	54,266	0.42	0	n/a

* SLD–UP: Alliance of the Democratic Left–Labour Union (*Sojusz Lewicy Demokratycznej–Unia Pracy*)
PO: Civic Platform (*Platforma Obywatelska*)
SO: Self-Defence (*Samoobrona*)
PiS: Law and Justice (*Prawo i Sprawiedliwosc*)
PSL: Polish Peasant Party (*Polskie Stronnictwo Ludowe*)
LPR: League of Polish Families (*Liga Polskich Rodzin*)
MN: German Minority (*Mniejszosc Niemiecka*)
AWSP: Solidarity Election Action – the Right (*Akcja Wyborcza Solidarnosc – Prawica*)
UW: Freedom Union (*Unia Wolnosci*).
The Alternative (*Alternatywa*)
+ Exempt from national threshold. ++ Coalition required 8%.
Source: *Panstwowa Komisja Wyborcza.*

blow. Finally, the nature and composition of parliament was radically changed by the entry of three new political formations – Civic Platform, Law and Justice, and the League of Polish Families – and the success of the hitherto marginalized radical populist Self-Defence.

Changes in 2001 to the electoral formula and constituency size, along with the abolition of the national list, were intended to prevent the SLD from gaining an outright majority, and in this regard they had the desired effect (Millard, 2003). It was less clear that this would prove beneficial for the political system as a whole. Leszek Miller became prime minister, but the SLD was once again forced into coalition with the PSL, as well as with its electoral ally the UP. The UP had done well enough to establish its own club of parliamentary deputies, and aimed to remain an independent political actor.

Institutions and State-Building

Poland's political institutions first took shape as part of the communist reforms of the mid-1980s, which established the Constitutional Tribunal and the Ombudsman, and at the Round Table, when both the new presidency and the Senate gained powers to challenge the dominance of the Sejm. The constitutional framework remained a matter of political controversy up to and even beyond the successful constitutional referendum of May 1997. The long genesis of a new Constitution meant a degree of legal confusion over the political institutions and their relationships, governed after 1989 by a series of further *ad hoc* amendments to the already unrecognizable 1952 Constitution and from December 1992 by the Little Constitution.

Institutions thus developed piecemeal in response to perceived problems at different stages of development. We have already noted this pattern in regard to the electoral system, in 1993 with measures designed to strengthen larger parties and in 2001 with changes intended to undermine the powerful position of the SLD. After 2001 it seemed likely to change again.

The Little Constitution included measures to strengthen government *vis-à-vis* the Sejm and to clarify the president's ambiguous powers. It succeeded in the former, notably with the introduction of the constructive vote of no confidence: the government falls only if the motion includes the name of the prime minister's successor. The role of the president in the process of appointing the prime minister was also spelt out in detail. It also facilitated the legislative process by weakening the Senate's legislative role. However, further clarification of presidential powers was less successful, and the 'presidential ministers' constituted an anomaly and an obstruction to cohesive government policy-making.

The 1997 Constitution was a major achievement of the SLD–PSL coalition. It was not a particularly coherent document, not least because of government concerns to generate the widest possible political consensus. Both main opposition parties, the Democratic Union and Labour Union, were fully involved in the constitution-making process. Outside parliament Solidarity opposed it. Its own version was overtly Christian-national and markedly syndicalist, with a strong role for the trade unions (Wenzel, 1998). Tensions between the government and the Episcopate remained salient at this time, not least because of the SLD's unwillingness to ratify the

Concordat (this was one of the first acts of Buzek's government), but also because of the Church's vigorous anti-abortion stance and protracted disagreements over the Constitution (Millard, 1999, pp. 137–9).

The new Constitution also reflected the experience of President Walesa's effective refusal to 'cohabit' with the SLD–PSL coalition. Not only were the 'presidential ministers' removed but the key presidential power, the veto, was weakened from a two-thirds override requirement to three-fifths. The president retained some important powers, and direct election made the office a major source of legitimacy; but Poland could no longer be viewed as a 'semi-presidential' system. The heart of the system remained parliament, and the Sejm in particular. Indeed, the SLD campaigned in 2001 in favour of abolishing the Senate, on grounds of cost and superfluity. But President Kwasniewski disagreed, and the PSL remained cool to the idea, calling into question the government's ability to gain sufficient support for a constitutional amendment.

Certainly there remained considerable problems with the quality of the Sejm's legislative work, its timetable, and its procedures, including the lack of automatic priority for government projects. The inexperience of deputies – 92 per cent were first-time parliamentarians in 1989, 73 per cent in 1991, 63 per cent in 1997, and 62 per cent in 2001 – also hindered the development of a routine, professional approach to parliamentary affairs. When Self-Defence entered parliament in 2001 it brought with it traditions of direct action and a lack of deference that soon disrupted normal parliamentary routines.

The Constitution strengthened the Constitutional Tribunal, which, along with the highly regarded Ombudsman, had amply demonstrated its role in securing the democratic process. Previously the Tribunal's decisions could be overridden by the Sejm; now the Tribunal's judicial review was binding on all institutions.

Aside from the broad provisions of the Constitution, other laws affected the structures of government. In 1990 in reaction to the centralization of the communist system, community (*gmina* or commune) governments gained considerable autonomy. Then in 1999 sixteen new provinces (*wojewodztwo*) replaced the existing 49, and the old county (*powiat*) tier was reintroduced. Major problems remained, not least because of existing inequalities and the inadequacy of resources to meet the increased functions of local and regional governments. At the same time central government also went through several phases of restructuring, with the SLD advocating further streamlining and measures to improve internal coordination in its 2001 election campaign. The Civil Service Law, with requirements for meritocratic competition for permanent civil servants, proved difficult to implement and was several times amended. In December 2001 the Sejm narrowly approved a government proposal that the Director-General should fill some 40,000 vacancies awaiting successful permanent appointments.

The real institutional gap lay, however, with the development of political parties and a coherent party system with predictable patterns of interaction. Leszek Miller's skill transformed the SLD from an alliance of numerous groupings united around the Social Democratic Party into a coherent, disciplined political party in 1999. No other party could match the SLD. The PSL had begun with the largest membership of all parties, extensive physical resources, organizational penetration throughout the countryside, and a clearly identified segment of the electorate. It was a governing party in 1993 and again in 2001. However, it squandered much of its political capital, and in 1997 it suffered massive losses. In 2001 it recovered somewhat, but suffered deep humiliation in being surpassed by Self-Defence (SO). SO had begun as a party of the rural disenchanted under Andrzej Lepper, with a radical populist appeal and penchant for direct action. In 2001 it became a truly national party, making the inroads into the towns that PSL had long sought. Self-Defence was undoubtedly aided by the general atmosphere of social pessimism and anti-establishment feeling, as well as the skilful transformation of Lepper's media image from that of streetwise thug to articulate spokesman for the oppressed.

The fragility of the parties was well illustrated by the fate of the Freedom Union in 2001. The party most closely associated with Solidarity's intelligentsia, it appeared the most stable and most highly institutionalized of the 'Solidarity parties' and (as the Democratic Union) the only one present in parliament throughout the 1990s. Its contribution both to the events of 1989 and the subsequent transformation programme was immeasurable. After the merger with the Liberals, when Balcerowicz became leader, the pragmatic free-market orientation prevailed; but the 'compassionate' wing of the party remained uneasy, particularly after the UW's poor performance in the 1998 local elections. In 2000 the UW neither fielded a presidential candidate nor endorsed Olechowski, the candidate closest to the party's own views. The UW's support further ebbed following its departure from Buzek's government. When Bronislaw Geremek became leader following Balcerowicz's departure to the National Bank after the presidential elections, the party seemed to be going backwards, not forwards. The liberal wing lost influence, and many joined Olechowski's new Civic Platform. With the party's own leaders deserting the sinking ship, it was not surprising that voters followed suit.

Nor did the smaller parties arising from the Solidarity movement prove effective in maintaining their political support. Krzaklewski drew them together in AWS, but he could not weld a single right-wing party from a pragmatic electoral alliance of squabbling leaders determined to croak loudest in their own small-party ponds. There were genuine ideological differences within AWS – liberal, conservative, agrarian, Christian democratic, nationalist – but these were overshadowed by the absence of effective leadership, a failure to develop as a coherent institution, and a public image of power-hungry, backbiting politicians, whether self-serving or downright corrupt. The departure of the Conservative-People's Party (SKL) to the Civic Platform in January 2001 sounded the death knell for AWS. Its major constituents, the SKL, the Christian Nationalist Union, the Christian Democrats, and the trade-union arm Social Movement (RS) all split, with departures to Civic Platform, Law and Justice, and the League of Polish Families leaving AWSP as a truncated mini-version of AWS.

Law and Justice (PiS) represented an attempt to capitalize on the extraordinary popularity of Lech Kaczynski, Buzek's Justice Minister after the UW's departure from government. Kaczynski's hard-line stance, with strong anti-corruption rhetoric and the promise of harsh penalties for criminals, provided the basis for this one-issue law-and-order grouping, orchestrated by his wheeler-dealer twin Jaroslaw. PiS touched a genuine chord of frustration and alienation from the new political class. Yet like PO, PiS was not entirely 'new'. Its foundation was the hard-core supporters of a defunct party, Jaroslaw Kaczynski's Centre Accord (PC), established in 1990 to support Walesa's presidential candidacy.

The final newcomer in 2001 was the League of Polish Families (LPR). This was another motley crew, drawn from discontented politicians of nationalist and clerical formations under the patronage of Radio Maryja, the voice of Catholic obscurantism. These parties offered little hope of cohesive, disciplined opposition in the 2001 parliament or as a future basis for the consolidation of the party system. PO, PiS and LPR were heterogeneous collectives, all displaying early tendencies to fray at the edges. They lacked clear profiles, organization, and social penetration. SO was the personal vehicle of Andrzej Lepper, who proved only too willing to disrupt parliament for publicity ends. SO's popularity rose further following the election, but it failed to mobilize the population for mass demonstrations in the summer. All the parties displayed internal tensions as they prepared for local government elections in late 2002.

Issues and Policies

The three-party government got off to a troubled start because of the uncertainties of the economic situation and the deep 'hole in the budget' inherited from the previous government, but also because of Prime Minister Miller's desire to accelerate negotiations with the European Union with a series of rapid concessions. The government's main priorities were to boost economic growth, especially through housing and road-building investment, and to achieve EU membership. Difficult decisions were required on public spending, and there were some immediate and unpopular changes in the tax regime. Planned savings through the streamlining of government administration became more difficult with three parties seeking the spoils of office, but there was some early restructuring of existing government agencies. During its first months in office the government waged a public but unsuccessful struggle with the independent Monetary Policy Council, with the president weighing in on the side of the latter. Proposed changes in labour legislation, designed to increase 'labour flexibility' and stimulate employment, generated new protests by trades unions in spring 2002. Social policy proposals, including restrictions on pensioners' earnings, also generated a mass outcry and a rethink of government strategy. The government suffered its first major casualty in July 2002 with the resignation of its respected Minister of Finance Marek Belka. However, Belka had done much of the hard work on public spending, and the return of the dynamic Grzegorz Kolodko (who had served in that post from 1994) was well received.

At the same time serious issues remained in the aftermath of Buzek's 'great reforms'. The health service was the central cause of concern. Indeed, all parties had campaigned in 2001 on platforms of 'repairing' the health service, including its new mechanism of insurance funding controlled by highly politicized health boards. Initial recentralizing proposals from the new health minister were met with scorn, and the SLD's preparations for government looked less impressive than they had seemed earlier. Concerns that the new mixed public–private pensions' system was still not functioning effectively and fears that it would in any case prove inadequate, especially for women, fuelled further popular anxieties. Thus the classic postcommunist dilemma of how to boost investment while allaying economic hardships and maintaining welfare spending did not disappear, and it created serious challenges for a purportedly left-wing government with a disparate electoral constituency.

On the EU, Miller's strategy was to push for rapid resolution of key issues, while mounting a sustained education–information campaign in anticipation of a referendum in 2003 and membership in 2004. He also began to construct a broad coalition of support, including the Catholic Church, to whom he proved remarkably conciliatory. If the referendum coincided with continuing economic problems, the Church's support could well prove vital. To this end the government effectively shelved plans for the mitigation of the existing harsh anti-abortion legislation, to the anger and dismay of the Parliamentary Women's Group.

The EU had scarcely been an issue before 2002, though commentators had warned of the dangers of 'shallow consensus' and eroding public support (Szczerbiak, 2000). Now parliamentary debates on both the EU and agricultural policy became a platform for open animosity to the EU. The nationalist LPR was stridently hostile to European integration, while both SO and the PSL were theoretically in favour but effectively Eurosceptic, anxious in particular to reassure their peasant constituencies. Agricultural modernization had remained little more than a slogan for previous governments, and the vast number of small peasant holdings represented a major social, economic, and political problem, as well as the thorniest issue of EU membership negotiations. However the strength of the government, the prestige of President Kwasniewski, the staunch pro-European stance of the PO, and the support of the Episcopate made it unlikely that Poland's populists would derail the accession process.

Poland's population often suffered a bumpy ride on their journey to democracy. Yet their vehicle negotiated safe passage for more than a decade and its drivers respected the rules of the road, if occasionally teetering on the edge or striking an unanticipated pothole. The institutional framework was in place, elites had proved their responsibility, civic freedoms were ensured. Instability, division, and protest were of the 'normal' variety, accommodated within the new democratic pluralism. Yet reforms were far from complete, particularly in the area of social policy. The quality of many institutions, including parliament itself, still demanded attention.

Above all, however, there remained a glaring institutional gap in the party system. New formations appeared in every parliament, and only the Alliance of the Democratic Left (SLD) could be regarded as fully institutionalized. It was still more appropriate to speak of 'the pluralisation of the party system than to proclaim the stability of a polyarchical party structure defined by strong parties with roots in the constituency' (Bielasiak, 1997, p. 41). Since political parties are key to the functioning of government, the structuring of parliament, and the linkage of the people to the polity, this problem should not be underestimated. Nor however, should it detract from the genuine achievements of Poland's political transformation.

3

The Czech Republic and Slovakia

KIERAN WILLIAMS

One oft-mentioned paradox of Czech and Slovak politics is that the two societies went their separate ways precisely when they had become more alike than at any point in modern times. By the early 1990s most of the old cliches about urban, secular Bohemia versus rural, Catholic Slovakia had lost their original validity, and the reality was of increasing convergence socioeconomically and culturally (Musil, 1995). It is true that they did not arrive by the same route at this common condition; Slovakia was modernized more recently and brusquely, under communist central planning, which left its mark on town–country relations and attitudes to the state. These differences, however, should not be so exaggerated as to attribute to them the collapse of the union at the end of 1992.

It appears instead that, the equalizing work of the common state apparently completed, political leaders saw little reason to perpetuate it, if endless fine-tuning of the constitution were to divert energy from other pressing matters. As the two nations' differences were probably not irreconcilable (Kraus and Stanger, 2000), we should not be surprised to discover a host of similarities in their subsequent development as separate states. After outlining the end of communist rule and of Czechoslovakia in 1989–92, this chapter will detail the institutions, parties and common political problems of the new states' first decade.

From Velvet Revolution to Dissolution

The chain of events that brought down one of the most rigid communist regimes in Eastern Europe started with the brutal dispersal of student demonstrators in Prague on 17 November 1989. Czechoslovak society had witnessed little protest in the previous twenty years, since the suppression of nationwide gatherings on the first anniversary of the 1968 Soviet-led invasion. That intervention had been prompted by fear that the planned liberalization of one-party rule announced by Communist Party leader Alexander Dubcek would spiral out of control, and its reversal was known euphemistically as 'normalization'. While expectations of change had risen in 1988, given the resemblance of Mikhail Gorbachev's *perestroika* to Dubcek's reforms, the 17 November 1989 student march was a meridian, marking the political arrival of a new generation that had experienced only 'normalization'.

The cuts and broken bones a relatively small group suffered that night became the stuff of wild rumour and legend, which inspired others to venture onto the streets of Prague, the Slovak capital Bratislava and other towns in the hundreds of thousands. They also became the core of a widely held conspiracy theory, according to which factions within the party and security service (StB) had organized a provocation to compel the resignation of the country's discredited leaders and replace them with Gorbachevian reformers. The flaw in this reasoning was its premise that the alleged conspirators had enough foresight to sense that, left unchanged, the system would be in peril. The surviving records so far declassified (admittedly, many were destroyed in late 1989) suggest no awareness of the gravity of the situation. Gestures were being considered akin to those offered in Poland several years previously, such as the introduction of a constitutional court, a new electoral law and a new constitution by October 1990. Such changes, however, were intended to fortify rather than change the nature of communist rule.

The complacency of the regime ensued from the conviction that the Czechoslovak economy, though torpid, was sufficiently able to deliver the basics that people needed, which translated into outward conformity and order. Periodically, elements of the intelligentsia could be mobilized for displays of support: in just two weeks in early 1977 around 7,500 artists, actors, architects, musicians and writers publicly endorsed the official denunciation of Charter 77, a dissident appeal for human rights that over the next twelve years only 1,742 brave souls dared to sign. Despite its difficulty in recruiting new members, the Party remained 1.7 million strong, embracing 16 per cent of the adult population in 1989, and had a paramilitary wing with thousands of armed workers. The StB still had

8,600 officers and at least 13,000 informers, thanks to whose efforts 340 people were sitting in prison for purely political reasons in the summer of 1989. The aging and unpopular president of the republic, Gustav Husak, had been unseated as party leader in 1987 not for obstructing reform, but for attempting to install a new coterie of proteges in the party's upper echelons; his marginally younger rivals had moved to protect and promote their own clients under the guise of 'rejuvenation' (Koudelka, 2000).

In view of the outward docility of Czechoslovak society on the eve of November 1989, the speed with which the regime fell was remarkable. The international context was critical, in that the swift course of events in other Soviet satellites, especially East Germany, left Czechoslovakia in the embarrassing company of Romania and Albania as the last holdouts against revolution. The Czechoslovak Communist Party in effect surrendered power when, only a week after the initial student march, it rejected pressure from the defence minister to protect socialism by 'all necessary means'. Unwilling to cause a massacre that would inevitably resemble the Tiananmen crackdown in China only months before, and with no sign of a Soviet intervention in their support, the party leadership resigned *en masse.*

Negotiations then commenced between the communist prime minister and the leaders of the emerging opposition movements, Civic Forum in the Czech lands and Public against Violence in Slovakia. Unlike the talks that had taken place in Poland and Hungary, these were not substantive deliberations over the constitution, electoral system or foreign policy, because the Czechoslovak Communist Party lacked the authority to set terms and conditions. Instead, the objectives were the formation of a non-communist interim government, the appointment of opposition representatives to seats in the legislature and the resignation of President Husak (Calda, 1996). In effect and probably in intent, the talks directed the revolution away from the city squares and into less populated institutions, out of the hands of students and into those of their parents. This process was completed on 29 December 1989 with the election of Vaclav Havel, the consummate dissident, to the presidency.

The interim administration finished with the founding election of June 1990, in which 96 per cent of eligible voters participated. The two movements of the revolution, Civic Forum and Public against Violence, triumphed and used their new ruling coalition to prepare legislation that would turn the country into a market economy.

Parliamentary business, however, was disrupted by a searing quest for StB collaborators in the new political elite, a process known as lustration, which in October 1991 was put on a statutory footing and extended to the entire public sector. Moreover, the broad political groupings that emerged in late 1989 were fragmenting along ideological lines, such that by 1992 there were eighteen factions in the federal legislature. Last of all, the passage of bills was subject to complex rules guaranteeing Slovak deputies the veto in key areas, so that they could not always be outvoted by the more numerous Czechs.

Despite such anti-majoritarian safeguards, Slovaks were quick to express dissatisfaction with the constitutional status quo, and not just because they equated it with the imposition by Czechs of a discriminatory economic policy. Grievances were already audible in the first quarter of 1990, well before the full impact of price liberalization, fiscal austerity and the loss of Soviet markets was felt in Slovakia. Instead, there resumed a quarrel dating back to the very foundation of Czechoslovakia in 1918, which concerned the degree of autonomy permitted within the union. Slovaks, with considerable justification, felt that Czechs had repeatedly reneged on promises of devolution, especially when the union was re-established at the end of World War II (although a German satellite, Slovakia had enjoyed nominal independence in 1939–45). Federalization in 1968 created distinct Czech and Slovak constituent republics with their own governments and legislatures but stopped well short of satisfying Slovak demands for near-sovereignty (Zatkuliak, 1996). The restoration of centralized party rule in 1969–70 only compounded Slovak disappointment. With many of the politicians and lawyers who argued the Slovak case in 1968 still alive and active in Public against Violence, it is not surprising that in early 1990 they returned to precisely the points not resolved 22 years before.

These veterans of 1968, joined by Slovak Christian Democrats rooted in Catholic dissident networks, manoeuvred to win the maximum possible power for Bratislava in successive rounds of negotiation in 1990 and 1991. While the Czech side at first freely yielded to many Slovak requests, they also looked for an endpoint at which federal institutions would achieve a new equilibrium. Such a settlement was not discernible in the ambiguous Slovak project, which was increasingly open to the Czech criticism that Slovak institutions would be given all the power and none of the responsibility; financial transfers and the protection of the Czech-dominated army would supply the safety net for an otherwise practically independent Slovakia. The intricate rules of federal law-making also made attempts at constitutional revision arduous and often futile (Olson, 1994a; Henderson, 1995).

What stymied the talks between the republics, however, was the politics of symbolism: Slovak Christian Democrats insisted on a virtual refoundation of the union through a treaty between the two republics, which would imply that Slovaks were as capable of self-government as the Czechs and had freely covenanted to delegate some power to the common state (Stein, 1997). The wording and legal status of such a treaty were the subjects of endless haggling in 1991 and early 1992; the defeat of a compromise text by one vote in the presidium of the Slovak legislature ensured the end of any further negotiations before the 1992 election and, ultimately, the end of Czechoslovakia itself.

The task of dismantling the union fell to two men who had not sought it when campaigning in 1992, but who had helped create an environment in which the Czech and Slovak elites could not easily govern together: Vaclav Klaus and Vladimir Meciar, the charismatic leaders of the strongest parties to emerge from the wreckage of Civic Forum and Public against Violence, respectively. Klaus was intimately associated with the economic reform package and thus with the hardships visited on Slovakia as unemployment shot up, which in turn gave Meciar the wherewithal to mobilize voters against Prague and neo-liberalism. Ostensibly attempting to form a federal coalition government in the summer of 1992, they concluded that separation was the easier option.

Brusquely dismissing Meciar's plan for a confederation, Klaus's team pushed through a set of intergovernmental agreements to maintain a customs union and common currency, in order both to affirm the end of the federation and cushion the economic blow. Also overridden was public opinion, which polls consistently found to be opposed to the split. No referendum on the fate of the union was held, and the state was terminated by a constitutional amendment. Attempts to stop the breakup were limited to a petition drive; although millions of citizens signed, this crusade did not mobilize the sorts of crowds that only three years before had brought down the Communist Party.

While few wanted to admit it, many ordinary people were suffering from the same lack of an ideological attachment to the federal idea that plagued their leaders. To survive, federations must not only generate material benefits or collective security but also a

VELVET RE DIVORCE
AGAINST POPULAR
SUPPORT OF THE
UNION

normative commitment, such that they are held to be intrinsically superior to nation-states (Franck, 1968). The opportunity to inculcate the ideal of a federal republic was squandered during 'normalization', when only the Communist Party, USSR and a fictional proletariat were glorified (Wright, 1984). So, on 1 January 1993, with velvet ease but little fanfare, the Czech Republic and Slovakia became independent states.

The New States' Institutions and Party Systems

Owing to the haste with which the new states' constitutions had to be drafted in 1992, and the legal continuity inherent in their successor status, the ratified documents drew heavily on the traditions of the Czechoslovak republic. The new countries were consequently parliamentary democracies, with the preponderance of executive power to be exercised by a prime minister and government relying on legislative confidence. In both cases the presidency was downgraded, becoming a rainy-day office to be activated mostly during ordeals of government formation and cohesion and to check the legislature gently by suspensive veto of bills, which in neither country required a supermajority to override. As in Italy, the presidency lent itself most freely as a bully pulpit from which to admonish the political class and teach the nation, but such forays invited retribution.

Following the Czechoslovak tradition, the first presidents (Havel in the Czech Republic and Michal Kovac in Slovakia) were initially chosen by the legislature; in 1999 Slovakia moved to direct elections when repeated attempts to choose a successor to Kovac failed. The experience of the first man to win a national presidential contest, Rudolf Schuster, suggested that having a mandate from the people did not automatically increase the authority of the office. More important were lacunae in the constitution interpreted to award the president extra room, for example to challenge the premier's request to dismiss a minister for corruption. Where the Czech president had a certified freedom, for which he answered to no one, was in certain appointments, such as of judges of the constitutional court and the top figures at the central bank, and he did not have to give the leader of the largest party the first chance to form a government after an election (Slosarcik, 2001). The exercise of this power often antagonized parliamentary parties, which attempted (unsuccessfully) to curtail it.

[margin handwritten: Gov Structure]

In the ten years after the 1992 elections, both states had four governments. Practically all were coalitions of a sort; even the single-party cabinets (in Slovakia in 1992–3 and the Czech Republic in 1998–2002) relied on semi-formal understandings with another party. Governments averaged in duration 29 months in the Czech Republic and 30 months in Slovakia. These rates, which are already good by any European standard, do not do justice to the full four-year terms served by cabinets under premiers Klaus (1992–6) and Milos Zeman (1998–2002) in the Czech Republic, and under Meciar (1994–8) and Miklulas Dzurinda (1998–2002) in Slovakia. While routinely buffeted by scandals and feuds, these cabinets endured from one election to the next unshielded by the constructive vote of no confidence that protects prime ministers elsewhere in Central Europe. Several factors account for this stability. One was the strong incentive to remain in government at a special time in the country's history, either to achieve milestone policy goals (such as membership of the EU and NATO) or to profit from privatization and state resources when everything was up for grabs and few controls were in place. Junior partners frequently agitated for disproportionate influence, but the difficulty with which early elections could be called discouraged attempts to convert momentary swings in opinion polls into higher seat totals. The other stabilizing factors relate to party organization and competition – the effective leadership and cohesion of the governing parties, and the polarization that reduced the set of possible combinations.

Although the premier was the very visible and often controversial embodiment of the government in both states, the coordination of duties and policy-making was largely delegated to deputy prime ministers (usually four) and interdepartmental committees run by state secretaries. Responsibility for transposition and implementation of the EU's *acquis* fell on the deputy premiers for legislation and foreign affairs, and on the justice minister; the premier intervened (as Zeman did in 1999) only if the job was not being done properly. Weekly cabinet meetings were lengthy and often decisive (Müller-Rommel and Mansfeldova, 2001; Müller-Rommel and Malova, 2001), although in the Czech case matters were increasingly settled in the smaller State Security Council (Horejsi, 2002). Even overbearing and opinionated leaders such as Klaus and Meciar were willing or forced to defer to colleagues on a range of issues; weaker, more consensual premiers, such as Dzurinda, had regularly to let matters reach crisis point before decisions could be taken (Lesko, 2000).

For most of the 1990s, the legislative agenda was set by the government. Although committees contributed meaningfully to the content of bills, the institution of parliament (bicameral in the Czech Republic, unicameral in Slovakia) displayed little autonomy. Except in periods of turbulence such as 1993 in Slovakia and 1998–9 in the Czech Republic, the parliament processed a steady stream of government-backed bills. Under pressure from the EU to step up transposition of the *acquis*, the Czech legislature of 1998–2002 passed or amended 465 laws, most of them in the last two years. Quantity, however, was often at the expense of quality, such that many new acts were 'semi-finished goods' in need of prompt revision (Korecky and Bilek, 2002).

This sort of output was made possible by the cohesion of parliamentary factions and, by extension, of clusters of likeminded parties (Kopecky, 2001). In both countries, especially from 1992 to 1998, one party overshadowed the rest. In the Czech Republic it was Vaclav Klaus's Civic Democratic Party (ODS), built on the liberal wing of the defunct Civic Forum and on a rhetorical blend of Thatcherism and nationalism (Williams, 1997; Hanley, 1999). Capturing 30 per cent of the vote in 1992 and again in 1996, its eclipse began in 1997, when the flaws in Klausian economics were exposed and a recession took effect. Although its share of the vote slipped in 1998 to 28 per cent and to 25 per cent in 2002, ODS remained the dominant voice of the right and one of the best developed party organizations.

In the shadow of ODS operated the Christian Democratic Union (KDU-CSL), descended from people's parties of the interwar republic and the communist period. Catering to distinct rural and Catholic constituencies, the party was an uneasy coalition partner in 1992–7, crossing swords with Klaus on such issues as social policy, restitution of church property and control of the security–intelligence service. Also on the right was Freedom Union, formed by defectors from the ODS in 1998. An electoral alliance ('Quad-coalition') of Freedom Union, the Christian Democrats and two miniscule parties excelled in elections to the upper chamber, the Senate, and to regional assemblies in 2000. However, their lacklustre 14 per cent in the 2002 election of the more important lower chamber, the Diet of Deputies, reflected maladroit alliance management and the general cooling towards the right that also hurt ODS (see Table 3.1).

After 1997, the left prevailed in Czech party competition. The Czech Social Democratic Party (CSSD), founded in 1889 and

TABLE 3.1   *Czech election results (lower chamber), 2002*

Party	% of the vote	Seats in Diet of Deputies	% of Diet seats
Czech Social Democratic Party	30.20	70	35.0
Civic Democratic Party	24.47	58	29.0
Communist Party of Bohemia and Moravia	18.51	41	20.5
Coalition (Christian Democratic Union–Czech People's Party and Freedom Union–Democratic Union)	14.27	31	15.5

Source: *www.essex.ac.uk/elections and www.volby.cz.*

forcibly merged with the Communists sixty years later, reappeared quickly in 1990 but acquired credibility only after 1993, under the leadership of economist Milos Zeman. Capitalizing on the discontent caused by a crisis of the banks and currency, Zeman took the CSSD to a 32 per cent share of the 1998 vote and into power. Holding only 74 of the 200 seats in the Diet of Deputies, the Social Democrats governed alone thanks to a special arrangement with Klaus's ODS, ensuring the latter a range of key portfolios and consultation on policy, combined with a commitment to institutional changes (revision of the electoral system and reduction of presidential power) that would enhance the power of the two parties.

This widely criticized undertaking worked poorly in its first 18 months: ODS often voted against government bills, including ones essential to EU accession, and an impasse over the budget in autumn 1999 paralysed the state for three months. When attempts by ODS to form its own coalition with other parties of the right failed, a new pact reaffirmed the relationship with the Social Democrats and helped start a legislative hurricane (Vachudova, 2001). While the deal was usually viewed as favouring ODS, ultimately the Social Democrats benefited more: they oversaw a return to economic growth, attracted floods of foreign investment, pleased Brussels and in the 2002 election won 30 per cent of the vote. One of the reasons for their repeated electoral success was a move as daring as the deal with ODS: Zeman, a bombastic centrist, agreed to stand down after just one term as premier, yielding to his more principled and sober deputy, Vladimir Spidla. CSSD voters could thus cast their ballots at once for continuity and change.

Flanking the CSSD on its left was the Communist Party of Bohemia and Moravia (KSCM). The scorn heaped on the Communists by dissidents and the West before 1989 concealed the party's social basis – elements of the working class, civil service, management and army that were truly sympathetic. Bolshevism had taken root as a political subculture in the 1920s and peaked in 1946, when 40 per cent of Czechs voted for the party in a relatively free election. After 1989, the approximately 200,000 members who stayed in the KSCM resisted the shift to social democracy that communist parties pursued in Slovakia and elsewhere. As a result, the KSCM remained untouchable for coalitions, stuck in permanent but vociferous opposition (Hanley, 2001). Never falling below 10 per cent of the vote, in 2002 it surged to 19 per cent and pulled in 200,000 additional voters when other parties were losing half a million each.

In Slovakia, the dominant party for the first six years of independence was Vladimir Meciar's Movement for a Democratic Slovakia (HZDS). Whereas ODS had been formed to compel Civic Forum to acquire sharper ideological definition, HZDS arose in 1991 as a reaction against the rightward shift of Public against Violence. Its eclectic blend of centrist economics and boisterous nationalism won HZDS 37 per cent of the vote in 1992, leaving it only two seats short of a majority. The fluidity of the HZDS programme attracted a diverse mix of supporters, primarily those most dislocated by the communist mode of modernization (Williams, 2000; Haughton, 2001).

Once in power HZDS became the instrument of industrial and commercial elites, which dictated the terms on which directors of public firms would be allowed to convert their insider positions into private wealth. Their influence translated into dozens of legislative acts that the constitutional court found to violate citizens' property rights, but HZDS rarely respected the judges' opinions. That disregard was a function of a general indifference to law when it conflicted with the party's power and interests, an illiberalism that provoked *demarches* from Western states. Denying the opposition any meaningful oversight through legislative committees, HZDS was able to plunder the state and abuse the offices of the security–intelligence service (SIS). At its worst, the party consorted with mafiosi and probably ordered the murder of an intermediary between journalists and a witness to the kidnapping of President Kovac's son by SIS officers (itself part of a plan to force the head of state to abdicate because of his opposition to Meciar). HZDS lost power in 1998 because of its reputation for corruption and its inability to reduce the high levels of crime and unemployment, but on 27 per cent it remained the largest party in that year's election and it topped opinion polls while subsequently in opposition. A last-minute schism and misconceived campaign pushed HZDS below 20 per cent in the 2002 election, yet it retained the largest share of the vote.

While Czech party competition stabilized in the mid-1990s, with minor changes on the margins, the Slovak was repeatedly shaken by splits, breakthroughs and disappearances. The two parties on which HZDS relied for a majority after 1994, the leftist Association of Workers and racist Slovak National Party, were already in no position to form another coalition in 1998, and were even less so in 2002. The Party of the Democratic Left (SDL), the Westernized successor to the Slovak Communist Party, found that Meciar had captured much of its potential electorate and was devastated by the 1999 departure of its rising star, Robert Fico. While Fico's new *Smer* (Way) movement clambered up the polls on a mix of *étatisme*, a tough stance on crime and occasional chauvinism (Haughton, 2002), and the hardline Communist Party of Slovakia broke through the 5 per cent barrier, the ineffectual SDL and a half-dozen other leftist fragments failed to win seats in the 2002 election (Table 3.2).

The situation to the right of HZDS was little calmer. The Christian Democrats, locked into a traditional, confessional niche, could neither expand their electorate nor contain the ambitions of their younger, more ecumenical functionaries. In 1998 they were pulled into a five-party electoral alliance, the Slovak Democratic Coalition, to maximize their chances of defeating Meciar in that year's election. Mavericks saw in the Slovak Democratic Coalition

TABLE 3.2   *Slovak election results, 2002*

Party	% of the vote	Seats	% of seats
Movement for a Democratic Slovakia	19.50	36	24.00
Slovak Democratic and Christian Union	15.10	28	18.65
Smer	13.46	25	16.66
Party of the Hungarian Coalition	11.16	20	13.34
Christian Democratic Movement	8.25	15	10.00
Alliance of the New Citizen	8.00	15	10.00
Communist Party of Slovakia	6.32	11	7.30

Sources: *www.essex.ac.uk/elections* and *www.evolby.sme.sk.*

the makings of a broader conservative party, but could not over-come the resistance of many Christian Democratic founders and activists. The result was a major division in early 2000 between the premier, Dzurinda, and his justice minister, Jan Carnogursky. Dzurinda gathered sympathizers into a new Slovak Democratic and Christian Union, while Carnogursky continued the more narrowly Catholic movement that he founded in 1990. The last development on the right before the 2002 election was the long-awaited emer-gence of a vehicle, the Alliance of the New Citizen, for media mogul Pavol Rusko.

A final attribute of the Slovak party system was the electoral suc-cess of the Hungarian minority. Constituting around 11 per cent of the population, Hungarian-speakers cast most of their votes for three parties that formed quickly in late 1989, which ensured a commensurate presence in the parliament. The three Hungarian parties often combined for elections and operated a joint parlia-mentary group, which in 1998–2002 was the only club not to lose a member. Leaning to the right of centre, the Hungarians joined the Dzurinda government and helped it survive, even though their Slovak partners often let them down. The only party besides Meciar's HZDS to win seats in 2002 under the same name as four years before, the Hungarian alliance joined the Slovak Democratic and Christian Union, Christian Democrats and Alliance of the New Citizen in forming a government of the right.

The development of the Slovak party system, and to a lesser degree that of the Czech, raises questions about systemic incen-tives: Was there something in the electoral process that encouraged flux? Both countries used proportional representation, with the Hagenbach–Bischoff formula and large multimember districts minimizing the advantage to bigger parties (the Czech Republic switched to the d'Hondt formula in 2002, with no dramatic conse-quences). This intrinsic fairness, however, was offset by a 5 per cent threshold that had to be crossed to qualify for seats; scaled thresh-olds were added in 1992 for alliances, to raise the bar somewhat higher. HZDS, in a bid to sideline the opposition in the 1998 Slovak election, imposed the requirement that each member of an alliance receive 5 per cent, hoping that three- or four-party clusters would fall short of the necessary 15 or 20 per cent and be disqualified. ODS introduced a slightly less punitive version of this scale for the 2002 Czech election. These devices, however, failed to exert their intended effect: in Slovakia the opposition simply converted alliances into unified shell parties, which needed only 5 per cent, and in the Czech Republic the Quad-coalition shrank to a tandem through merger and the departure of one of its mini-members (Birch, Millard, Popescu and Williams, 2002). Once over the hurdle, these expedient associations rarely held together. A truly drastic measure, such as the ban on electoral coalitions found in Germany and Austria, may be required to induce a lasting aggregation.

The Czech case, however, provides evidence of stabilization owing not to a rational response to incentives, but to the emotive success of parties in generating identities and loyalty. After a last burst of splintering in 1994, the departure of deputies or whole factions slowed and became the extraordinary event (such as befell ODS in early 1998) that it is in Western Europe. In the 1998–2002 Diet only two deputies quit the party on which they had been elected, compared with more than 30 in Slovakia during the same period. There is no simple formula for this Czech sense of belonging; rather, it can be attributed to the air cleared by the earlier schisms, the replacement of overt discipline with more subtle forms of intraparty surveillance and reward, and the pronounced personalities that parties acquired thanks to able leaders (Kopecky, 2001). In this regard, the two countries diverged sharply after becoming independent.

Common Problems in Separate States

This difference notwithstanding, much continued to unite the political lives of the new states. The rest of this chapter will focus on two general commonalities.

The first is the awkward place occupied by fading giants such as Klaus and Meciar, and more generally by the first post-1989 wave of leaders. After the watershed of 1998 the unseated premiers' mass appeal dwindled and, perhaps more important, other parties did not want to sit in government with them. Klaus irritated many at home and abroad with his increasingly strident nationalism, while Meciar was internationally ostracized for his illiberalism. In 2002 American officials informed the Slovak people that an HZDS victory in that year's election would deprive the country of an invitation to NATO.

Still able to command a solid fifth or quarter of the vote, however, Klaus and Meciar were not entirely spent forces. Once *primus inter pares* in their parties, by the late 1990s they had broken with the other founders and were surrounded by outwardly loyal, dependent juniors. For all the resouces ploughed into the formidable ODS and HZDS organizations, the future of the parties was considered contingent on the ability of their chairmen to hold various factions together. Kept in place if only to postpone the bloodletting of a succession struggle, their continuing presence (like that of the Communists) limited the set of likely coalitions by removing a large share of the seats from consideration.

The incremental cutting down to size of the men who founded the new states was part of the phasing out of the veterans of 1989. A few familiar faces remained, and high-profile positions such as the presidency were likely to remain in the hands of elders (Havel stood down in January 2003, while Schuster's first term ends in 2004), but practical power was shifting to thirty- and fortysome-things, especially in the Czech Republic. Even though Zeman gave way to Spidla (born 1951), the most powerful figure in the Czech Social Democratic Party was arguably Stanislav Gross, who became interior minister in 1998 aged only 28, while its most popular member, Petra Buzkova, was born in 1965. The upper echelon of Klaus's ODS was filled by Ivan Langer (born 1967), Petr Necas (1964), Jan Zahradil (1963) and Vlastimil Tlusty (1955).

Slovak party leaders tended to be older, and despite a declared effort during the 2002 election to promote younger faces the average age of candidates within electable range was 46; many, at least, had never sat in parliament before, so a watershed of sorts did occur. Some attempts at generational turnover had unintended consequences: Meciar used the pretext of rejuvenation to put unknowns on his party's 2002 list of candidates in place of older colleagues, who thereupon quit to found their own movement and took with them a sizeable share of the HZDS support base.

Whether the existing party labels will suffice for the next generation or undergo realignment and rebranding will reveal just how deeply parties were institutionalized in the 1990s. One challenge for the new political elite will be to stir voters succumbing, as across Europe, to apathy. Turnout was vibrant in the first four elections (surging up to 84 per cent in Slovakia in 1998), but crashed to 58 per cent in the Czech Republic in 2002. An even more sobering fact of that Czech election was that only 40 per cent of eligible voters turned out to cast ballots for the major pro-system parties (excluding the KSCM). The 2002 Slovak poll drew a more respectable 70 per cent, owing to the special effort of non-party civic groups to mobilize voters and to the significance of that election for Slovakia's chances of joining the EU and NATO. As the danger of exclusion from the international community recedes, the imperative to participate may also wane. A related challenge will be to improve the representation in both states of the Roma minority and of women, the latter's share of legislative seats having been halved from 30 per cent in the last communist legislature to around 15 per cent by the late 1990s. Only 34 of 200 Czech deputies elected in 2002 were women, while in the 2002 Slovak election the ratio of men to women within electable range on party lists was 5 : 1 (Kaliska, 2002), as a result of which only 22 women secured seats. The second commonality is the quality of governance. Neither state found it easy to craft a post-privatization public sector. Although some ministries were abolished along with central planning, other departments had to grow or be created to address the new needs of a market economy. Slovakia had to kick-start services, such as diplomacy and defence, which Czechs had dominated in the federation. In any revolution, the new elite claims the discretion to install supporters who will implement change. Neither the allegedly anti-state Klaus nor the allegedly pro-state Meciar wanted to so professionalize the civil service that partisanship would disappear as a factor in hiring and promotion. The result was an unregulated recruitment regime that did not always prioritize ability.

Moreover, governance of both states was highly centralized. With a powerful cabinet office at the hub, ministries concentrated policy-making in the capitals and enforced decisions through branch offices at the district level. Little power fell to local elected authorities, despite the fine talk in 1989 of participation and citizenship. Campaigns by President Havel and his late wife Olga to promote non-governmental organizations were derided by Klaus as the back door to state capture by special interests. Meciar, though no less hostile to the NGOs championed by President Kovac and his gifted advisor Pavol Demes, counter-attacked by funding a Potemkin civil society around his HZDS.

After 1997, however, governance was not a purely domestic matter: the EU took it into account when considering applicants' readiness for membership, and its initial opinions of Czech and Slovak public administration were scathing. In response, the Zeman and Dzurinda governments that came to power in 1998 made a more effective and less corrupt state a top priority. Decentralization also started, albeit haltingly after battles over the number and boundaries of regions, and over the powers of their assemblies and chief executives; the Hungarians in Slovakia bitterly resented the rejection of a 'majority–minority' region covering their area of concentration. Although the Czech Republic enacted a civil-service statute only in 2002, and the various anti-corruption drives could never meet the high expectations they raised, sufficient progress was identified to allow Brussels to downplay governance as a problem.

One acclaimed development in both states was the growth of counter-majoritarian institutions such as the very active constitutional courts (Schwartz, 2000; Slosarcik, 2001) and, since 2000, the Czech ombudsman. (The first Slovak ombudsman was elected in March 2002, so the office's impact has yet to be felt; parliament's choice of an HZDS deputy disappointed the NGO activists who had backed a non-party attorney.) Beyond the constitutional court, however, the judiciaries of both states caused great concern to the EU, which found them to be overloaded, understaffed and vulnerable to corruption or politicization (Vachudova, 2001). Recent reforms have made the judiciary a more attractive profession, commanding life tenure and a respectable salary, but around 300 of the planned 2,893 judgeships remained unfilled in the Czech Republic as of 2001. In Slovakia, 1,278 judges had to contend with 900,000 new cases a year. Vacancies on the bench and laborious prosecution procedures created massive backlogs; civil cases lasted on average 13 months in Slovakia and even longer in the Czech Republic. Lack of foreign language skills was preventing retraining in EU law, but in both countries the judiciary was acquiring more corporate autonomy and thus more control over judges' ongoing education. Although the rule of law is a vital myth in the legitimation of the postcommunist state (Priban, 2001), its realization in an effective judiciary will be the most challenging task of the next decade.

4

Hungary

MARK PITTAWAY

The development of Hungary's postcommunist political system and the dynamic of politics in the country during the 1990s cannot be understood without reference to communist politics as they were practised between the suppression of the 1956 Revolution and the late 1980s. During this period the country was ruled by Janos Kadar, who had been installed by Soviet troops in 1956. Though the early years of Kadar's rule were marked by the repression of groups and individuals that had supported the Revolution, beneath the hardline exterior, even in the early years, Kadar quietly reformed the socialist system. The state abandoned its Stalinist policies in the workplace and sought an accommodation with the industrial working class by recasting the identity of the ruling party, the Hungarian Socialist Workers' Party (*Magyar Szocialista Munkaspart*, or MSZMP), as a genuinely 'workers' party', and making improvements in social policy and living standards that were central to its appeal (Foldes, 1993). While agriculture was finally successfully collectivized in 1961, the changes that took place were accomplished through the pursuit of flexible agricultural policies that allowed peasants more opportunities for improving their living standards, thus reconciling them to the new cooperatives (Swain, 1985; Varga, 2001). Furthermore, throughout the 1960s a compromise between party and intelligentsia emerged which provided a basis for one of the most liberal cultural policies in East-Central Europe. More practically the regime came to rely on expertise from the social sciences for policy formation to a degree unprecedented in the region (O'Neil, 1998).

While the state continued to maintain a large political police force it withdrew from a prominent role in everyday life, concentrating instead selectively on acts of explicit political dissidence

(Kenedi, 1996). Kadar himself described his policy towards political opposition in 1962 as follows:

> Everyone who is striving for the cause of socialism and peace must be united on the basis of the socialist policy of national unity. We must bring together Communists and those outside the party, politically active supporters of the regime and those who today are still wavering, the indifferent, those who hold to a materialist world-view and people of a religious disposition alike. The construction of socialist society is a matter for the nation as a whole. (Quoted in Romsics, 1999, p. 333)

Conciliatory policies directed towards social groups who opposed socialism were combined with economic growth underpinned by successive waves of economic reform that allowed spectacular growth in living standards during the 1960s and 1970s. This growth was underpinned by a growth in real wages, a major expansion of social benefits and increasing opportunities to earn money in the so-called 'second economy', that is to say, semi-legal private sector activity. By the mid-1970s, the golden years of Kadar's social pact with Hungarian society, living standards were high, and in contrast to some of Hungary's immediate neighbours, there were no real food and goods shortages.

Beneath the surface there were serious problems. There was a small dissident opposition based in Budapest that was an irritant to the socialist regime. There was broader criticism of the limited effectiveness of state social policies. The major difficulty was that despite successive waves of economic reform the Kadar compromise rested on a weak economic base and had been bought by steadily accumulating debt (Foldes, 1995). By the late 1970s this had led to economic crisis. The slow beginnings of Hungary's economic transformation quickly followed. Price subsidies were cut in 1979 while the early 1980s were marked by measures to privatize retail services and introduce entrepreneurial elements into the state sector. The 1980s were for most ordinary Hungarians a decade of austerity as living standards stagnated and key elements of socialism's social contract, such as full unemployment, were abandoned. This climate led to increasing levels of popular discontent. In 1985 the party allowed multi-candidate elections for the first time; although no party other than the MSZMP was permitted to stand, independent candidates were elected in opposition to party officials for the first time.

With Mikhail Gorbachev's accession to the Soviet leadership in 1985 Hungary's international position changed in a way that opened the door to greater political change. This shift occurred at a time of greater political activism in society and a gradual withdrawal of trust on the part of the population from official institutions. From the early 1980s the small dissident opposition had been able to expand as a result of its publication of *samizdat*. Furthermore it had been joined by other groups advocating environmentalism, nuclear disarmament and pacifism. Nationalist, conservative and liberal elements within the opposition had begun to develop common ground, which was demonstrated at a meeting of opposition figures at Monor in 1985. Within the party there was growing pressure for reform, particularly among younger members and officials. In September 1987 the party's monopoly over political life was broken when in the provincial town of Lakitelek a group of nationalist writers, with some cooperation from local party officials, founded the Hungarian Democratic Forum (*Magyar Demokrata Forum*, or MDF).

While the formation of the MDF was made possible by cooperation between certain elements in the party apparatus and the nationalist wing of the opposition, it opened the door to the formation of organizations that explicitly opposed the party-state. Early 1988 saw the foundation of the Network of Free Initiatives by members of the dissident opposition based in Budapest. Thirty-seven students at Budapest's Karl Marx University of Economics launched a youth organization – the Alliance of Young Democrats (*Fiatal Demokratak Szovetsege*, or FIDESZ) – to provide young Hungarians with an alternative to the party's youth organization. In May, employees in the universities and research institutes founded a trade union in opposition to the official union federation. Attempts by the police to hinder the operation of the new organizations met with little success and during the course of 1988 they grew in confidence. As organizations independent and opposed to the party-state multiplied, some began to explicitly transform themselves into political parties. In November the Network of Free Initiatives transformed itself into a radical liberal party, the Alliance of Free Democrats (*Szabad Demokratak Szovetsege*, or SZDSZ). The same month saw the re-foundation of the Independent Smallholders' Party (*Fuggetlen Kisgazdapart*, or FKGP), the conservative party that had won the first postwar elections in 1945 that preceded the creation of socialist dictatorship.

The growing assertiveness of the opposition was paralleled by a widening split within the party between Kadar and his allies, and those committed to radical economic and political reform. This split became visible at the party congress in May 1988 which not only removed Kadar but also transformed the party leadership, dismissing most of the Politburo and around a third of the Central Committee. While Kadar's successor as party secretary, Karoly Grosz, was unconvinced of the need for reform, the congress strengthened the position of leading reformers including Imre Pozsgay, who had encouraged the foundation of the MDF. During the second half of 1988 the party responded slowly to events as groups within it committed to more radical reform began to form 'reform circles' in order to democratize the party from below. By the end of 1988 the leadership of the MSZMP began to discuss the end of the leading role of the party and democratization of the political system. The reformist wing of the party forced the pace of change during early 1989. The young prime minister Miklos Nemeth asserted his willingness to enter talks with the opposition; and Imre Pozsgay broke one of the taboos of the Kadar era by declaring that the 1956 Revolution had been a a 'popular uprising' and not a 'counter-revolution'. By February the Central Committee had expressed its support for the introduction of a multi-party system. These shifts concealed deep and bitter disagreement between those, led by Grosz, who sought to preserve as much of the socialist system as possible, and more radical reformers.

The growing disarray within the party increased the confidence and the unity of the opposition. A variety of opposition groups including the MDF, FIDESZ, the FKGP and the SZDSZ demanded that a 'national roundtable' be convened to discuss the election of a 'constitutional convention'. A large opposition demonstration followed in the capital on 15 March – the anniversary of the beginning of the 1848 Revolution. Growing cooperation between opposition organizations resulted in the formation of 'an opposition roundtable', convened to prevent the party from attempting to play different organizations off against each other. In June 1989 a 'national roundtable' was convened to discuss the transition from authoritarian to democratic rule. On one side sat representatives of the party, on another sat the 'opposition roundtable' delegates, while a 'third side' was made up of the various 'social organizations' that had begun to assert their independence from the party-state. Meanwhile, in a deeply symbolic move, Imre Nagy,

Hungary's prime minister during the 1956 Revolution who had been executed in 1958, was given a public reburial; Janos Kadar, who had succeeded him and who had been ousted from the party leadership the previous year, died in July. With the conclusion of the 'national roundtable' negotiations in September, agreement was reached on amendments to the constitution necessary to effect Hungary's transition to competitive politics, and an electoral law for the new multi-party national assembly. Opposition representatives, however, were divided on whether direct presidential elections should precede parliamentary elections, which was favoured by the representatives of the ruling party. The MDF took the same view, yet the SZDSZ, FIDESZ, the FKGP and the re-founded Social Democratic Party were opposed, believing that only a new parliament should decide on the role of the president in a new republic. Behind this disagreement lay several factors. The first was a difference in principle as to whether Hungary should become a presidential republic on the French model, or a strictly parliamentary republic, where the president's role would be largely ceremonial and power would instead be held by parliament. The second was motivated more directly by political considerations. The SZDSZ and its allies believed that direct presidential elections would result in the victory of Imre Pozsgay who would then rule in concert with the MDF, thus allowing the party to hold onto power in a new system, co-opting part of the opposition. Behind this lay a third reason in that the SZDSZ believed that a clean break was necessary for successful transition to democracy, which was more likely to be achieved in the context of a parliamentary republic. They were also worried about a possible repetition of the inter-war experience when the country's then head-of-state, Miklos Horthy, had played a central role in the political system, limiting the power of parliament.

The SZDSZ and its allies began to collect signatures to force a referendum to modify the 'national roundtable' agreement. It cleverly combined the controversial issue of the presidency with three other less controversial issues that would enable it to mobilize anti-communist votes, namely the banning of party activity in the workplace, reallocating party property and banning the party's paramilitary organization – the Workers' Guard. It successfully forced the referendum that was held on 25 November. The campaign was held against the background of the crisis of the communist regime in the German Democratic Republic, which had in part been sparked by the decision of the Hungarian government to allow East German tourists to travel freely to the west in September. The winds of change blowing through the socialist bloc contributed to a climate in which the SZDSZ's proposals, despite the fact that the MDF boycotted the referendum, were all carried, including the crucial provision that the president be elected only after parliamentary elections had been held.

The referendum had major implications for Hungarian politics. Prior to November 1989 opinion polls had shown the SZDSZ as a small radical liberal party with little support outside the capital's middle classes. The SZDSZ's championing of a clean break with the recent past allowed it to mobilize the anti-communist middle class outside the capital, thus turning it into a mass party. Its promise of a radical break with socialism in politics and economics, and its programme, which promised the creation of a 'bourgeois/civic' Hungary, made it a major political force. It also effectively destroyed Pozsgay's strategy of preserving some of the party's power through an alliance with MDF by removing the prospect of his being elected president, while creating a climate in which the MDF was forced to distance itself from the regime. Thirdly it further contributed to the fragmentation and marginalization of the left in the run-up to the first free elections.

The fragmentation of the left had, in fact, already begun. During the summer, reform circles within the MSZMP had pressed for the wholesale transformation of the party into a left-of-centre social democratic party, a measure bitterly resisted by the old guard within the membership. At the final, special party congress in September 1989 a deal was brokered between the reformers and the more pragmatic of the old guard that led to the transformation of the MSZMP into the Hungarian Socialist Party (*Magyar Szocialista Part*, or MSZP). The failure of the party to break unequivocally with the past contributed to a decline in public support for the MSZP during the later months of 1989 as Hungarian public opinion reacted to the tumultuous events elsewhere in the region (O'Neil, 1998). This perception was strengthened in January 1990 by revelations that the internal security services continued to bug the telephones of senior members of the opposition parties. Furthermore the compromises necessary to bring the MSZP into being failed to satisfy all the factions that had emerged within the MSZMP during the final year of its existence. This initiated a process of fragmentation on the left as both members of the old guard and reformers left the party to form new political organizations.

In the run-up to the elections the MSZP found itself isolated. The competition for first place was fought chiefly between the SZDSZ, who advocated a radical break with the past, and the MDF, who under the leadership of Jozsef Antall had identified themselves as a party of the moderate centre-right committed to national values. While the MDF advocated a gradual economic transformation that would preserve much of the welfare state of the Kadar era, the SZDSZ argued for radical market reform. The campaign was largely dominated by the two leading contenders demonstrating their anti-communist credentials. Parliamentary elections took place over two rounds, held in March and April 1990, under a complex electoral system that combined majoritarian and proportional elements. In the first round voters cast two votes – one for the local representative in an individual constituency and the other for a party list. If a candidate secured 50 per cent in an individual constituency on the first round they were deemed elected; however if no candidate secured this then the top three candidates, or all those candidates securing over 15 per cent, qualified for the second round. In the second round a simple plurality was necessary for election. To win seats under the party list, a list had to win at least 4 per cent of the national vote (in subsequent elections the hurdle was raised to 5 per cent), and seats were allocated proportionally according to the share of votes cast in each county.

The votes cast in the first round revealed a political field that could be divided into three camps. The largest camp was that of the national-christian centre-right, consisting of those parties that argued Hungary's future development should be built on a restoration of elements of the country's pre-socialist past. Central to national-christian ideology was a belief in the social and moral reconstruction of the Hungarian nation. Raising the birth rate, restoring the traditional family unit and the cultural influence of the 'historic' Christian churches were central to this vision. Members of the national-christian camp also believed that the Hungarian government had a responsibility to the whole of the Hungarian nation, including those ethnic Hungarians who lived beyond the borders of Hungary proper. There were some in the national-christian camp who dreamed of extending the country's borders to include all those territories where Hungarians lived, as had been the case before World War I. The most radical advocates of this vision were the FKGP, who placed the restitution of all nationalized and collectivized property to its original owners at the centre of their programme. The Christian Democratic People's Party (*Kereszteny Demokrata Neppart*, or KDNP), along with the MDF, were both more moderate. The 'bourgeois' liberal camp, marked by a mixture of radical anti-communism, a strong commitment to the market economy and social liberalism, emerged as the second largest camp. The left-wing camp appeared to have suffered almost total defeat, given that its only parliamentary representative – the MSZP – had polled only slightly more than one vote in ten. This certainly understated its strength, as the left was the most fragmented of the three blocs; parties that could be identified as left-wing had together taken around one vote in four – a defeat nonetheless, but one that was less great than a concentration on the share of the MSZP alone would suggest (Racz, 1993). With turnout at 65 per cent, opinion surveys suggested that there were many potential supporters of a left-wing party among the non-voters (Szelenyi and Szelenyi, 1991).

With the left clearly eliminated from the race to form the next government the national-christian and 'bourgeois' liberal camps formed electoral pacts to maximize their chances of winning individual constituencies in the second round. The national-christian camp, led by the MDF, fought a campaign that combined anti-communism with a promise of gradual transition and the maintenance of much of the welfare state. Distrustful of the radicalism of the liberal parties (the SZDSZ and FIDESZ) most voters rallied behind the national-christian camp (the MDF, the FKGP and the KDNP), giving them a comfortable majority in the new parliament. This allowed the MDF president, Jozsef Antall, to form a three-party centre-right coalition government. The new government, in the interests of resolving outstanding constitutional issues, negotiated a pact with the SZDSZ as the largest opposition party. This allowed the SZDSZ candidate, Arpad Goncz, to be elected president of what was to be a parliamentary republic, while the SZDSZ supported Antall's proposals to strengthen the office of Prime Minister *vis-à-vis* parliament.

Postcommunist Patterns of Government

The nature of Hungary's political transition had created a party system that reflected clear divisions within society by the time of the 1990 elections. This party system, and the divisions that it reflected within Hungarian society, were very different by the time of the 2002 elections. The MSZP, which came fourth in 1990, was to take most votes in the first rounds of the three subsequent parliamentary elections; the 'bourgeois' liberal and national-christian camps that emerged in the first elections all but collapsed. While liberalism survived as a peripheral force in Hungary politics, most of the 'bourgeois' liberal and national-christian camps were merged into a new right-wing bloc dominated by FIDESZ, which took fifth place in the first postcommunist elections.

The period between 1990 and 1994 was marked by the fragmentation of the national-christian camp and the recovery of the left. Economic crisis and widespread popular discontent provided the backdrop to this shift. The Antall government inherited an economy that was in severe crisis. Hungary's domestic circumstances alone would have made transition to a market economy painful but they were exacerbated by the impact of economic transformation in neighbouring states, recession in Western Europe and the collapse of the rouble-based trading system within the Soviet bloc. The economy contracted by 17 per cent between 1990 and 1993, resulting in an increase in unemployment from virtually nothing in 1990 to a peak of 12 per cent in 1993. Inflation accelerated to 22 per cent in the same year and real wages fell dramatically. Recession led to falling tax receipts and a substantial budget deficit, which restricted the ability of the government to relieve acute social stress. Furthermore it forced the government to continue with policies of privatization that became increasingly unpopular as its period in office progressed.

The Antall government, elected on a promise of gradual transition, faced a backlash. Warning signs of a withdrawal of public trust in the government came as early as the later months of 1990, with taxi drivers mounting a blockade to protest against rising petrol prices, and victories for the liberal opposition in local elections. The government's unpopularity rose to record levels. Loss of confidence in the government brought about and was fuelled by two political trends: a rise in support for the left and a growing fragmentation of the national-christian camp.

The fragmentation of the national-christian camp had major consequences for the conduct of politics. Its first major manifestation was in 1991 with a major crisis within the FKGP – the junior partner in the governing coalition – brought about by the election of right-wing populist Jozsef Torgyan to the presidency of the party. Torgyan's radicalism and his refusal to accept the need for compromise with Antall over the issue of land restitution split the party. Conservative members of the FKGP remained within the governing coalition, while Torgyan and his allies went into opposition. Thus the government faced not only opposition from the left, but also, increasingly from the populist right. A more serious threat came from within the MDF itself. Against the background of social tension the populist right within the party around its vice-president, Istvan Csurka, demanded a more assertive nationalist policy, an end to the privatization of state companies to foreigners and more radical measures against 'former communists'. Csurka gained notoriety when he attacked the government publicly in an article in the newspaper *Magyar Forum* in 1992, demanding that it take an explicitly populist and anti-semitic course. His stand caused a crisis within the governing party, as it became evident that Csurka's stance had the support of a substantial number – though not a majority – of party members. This crisis was only resolved when the MDF leadership successfully expelled Csurka from the party in May 1993. He responded by founding the Hungarian Justice and Life Party (*Magyar Igazsag es Elet Partja*, or MIEP), which was committed to a strongly anti-semitic and extreme right-wing stance.

By 1993 it had become clear that the MSZP was gaining in support. It had demonstrated an ability to win parliamentary by-elections. The party was partly able to feed on growing nostalgia for the material security of the Kadar era, particularly among working-class voters. It was able also to draw on its reformist credentials to deflect criticism that it would seek a restoration of the communist system. Growing concern with the authoritarian policies of the Antall government, particularly towards state television and radio, and the apparent threat of the far right, helped end the MSZP's isolation. Political figures in the liberal SZDSZ founded the Democratic Charter organization in 1991, which came to act as a forum for cooperation between liberal and socialist politicians.

In the year prior to the 1994 elections the centre-right government was in a state of near total collapse. It had all but lost its parliamentary majority by the summer of 1993. FIDESZ, the formerly liberal anti-communist youth organization, transformed itself into a political party in 1993 and positioned itself to profit from discontent with the government on the centre-right. Antall was seriously ill with cancer and died in December 1993; his replacement, Peter Boross, an authoritarian conservative on the right of the MDF, was regarded by many as little more than a caretaker prime minister. Faced with imminent defeat at the hands of the MSZP Boross sought to rally anti-socialist votes with a negative campaign directed against the leader of the MSZP, Gyula Horn, who had served in a paramilitary unit during the suppression of the 1956 Revolution. The first round of the elections in the spring of 1994 demonstrated that nostalgia for the socialist system, however, could mobilize as many voters as could anti-communism.

With the right effectively eliminated in the first round the campaign turned into a fight between the MSZP and SZDSZ, with the SZDSZ attempting to mobilize anti-communist voters to stop the MSZP. Right-wing voters abstained rather than back the liberal SZDSZ, handing the Socialists a landslide victory. Having sought to capitalize on anti-communism by promising not to share power with the MSZP if it won an absolute majority, the SZDSZ accepted Gyula Horn's offer of partnership in a coalition government. Though this was not immediately apparent, this volte-face fatally undermined the SZDSZ's appeal among the anti-communist provincial middle classes who had made the party a major political force with appeal beyond the restricted ranks of Budapest intellectuals. This would pave the way for major realignment in Hungarian politics.

The Horn government, elected to ease the social crisis that had arisen with the collapse of the socialist system, came to power facing a severe economic crisis of its own. Its right-wing predecessor during its last year in office had relaxed public expenditure controls and sought to stimulate the economy. This led not to economic growth but to accelerating inflation and a deteriorating current account. Meanwhile the new government was split over solutions to these difficulties between economic liberals led by Socialist finance minister Laszlo Bekesi and members of the SZDSZ on the one hand, and more left-wing figures around prime minister Horn. Consequently the government drifted until Bekesi walked out in frustration in early 1995; the country plunged at the same time into financial crisis as a result of capital flight and a weakening currency. Bekesi's successor, Lajos Bokros, insisted on implementing the programme of the economic liberals. In March 1995 the so-called Bokros package was unveiled to overcome the crisis. This austerity programme cut welfare spending, increased taxation, devalued the forint and introduced a temporary 8 per cent levy on imports. Though Bokros was to be replaced by the pragmatic Peter Medgyessy in 1996, the Bokros package was to prove the defining act of the Horn government, laying the foundations for strong economic growth from 1996 onwards. Growth, however, was bought at the cost of tremendous discontent and accelerating social polarization. Real wages fell by 9 per cent in the last nine months of 1995 alone, and poor families, the MSZP's natural constituents, were directly hit by the cuts in welfare benefits. Accelerated privatization, particularly of public utilities, led to similar effects as poor consumers had to bear the brunt of above-inflation price increases for basic public services. Furthermore a series of corruption scandals connected to the privatization programme generated considerable public anger.

The right of the political spectrum underwent almost complete realignment. The parties that had supported the Antall and Boross governments were in a state of almost total collapse between 1994 and 1998, with the MDF experiencing a damaging split in 1996 and the KDNP experiencing similar fragmentation in 1997 and 1998. Initially in the Horn government's term it seemed that the populist right in the shape of Torgyan's FKGP and Csurka's MIEP would fill the vacuum left by the collapse of the national-christian parties. Eventually, however, the once liberal FIDESZ emerged as the eventual beneficiary of this process. The leadership of the party around its president Viktor Orban reacted to their 1994 election defeat by decisively positioning themselves on the right, forming the fulcrum of a right-wing electoral alliance in the 1994 municipal elections that won control of several major provincial cities. Over the course of the Horn government's tenure FIDESZ adopted a political language designed to extend their appeal beyond the traditional right, speaking of the creation of a 'civic' Hungary in language that appealed particularly to former SZDSZ voters who were disillusioned with their party's coalition with the MSZP.

With the approach of elections in 1998 the Horn government seemed clear favourites to win, aided by the improvement in the economy and a successful referendum on Hungarian entry into NATO in November 1997. These advantages concealed deeper problems that the leadership of the governing parties seriously underestimated. FIDESZ, in opposition, skilfully positioned itself in the run-up to the 1998 election in order to profit from them. It opposed measures to allow for foreign ownership of agricultural land and formed a limited electoral pact with the remnants of the MDF in order to appeal to right-wing voters who had deserted the national-christian parties. Its rhetoric of a 'civic Hungary' consciously appealed to disillusioned former SZDSZ voters. At the same time its stance on economic and social issues exploited the real discontent that the Horn government's liberal economic policies had generated by abandoning its own neo-liberalism. At the heart of its new economic policy was a policy of boosting the economy to achieve an average growth rate of 7 per cent per annum. This growth-oriented economic policy was combined with several symbolic social policy measures designed to exploit popular discontent with the Bokros-inspired welfare expenditure cuts – it promised the abolition of university tuition fees introduced in 1995 and the reversal of the Horn government's cuts to child support.

Disillusion with the social policies of the Horn government contributed to a low turnout, particularly among working-class voters, in the first round of the elections that took place in May 1998; only 56 per cent of those eligible turned out to vote. Though the MSZP share of the vote held up, that of its coalition partner – the SZDSZ – collapsed as the provincial middle classes defected en masse to FIDESZ, ensuring that the right-wing parties, including the far-right MIEP, entering parliament in its own right, won an absolute majority of votes cast.

Following the first round FIDESZ extended their pact with the MDF to include the right-wing populist FKGP, though excluding the MIEP. This right-wing coalition won a convincing though not overwhelming victory in the second round, allowing Viktor Orban to form a government in the wake of the elections. The new prime minister signalled a shift in political style by promising that the advent of the right-wing coalition would represent 'more than a change of government, but less than a change of system'.

This was not immediately evident in the field of economic policy, where the government under its economics minister Attila Chikan pursued a much more cautious policy than it had promised in the election campaign. With Chikan's replacement by Gyorgy Matolcsy in 2000, the Orban government eventually shifted radically away from the neo-liberal orthodoxy of the 1990s and introduced a self-consciously neo-Keynesian policy of expanding domestic demand through measures like raising the minimum wage and increasing public spending. It was, however, in the field of cultural policy where the Orban government introduced its most radical and controversial changes. This policy was based on the assumption that the left of the political spectrum and especially supporters of the MSZP had accumulated enormous power over the media and the cultural sphere. It sought to break this assumed 'monopoly' using state power. It tightened government control over state-run television, radio and the regulatory bodies that supervised commercial media. It used its control over a bank to ensure that the national newspaper *Magyar Nemzet* became a mouthpiece for the government, and unsuccessfully threatened the independence of another daily, *Magyar Hírlap*. Commercial radio franchises were awarded to groups closely associated with the right, including the churches, and one was allocated to a group associated with Csurka's MIEP.

In addition to extending the influence of the right over culture and the media, FIDESZ and its leadership sought to extend their influence over the right of the political spectrum as a whole. While the MDF managed to preserve its political independence, the remnants of other conservative parties like the KDNP were incorporated into FIDESZ. The most dramatic act in this process was the effective destruction of the FKGP, the marginalization of its leader Jozsef Torgyan and the incorporation of some of the party into Orban's political bloc. While the government made no open agreements with Csurka's MIEP, the small far-right party generally operated as an ally of the government without openly being a member of the governing coalition for much of the government's term. The cumulative result of these changes was that FIDESZ itself changed further, becoming less of a political party in any traditional sense and more a right-wing electoral alliance that bound a variety of interests to the government.

Furthermore during its term in office it shifted perceptibly further to the right. In foreign policy it pursued an openly nationalist agenda, introducing a status law in 2001 to bind Magyar minorities living beyond Hungary's borders to the Hungarian state. Its relations with neighbouring states deteriorated. It acted aggressively towards its political opponents, eschewing the politics of compromise that had, to some extent, been practised by its predecessors. In distributing funding to local authorities and investment projects, areas that had voted for the opposition – particularly Budapest – faced open discrimination. The government's divisive style poisoned the political atmosphere in the run-up to the 2002 elections.

It governed, however, in a more stable economic climate than any of its predecessors had been able to enjoy. Though economic growth peaked at 6 per cent in 2000 and fell back to 3 per cent by late 2001, economic growth continued throughout its term in office enabling middle-class incomes to rise and allowing for the emergence of Western-style mass consumerism. Shopping malls, out-of-town hypermarkets and multiplex cinemas opened not only in the capital but in many major provincial towns as well. The reductions in inflation, and welfare measures such as subsidies for private housebuilding (which mainly benefited the middle classes), contributed to a greater sense of well-being. Although official unemployment was recorded at only 7 per cent by the end of 2001, it had become clear that many had not benefited from the economic boom. Pensioners and those employed in the public sector had done particularly badly, while growth in eastern regions of the country lagged significantly behind Budapest and the north-west. Furthermore among the poorer half of the population job and income insecurity was still widespread.

Current Issues

Increasingly social polarization generated by the differential effects of economic growth on different economic groups combined with political polarization caused by the divisive style of the Orban government. This tense atmosphere formed the background to the 2002 elections; in the aftermath of those elections social and political division forms perhaps the major challenge facing the country. The depth of these problems and their potential for generating political instability should not be underestimated.

During the April 2002 elections an ugly and ill-tempered campaign polarized Hungarian society between supporters of Orban and those of the centre-left led by former finance minister Medgyessy. The right appropriated national symbols during its campaign and sought to brand its opponents as unpatriotic. Though this tactic successfully mobilized the right, it also mobilized their opponents. The first round of the elections held on 7 April gave the centre-left a narrow advantage, but also revealed the depth of political division in the country. Budapest and urban industrial areas voted heavily for the MSZP, while much of rural Hungary voted for the electoral pact of FIDESZ and the MDF. The polarization of the electorate squeezed smaller parties, ensuring that MIEP lost its parliamentary seats and that the SZDSZ only just scraped in (Table 4.1). Between the two rounds the MSZP and SZDSZ formed an electoral pact. The campaign between the two rounds diverged from the practice of the previous three parliamentary elections in that

TABLE 4.1   *Results of the Hungarian parliamentary elections, 2002 (parties winning seats only)*

Party	1st round list votes	1st round list %	Individual constituencies won	Regional list seats won	National list seats won	Total seats won
MSZP	2,361,997	42.05	78	69	31	178
FIDESZ–MPP–MDF	2,306,763	41.07	95	67	26	188
SZDSZ	313,084	5.57	3	4	13	20

Source: adapted from *http://www.valasztas.hu/so02/v02din1/1403.htm;http:// www.polhist.hu/voks2002/vtort02.htm.*

Orban and his supporters intensified their campaign of mobilization. FIDESZ launched a negative campaign against their opponents in which Orban explicitly appropriated the rhetoric of the populist far-right, warning that the Hungarian middle class was threatened by the prospect of a government of 'foreign capital'. FIDESZ brought several hundred thousand of its supporters onto the streets of Budapest between the two rounds in a show of strength.

Orban's campaign of mobilization, though insufficient to save his government, did bring some results. More voters – 74 per cent of those eligible – turned out in the second round than in the first, and FIDESZ-supported candidates won most of the individual constituency seats being contested and just under 50 per cent of the total second-round vote. The centre-left won a parliamentary majority because of the weight of the votes cast for proportionally allocated seats in the first round. While the result allowed Medgyessy to form a new centre-left coalition government, the result was virtually a dead heat between right and left.

While Orban personally conceded defeat on the night of the election, many of his supporters refused to accept the result. Immediately following the elections the authorities were deluged with an unprecedented number of complaints and threats of legal action from the supporters of narrowly defeated candidates holding up the final official declaration of the result. Allegations of electoral fraud were made by supporters of the far right and of FIDESZ. One small right-wing group staged an illegal demonstration, blocking a Budapest bridge during rush-hour, to demand a recount of the ballots. The atmosphere was further poisoned by allegations made in the *Magyar Nemzet* newspaper against Medgyessy, accusing him of having a secret police past.

This political polarization demonstrates not so much consolidation as deep-seated division and a new stage in the evolution of the political system. The 2002 election broke the pattern of the previous three where power was transferred peacefully and without much controversy. Furthermore, for much of the 1990s it could be plausibly claimed that Hungary was undergoing a 'transition' to some form of democratic, liberal political system. Behind the current polarization lies deep-seated disagreement in Hungarian society about the meaning of that 'transition' and its relationship to the late socialist period that preceded it. For the left the shifts to parliamentary democracy and a market economy are a natural evolution of the reformism of the Kadar era. For them 1989 represents no decisive break and the survival of a large party with its roots in the socialist dictatorship is perfectly compatible with a change of system. The right, however, denies that the survival of the MSZP in a governing role is in any way compatible with a change of system – they would seek to build a political system in which the former communist party was denied any power at all. Because of the extent to which these divisions are rooted in Hungarian society it is difficult to see how they can be overcome in the short term.

The questioning of the meaning of the change of system has gone together with a move away on both sides of the political spectrum from another aspect of politics during the 1990s, namely the commitment of Hungary's political elite to neo-liberalism. FIDESZ, during their last two years in office, decisively abandoned neo-liberalism in favour of a neo-Keynesian *dirigiste* approach to economic management. Orban's almost anti-capitalist rhetoric in the campaign between the two rounds suggests that this shift is likely to become even more marked. The Medgyessy government seems intent on substantially increasing public sector investment and envisages an enhanced role for the welfare state. Its first measures in office have been to substantially increase pensions, as well as wages and salaries for those employed in the health and education sectors. These seem likely to continue and reflect growing discontent with the social costs of economic restructuring during the 1990s. The question does however remain as to whether the country's economy, based as it is on a booming financial sector and substantial foreign direct investment in manufacturing, can support the welfarist aspirations of both the Hungarian electorate and the country's political class.

COLLAPSE OF NEO-LIBERAL CONSENSUS

5

The Balkans since 1989: The Winding Retreat from National Communism

TOM GALLAGHER

Important differences between the states of Central Europe and the Balkans emerged as the communist era drew to a close that would shape their divergent evolution. In all the Balkan states, durable personal autocracies enjoyed lengthy terms of office. Josip Broz Tito and Enver Hoxha dominated Yugoslavia and Albania respectively from 1944–5 until their deaths in 1980 and 1985. Todor Zhivkov and Nicolae Ceausescu were undisputed rulers of Bulgaria and Romania from the mid-1960s until 1989. There were few checks on their powers, even in Yugoslavia with its elaborate forms of decentralization and concessions to capitalism and other forms of Western influence. Everywhere, political systems dominated by a single personality whose authority derives from charisma or the ability to intimidate or coerce are more prone to policy errors than relatively impersonal and consensual regimes. The mistakes of Balkan communist leaders were on a more grandiose scale than was the case in the other Soviet satellites where leaders could usually not indefinitely override their senior colleagues' views on policy issues.

In each Balkan country, there was a much larger industrial sector and a smaller service sector than in Central Europe. Heavy industry was promoted on ideological grounds to create a numerically dominant industrial proletariat in what had previously been overwhelmingly agrarian societies. Despite secondary concessions to capitalism, much of Yugoslavia still possessed an unwieldy command economy based around heavy industry and mineral extraction. Such economic activities, promoted in the poorer

Yugoslav republics, only accentuated their lack of competitiveness and contributed to the crisis of the federation in the 1980s. Nationalism increasingly compensated for economic failure across the region in the later years of communist rule. In Bulgaria and Romania, ethnic minorities lost ground as appeals to ethnicity began to drown out the references to proletarian solidarity. In Yugoslavia, socialist 'Yugoslavism', overriding the diverse national identities of the Yugoslav peoples, was starting to fail as an integrative mechanism even before the death of Tito in 1980 (Ramet, 1992). In many ways, Yugoslavia remained a traditional state whose sinews were the clienteles of individual leaders, not working-class consciousness or a commitment to equality. Recruitment, promotion and the allocation of resources were often based on kinship and localism (Allcock, 2000, p. 366). The same was largely true in Bulgaria, Romania and Albania, which were not federations, but whose political systems allowed ample oppor-tunities for patron–client relations. These, in turn, provided a basis for populist politics in the 1990s and beyond.

In Yugoslavia, the manipulation of nationalism occurred at the very end of the communist era, when the communist party in Serbia was captured by individuals who sought a new lease of life and a clean political identity by issuing uncompromising ethnic appeals. Slobodan Milosevic became the prototype '*nomenklatura* nationalist', a former communist bureaucrat who turned to nation-alism once the bankruptcy of communist ideology had been exposed. He was determined to remain a pre-eminent player under new quasi-democratic rules of the game by exploiting mass fears of a range of internal 'enemies' against which the nation must rally. First the Kosovar Albanians, and then the Slovenes and Croats were allotted the role of villain. Thus Yugoslavia, whose viability as a political entity depended on elites refraining from such ethnic appeals, was tested to destruction in the years up to 1991 when the federation started to break up.

Contested and Stalled Transitions

The Balkans entered the postcommunist era between 1989 and 1992: the Bulgarian and Romanian dictators were removed (Zhivkov peacefully and Ceausescu violently) in 1989; multi-party elections took place in all Yugoslav republics in 1990; and by 1992

the Albanian communists had given up power in the face of economic collapse and mounting unrest. The whole region faced
broadly similar problems due to the intensity of communist rule, the
misuse of resources, the elevation of deeply flawed individuals to
positions of absolute power, and the absence of mechanisms
designed to regulate conflict. Yugoslavia from 1991 to 1999 experienced four internal wars as Milosevic sought to create a greatly
enlarged Serbia upon the ruins of the federation. In the end he failed,
but several factors operated in his favour until at least the mid-1990s.
The Serb-dominated army (where Tito had neglected to preserve
an ethnic balance) was willing to rally behind a leader who broke
with incoherent and quarrelsome federalism. The West showed no
readiness to intervene, policy-makers believing erroneously that
Milosevic was trying to preserve a united Yugoslavia, or that a strong
Serbia was necessary for the stability of the Balkans. Finally,
Milosevic was assisted by the rise to power of a vocal nationalist in
Croatia, Franjo Tudjman, who attempted to crack down on the Serb
minority, and thus popularized the internationally held view that
nationalism was the natural political condition of the region. Wars of
differing intensity and duration at their worst radically altered human
geography, as in Bosnia, creating several million refugees and,
almost everywhere, undid the economic advantages Yugoslavia had
previously enjoyed over all other eastern bloc countries due to its
considerable economic ties with the West.

A readiness to view the whole region as one in the resolute grip
of hardline nationalism and entrenched authoritarianism was apparent among policy-makers, diplomats and not a few academics. But
the Balkan countries that remained at peace responded to the challenges of building new political institutions in sometimes very contrasting ways. Bulgaria was perhaps best placed to make a decisive
break from the totalitarian era. Before 1989 there had been several
'thaw periods' allowing for economic experimentation and a relaxation of the media. Political dissent in the 1980s allowed for the
emergence of an embryo civil society and there were experienced
political activists who, by 1990, were ready to effectively oppose
the former communists, who had regrouped into the Bulgarian
Socialist Party (BSP). Despite their many differences, the main contenders from left and right agreed over the broad outline of institutional reform in 1990. All parties pledged to promote a democratic
transformation in an 'unforced, bloodless, and civilized manner'
(Bell, 1997, p. 364). The country's first elected President, Zhelu
Zhelev, had support from both the BSP and its centre-right rival, the

Union of Democratic Forces (UDF). In the first half of the 1990s, he stood for balance and moderation during periods of turbulence when neither party enjoyed an outright majority.

In Romania, the largely unreformed party and state bureaucracy enjoyed continuing influence through the National Salvation Front (FSN). In 1990, it won early elections by relaxing the harsh austerity that the population had endured for the previous decade. But there was plenty of evidence that the FSN was intent on maintaining a political monopoly while paying lip-service to pluralism. Opponents were harshly dealt with if their dissent threatened the FSN's grip on power. Unlike the BSP in Bulgaria, the FSN manipulated sentiments against ethnic minorities in order to discredit the opposition parties with which the minorities were allied. In Bulgaria, there was no counterpart to Romania's Corneliu Vadim Tudor who praised Ceausescu's record and by 2001 was leader of the second largest party, the extreme nationalist Greater Romania Party. Unlike Romania, a virulent nationalist media was conspicuous by its absence in Bulgaria where intellectuals had largely rejected the shrill tones of the communist regime's later years and its persecution of the country's Turkish minority.

Albania was largely an ethnically homogeneous country where the communist elite was supplanted by the centre-right Democratic Party under Sali Berisha. By the mid-1990s his regime was using electoral malpractice and intimidation of its political opponents and the media to remain in power. But Berisha's relations with his international sponsors in the major democracies remained unruffled. Albania illustrated the tendency in the West 'to equate a particular leader with democracy and to assume that steadfast support for that leader is the best means of promoting democracy' (Carothers, 1995, p. 23). It was a policy that would rebound badly, particularly on the major EU states, when the Berisha regime collapsed following a banking scheme that defrauded much of the population. This sparked off a revolt in 1997 which only abated with the despatch of an Italian-led peace-keeping force to supervise new elections and a return to fitful stability under the former communists, now repackaged as the Socialist Party.

The Economic Context of Fragile Transitions

Economic factors undermined the transition states of the Balkans in the 1990s and beyond, just as they had their communist predecessors. The states that avoided war nevertheless suffered massive blows as a result of the disruption to trade and communications brought about by the Yugoslav conflicts. But much worse problems were caused by corruption, usually involving the diversion of state assets into private hands. State firms and banks were plundered by well-connected insiders, their debts being covered by the state. Sometimes, though not always, these insiders had a background in the pre-1989 regimes, often in the intelligence services, which had directed much of external trade. Irresponsible credit policies fuelled runaway inflation that hit low-wage earners, pensioners and others on fixed incomes the most. By the end of 1993, real wages in Romania stood at only 63 per cent of their level in January 1990 (Ronnas, 1995, p. 20). New economic oligarchies, based on speculation and theft, managed to redistribute wealth upwards in part because this pattern of behaviour reflected a deep-seated belief that the state should be an automatic provider of economic benefits. In no part of the Balkans did substantial improvements occur in the public administration that could have limited if not prevented such systemic corruption. Low salaries in major ministries and the judiciary made officials susceptible to bribery and meant that unscrupulous figures looting the state often faced no sanctions other than exposure in the media.

The absence of a system of financial regulation in which property rights and contracts were protected and the rule of law upheld prevented Romania and Bulgaria acquiring functioning market economies. Foreign investors were scared off: out of the total amount of foreign direct investment channelled to Eastern Europe and the Baltic States between 1990 and 1997, Romania and Bulgaria obtained less than 8 per cent compared with Hungary's 37 per cent and Poland's 20.5 per cent (Done, 1998). Private banks and investment firms crashed on a regular basis in the 1990s in all the states of the region, with millions of investors losing everything. In Bulgaria (under the rule of the BSP after it won an outright electoral majority in 1994), the currency collapsed and inflation hit stratospheric levels after bank failures in 1996. Public outrage then forced out a government that had worked closely with economic conglomerates to asset-strip the economy. The crisis subsided with new elections in the spring of 1997, convincingly won by the right-wing UDF. The IMF also extended a loan designed to restore Bulgaria's battered credibility on world markets, on condition that a currency board was set up to oversee the country's financial and monetary systems.

In Romania, President Ion Iliescu and his party were out of office before the worst effects of their economic misrule became obvious. They lost the presidential and parliamentary elections of 1996 because they had been unable to shelter their working-class supporters from the economic effects of their incompetence and opportunism. The postcommunists were replaced by an unwieldy coalition of all the opposition parties minus the ultra-nationalists. The coalition lacked the common ground and clarity of vision to confront the Romanian electorate with the scale of the damage done to the country in the previous six years. Emil Constantinescu, the new President, failed to become an effective rallying force for change. Capitalists with a background in the old communist *nomenklatura* continued to divert large amounts of state funding for their own private use under the eyes of incompetent and quarrelsome 'reformers' who soon lost the respect of the vast bulk of the Romanian public.

Bulgaria's reforming push was more sustained. The 1997–2001 government of Ivan Kostov was a single-party (UDF) one with a parliamentary majority. It secured high growth rates and won praise from international financial bodies for reforming its financial structures. The EU found the public administration in Sofia more professional and easier to work with than its Romanian counterpart when both states opened negotiations for accession to the EU after 2000. But the Bulgarian electorate, tired of austerity, rejected the UDF and voted for the National Movement for Simeon II, led by the ex-king Simeon, who had returned from exile and became prime minister in June 2001. He promised to restore the country to economic and political health within 800 days of taking office, intensifying the UDF's reform programmes but pursuing a more consensual course.

In Romania, instead of opting for a different brand of reformer, voters in 2000 re-elected Iliescu's party, now renamed the Social Democratic Party (PSD), with the ultra-nationalists in a strong second place. The PSD is reconciled to capitalism and appears on the verge of taking Romania into NATO, having convinced the USA of its readiness to act as a bridgehead for US-led military operations in the Middle East. But corruption has increased and the party shows plenty of evidence of wishing to exercise a political monopoly if it can get away with it. Bulgaria's stronger engagement with democracy perhaps reflects the milder nature of the totalitarian system before 1989 and the greater capacity of reformers to take on the postcommunist oligarchy.

The Corrosive Effects of War

In war-torn parts of the former Yugoslavia, ordinary citizens faced far greater dangers. From 1992 to 1995, multi-ethnic Bosnia, shared by Muslims, Serbs and Croats, was the scene of the worst fighting in the post-1991 Yugoslav wars. Bosnian Serb forces, financed and armed by Milosevic, attempted to drive out the Muslims in order to create an 'ethnically cleansed' territory that could be attached to Serbia. In the first year of war, one-third of the population fled or were forced from their homes. Tudjman and Milosevic at times were close to carving up Bosnia between them. The Croatian leader was a true nationalist believer whereas Milosevic was an arch-manipulator of nationalism who was prepared to abandon the tactic when it ceased to earn rewards for him. He shelved his Greater Serbia project when economic sanctions pulverized his economy and he lost control of the Bosnian Serb leadership. Deciding to transform his image from 'the butcher of the Balkans' to the indispensable peacemaker, he supported belated NATO efforts to end the war in Bosnia in 1995, as long as his own position was not threatened. In the process he abandoned the Serbs of Croatia and many of those in Bosnia when the war turned against them.

In 1995, the internationally sponsored and US-directed Dayton Peace Agreement ended the Bosnian war. A single Bosnian state was created, supervised by the United Nations. In practice, Bosnia consists of three ethnic entities which have their own armies and police forces. The Republic of Srpska (mainly inhabited by ethnic Serbs) has refused to cooperate with the central authorities (which besides have only weak powers) unless pressurized by the UN. International officials increasingly ran Bosnia as a UN protectorate in order to prevent the collapse of a fundamentally unstable peace. The Muslim and Croat entities supposedly operate as a single federation but in practice their ten cantons have become the real centres of economic and political power. Dayton's architects promoted sweeping devolution of power and early elections in the hope that it might promote trans-ethnic powersharing, but in practice it has allowed wartime nationalist elites to consolidate their authority. What has been the most ambitious and expensive UN-led exercise in post-conflict political reconstruction has produced meagre gains and left many pressing problems that could be the trigger for fresh violence.

Warfare, mainly directed against civilians in order to radically alter the human geography of parts of Croatia and most of Bosnia, had a devastating effect on politics and society even beyond these regions. The destruction of infrastructure and the disruption of trading links led to a collapse in economic activity. Much of the Yugoslav middle class was politically marginalized and became trapped in poverty. A huge brain-drain occurred, well-qualified and often liberal-minded young people fleeing abroad to avoid being conscripted to fight nationalist wars. Groups committed to a multicultural existence also suffered. If not the direct victims of persecution and violence, they were given little by the various Western-sponsored peace plans in Bosnia (up to and including Dayton), which were all centred on accommodating ethnic elites.

Against such a background, liberal civil society groups hoping to democratize political systems in Serbia and Croatia, which had become little more than ethnic autocracies, were in very poor shape. Instead, a new economic elite emerged, often composed of people from marginal or obscure backgrounds who had successfully acted as enforcers for the repressive strongmen ruling Serbia and Croatia. They may have seized private property in war conditions, smuggled arms, drugs or people, engaged in dubious privatization schemes, or carried out a range of services for their patrons at the apex of Serbian and Croatian politics. Those ordinary citizens with connections among the newly powerful, whether they were state bureaucrats or local economic moguls, managed to get by or avoided the discrimination and disadvantage which is the lot of the powerless (International Crisis Group, 1999, p. 73). It should not be forgotten that such clientelist practices had prevailed in Tito's supposedly egalitarian state, but they were enormously reinforced following its demise.

The overall effect of the Yugoslav wars has been to postpone the emergence of developmental economies – that is, ones which supply the needs of the domestic market, employ large numbers of citizens in productive rather than speculative activities, and earn revenue from legitimate trading abroad. Instead, there is a thriving subterranean economy and organized crime is a new and well-established social formation, with a vested interest in promoting nationalism. Gangsters and entrepreneurs dealing in illegal commodities need to ensure that international conventions and laws do not impede their activities. In 1995–6 a power struggle in the

Bosnian city of Mostar, between Croatian gangsters linked to Tudjman's Croatian Democratic Union (HDZ) and the EU, ended in victory for the former. The EU had agreed to try and reintegrate the city, which was previously the scene of an attempt by Croat extremists to drive out its Muslim inhabitants. It was the EU's first large engagement in post-conflict peacebuilding, but it ended in a fiasco when EU political leaders refused to back local EU officials when they came under fierce attack from local hardliners. The EU pulled out in humiliation in 1996. It was a sign of their failure that, during their tenure, Mostar became known as 'the car theft capital of the world' with police officials from EU countries apparently powerless to prevent thousands of luxury cars stolen from West European countries ending up there.

With industrial output slashed and tourism at an end, illegal activity and the black economy generally became the chief areas of economic activity in most of what had been Yugoslavia, with the large international presence in Bosnia, and later in Kosovo and Macedonia, generating only a feeble recovery.

Ethnic Autocracies: A Comparison of the Serbian and Croatian Regimes

The regimes of Milosevic and Tudjman were far from being duplicates, but they used very similar methods to entrench themselves in power and prevent opposition expressing itself in the normal democratic way. These were hybrid political systems that fell short of being outright dictatorships, but in which authoritarian practices made a mockery of any pretensions about being democratic. Despite their growing unpopularity at home, the ruling groups had little to fear from elections, and outright defeats could be evaded by fraud or simply by annulling the results. Both the Serbian and Croatian regimes became personalized ones in which the dividing line between private and public property became unclear. At the outset, in 1990, the Serbian leadership set an example for their minions to follow by simply taking an estimated $4 billion from private hard currency accounts in the Yugoslav National Bank, part of which was used to pay for various wars. In Croatia, allies of Tudjman captured the lucrative retail and tourist sector when they were allowed to borrow large sums from compliant banks in order to purchase companies, using only its assets as security.

Mira Markovic, Milosevic's wife, had always been his closest confidante and gradually emerged as his co-ruler. She formed her own party in 1994, the Yugoslav United Left (JUL). Committed to creating 'a wealthy, just and modern socialist state, unlike socialism in the past', it soon became a cover for systematic graft, in which government licences for any significant economic activity could not be obtained without a hefty contribution to its swelling coffers. Markovic tried to make light of a Marxist party dominated by the nouveaux riches in a land of mounting poverty by remarking, 'Friedrich Engels was an industrialist but he was also a communist' (Doder and Branson, 1999, p. 202). Tiny Slovenia was the only country to avoid significant abuses of power. Privatization was pursued, but more slowly than elsewhere, and the social structure remained largely intact in a consensual political atmosphere in which multi-party coalitions were the norm. It is not beyond the bounds of possibility that much of the rest of Yugoslavia could have achieved a similar soft landing if opportunities to strengthen links with the West had been taken before the end of the Cold War and the power-grab of radical nationalists had met stiffer resistance.

In neither Serbia or Croatia was a proper separation of powers permitted. Tudjman dominated the judiciary and Milosevic increasingly packed the courts with obedient supporters. Important ministries were populated by officials whose key priority was to serve the ruling few rather than the wider public good. Opposition parties in both states were fragmented and usually lacked professionalism. Sometimes they latched onto nationalism in a desperate bid to outflank the ruling party in patriotic zeal. Both regimes did not hesitate to manipulate elections, or steal them outright, so as to extend their hold on power. In Serbia this happened in the 1992 presidential elections and again in 2000 for those to the Federal Presidency. Before elections in Croatia in 1994, Croats from Bosnia were allowed to vote, which assured the HDZ of 10 per cent of the seats in advance. However, in 1995, Tudjman's opponents captured Zagreb in municipal elections; but the President refused to allow the capital to elect a mayor who would oppose state policy and imposed his own nominee. Both regimes dominated state television and radio, rarely allowing any dissenting voices to appear. Milosevic's control of the electronic media was arguably the key factor helping him to stay in power when political setbacks mounted. Tudjman used the banks to ensure his supporters bought up the press. They were instructed only to give credit to HDZ loyalists so that newspaper staff, or would-be independent owners hoping to buy state newspapers earmarked for privatization, were frozen out.

The return of a semblance of normality in the mid-1990s enabled political competition to revive in both countries, the strongest challenge being faced by Milosevic. Both leaders alienated collaborators by high-handed behaviour, abrupt policy changes, and withdrawal of privileges. A long list of top Milosevic aides and former allies were assassinated in 1999–2000 in unexplained circumstances. Earlier, during the winter of 1995–6, he had survived massive street protests over local election fraud and state control of the media. Forthright international backing for those opposing electoral fraud and malpractice in both countries during 1996–7 might have destabilized authoritarian rule but, especially in Serbia, the mainstream opposition was largely cold-shouldered abroad.

An embarrassing blow to Milosevic's authority came from Montenegro. Since 1992 it and Serbia had comprised a truncated Yugoslav federation shorn of the four other republics that had seceded in 1991–2. But the junior partner in rump Yugoslavia grew increasingly disaffected and open defiance towards Belgrade started to occur with the election in 1997 of Milo Djukanovic, who was keen to establish a power base independent of Belgrade. The Serbian leader's isolation intensified further when US officials in the second Clinton administration altered their view about his usefulness and started to declare openly that he was the chief obstacle to the normalization of politics in the Balkans. Washington was dismayed by the indiscriminate violence used to crack down on unrest in Kosovo. The West had largely ignored the Albanian opposition when it pursued non-violent protest. But when the Dayton accord of 1995 left Milosevic's repressive system largely intact, the Albanians quickly became radicalized. NATO finally launched a bombing campaign in the spring of 1999 as the Serbian crackdown extended to driving much of the Albanian population from Kosovo. A peace accord in June 1999 turned Kosovo into a virtual UN protectorate with a large NATO force on the ground (even though technically the state still remained part of Yugoslavia).

Peaceful democratic transitions soon got under way in both Croatia and Serbia. The death of Tudjman on the eve of elections was followed by victory for a centre-left coalition in December 1999 and the election as president of Stjepan Mesic, who was committed to restoring rights to minorities and mending fences with estranged neighbours, especially Bosnia. In Serbia, blatant electoral fraud in September 2000 brought onto the streets groups such as industrial workers, who had previously remained on the sidelines. The military and police refused to obey orders to deal ruthlessly with protests, many of which were spearheaded by university and secondary-school students whose bold tactics unnerved the authorities. Milosevic was swept from office and placed first in local and then international custody, but in neither Croatia nor Serbia has a clean break with the past occurred.

Makeshift ruling coalitions have found it difficult to establish their authority over unaccountable power centres in the army, police, and intelligence world. They have neither governed effectively nor instituted economic recovery, the latter being a vital requirement if most citizens are to be fully convinced that democratic government is preferable to the authoritarianism of the recent past. The former ruling parties in Serbia and Croatia continue to enjoy a degree of influence that opposition parties do not normally possess in the Balkans or elsewhere. This is due to their having well-placed allies in both the private and state-run sectors of the economy, in the media, and in the judiciary and security services. A freer atmosphere, the absence of glaring corruption, and the benefits of external aid may allow pragmatists to hang on in Serbia and Croatia. But nor can a realignment be ruled out, with parties such as the Croatian Social Liberals and Yugoslav President Vojislav Kostunica's Democratic Party of Serbia forming a new ruling coalition with elements who held power during the Tudjman and Milosevic eras. Desire to enjoy the trappings of office and access to state resources may prove strong enough to overcome normal political divisions, or even memories of harassment at the hands of authoritarian parties now out of office.

EU Efforts to Stabilize the Balkans

The demise of Tudjman and Milosevic coincided with the European Union acquiring far greater visibility in the Balkans. The United States has downgraded its role in the region, especially since the change of administration in Washington at the start of 2001. This means that the EU has assumed much greater responsibility for crisis management. The EU's Commissioner for External

Relations has admitted that the Balkans will be a critical test for the Common Foreign and Security Policy gradually taking shape.

Without purposeful EU intervention in 2001, it is difficult to see how Macedonia could have avoided a descent into full-blown civil war. A limited consensus between the ethnic Macedonian majority and the large Albanian minority had survived Macedonia's first decade of independence. It was based on a common interest in staying out of the wars that engulfed much of the rest of what had been Yugoslavia. Under the leadership of President Kiro Gligorov (1991–8), Macedonia showed skill in limiting the ability of Serbia to destabilise its fragile independence. A United Nations Preventive Deployment Force (1995–9) contributed to strengthening Macedonia's sovereignty by patrolling the undefined border between Macedonia and FRY. But the European Union failed to take resolute action to counteract the effects of the economic boycott which one of its members, Greece, imposed on Macedonia for 18 months in 1994–5. The economic damage was compounded by the impact of international sanctions on rump Yugoslavia and by the Kosovo conflict in 1999.

During the initial phases of the Yugoslav conflict, there was deep apprehension that Macedonia's ethnic configuration and the absence of well-wishers among the states bordering it would make its peaceful existence shortlived. But when predictions of doom were not fulfilled, global attention was directed elsewhere, despite the implications for regional stability in the southern Balkans if Macedonia unravelled as a state.

The business of government became very much a holding operation during recurrent crises. Actions designed to remove some of the grievances of ethnic Albanians, who were denied access to a wide range of public employment and prevented from having Albanian-language educational institutions at university-level, could hardly proceed in such a fraught atmosphere. Increasing numbers wanted Albanians to enjoy constitutional parity with the shrinking Slavic majority. In 1998, the retirement of President Gligorov and the electoral victory of the Internal Macedonian Revolutionary Organization (VMRO) led to mounting instability. This nationalist party was prepared to form a coalition with an Albanian nationalist party, but it was deal-making and an interest in enjoying the spoils of office which created the momentum rather than a desire to regularize relations between the two communities. After February 2001 Macedonia's uneasy peace was shattered by direct hostilities between Albanian rebels who proclaimed themselves the National Liberation Army (NLA) and the unprepared Macedonian security forces.

Macedonia's stability had been undermined by events hailed by much of the rest of the world as preparing the way for the normalization of the region: the ending of Belgrade's oppression of the Albanian majority in Kosovo in 1999 and the fall from power of Milosevic in 2000. The disappearance of the threat of an expansionary Serbia removed the thin layer of glue binding the two main national communities together. Perhaps most ethnic Macedonians now identified a new external threat: an Albanian-dominated Kosovo which would release forces resulting in the federalization of their state or else its partition with large segments joining Kosova and Albania to form a 'Greater Albania'.

Months of shuttle diplomacy by the EU culminated in the Framework Agreement for Macedonia signed at Ohrid on 13 August 2001 and the despatch of a NATO force designed to enforce and safeguard a new internal political settlement. In the face of continuous obstruction from radical members of the VMRO-led government, the EU Commission worked hard for the adoption of measures that would give the large Albanian minority and others a much greater role in decision-making. The changes to the constitution in November 2001 and the adoption of a law on local self-government in January 2002 were important steps in that direction. An amnesty, allowing Albanian militants who had renounced violence to avoid criminal charges and play a role in public life, was also wrung from the government of Ljubo Georgievski.

Shortcomings of the International Approach

The EU hopes that the multi-level process of political and economic recovery in the Balkans will become a self-sustaining one. But clearly that is not possible in Macedonia in the foreseeable future due to the brittleness of the state and the incapacity of public institutions. The EU will need to oversee a process of economic and political reconstruction if Macedonia is to become a viable entity enjoying a minimum degree of internal cohesion. But it appears reluctant, as do other partner organizations, to become a lead organization fighting the endemic corruption which was a strong contributory factor to the civil war that took place in 2000.

It appears to prefer the approach tried in Bosnia where 'seven years of seminars, training sessions and "capacity building" have not yielded a single major corruption or organized crime conviction – even where the international community has supplied the evidence' (*International Crisis Group*, 2002, p. 35). The same source has warned that 'Ohrid risks becoming a paper peace, awaiting the next conflict to be torn up and rewritten.'

The plethora of international organizations involved in the Balkans, with diverse and often incompatible institutional cultures and management styles, makes effective coordination of externally led efforts to stabilize the region difficult. Authoritarian forces can sometimes exploit the turf-wars and short attention-span of international bodies to remain powerful local players. In 1999, the Stability Pact for the Balkans was launched by NATO and EU states (and also Japan). External funds were injected to promote regional development and revive cross-border trade. But at least until 2002 its performance was criticized because of its failure to engage with local forces committed to meaningful democratic change, and its unwieldy bureaucratic character.

Whether the EU can upgrade its performance in the Balkans and help restore the basis for long-term cooperation between two currently estranged ethnic groups in Macedonia will be a critical test of its competence and resolve to undertake difficult foreign policy responsibilities. The core of the EU's Balkan strategy is to conclude stabilization agreements with reform-minded governments, offering assistance to those ready to introduce a market economy, build a public-service-orientated bureaucracy, tackle corruption, and improve relations with their neighbours. The prospect of integration with mainstream European institutions for those states prepared to embrace this agenda opened up considerably in the late 1990s.

Now two of the eight territorial units formerly comprising Yugoslavia (Bosnia and Kosovo) have UN-mandated civil and military missions with substantial authority over local political bodies. Innovative strategies needed to be devised for the sub-state entities that are connected to Serbia through the existence of the Yugoslav Federation (Montenegro, Vojvodina and Kosovo), to shake off the overlordship of Belgrade without embarking on the path of complete independence which is likely to be strewn with problems. It looks as if the EU wishes to preserve a rump Yugoslavia in which its component parts enjoy differing degrees of autonomy.

The relationship between Kosovo and Serbia might become similar to that between Britain and Gibraltar or Denmark and the Faroe Islands. Active EU mediation in 2002 produced agreement on a less one-sided relationship between Montenegro and Serbia.

Nationalism, Democracy and Crossnational Politics

The tendency on the part of the West to have profoundly negative views about the capacity of Balkan elites, and their populations to rise above narrow nationalism, as well as those elites' and peoples' preference for authoritarian politics, is now over a century old. But the contrasting performance of Bulgaria and Romania since 1989, and the ability of some ex-Yugoslav countries to resist ethnic conflict better than others, suggests that such fatalistic judgments can be overdrawn.

Yugoslavia could have evolved in different ways at the end of the Cold War. Human agency, as well as defective economic and administrative structures, hastened the end of Tito's experiment. But its destruction at the hands of ethno-nationalist political forces was by no means inevitable. Nor was a descent into full-scale violence when the political edifice Tito bequeathed to his successors proved incapable of reforming itself. The timing of the Yugoslav crisis was dependent on external as well as internal developments. A clearer Western understanding of what was at stake if Yugoslavia violently broke up could have prevented the initiative swinging so completely to those forces intent on homogenizing the federation and, through radical alteration of the human geography, creating rival ethnic statelets.

Romanian and Bulgarian communist despots licensed ultra-nationalism to mask critical failures in the economic realm. But the impact on Bulgarian society was less harmful than in Romania. Despite the mass exodus of Bulgarian Muslims in 1989, postcommunist rulers frowned on excursions to the wilder shores of nationalism, while in Romania ethnic politics remained a going concern for at least another decade. Human agency once again intervened, allowing for 'an aborted "clash of civilizations"' in Bulgaria, according to one commentator (Ragaru, 2001).

Nationalism is undeniably an important feature of Balkan political culture in most states of the region. The strength of the intransigent variety has been reinforced by the bitter memories left

by bloody internecine conflicts, the continued existence of disputed
boundaries, and the presence of large numbers of people who are
victims of economic collapse and who can be persuaded to blame
their plight on ethnic rivals. But it is not necessarily a permanent
condition; national identities do not remain unchanging but mutate
according to the pressure of events, such as the outcome of wars
and, not least, economic forces. The lack of common ground
revealed between the Serbs of Serbia proper and those located in
other republics became hard to disguise as the post-1991 conflicts
intensified. Important cleavages also exist between Croats in
different parts of their scissor-shaped country. And the degree of
differentiation between Albanians spread across three states in the
southern Balkans, suggests that the spectre of a 'Greater Albania'
is unlikely to become reality if it depends on the solidarity of
co-ethnics in Albania, Macedonia and Kosovo to bring it about.

   Apart from the ethnic standoff in Macedonia, most of the critical
internal political struggles in the region in the early years of the
new century were taking place between political parties representing the same ethnic groups: Montenegrins were divided about
whether to opt for independence or renegotiate the federation with
Serbia; Croats were sharply at odds about the degree to which centralist, and ultra-nationalist policies isolating the country from the
rest of the region should be replaced; Serbs in the post-Milosevic
era are likely to be divided about the direction the country should
take for a long time to come. Groupings belonging to opposing
nationalities have shown the capacity to work together. Sometimes
this is unsettling as when the Serb and Albanian underworlds close
ranks to keep open the clandestine routes through which people
and drugs are shipped westwards; or when nationalist parties from
the chief majority and minority groupings in Macedonia find common ground by sharing out state resources among themselves on a
massive scale. More happily, in Romania and Bulgaria, the parties
of the Hungarians and Muslims have participated in government
along with parties that sometimes express majoritarian nationalism, without going down the path of wholesale corruption.
Nevertheless, it is often economic concerns that prompt these
unlikely bedfellows to cohabit. And economic frustrations can
sometimes better explain the successes of chauvinist parties than
the existence of ethnic antagonisms.

   The deepening economic plight of the region, thanks in no
small measure to the baleful legacy of the communist era and the

inexperience or dishonesty of postcommunist rulers, is a recipe for political volatility. Opinion polls nearly everywhere in the Balkans show far greater concern with unemployment, poverty, and corruption than with the identity issues supposedly uppermost in the thoughts of Balkan peoples. But economic desperation sometimes finds an outlet in populist politics with a destabilizing ethnic agenda. In the year 2000, the combined GDP of Albania, Bosnia, Bulgaria, Romania, Macedonia and Croatia was equivalent to that of the city of Hamburg (*Kosovo Report*, 2000, p. 246). A declining population and a growing proportion of elderly people across much of the region is compounding the socio-economic crisis with a demographic one.

The region is unlikely to recover quickly if global institutions, with the EU to the fore, insist on macro-stabilization policies based on hasty bids to create market economies. Rapid privatization may have enjoyed a certain success in Central European states such as Poland and Hungary but will be difficult to implement properly, particularly in the context of the postwar parts of ex-Yugoslavia. In the absence of a middle class, which has been greatly weakened by the conflict, it is likely that those who will emerge as the new economic and political powerbrokers are speculators, black-marketeers, and outright gangsters who have already flourished in wartime conditions. In some important ways, the cultural differences between peoples in the south-east corner of Europe are less great than those that confronted the architects of the future EU when trying to rebuild much of Western Europe fifty years ago. Poverty, misrule and totalitarianism have exacerbated such differences, but they may well recede if the peoples of the region have the chance to rebuild their societies with help from the rest of Europe. However, until these factors start to be significantly eroded, politicians ready to challenge and undermine democracy in the name of ethnic exclusivism are likely to find plenty of opportunities to wield power and influence again in local and possibly also national politics.

6

Ukraine and Post-Soviet Europe: Authoritarian Consolidation or Renewed Reform?

ANDREW WILSON

Independent Ukraine has suffered not just the pains of transition, but of transition inflation. Since 1991 it has variously been described as simultaneously making the transition from empire to nation-state, from totalitarianism to democracy, command to market economy, and object to subject of international relations. Ukraine's situation has indeed been complicated by this daunting array of tasks, but this chapter will argue that its problems – and those of adjacent post-Soviet Europe – can only partly be understood via a 'transition' framework. Not only is modern Ukraine strongly marked by continuities with the past, but also a certain consolidation of a semi-reformed polity and economy was evident by the mid-1990s, which has only recently begun to be challenged (Wilson, 2002). The chapter is in three sections. The first discusses the background to Ukraine's declaration of independence in 1991. The second looks at political developments over the following decade; and the third examines the key policy dilemmas faced by the new state, including the still contested nature of Ukrainian national identity, the constitutional system, economic reform and the development of Ukrainian foreign policy. Finally, some limited conclusions are drawn.

Historical Background and Independence from the USSR

Ukrainians were not expecting independence when Mikhail Gorbachev assumed the Soviet leadership in 1985. Even radical nationalists were not anticipating it any time soon when serious political reform began in 1989–90. The events that led to the Ukrainian parliament declaring independence on 24 August 1991 and the overwhelming endorsement of that decision by popular referendum on 1 December 1991 therefore took place in accelerated time. Perspectives changed as rapidly as events, which often ran ahead of participants' plans. However, many of the arrangements and decisions then made in haste are still a powerful influence a decade later.

Soviet Ukraine was a hybrid entity. Most obviously, the westernmost territories of Galicia, Transcarpathia and Bukovyna had been part of the Habsburg Empire until 1918, and then of the new Central European states (mainly Poland, plus Czechoslovakia and Romania) until 1939. They therefore had a very different historical experience before their relatively late incorporation into the USSR, including most importantly relative political freedom, the consolidation of national identity under a degree of official sponsorship and through the persistent national and social conflict with the local Poles, and the growth of a far-right movement in the interwar period. Most of modern Ukraine, however (central Ukraine either side of the river Dnipro, the industrial east, Crimea and the southern coast), was part of the Russian Empire until 1917. National consciousness and a national movement were only nascent forces in 1917, and were in any case largely confined to the former Hetmanate and peasant heartland regions of central Ukraine. (The Hetmanate was the name given to the polity carved out of the Polish Commonwealth after the great Cossack Uprising of 1648; although linked to the Tsar by the Pereyaslav Treaty of 1654, it retained a degree of autonomy until 1785.) The south (dubbed 'New Russia' or *Novorossiya*) was regarded as virgin territory for the official administration of multi-ethnic settlement. In the eastern Donbas a Russified working class developed a strong regional and labour consciousness. Crimea, in a separate decision, was transferred to Ukraine as late as 1954; accordingly, it missed the half-hearted promotion of the Ukrainian language and culture that the Soviet authorities briefly encouraged in the 1920s.

With the exception of the former Habsburg territories therefore, most Ukrainians supported aspects of Soviet rule and welfare socialism, and their Ukrainian identity was a Soviet Ukrainian one, nested in larger identities of great power patriotism and/or East Slavic unity. Furthermore, West Ukrainian and Soviet

Ukrainian political cultures remain very different. Patrimonial communism and its characteristic features – the suppression of civil society, clientelism and authority worship – put down strong roots outside of west Ukraine, where habits of social self-organization were more easily recovered in the late 1980s. Soviet rule also inverted Ukraine's traditional socio-economic geography. The west and the central Ukrainian heartland remained relatively underdeveloped. The former periphery, the steppe region in the south and east, was now home to most of Ukraine's industry and most of its larger cities. This was also where the Russian minority (11 million at the time of the 1989 census) was concentrated, and where the Russian language remained hegemonic over Ukrainian 'newcomers' (new in the sense of newly urbanized) – even during the brief 'Ukrainianization' campaign of the 1920s (Martin, 2001, pp. 122–4). Nationally, although ethnic Ukrainians made up 73 per cent of the population in the 1989 census (and 78 per cent in 2001), roughly a third of these were habitual and/or preferential Russophones and only 45–50 per cent of the population were Ukrainophone (though there was enormous overlap) – a large majority in the countryside, but a minority in the cities.

In 1989–91 therefore the national 'Popular Front' *Rukh* (the Ukrainian for 'movement') developed a strong base in the west and in the capital Kyiv, but was only able to win a quarter of the seats in the first free elections to the Ukrainian parliament (*Verkhovna Rada*) in March 1990. In Gorbachev's March 1991 referendum on the preservation of the USSR as a 'renewed federation', 70.5 per cent of Ukrainians voted in favour, and only 29.5 per cent said no (again, mainly voters in Kiev and the west). Unlike the Central Asian republics or Belarus, therefore, Ukraine had a powerful opposition movement; but, unlike the Baltic republics, South Caucasus or Moldova where local Popular Fronts won absolute majorities in 1990, Rukh was not about to win power or secure independence on its own.

Nevertheless, the number of Soviet diehards and/or committed opponents of Rukh was also small. In Ukraine there was a huge middle ground – the 'Soviet Ukrainians' – whose identities and political loyalties were flexible and often contradictory. Many wanted both the USSR and a 'sovereign' Ukraine. Even the communist party was split. Its official leadership – the so-called 'imperial communist' group led from 1990 by first secretary Stanislav Hurenko – tended to side with Gorbachev's conservative opponents in Moscow. On the other hand, Leonid Kravchuk, the chairman of parliament, led a 'national communist' group; and the alternative question he manoeuvred onto the March 1991 ballot (proposing a loose confederal 'Union of Soviet Sovereign States ... on the basis of Ukraine's ... sovereignty') won even more support (80.2 per cent) than Gorbachev's question.

The contradiction was real, but typical. Rukh had already accepted it would have to work with the national communist group before August 1991, but their 'grand bargain' took on broader dimensions after the failure of the Moscow coup. Rukh still depended on former Communists to exploit what might have proven only a temporary opportunity (had Yeltsin sought to replace Gorbachev as *Soviet* rather than Russian leader after August 1991, many Ukrainians would have supported him). In return for converting their support for 'sovereignty' into 'independence', Rukh agreed not to seek to force the former communist elite from power. Kravchuk therefore easily defeated his divided and half-hearted nationalist rivals in Ukraine's first presidential election in December 1991, winning a comfortable 62 per cent in the first round. All sides now backed independence for different reasons, while Yeltsin's Russia was preoccupied with its own affairs, resulting in a euphoric majority of 90 per cent in the referendum held on the same day. The 'confederal' option Kravchuk had backed in March had now seemingly vanished, although politicians' rhetoric was still guilty of blurring distinctions, both before and during the campaign. The dramatic transformation since March 1991 was therefore both apparent and real.

Politics in Independent Ukraine

First President Leonid Kravchuk, 1991–4

Unlike other 'Popular Fronts' of the late communist period (Solidarity in Poland, Sajudis in Lithuania), Rukh has survived; in large part because its agenda remains uncompleted. The 'grand bargain' still shapes Ukrainian life. Although Rukh helped to win independence, it has been unable to displace the remodelled Soviet order in most of Ukraine. In the first years of independence, therefore, many of the issues of the late 1980s were replayed. Feeling itself a cultural minority, Rukh remains committed to a thorough

Ukrainianization of all aspects of public life. Its foreign policy is resolutely pro-Western. Its economic policies are less clear-cut, with Ukrainian nationalists claiming to support both the creation of a market and a 'national' (potentially protectionist) economy.

The Communist Party of Ukraine (CPU) was banned in August 1991, but allowed to revive in 1993 as a 'new' party. (The Constitutional Court annulled the 1991 decision in December 2001; the 'old' party was therefore formally revived and promptly merged with the 'new' party at a special 'unity congress' in May 2002.) The CPU was dominated by Kravchuk's former 'imperial communist' opponents and remained one of the most left-wing parties in the former communist region. It opposed all economic reform, and its leaders rarely used Ukrainian. As late as 2002, the party still campaigned unequivocally for the restoration of the USSR. Rukh therefore regards the party's very existence as a breach of the 'grand bargain', and has frequently called for it to be banned.

The former 'national communists', on the other hand, had no party of their own. As first president of the new state, Kravchuk's main priority was to give real meaning to the 'sovereignty' on which he had based his rise to power in 1990–1. Kravchuk found it easiest to concentrate on the formal attributes of statehood – rather more important to the elite than to the public at large. International recognition was secured, armed forces established, uniforms were changed. However, his consensual style and reluctance to embrace risky reform programmes meant that the momentum from his impressive victory in 1991 disappeared surprisingly quickly. Moreover, Kravchuk's initial desire to seek 'sovereignty' through economic autonomy from Russia (the two economies were so intertwined, they were not really separate entities at all) and his failure to launch any real project of domestic reform (see the discussion on economic policy below) led to catastrophic disruption and a huge strike wave in eastern Ukraine in the summer of 1993; forcing the concession of early elections, and further economic difficulties after Kravchuk settled the crisis through resort to the printing press.

At the parliamentary elections in March 1994, Rukh and the Communists revived their rivalry, with the latter the clear winner, taking 86 seats to Rukh's 20 (for the detailed results of all but the most recent elections, see the chapter by Sarah Birch in *Developments in Central and East European Politics 2*). Other parties were not yet well developed, particularly in the centre ground. One exception was the Socialist Party set up during the Communists' temporary absence in October 1991, which was then anti-market but pro-independence, and won 14 seats. Ukraine's underdeveloped party system meant that most (168) of the deputies were (ex-communist) 'independents'. Another defect was 112 empty seats. The electoral system retained Soviet practices, with single territorial constituencies (*okruhy*) requiring *both* a 50 per cent plus one turnout and a 50 per cent plus one majority. As a result initially mainly of the latter stipulation, only 338 of the 450 seats were filled at the first attempt. Even after many rounds of repeat elections, 36 were still empty on the eve of the next poll in 1998. The new parliament was therefore no more capable of pushing reform forward than the last.

The revanche of the left in 1994 served as a prelude to Kravchuk's loss of office in the pre-term presidential election in the summer. The deepening economic crisis forced Kravchuk to stand on his achievements in 'state-building', and paint his main opponent, former prime minister Leonid Kuchma (served 1992–3), as a dangerous Russophile. Kuchma did indeed campaign on a platform attacking Ukraine's 'isolation' from Russia and defending the rights of Russian-speakers, as well as contrasting his promises of (unspecified) reform with Kravchuk's inaction; but this mix of policies was designed to appeal to archetypal Russified and/or Soviet Ukrainians (Kuchma being both) rather than the Russophile extreme. It therefore won him victory by 52 to 45 per cent in the second round. Most commentators noted the obvious fact that the second round results were highly polarized, Kravchuk winning every region west of the river Dnipro apart from Poltava, Kuchma every region further east and south. Fewer noted the corollary: that Kuchma's broad coalition of support was extremely diverse, initially including even the Communists, who detested Kravchuk for his role in ending the USSR.

Kuchma, moreover, was elected to rebalance Ukraine's balancing act – to de-emphasize sovereignty and rebuild links with Russia, but not to abandon the former. Moreover, his margin of victory was relatively narrow. In neighbouring Belarus, where the Popular Front won only 8 per cent of the seats back in 1990, the sovereignty drive had seemingly run out of steam by 1994; and Alexander Lukashenka was elected president with 75 per cent of the vote on a platform explicitly advocating the 'reunion' of Russia and Belarus.

Second President Leonid Kuchma, 1994–1999–2004

After the election Kuchma chose to de-emphasize Russian speakers' language concerns, although by freezing the linguistic status quo he delivered most of what they wanted by enshrining Russian's de facto dominance. Impending state bankruptcy forced him to change priorities and launch Ukraine's first serious economic reform in October 1994, which quickly earned official IMF approval with a Systemic Transformation loan. The economic system was only partially transformed, however. The plan's early achievements were considerable: macroeconomic stabilization culminating with the successful introduction of a proper hard currency (the *hrivnya*, to replace the emergency 'coupons' used since Ukraine's ejection from the rouble zone in 1992) in 1996, price liberalization and the privatization of 'small' enterprises (such as restaurants and shops). However, backsliding was evident as early as 1995, and things began to go seriously awry when former Kuchma ally Pavlo Lazarenko served as prime minister in 1996–7. 'Soviet Ukrainian' habits of clientelism and authoritarian rule became increasingly entrenched, and corruption exploded to endemic proportions as the prime minister tried to bring whole swathes of the economy, particularly the energy sector, under his personal control.

Nevertheless, early in his first term compromises were necessary. Kuchma's main domestic achievement was to ensure the belated approval of a new constitution in June 1996, which enshrined a delicate balance between Rukh on cultural questions, the left on welfare issues, and Kuchma's own preference for enhanced presidential authority. The two treaties signed with NATO and Russia in 1997 also seemed to secure a delicate equilibrium in foreign policy (see below). However, it soon became apparent that Kuchma's growing personal power would be the unstable element in this balance of balances. The parliamentary elections held in March 1998 were a first sign that Ukraine's 'democratization' transition was beginning to go awry. Kuchma manipulated the opposition and backed an array of new 'centre' parties that were in fact fronts for Ukraine's new 'business' interests (similar to the client or 'oligarchic' networks produced by Russia's distorted privatization process). The 'National-Democrats' were the party of government, Hromada ('Community') represented Lazarenko (now out of office, but retaining economic power) and his power base in Dnipropetrovsk, the 'Social Democrats' were the Kiev business elite, the 'Greens' a younger group of energy traders and bankers. The Progressive Socialist Party – a breakaway from the Socialists, widely rumoured to be secretly supported by the authorities – was the other suspicious newcomer. Kuchma also agreed to change the electoral system. Half of all deputies (225) were now elected from a national party list – with a 4 per cent barrier for representation; and half by plurality voting in enlarged territorial constituencies – with the majority requirements thankfully abolished. However, the new system failed to benefit the 'centre' parties as he had hoped, none of whom won more than 6 per cent. The Communists once again topped the poll with 24.7 per cent and 122 seats, and with the support of sympathetic independents, the three parties of the 'left bloc' (the Communists, Socialists and Rural Party) were close to a majority – though the Progressive Socialists (16 seats) remained unpredictable. Rukh, which recovered on its dip in 1994 to win 9.4 per cent and 46 seats, therefore renewed the 'grand bargain' by allying with the centre parties.

Within the centre camp, however, former prime minister Lazarenko and his Hromada party (23 seats) staged a bitter war for influence with the pro-presidential National Democrats (29 seats). When Hromada eventually allied with the left to give Oleksandr Tkachenko of the Rural Party the parliamentary leadership, Kuchma feared the same balance of forces might unseat him at the next presidential election due in 1999. Like Berezovsky in Russia or Kazhegeldin in Kazakhstan, Lazarenko over-reached himself and broke implicit rules about the elite's division of the spoils. Lazarenko's business and media empire was therefore ruthlessly undermined, followed by the *coup de grâce* of his arrest for entering Switzerland on a false passport, loss of parliamentary immunity and final flight to the USA via Greece. Thereafter, Kuchma made sure that presidential favour was the key to influence in the new economy.

After Lazarenko's exile, Kuchma was able to proceed with his re-election plans, which were really nothing more than simply copying Yeltsin's victory strategy in Russia's 1996 election. Rukh was split to ensure Kuchma faced no effective opponents to his right (see Table 6.1). Former security chief (1991–4) and prime minister (1995–6) Yevhen Marchuk ran on the centre-right, before

TABLE 6.1　*Ukraine's October/November 1999 presidential*
election (main candidates only; percentages)

	First round	Second round
Leonid Kuchma	36.5	56.2
Petro Symonenko (Communist)	22.2	37.8
Oleksandr Moroz (Socialist)	11.3	
Nataliya Vitrenko (Prog. Soc.)	11.0	
Yevhen Marchuk	8.1	
Yurii Kostenko (Rukh)	2.2	
Hennadii Udovenko (Rukh)	1.2	

accepting Kuchma's 'surprise' offer to copy Aleksandr Lebed in
1996 and take over as National Security Adviser between the election's two rounds. The country's leading liberal, National Bank
Chairman Viktor Yushchenko, and other strong potential centre
candidates were dissuaded from running. On the left, the
'Progressive Socialist' leader Nataliya Vitrenko was used to divert
votes from the relatively moderate Socialist leader Oleksandr
Moroz and ensure that Kuchma faced the easily defeatable
Communist leader Petro Symonenko in the second round. Given
the manoeuvring, Kuchma would have won anyway, but widespread accusations of media bias and abuse of 'administrative
resources' to enhance the final result indicate that he made doubly
sure (see Table 6.1).

Kuchma's Second Term

After the election, Kuchma's authoritarian tendencies seemed to
get worse. In January 2000 the 'Velvet Revolution' – in effect a
parliamentary coup – removed the left from the leadership of the
Rada. Tkachenko was replaced as chairman by a triumvirate of
'oligarchs', fronted by Ivan Plyushch, who had held the post in
1992–4. In April, Kuchma staged a much-criticized referendum to
expand presidential power, although the 1996 constitution states
that two-thirds of the deputies must support such proposals, implic-
itly before any referendum takes place. Even the normally docile
Constitutional Court struck out two questions (no confidence in the
existing Rada, and approval of the 1996 constitution by referendum); but the four that remained (abolition of deputies' blanket

legal immunity, a reduction in their numbers from 450 to 300, enhanced dissolution powers and the introduction of a second chamber, probably to be made up of regional governors appointed by the president) officially received 82 to 89 per cent approval on a turnout of 81 per cent. If the 1999 election had been carefully manipulated, this looked more like simple fraud. Securing the Rada's approval was another matter, however. Even when the president's powers of persuasion were at their height in July 2000, only 251 voted in favour of the proposed amendments – and then the Gongadze affair changed everything (see below). With the 2002 elections failing to deliver the president's supporters anything like a two-thirds majority, the referendum was quietly forgotten. Kuchma's increasing heavy-handedness after his re-election was only part of the story, however. Kuchma was unable to consolidate authoritarian rule as decisively as Lukashenka in 1995–6. Ukraine is more important geopolitically, and, without Russia's subsidies to Belarus, was in a much tighter economic bind after the local financial crises in 1998. Kuchma therefore came under heavy American pressure to resume reform and, in particular, to appoint the well-regarded Yushchenko as prime minister. The new government set about its task with surprising vigour, slimming bureaucracy and reducing many burdensome controls, clamping down on oligarchs' business scams and cleaning up the privatization process. Government finances improved, pensions and salary backlogs were cleared and 2000 became the first year of economic growth since independence. The various clans around Kuchma were incensed, however, taking particular umbrage at the upheavals launched by deputy prime minister Yuliya Tymoshenko in the energy sector. As a longstanding associate of Lazarenko, she had previously been one of their own – hence the biting edge of her reforms.

As the clans manoeuvred to replace one or both of the Yushchenko–Tymoshenko tandem, trouble came from an unexpected quarter. In September 2000 a leading opposition internet journalist Hryhorii Gongadze disappeared. In October what all bar the authorities accepted was his headless corpse was found in a wood near Kyiv. But the real sensation came in November, when at a special Rada session the Socialist leader Oleksandr Moroz played tapes supposedly secretly made in the president's office by a disgruntled officer in Kuchma's own security detail (Major Mykola Melnychenko) that seemed to implicate the president in

Gongadze's disappearance. Even worse, Melnychenko, who fled first to Central Europe and then the USA, claimed to have hundreds of hours of tapes, uncovering electoral fraud in 1999 and 2000, manipulation and intimidation of the opposition, corruption in the president's entourage and more.

Kuchma denied (most of) the tapes' authenticity and faced down demonstrations calling for his resignation. Instead, first Tymoshenko was removed from office in February 2001 (briefly ending up in prison) and then Yushchenko himself in April. As with Yushchenko's predecessors as prime minister, his successor Anatolii Kinakh was again a representative of the business elite, albeit one safely neutral between the clans. Kuchma survived to welcome the Pope on a historic visit to Kiev and Lviv in June 2001, after which the regime seemed to stabilize internally – although Kuchma was unlikely to be received abroad. Even more damaging allegations of arms trading to 'rogue states' (Iraq, the Taliban) surfaced in 2002.

The 2002 Elections

At the next (parliamentary) elections in 2002, Kuchma faced a triple challenge. The 'Gongadze affair' had led to the divorce of the Communist and Socialist parties, with the later now firmly in the opposition camp. Viktor Yushchenko's supporters, including Rukh, formed the 'Our Ukraine' block, which outpolled the coalition of the president's supporters calling itself 'For a United Ukraine' (and their allies of convenience, the United Social-Democrats) and pushed the Communists into second place (see Table 6.2). Tymoshenko ran her own list in more radical opposition to the president, and like the Socialists, tapped the new protest vote to clear the 4 per cent barrier with surprising ease.

Table 6.2 continues to use the orthodox classification of Ukrainian parties into left, right and centre, but this is often a serious simplification. First of all, as already mentioned, the 'virtual' parties of the centre that first appeared in 1998 were almost all business fronts. Moreover, by the time of the 2002 elections, the influence of the clans was beginning to extend outwards to right and left. The Communists had nascent business interests to protect, and provided useful support to the president and his allies during the Gongadze affair. Our Ukraine had its fair share of business

Andrew Wilson 103

TABLE 6.2   *Ukraine's March 2002 parliamentary elections (initial alignment only)*

	List vote %	List seats	Okruhy	Total seats
Left				
Communists	20.0	59	6	65
Socialists	6.9	19	3	22
Centre				
For a United Ukraine	11.8	35	66	101
Social-Democrats (United)	6.3	19	5	24
Right				
Tymoshenko block	7.3	22	–	22
Our Ukraine	23.6	70	42	112
Other parties	16.1	–	9	9
Independents	–	–	83	83
Total		225	225	450

'sponsors' and 'cuckoos' from the presidential administration, including the bloc's campaign head Roman Bezsmertnyi and Sumy governor Volodymyr Shcherban. Rukh was deeply distrustful of Yushchenko's pragmatic relations with both types, and fearful that the cuckoos could easily be persuaded to leave the nest (seven duly defected to ensure the election of Kuchma ally Volodymyr Lytvyn as parliamentary chairman in May 2002).

Second, with little or no ideological commitment to restrain them, Ukrainian politicians are extraordinarily mobile. In the 1998–2002 parliament the 450 deputies changed allegiances more than 600 times (and most of the originally 122 communists stayed where they were). Factions changed with bewildering speed. Only four out of 33 parties or party blocs on the list for the 2002 elections were the same as in 1998. It was obviously impossible to establish any kind of stable majority amidst all this Brownian motion (Wilson, 2001). The 'New Majority' stitched together with great fanfare in January 2000 fell apart within a year. Even after swallowing scores of independents to reach 177 seats by May 2002, For a United Ukraine had no guaranteed majority in the 2002 parliament. After combining with the Social-Democrats to elect Lytvyn, the coalition duly disassembled into its constituent parts. Nevertheless, the various strands of opposition – particularly the ever-vigorous Tymoshenko – sought to revive the campaign against Kuchma after the elections. A new wave of demonstrations against the president began on 16 September, the second anniversary of Gongadze's disappearance, and it was far from certain that Kuchma would survive to see out his term until 2004. As with Yeltsin in his last days in office, he was in any case now preoccupied with securing a safe succession and retirement.

Dilemmas and Choices

Jackdaw Nationalism

In part, the divisions in parliament and between parties simply reflect those in Ukrainian society. Because 'nationally committed' elements (Rukh) command the support of no more than 25–30 per cent of the population – a regional (western) and social (the Ukrainian-speaking intelligentsia) minority – Ukraine lacked a clear trajectory towards independence in 1989–91, until the failure of the Moscow coup delivered it anyway. Nationalists hoped for 'consolidation' after 1991, but results have been mixed. First president Leonid Kravchuk alienated many Russophones with his education policy and choice of national symbols. Leonid Kuchma, his successor after 1994, initially promised a more 'Eurasian' identity, but soon settled for an eclectic approach that masked a highly contradictory situation on the ground. In some state bureaucracies, formal Ukrainianization has been applied; although the programme 'On broadening the functioning of the Ukrainian language as the state language' introduced in February 2000 both promised to take further measures and admitted previous only partial success. In education, the number of children in Ukrainian language schools rose from 47.5 per cent in 1988–9 to 65 per cent in 1998–9 – an advance on the Ukrainophone share of the population. In publishing and popular culture, however, Ukrainophones continue to be underserved. If anything, writing or singing in Ukrainian became more difficult in the late 1990s. In the broadcast media the situation was more complex. Kuchma had more success than Kravchuk in creating a national 'information space' after 1994 – but largely for propaganda purposes. Ukrainian TV is notoriously biased.

At a broader level, the nature of Ukrainian identity continued to be contested. The state paid homage to elements in traditional Ukrainian nationalism and anti-communism: putting up a new statue to the national historian Mykhailo Hrushevskyi in Kiev; rebuilding the St Michael's Monastery and Assumption Cathedral; abolishing the October Revolution holiday and removing Soviet symbols from the parliament building – but only in 2000, after nine years of nominal independence. Moreover, Kuchma combined such gestures with the rhetoric of East Slavic fraternity and suitably remodelled Soviet Ukrainian traditions. 'Victory Day' is still a huge pageant to celebrate 1945, but with rather more focus on the Red Army's Ukrainian Front. No serious attempt was made to clear up the ambiguities of the 'middle ground' – in part because it suited the authorities to preside over an amorphous society from which no organized challenge to their rule seemed likely to emerge. If Yushchenko were to win the presidency in 2004, however, then Rukh would be close to real power for the first time.

Shaping the New Polity

In 1991–6 Ukraine's political arrangements were also amorphous and provisional. The long debate over adopting a new post-Soviet constitution (Ukraine was the last post-Soviet state to do so) was itself a factor muddying the waters and diverting time and energy from other reform vectors. The belated approval of a new constitution by the Rada in June 1996 (based on the earlier 'constitutional agreement' of 1995) therefore marked a key turning-point.

Since 1995–6 Ukraine has had a semi-presidential system in which the balance of power favours the president. The president appoints the prime minister. The Rada must approve, but the president's choice is not formally dependent on the balance of forces in parliament. Moreover, limits are placed on the Rada's removal powers. In particular, no-confidence motions cannot be tabled for a year once the government's programme had been approved. The president has wide appointment powers, only some of which are shared with parliament or subject to parliamentary ratification. Authority in the regions is directly exercised by the president's appointed governors. The 'power ministries' (defence, security and the interior) are under the president's direct personal control. Presidential patronage also extends to the National Bank, the Constitutional Court (one-third, but another third are also picked by existing judges) and State TV and Radio. In 2001, after the failure of the aborted referendum, Kuchma introduced a system of

'State Secretaries' (totally unknown to the constitution) to act as his eyes and ears in all major departments.

Given Ukraine's highly fractured parliament, it is extremely hard to win the two-thirds majority necessary to override presidential vetoes (a power that Kuchma has used extensively). Impeachment ultimately requires a majority of four-fifths – so the Rada found its criticism impotent during the Gongadze affair. In fact, all attempts to censure administration officials were failures. Unlike Russia, the president's dissolution powers are limited. In practice, however, the presidential administration sits at the head of a dense network of post-Soviet clientelism and government 'by telephone', and Ukraine, like Russia, inclines towards 'hyper-presidentialism'.

Kuchma therefore shocked most observers by using his 'state of the nation' speech on the eleventh anniversary of independence in August 2002 to propose that Ukraine move towards a parliament–presidential system, with a proper 'parliamentary majority' and a prime minister answerable to that majority, not to the president. As this ran counter to the whole tenor of his policies since 1996 – the 2000 referendum in particular – most saw only a cynical move to divide and distract the opposition from its second campaign to force Kuchma's resignation. Nevertheless, academics in Kyiv took the proposal sufficiently seriously to draw up a detailed programme of point-by-point constitutional amendment. If neither Kuchma nor the opposition were to emerge a clear winner from the protest campaign, then a compromise which reduced the president's formal power was possible.

Economic Policy: No Recovery until 2000

In the first two years of independence, Ukraine's economic policy was delusional. The one minister who advocated market reform (Volodymyr Lanovyi) was sidelined, as Ukraine instead pursued the chimera of economic autonomy – meaning maximum distance from Russia. At the same time, the authorities attempted to forestall recession via subsidy and the printing press. Fiscal discipline was non-existent. For a country so integrated in the hyper-centralized Soviet economy, the result was collapsing production (huge falls in GDP of −9.9 per cent in 1992 and −14.2 per cent in 1993) and rampant inflation (1,210 per cent in 1992, a colossal 5,371 per cent in 1993). As prime minister from October 1992 to September 1993,

Leonid Kuchma attempted some U-turns; but his putative signature to an 'economic union' with Russia and Belarus in July 1993 was a step too far for Ukrainian nationalists. The huge wave of miners' strikes in the Donbas in June 1993 resulted in the parachuting into government of leading politicians from eastern Ukraine; but the government of former Donetsk mayor Yukhym Zviahilskyi (September 1993 to May 1994) combined its overtures to Russia with an ill-conceived reassertion of arbitrary state controls that only helped stimulate increasing corruption. Nevertheless, since 1993 – unlike the Baltic states – Ukraine has made no real effort to wean its trade away from Russia. Ukraine also remains dependent on Russia, and to a lesser extent Turkmenistan, for imported oil and gas. Russia in turn depends on Ukrainian territory for its own energy exports, but has threatened to expand the Yamal pipeline that bypasses Ukraine through Belarus if Ukraine steps up its attempts to obtain alternative supplies from Azerbaijan and elsewhere.

Ukraine's frustrated autonomy plans helped the revanche of the left in the March 1994 elections. Kravchuk's response, announcing that there was insufficient political space for any new reform initiative and appointing the leftist dinosaur Vitalii Masol as premier, could do nothing to stave off the president's defeat in July. In 1994 GDP decline accelerated to a scarcely credible −22.9 per cent. Something had to be done. Kuchma's campaign rhetoric had concentrated on language and geopolitics. He had mocked Kravchuk's economic record and genuflected towards 'reform', but never spelt out what it might involve. He therefore deserves credit for preparing and launching Ukraine's first real reform package relatively quickly in October 1994, without any real mandate to carry him forward, although this was also one of the reasons that led him to yield fairly quickly to pressure to water the programme down. Most prices were freed, some irksome government restrictions lifted and (initially) foreign trade liberalized, some basic fiscal discipline was accepted and monetary emissions curbed. After an initial spike, inflation tumbled. The exchange rate stabilized, allowing the successful introduction of a proper national currency, the *hrivnya*, to replace the temporary 'coupon' in September 1996.

Privatization, however, was confined to small-scale and service sectors; and under prime ministers Yevhen Marchuk (1995–6), Pavlo Lazarenko (1996–7) and Valerii Pustovoitenko (1997–9) many controls were reintroduced, and an increasingly etatist, semi-reformed economy developed a worsening reputation for corruption. The privatization programme moved into a large-scale cash phase in 1997–8; but as in Russia, sales were too often made to preferred bidders at knockdown prices. Zviahilskyi fled the country on corruption charges – though he was allowed back in 1997. Lazarenko, accused of embezzling over $800 million, followed him abroad in 1999. In August 1998 Ukraine suffered the same currency confidence and currency collapse as Russia – not quite as severely, but effectively closing off access to foreign bond markets and IMF lending. Thanks to the discipline imposed by Yushchenko at the National Bank inflation remained low, but GDP decline merely levelled out and hopes of real recovery were constantly postponed.

Ukraine therefore faced another crucial turning-point after Kuchma's re-election in late 1999, but once again pulled itself back from the brink. Yushchenko and Tymoshenko now headed a second-chance reform government and moved swiftly to clamp down on the more obvious corruption scams, particularly in the notorious energy sector, as well as removing the most odious or blatantly political government controls. Long-delayed agricultural reform was launched in summer 2000, with a promise to overhaul the grossly inefficient system of state and collective farms. The new Land Code approved in October 2001 promised to allow the buying and selling of farm land from 2004. Privatizations (of regional energy companies) were conducted more openly, and raised more money. Fiscal reform aimed to 'monetize' the state budget, replacing barter or payment in kind with cash, allowing the backlog of wage and pension payments to be cleared and stimulate consumption-led growth. Ukraine also benefited from the delayed effects of the 1998 *hrivnya* devaluation, as well as piggybacking on Russia's parallel rouble slide and subsequent growth. As a result, 2000 was not only the first year of real growth since independence, but an impressive 5.9 per cent was posted, followed by 9.1 per cent in 2001.

Western governments were accordingly dismayed when Yushchenko was forced out of office in April 2001 by the oligarchs whose rent-seeking opportunities were being closed down. The new prime minister Anatolii Kinakh pledged to continue the basic thrust of his predecessor's policy, but made several quiet U-turns to please his oligarchic supporters. Yushchenko, meanwhile, chose to remain in 'loyal' opposition, assuming that growth and piecemeal reform would maintain sufficient momentum for yet another restart in 2004.

Ukraine's Pendular Foreign Policy

For most of the 1990s Ukraine stuck to its declared aim of a 'multi-vector' foreign policy. This was a useful metaphor for the existential dilemma of Russia or the West, Europe or Eurasia – which is still far from resolved. Like Moldova, there is no simple pro-Western (as with the Baltic states) or pro-Russian majority (Belarus). Foreign policy thinking was also initially dominated by deep-felt security fears, but in this sphere at least the twin agreements with Russia and NATO in 1997 marked a decisive turning-point.

Under first president Kravchuk (1991–4), as with economic policy, foreign policy was dominated by the search for autonomy from Russia. Unlike economic policy, however, that search was less subject to sharp correction in 1993. Ukraine has always been a reluctant member of the CIS at best, and has opposed all efforts to give the Commonwealth more independent authority. Instead, Ukraine initially sought security by picking up membership cards to as many Western institutions as it could, including the IMF and World Bank (1992), CSCE, later OSCE (1992), and the Council of Europe (1995). Ukraine also attempted to forge special relationships with its own historical west. Bilateral relations with Poland were initially good, especially under Kravchuk, but grander schemes for a Baltic–Black Sea Alliance or nuclear-free East-central Europe were rebuffed.

At first, the Kravchuk administration assumed security and autonomy were the same thing, but some of the potential conflicts were soon exposed by the nuclear issue. With some territorial rights but no operational control over its share of the Soviet nuclear arsenal stationed on its territory, Ukraine was briefly tempted in 1992–3 to boost its international standing by hanging on to the weapons and trying to acquire control. The existing nuclear powers, however, thought no further than the proliferation issue, and Ukraine was unable to make any serious foreign policy progress until it abandoned its nuclear pretensions in the January 1994 Trilateral Agreement with Russia and the USA. All weapons were gone by 1996.

Thereafter, Washington was Ukraine's most important Western ally. From 1994 to 1998, it encouraged Kyiv to redefine its goals as 'cooperation with the CIS, integration with the West'; although, with the nuclear issue out of the way, the USA never upped its commitment as many Ukrainians had thought and hoped it might.

The high point of the relationship was the Charter on Distinctive Partnership signed with NATO in 1997, but progress in other multilateral areas was limited, and most EU governments preferred to concentrate on Ukraine's patchy reform and human rights record. With the EU itself Ukraine has been unable to advance beyond the Partnership and Cooperation Agreement that was signed in 1994, but only finally ratified in 1998.

A change in Ukraine's priorities was therefore apparent by 1999–2000, *before* the Gongadze affair worsened relations with the West. After the 1998 regional economic crisis, it was clear that hopes of large-scale international financial assistance were dead. Russia was also forced to refocus its ambitions closer to home, and the emergence of Putin as president heralded the adoption of a more pragmatic foreign policy no longer overshadowed by the mythologies of 1991. Moreover, the 1997 treaty between Russia and Ukraine helped defuse many fears – precisely by accepting the independent existence of a Ukrainian state, Russian elites have since been able to wield more influence within its borders. In 2000 the pro-Western Borys Tarasyuk was replaced as foreign minister by the more flexible Anatolii Zlenko. In 2001 Viktor Chernomydrin's arrival as Russian ambassador confirmed a new era of opportunity for Russian capital in Ukraine. Russian companies are now important players in Ukraine's oil refining, aluminium, power and banking sectors – because of the common language, their role in press, TV and mass culture (music, video, pulp fiction) has always been strong.

The rapprochement with Russia was undoubtedly further encouraged by Kuchma's informal isolation in the West after the Gongadze scandal, even if it was not begun by it. However, the events of 11 September 2001 further muddied the waters. Ukraine now faced the risk that America's and NATO's upgraded relations with Russia would come at the expense of less attention to its concerns, or even give a green light to Russia to reassert itself regionally. Despite opening its airspace to assist the USA in supplying its new Central Asian bases during the Afghan campaign, Ukraine had much less to offer than Russia to the new anti-terrorist geopolitics. On the other hand, Russia now no longer saw NATO expansion in the same threatening terms, and Ukraine was able to announce its long-term aim of NATO membership in May 2002.

The new slogan 'To Europe with Russia', already fashionable in early 2001, survived into 2002 to serve slightly different purposes as Russia seemed to move ahead in the queue. Kyiv was aware, however, that its room for manoeuvre was not large. Kuchma has continued to restate Ukraine's desire for an association agreement with the EU, leading to eventual membership, but Brussels will no doubt prefer to wait for a possible Yushchenko presidency in 2004. Ukraine may also have missed the NATO boat. The USA confirmed its disillusion in September 2002 by announcing that it would suspend $55 million in aid and 'review' its relationship with Ukraine, after it concluded claims by Melnychenko that Kuchma had ordered the sale of the 'Kolchuha' radar system to Iraq in 2000 were genuine.

Conclusion

Nation building is not necessarily a unilinear process. Under Kuchma, Ukraine seemed to have settled for a highly eclectic form of heterogeneity. The process of democratization has also had twists and turns. Ukraine scored well for the peaceful handover of the presidency to Kuchma in 1994 – but there was no real possibility of a transfer of power in 1999, and every likelihood of a bitter struggle between Yushchenko and the 'oligarchs' over the nature of Ukrainian democracy in 2004. Unlike Belarus, where Lukashenka triumphantly staged his re-election over an impotent opposition in 2001, Ukraine's parliamentary elections in 2002 showed there will be a much closer contest in the presidential election that is due in 2004.

Economic reform has meanwhile proceeded in fits and starts: with the pursuit of 'autonomy' in 1992–3, recentralization in 1993–4, liberal reform in October 1994, backsliding in 1995–9, the relaunch of reform under Yushchenko's premiership in 2000–1, and another pause under Kinakh. Foreign policy has been inconsistent, and Ukraine's goals have been regularly redefined. This is in part due to the conflicting pressures within Ukrainian society, but it also a useful corrective to the idea that 'transition' has its own momentum. In Ukraine, all eyes are on the presidential election due in the later months of 2004, when once again key choices will have to be made.

PART TWO

The Framework of Politics

7

Executive Leadership: Presidents and Governments

RAY TARAS

What models of a political system are there to choose from when an *ancien regime*, like communism in Central and Eastern Europe, collapses? Assuming that the choice is likely to be a democracy under conditions where most other alternatives have been discredited, as was the case for Central and Eastern Europe in the 1990s, what institutional configurations are available for new democracies to experiment with? One leading specialist has underlined how in practice 'our cultural repertoire of political institutions is limited. In spite of minute variations, the institutional models of democracy are very few' (Przeworski, 1992, p. 99). To be sure, there are quasi-democratic variants, such as bureaucratic-authoritarian (O'Donnell, 1979), corporatist (Lehmbruch and Schmitter, 1982), and sultanistic (Chehabi and Linz, 1998), which have been more closely identified with politics in the developing world – and Latin America in particular – than politics in Central and Eastern Europe. But we do find here examples of personal dictatorships and one-party rule surviving into the late 1990s, and cases of neo-patrimonialism involving 'the capture of the state by ruling clans' (Van Zon, 2001, p. 72), as well as super-presidentialism, under which leaders garner enormous power after winning non-competitive elections (Fish, 2000, p. 178).

Models of the Political Executive

These various models refer to the political system taken as a whole – its institutions, their interrelationships, who the rulers are and how they govern, where average citizens fit into the picture. In this chapter we focus only on the executive branch of government, the historical core of a political system. Before there were parliaments, judiciaries, and bureaucracies, there were executive rulers: absolute monarchs, emperors, proconsuls. The political executive was and is the seat of authoritative power in any political system. There may be greater or lesser power-sharing required of the political executive, more or fewer institutional checks on the executive, but the existence of a political executive to discharge leadership and formulate policy – in short, to govern – is discernible in all models of a political system. Political executives in Central and Eastern Europe today, we shall see, differ widely in terms of the process by which they attain power, the powers they hold, the policies they pursue, and the people they recruited. To begin, we need to start with various models of a political executive.

The simplest typologies of political executives posit the dichotomies of whether they are effective (for example, the US president) or ceremonial (like the King of Spain); and whether they are individual (as the German Chancellor) or collective (as the British Cabinet) (Almond and Powell, 1983, p. 106). In practice, institutional arrangements for leadership differ widely, even within a close-knit geopolitical region like the European Union. Moreover executive power also changes over time, as in the case of the United States, where a constitution over 200 years old has not prevented the president from enhancing the powers of the office. Similarly in Britain the role of the prime minister, in both style and substance, has evolved to the point where the system is viewed by many observers as a quasi-presidential type of government. It should be no surprise, then, that since the collapse of communism there have been radically different approaches to constructing executive power in Central and Eastern Europe. Poland and Belarus are neighbours, for example, but the many constitutional, electoral, and political checks on the Polish prime minister contrast starkly with the virtual unaccountability of the political executive, the presidency, in the former Soviet republic on its eastern borders.

Generally we can identify three types of executive government in modern democracies. The first is *cabinet government* where political leadership is entrusted to a prime minister and a group of colleagues who head the important departments of government. The composition of the cabinet in large part reflects the balance of political power in the legislature, which in turn is the product of legislative elections. A test of whether cabinet government really exists is whether the cabinet accepts collective responsibility to parliament for the policies it pursues. The Czech Republic, Hungary, Poland, Slovakia, and Slovenia are countries that best fit the model of cabinet government. There have been examples of strong prime ministers in these new democracies (Vaclav Klaus in the Czech Republic and Janez Drnovsek in Slovenia were two) but, arguably, none has come close to building the prime ministerial system of government that Margaret Thatcher and Tony Blair did in Britain.

(2)

A second type of executive government is the *presidential sys-* *PRESIDENTL*
tem. It is distinguished by the fact that there is a single head of the political executive who is elected to office directly by the people. In this model, the president usually combines the roles of head of government and head of state – the second a largely ceremonial role that in a cabinet or parliamentary system would be assigned to a political figure of secondary importance. Under this system the president also appoints the key members of the administration who are regarded as members of the executive branch. In the United States – the paradigmatic presidential system – this is symbolized by the fact that these appointees occupy the Executive Building that stands near the White House. Belarus under Alexander Lukashenka, Ukraine under Leonid Kuchma, and in the 1990s Croatia under Franjo Tudjman and Yugoslavia under Slobodan Milosevic had presidential systems of government (see Figure 7.1). Some scholars would classify these cases as super-presidential systems: 'a huge apparatus of executive power that overshadows other state agencies and the national legislature in terms of its size and the resources it uses; a president who controls most or all of the levers of public expenditure; a president who enjoys the power to make laws by decree; ... a legislature that enjoys little real oversight authority over the executive branch; and a judiciary that is appointed and controlled largely by the president and that cannot in practice check presidential prerogatives or even abuse of power' (Fish, 2000, pp. 178–9).

(3)

A third type of executive system consists of *assembly, or parlia-* *PARLI GOVT*
mentary, government. Here the elected legislature is politically dominant and is able, paradoxically, to wrest executive power from the executive branch. The classic cases of such a system are the Third (1875–1940) and Fourth (1946–58) French Republics, where the legislature was able to overthrow cabinets with consummate

FIGURE 7.1   *Type of political system and extent of leadership turnover*

ease: 102 and 24 governments respectively were formed and then fell in the two Republics. Post-1989 Poland seemed to be heading towards a parliamentary-dominant system with eight prime ministerial appointments heading governments over an eight-year period, but the enactment of a new constitution in 1997 crafted a cabinet form of government. Today assembly governments are rare anywhere in the world.

As the example of Poland shows, executive systems can be fluid. They can also be hybrid, and the states of Central and Eastern European have for the most part opted for some mix of *presidential–parliamentary government*. This is a safe choice and is explained by a number of considerations. First, a pure presidential system generates a zero-sum game, with the winning candidate taking all and the losers receiving nothing. Parliamentary systems, by contrast, increase total payoffs, with many parties and their candidates 'winning' influence even while losing elections. Even clear losers in this system have an incentive to stay in the parliamentary game: they have the prospect of expanding their representation or gaining positions of power next time around. The mixed presidential–parliamentary system also produces a greater rotation of leaders, with more frequent changes of prime minister and cabinet reshuffles, than either a strong presidential or strong parliamentary one.

Qne system that may today be described as presidential–parliamentary, where a political equilibrium is struck between the two branches of government, is Yugoslavia under president Vojislav Kostunica. In a historic election in October 2000, he defeated the strongman Milosevic only to find his executive power limited by a rejuvenated parliament and the government that emerged from it, headed by an ambitious prime minister in Zoran Dzindjic. Adding to the complexity of the country and the institutional checks on the presidency is the still far from finally resolved question of the future of the union of the Yugoslav Federation's two constituent parts, Serbia and Montenegro. It is remarkable that a system that was so clearly super-presidential could so quickly be transformed into a hybrid presidential–parliamentary one with a change in the persons in office.

Another closely related hybrid system is *semi-presidentialism*, which is often used to describe the Fifth Republic in France. The French presidency is constitutionally powerful – it had, after all, been drafted to suit the needs of its first incumbent, General Charles de Gaulle. Its Achilles heel, however, was the possibility that parties of the left and right would capture different institutions – the presidency and the legislature – thereby generating political tensions and even constitutional crisis over whether the president or the prime minister and government really embodied executive power. In practice the Fifth Republic has weathered uneasy periods of 'cohabitation', such as between a socialist president and a conservative government (1986–8), and a conservative president and socialist prime minister (1997–2002). These episodes of cohabitation have established the convention that under such political circumstances, the strong presidency envisaged by the constitution will be set aside in favour of a diminished semi-presidential system. 'Cohabitation' in the more fragile and volatile conditions of postcommunist Europe has not always worked as smoothly. The election of a democratic president in Bulgaria in 1996 precipitated a wave of

SEMI -PRESIDENTIALISM

anti-socialist demonstrations demanding the resignation of the socialist government even though it had a mandate to rule to the end of 1998. By contrast in Poland a former communist, president Aleksander Kwasniewski, encountered few difficulties in working with a prime minister from the Solidarity camp between 1997 and 2001.

What are other possible examples of semi-presidentialism in Central and Eastern Europe? There has been a slight preference in postcommunist states to elect the president directly along the lines of the Fifth Republic semi-presidential model. Where this is not the case – Albania, the Czech Republic, Estonia, Hungary, Latvia, and Moldova after 1996 – cabinet government has flourished (for other reasons Moldova does not fit this description). On the other hand, Romania after Iliu Iliescu returned to office in the presidential election of 2000 may furnish another example. Out of power for four years after serving as the country's first postcommunist president, Iliescu took over a very different presidential office after 2000: he could no longer accumulate the extensive executive powers that he had commanded following his election victories in 1990 and 1992.

Central and Eastern European presidents generally serve for five years, like the French president (although Romania has a four-year term). Like the French National Assembly, their parliaments have a four-year mandate (the exception here is Slovenia where it is five). The extra year in most presidents' terms is suggestive of semi-presidentialism in that it seems to privilege that office. But this alone does not account for semi-presidentialism. The distinction between presidential–parliamentary and semi-presidential hybrid systems is not hard and fast. In many ways the Baltic republics may be characterized as hybrids of either a presidential–parliamentary (Estonia and Latvia) or semi-presidential (Lithuania) kind. One factor distinguishing the two types may be the greater formal powers that the president is assigned in the latter, powers that he may be hard pressed to exercise under certain political conditions.

It is to be expected that our typology of political executives will not capture the entire range of variation across the entire postcommunist universe. In the first years of political transition, prospective constitutional framers had to address a central dilemma inherent in any political system: resolving the ever-present tension between imperatives of democracy and those of efficiency. The choice they made would have a direct impact on the shape of the political executive. A preference for a deliberative democracy would favour the legislative branch at the expense of the political executive, while priority given to the virtues of efficiency, management, and decisiveness would, conversely, put the executive branch in a favourable position. In each country, specific historical, economic, and social conditions predisposed the emergent system to emphasize one of these imperatives over the other. To be sure, in a handful of states, particularly former Soviet republics outside the Baltic region, the deck was stacked almost equally against both democracy and efficiency. Some leaders even seemed to ignore the issue of regime change, preferring more 'muddling through' to any combination of democracy and efficiency.

There is thus no formula or general law about how the political executive emerges during political transitions. What is clear is the importance of judicious institutional experimentation in the search for the optimal result for a given society. When economist Douglass North asked why some societies developed efficient, adaptive, growth-promoting institutions and others did not, he was forced to conclude that a society's willingness to abandon institutions that did not work was of overriding importance. 'It is essential to have rules that eliminate not only failed economic organization but failed political organization as well', he wrote. 'The effective structure of rules, therefore, not only rewards successes, but also vetoes the survival of maladapted parts of the organizational structure.' It follows that 'the society that permits the maximum generation of trials will be most likely to solve problems through time' (North, 1992, p. 81).

Not surprisingly, countries that opened up the debate over institutional arrangements to the greatest number of participants – for example, roundtable talks at the key moment of regime change – allowed consideration of alternative institutional possibilities (as when Hungary held a referendum on whether its president should be directly elected). And the countries that changed governments frequently in the early transition years (often the result of competition between institutions) were best able to carry out institutional engineering. Hungary and Poland led the way in this regard, but nearly a decade later Croatia, Romania, and Yugoslavia also reaped the benefits of institutional experimentation. If there was a general lesson learned about the nature of the political executive, it was that, to use North's terminology, the maladapted parts of the organizational structure that had to be eliminated were usually features of super-presidentialism.

Factors Shaping the Structure of Executive Power

After the fall of communism, Central and Eastern European states were faced with conflicting imperatives. On the one hand, they were expected to construct a checks-and-balances system that would limit executive power, which had gone unchecked under communism. On the other, the new political systems had to ensure sufficiently strong leadership to govern politically and sometimes ethnically divided societies, with disaffected social groups reeling from shock therapy, and fragmented party systems. The choice of the structure of executive power has been credited with, and blamed for, many of the major developments that have taken place in the region from the 1990s: Poland's highly successful transition to a market economy and Romania's reform failures, Czechoslovakia's velvet divorce and socialist Yugoslav's violent end, the Baltic states' improving credentials for admission into NATO, and the EU and Belarus and Ukraine's inability to integrate into Western structures.

An array of factors influences the choice of model of a political executive. The Central and Eastern European constitutions adopted in the 1990s were based on many considerations: the backlash against communism and its centralized system of executive power, a new set of public expectations about the role of society in government, the different political traditions of the individual states, the preferences of actor–agents, and the international normative regime dominant at the time. Let us look more closely at these.

Backlash Against Communism and New Public Expectations

The backlash against authoritarian regimes triggered by the experience of communism provided the backdrop for valuing representative institutions more highly than strong rulers. The pull of the more authoritarian arrangements of the past was offset by the appeal of the Western system of representative government that had proved its political and economic superiority in the Cold War. Even granting that historically most Central and Eastern Europe societies preferred being ruled by strong leaders – and this is a controversial proposition anyway – the political environment was very different when these societies were asked to design a new system. Survey results from the 1990s up to the present confirm that ordinary citizens have increasingly prized representative government. Some societies fully embraced representative democracy in 1989, in others democratic processes grew on them. In a handful of states, democracy remains a suspect system even today. The general shift from authoritarian preferences took a variety of forms across the region.

Already in the early years of the political transition, attitudinal surveys in a number of countries indicated that the importance of leaders was declining relative to representative institutions. Data from nine states in the region compiled during 1992–3 led to this finding: '*Representative democrats* [who] disapprove of the suspension of parliament and reject the appeal of strong leaders ... are the largest group in six of the nine postcommunist societies surveyed' (Rose and Mishler, 1996, p. 233). These six were the Czech Republic, Hungary, Poland, Romania, Slovakia, and Ukraine. Only in Bulgaria, Slovenia, and Belarus did *leadership democrats* – respondents favouring a reform of parliament to allow a strong leader to emerge – comprise a plurality. Similarly *authoritarians* – those calling for the suspension of parliament and the appointment of a strong leader – were rare in any part of the former communist world surveyed, apart from the former Soviet republics of Belarus and Ukraine, where they made up as much as one-quarter of the total. Where the representative-democratic preference evoked substantial majority support, as in the Czech Republic, Hungary, Poland, Romania and Slovakia, the balance of power between executive and legislative branches of government became slanted towards the latter. The institutional choice in favour of parliamentary democracy and cabinet government was taken early in the Czech Republic and Hungary. By contrast, in Romania and Slovakia (where a majority of respondents had favoured such a system as early as 1992–3), the process of subordinating strong leaders to the legislature was more protracted and was completed only by the late 1990s. In the first years of the new century the rest of the Balkans – from Albania to the Yugoslav federation of Serbia and Montenegro – witnessed strong leaders giving way to the free play of institutional forces. That leaves the two former Soviet republics of Belarus and Ukraine, where support for an authoritarian system had been significant during the formative years of institution building, as outliers, with their super-presidential systems.

The very nature of democracy signifies that citizens must support the institutions that are created and give consent to the leaders that emerge from them. If institutions are the 'hardware' of democracy, what people think about them makes up democracy's 'software' (Agh, 1996, p. 127). Ensuring democratic rule and efficient government are not irreconcilable tasks: 'The ideal democratic system is representative and has effective leaders. Logically, the two criteria can be mutually reinforcing, in so far as leaders may gain effectiveness by mobilizing popular support, and effective action increases a leader's popular support' (Rose and Mishler, 1996, p. 224). Of particular importance in designing the architecture of power, then, was setting up safeguards to control the actions of leaders. Otherwise, as one long-time analyst of Soviet politics conjectured, 'we can see the possibility of an authoritarian personality serving as leader in the regime of a constitutional democracy, and, conversely, of a democratic personality serving as the leader in an authoritarian system of rule' (Tucker, 1981, p. 68).

Public opinion can act as one of the safeguards against a return to authoritarian practices. At the same time it can be manipulated to serve those in power. On the basis of a study of Bulgaria, one author concluded that a decade after communism's collapse, 'political elites use opinion polls not to extend political power to citizens, but to concentrate it in their own hands' (Henn, 2001, pp. 67–8). Instead of 'populist government', which pollster George Gallup idealistically thought would result from elites knowing voters' preferences better, Joseph Schumpeter's notion of 'competitive elitism', under which leaders acquire information about the electorate's views in order to obtain a competitive advantage over adversaries, has become the more common practice (Schumpeter, 1976).

Different Political Traditions

Another influence shaping the emergence of executive structures is a country's earlier experience with different forms of government. The political structures of the inter-war period have been particularly important in affecting thinking about new structures. Thus advocates of a presidential system in Czechoslovakia and Poland held up the examples of dominant inter-war state-builders, like Tomas Masaryk and Jozef Pilsudski respectively. Yet if Czech president Vaclav Havel was content to serve in the role of moral authority and sometimes political broker, president Lech Walesa of Poland self-consciously strove to be an imperial president. Despite the contrasting readings by these presidents of their countries' inter-war experience, in neither case was a presidential system created. In the case of Hungary, the authoritarian inter-war leader Admiral Miklos Horthy was a controversial figure. Some political activists – in particular those campaigning against the direct election of a president in the 1990 referendum – invoked his experience to highlight the need to avoid returning to such an executive model. Hungarians on the right, by contrast, favoured his rehabilitation, which exacerbated the polarization of politics in Hungary in the 1990s. Today the Hungarian president is indirectly elected and therefore rather weak. A succession of prime ministers has seemingly turned the country into a less leadership-oriented system than elsewhere in the region. By the late 1990s, a prime minister with broader leadership ambitions, Viktor Orban, was, significantly, not re-elected to a second term by Hungarian voters in 2002.

Both Bulgaria's and Romania's inter-war experience of illiberal politics and authoritarianism offered a negative model for postcommunist leaders but, nevertheless, both countries languished under quasi-communist rule until late 1996. In what used to be socialist Yugoslavia, South Slav nations escaping from a Serb-dominated federation established strong presidencies in Croatia, Macedonia, and Bosnia-Herzegovina. In Croatia's case, however, the death in 1999 of Tudjman, who personified the wartime nationalist *Ustasa* culture, ended the experiment with an all-powerful presidency, and the country scrambled to remake its democratic image more in keeping with EU criteria. Slovenia was exceptional in that its breakaway from Yugoslavia in 1990 was relatively swift and bloodless. As a result, it could afford to forgo a powerful executive. Tellingly, its prime minister, Drnovsek, held office much longer than the autocratic rulers of the other Balkan states.

Actor–Agent Preferences

Legal experts who draft a constitution and the political actors themselves – in both executive and legislative branches of government – are the most direct agents determining what executive power will look like, so the self-interest of the architectural team needs to be taken into account. As Adam Przeworski argued, '[t]he decisive step toward democracy is the devolution of power from a group of people to a set of rules' (Przeworski, 1992, p. 14). Taking this step is hardly a purely technical affair, because '[e]ach political force opts for the institutional framework that will best further its values, projects, or interests' (ibid., p. 80). Especially in the transitional situation, 'the chances of the particular political forces are very different under alternative institutional arrangements' (ibid., p. 40). Not surprisingly, in the transition period political forces battled to tailor institutions to their own needs. The different types of executive structures that emerged in the 1990s were the products of bidding and bargaining among interested parties, not purely rational outcomes arrived at by disinterested state-builders.

Let us review a few illustrative cases. Those who favoured a strong presidency (like Walesa in Poland) were often the politicians who were the strongest candidates for such an office. The direct election of the president gave the office greater prestige and usually imbued it with greater powers and, accordingly, the best candidates tried to look 'presidential': decisive, dignified, and visionary. Those who felt comfortable under cabinet government (like Klaus in the Czech Republic) were often skilful party leaders who performed best in a parliamentary system. Self-styled parliamentarians were ambitious politicians, to be sure, but they felt most comfortable where bureaucratic, technical, and brokering skills were at a pre-mium, as in the context of a legislature.

Instructive cases of how quality of leadership affected different institutional outcomes are provided by the two constituent parts of former Czechoslovakia. One study explored why Czech democratization occurred more rapidly than Slovak. Structural factors such as differing levels of economic development and prevailing cultural pathways, and institutional ones such as better design of executive–legislative relations and of electoral and party systems, were less influential in accelerating democratization than the actor-behavioural variable. The conclusion drawn by the authors of this study was noteworthy: 'Rather than deep cultural differences between the two countries on the mass level, differences in economic performance, or a previous communist regime of differ-ent nature, it is the elite and political competition which function in a different way, and this is what accounts for the different political outcomes' (Kopecky and Mudde, 2000, p. 77). The Czech political elite united in favour of fundamental democratic principles, while the Slovak elite was polarized over the ways to promote national and regime identity. Thus leaders, their styles, and their personali-ties affect the character of a political system. Especially critical in a transition period is the emergence of 'leaders with the personality formation appropriate to democracy' (Lasswell, 1986, p. 196).

International Norms

The global ascendance of liberal political and economic values in the 1990s was both a product of communism's defeat and a force promoting a normative shift that would remake the 'deep structures' of a society and anchor regime change in more than institutional reforms. Undergoing political transitions at a time when an age of unrivalled American power had dawned exerted an important influence on Central and Eastern European normative and institutional choices. Both the American worship of individual freedoms and its presidential system were widely admired in the new democracies, but it became clear to constitutional framers that it would be problematic to graft such features onto other societies. While individual freedoms could be embedded in new constitutional frameworks with relative ease, the US presidential system could not, for it was predicated on federalism, an alternating two-party system that pervaded politics from the national to local levels, and an executive office that bargained with the legislature. These institutional arrangements were largely absent in the former Soviet bloc.

The result was that constitutional framers looked to the political experience of Western Europe, which offered more salient and viable models of institutional architecture also based on the norms of liberalism. A cabinet system of government seemed *de rigueur* in European Union member-states – states that were exemplary in their political stability, consensus, and prosperity. But the West European experience signified more than a particular kind of political system: it also embraced liberal democratic values, free markets, and a universal ideal of citizenship. Some writers have therefore claimed that a process of 'executive Europeanization' has begun that will help integrate both parts of Europe (Goetz, 2000, rejects this claim). The fact that leaders in Central and Eastern Europe want to remake their states in the image of EU members does not signify, of course, that they have turned their backs completely on their national political traditions, as discussed earlier.

Apart from institutional design and political values, the leadership culture of contemporary Western Europe is distinctive, and numerous politicians jockeying for power in the new democracies have sought to imitate it, often adopting individual Western leaders as role models depending on their ideologies and styles. In the early 1990s, the memory of British prime minister Margaret Thatcher and her driven leadership style was fresh in the minds of conservative groups in Central and Eastern Europe. Possibly more than any other Western leader, it was her authority that was most often invoked by the region's politicians in the early years of transition. The plodding but reassuring style of long-serving German Chancellor Helmut Kohl, who had presided over unprecedented prosperity and German unification, had an appeal to the region's politicians who lacked charisma but possessed resilience. Hungarian prime minister Jozsef Antall made references to an earlier German Chancellor, Konrad Adenauer, who had consolidated the West German state and secured its prosperity. For politicians with messianic aspirations – and there were many among those who had spearheaded the victory over communism – Charles de Gaulle of France, founder and centrepiece of the Fifth Republic, cut an imposing figure. For more authoritarian-minded 'democrats' in some former Soviet republics, Chilean dictator Augusto Pinochet, who had crushed Marxism and expanded trade with the US, became an acknowledged model. The paternal figure of US president Ronald Reagan had an appeal throughout the region, too, but other leadership qualities also proliferated – political brokers and consensus-builders, chief executive officers and anti-leaders, charismatic and traditional leaders. The political executive thus incorporated a human dimension that could not entirely be obscured by issues concerning institutional design.

The Background of Central and Eastern European Leaders

An issue that one might expect to be of paramount importance in choosing democratic leaders in Central and Eastern Europe is what these prospective leaders were doing under the communist regime. Yet even today many postcommunist leaders – and not just in post-Soviet republics – have links to the communist system: 'In virtually all postcommunist countries, including those which abandoned old political habits, familiar faces from the communist past dominate the landscape. ... Everywhere, individuals who have dropped out of the elite since the fall of communism are outnumbered by those who have maintained or improved their positions, by a ratio of almost nine to one in Russia and over two to one in Poland and Hungary. Until age attrition takes its toll, the best prospects for success under democracy will belong to those who were successful under communism' (Liebich, 1997, p. 68).

The ex-communists who have attained leadership posts in the young Central and East European democracies bring with them attributes that 'post-totalitarian' elites generally share. Such 'post-totalitarian leaders tend to be more bureaucratic and state techno-cratic than charismatic' (Linz and Stepan, 1996, p. 47). Post-totalitarians include men like Iliescu in Romania and Milosevic in Yugoslavia who were recruited from and made use of former communist organizations in order to stay in power. But marked differences are discernible among post-1989 leaders who were 1980s communist officials. Thus, leaders like President Kwasniewski in Poland and prime minister Gyula Horn in Hungary came to power *after* breaking with the communist apparatus; they tapped a broader political constituency to gain political office. While these men were ex-communists who, to varying degrees, embodied bureaucratic leadership values as well, the crucial dis-tinction to be made between postcommunists and post-totalitarians is that the former have embraced the rules of the democratic game.

Dissidents from the old communist regime have not, as a group, been as successful in taking power as the former communists. Winning popular elections today requires different political skills and resources from those developed in the struggle against com-munism yesterday. The list of political executives who were for-merly communist party members is long, while only a few post-1989 presidents and prime ministers can 'boast' of having been incarcerated by the former communist regime; the most promi-nent were Antall, Havel, and Walesa. It may seem puzzling that rel-atively few 'old warriors,' hardened by years of struggle against communism, held power for very long in the 1990s. Some never could get away from their combative, ideological ways (Havel was an exception), but others turned from politics to capitalism during the transition. Just as much of the communist *nomenklatura* sought to enrich itself, so many dissident intellectuals did the same (see Eyal *et al.*, 1998). The chief *desiderata* for leadership changed to having the right managerial and economic qualifications. A type of 'liberal–national' leadership grounded in both Western liberal democratic values and Central and Eastern European culture, was particularly well positioned to promote political and economic development (Wesolowski, 2000).

The rise of a professional political class, as Schumpeter (1976) called for decades ago, seems to have begun. Many young professionals whose formative experience was of 'goulash communism' in the 1970s, when a more Western-oriented economic system was promoted, for example in Poland and Hungary, were catapulted to executive power after 1989. Regime transition in some ways also involved generational change. Some very young politicians enjoyed meteoric careers (like prime minister Waldemar Pawlak in Poland) as did, paradoxically, old politicians (Tudjman in Croatia). These cases obscure the fact that power was being assumed largely by a generation in their forties (for data from the Czech Republic, Hungary and Poland, see Hanley *et al.*, 1998, p. 39).

Regime transition did not, however, bring a corrective to the under-representation of women in the political executive. If women had been totally excluded from executive power under communism, they fared only marginally better in the emerging democratic systems; two exceptions were Prime Minister Hanna Suchocka in Poland and President Vaira Vike-Freiberga of Latvia. Cabinets remained primarily a male preserve, although in most a handful of women might be included. The optimistic interpretation for the continued under-representation of women in executive power is that women prefer to 'express their presence and political will in ways that are different from those of men – or of their sisters in long-established Western democracies', for example, through well-timed protest actions (Szalai, 1998, p. 200). But not everyone would agree that women's absence from executive office-holding was primarily the result of women's choice.

In the Baltic republics (but elsewhere too), a long, successful professional career in the West was an asset in seeking high office, and returning émigrés were appointed defence, foreign, and finance ministers, and in some cases even presidents and prime ministers. Other émigrés were more nationalistic than native politicians themselves and used various means to support authoritarian right-wing groups, especially in Croatia and Slovakia. Probably the single largest group of émigrés consisted of those who tried to make political careers in their land of birth and failed.

What have been the social origins and demographic characteristics of postcommunist political elites? A comparative study of elites in three Central European states in 1993 discovered that members of the political elite had more privileged social origins than their counterparts in the economic elite. Furthermore, circulation into the political elite in the Czech Republic, Hungary, and Poland was substantially higher than that into the economic elite. However, as the authors of this research noted, 'greater circulation into the political elite has not translated into a change in the class character of that elite. Post-communist administrators and legislators are as likely to report intelligentsia origins as are the directors of economic enterprises. In other words, elite circulation does not appear to be accompanied by class circulation' (Hanley *et al.*, 1998).

Conclusion

Writers, electricians, economists, philosophers, geologists, and communist bureaucrats have ruled in Central and Eastern Europe since 1989. While occupationally diverse, they have been predominantly male and somewhat younger than the preceding ruling elite. They have used free market, nationalist, pan-European, socialist, and third way rhetoric to get elected. They have almost never used political violence to stay in power. Most have learned to be expert in the art of coalition building.

At first Central and Eastern European leaders did not stay in office very long. A short election cycle in the early 1990s led to considerable turnover among political leaders. But since the mid-1990s, elections have commonly been held four or five years apart, leading to a lower rate of turnover. Getting reelected is a skill that leaders only recently have mastered. To be sure, winning a majority of seats in parliament in two successive elections in a EU member state is a rare accomplishment too; it occurs just as rarely in the new Central and Eastern Europe. Even the former communists who returned to power through the ballot box nearly everywhere in the region are nowhere *entrenched* in power.

The likelihood of political instability returning to the region differs from one country to another. The conditions that could engender instability also differ. Dispersal of power inherent to a parliamentary system carries certain risks, just as empowering executives with too many prerogatives does. Holding executives accountable to representative institutions while giving them the chance to provide strong leadership has been a perpetual dilemma of governance. More than a decade after the *annus mirabilis* of 1989, Central and Eastern European states have reached a functional equilibrium. There is scant evidence that intolerance in Central and Eastern Europe is greater than in the original six EU member states. The skilful construction of executive power in the region can in large part be credited with this achievement.

THIS CHAPTER IS
NOT SO GREAT.

8

Structures of Representation: The New Parliaments of Central and Eastern Europe

PETR KOPECKY

Parliaments are core state institutions of modern democracy. Parliaments provide the forum for interaction of intermediary agencies: the parties, interest groups, or social movements that link them to society. Parliaments also link society with other democratic institutions – the executive, judiciary or state bureaucracy. In that sense, parliaments are the key structure of representation. They are, to use Phillipe Schmitter's (1988) term, an important and large 'partial regime' of a political system, which encompasses a wide range of institutions, rules and procedures, as well as political organizations. The parliaments can thus be viewed as a focal point around which all crucial questions of political style, legitimacy and democratic accountability revolve. In addition, parliaments are multifunctional. They of course legislate (hence the term 'legislatures'): that is, they make laws. However, parliaments also socialize and train political elites, integrate diverse social strata and nationalities in one state, oversee national administration, and help to articulate societal interests.

Many studies of (West) European politics and government have for a long time advocated a thesis of parliaments in decline. Parliaments came to be seen no longer as supreme legislative and representational institutions – a view heavily biased towards nineteenth-century democratic theory – but instead became stigmatized as rubber-stamping bodies, dominated by executives, bureaucracies and strong political parties (see Norton, 1990). The parliaments in non-democratic communist Eastern Europe fitted to this pattern. Although none of the Eastern European countries abandoned parliament during the communist period, they were so subordinated to the communist party apparatus that their law-affecting activities and oversight functions were minimal, at least until the 1980s, when the communist leadership began to lose their grip on their respective societies (see Nelson and White, 1982).

The wave of political change that swept across Eastern Europe in the early 1990s has therefore presented parliaments with a new opportunity to reassert themselves as important platforms in the political life of the newly emerging democracies in the region. They were almost overnight propelled from institutions with very limited autonomy in decision-making to bodies that had initially become something of a linchpin of transition to democracy, in the eyes of political elites and publics alike. However, like all other institutions in Eastern Europe, parliaments, too, experienced numerous problems typical for new institutions. They lacked institutional resources, infrastructure and experienced members, which constrained their capacity to act. Moreover, with the reassertion and development of both political parties and executives since the second half of the 1990s, the centrality of parliaments in political life may have waned further.

This chapter shows Central and East European parliaments in their full political context. Parliaments obviously have their own internal life and procedures, but at the same time they do not exist in a vacuum. The constitution of each country determines their basic powers. They are often externally constrained by political parties, executives, courts or even supranational organizations. Therefore, following a review of the basic profile of parliaments in the region, this chapter provides an analysis of parliaments in terms of their relations with the polity: that is, with both the electorate and with the other state institutions, such as governments and presidents. It also looks at several aspects of their internal life, like the individual members, parliamentary parties and parliamentary committees. Processes of parliamentary institutionalization, as well as the place of parliaments in new democracies of Central and Eastern Europe, are assessed in the conclusion.

Institutional Origins and Profile

Table 8.1 presents a basic profile of parliaments in Central and Eastern Europe. We can see, firstly, that the majority of legislatures

TABLE 8.1   *Profile of Central and East European parliaments*

Region and country	Chamber structure	Election years (all elections)	Chamber names	Size	Term
Central Europe					
Czech Republic	Unicameral	1990 and 1992	Czech National Council	200	2 (4)
	Bicameral	1996,	Chamber of Deputies	200	4
		1998 and 2002	Senate	81	6
Hungary	Unicameral	1990, 1994, 1998 and 2002	National Assembly	386	4
Poland	Bicameral	1989, 1991, 1993	Sejm	460	4
		1997 and 2001	Senate	100	4
Slovak Republic	Unicameral	1990 and 1992	Slovak National Council	150	2 (4)
		1994, 1998 and 2002	National Assembly	150	4
Baltic States					
Estonia	Unicameral	1990	Supreme Council	105	4
	Unicameral	1992, 1995 and 1999	State Assembly	101	4
Latvia	Unicameral	1990	Supreme Council	201	4
	Unicameral	1993, 1995 and 1998	Saeima	100	4
Lithuania	Unicameral	1990	Supreme Council	141	2
	Unicameral	1992, 1996 and 2000	Seimas	141	4
Balkans					
Albania	Unicameral	1991	People's Assembly	250	4
	Unicameral	1992, 1996, 1997 and 2001	People's Assembly	140	4
Bosnia & Herzegovina	Bicameral	2000	House of Representatives	42	2
			House of Peoples	15	2
Bulgaria	Unicameral	1990	Grand National Assembly	400	4
	Unicameral	1991, 1994, 1997 and 2001	National Assembly	240	4
Croatia	Bicameral	1992, 1993, 1995 and 1997	House of Representatives	138	4
			House of Municipalities	63	4
	Unicameral	2000	House of Representatives	151	4
Macedonia	Unicameral	1998	Sobranie	120	4

(cont. overleaf)

TABLE 8.1   (continued)

Region and country	Chamber structure	Election years (all elections)	Chamber names	Size	Term
Romania	Bicameral	1990	Chamber of Deputies Senate	385 119	4 4
	Bicameral	1992, 1996 and 2000	Chamber of Deputies Senate	345 140	4 4
Slovenia	Bicameral	1992, 1996, 1997	National Assembly	90	4
		2000 and 2001	National Council	40	5
Yugoslavia	Bicameral	2000	Vece Gradjana Vece Republika	138 40	4 4
Former USSR					
Ukraine	Unicameral	1994, 1998 and 2002	Verkhovna Rada	450	4
Moldova	Unicameral	1994, 1998 and 2001	Parlamentul	101	4

Sources: derived from Olson (1998); and Inter-Parliamentary Union (*www.ipu.org*).

are unicameral – a trend apparent in new democracies worldwide (see Woldendorp *et al.*, 2000). Second or upper chambers are usually established to represent territorial and/or functional interests. The representation of territorial interests is the case of second chambers in both Bosnia and Herzegovina and Yugoslavia, the countries that emerged from the violent disintegration of the Yugoslav Federation. It also includes the Polish Senate, which was established to represent that country's territorial-administrative units. An example of the representation of functional interests is provided by the corporatist second chamber in Slovenia (the National Council), to which councillors are (s)elected to represent economic, local, trading and other professional interests.

However, second chambers, in addition to their specific representational tasks, are also established to provide a system of checks and balances and to ensure horizontal accountability among the institutions of the state. This idea has strongly influenced the creation of upper houses in both the Czech Republic and Romania. Yet it is only in Romania where the upper house – the Senate – exercises legislative powers that are on a par with those of the lower house, the Chamber of Deputies. In the Czech Republic, as well as in Slovenia and Poland, second chambers have some legislative and appointive powers, but can mainly delay or suspend policies and legislation, rather than block them or even propose them. In all these countries, we therefore talk about weak bicameralism. The size of legislatures varies greatly across the region. The upper chambers are smaller than lower houses in all countries with bicameral parliaments, which is usual for legislatures in established democracies as well. The size of lower chambers ranges between 42 MPs in the House of Representatives in Bosnia and Herzegovina to a rather mighty number of 460 MPs in the Polish Sejm. Larger countries (Poland, Ukraine, Romania) have, not surprisingly, larger lower chambers than smaller or medium-sized countries, which are relatively more numerous across the region.

Table 8.1 also shows that the parliamentary term is almost uniformly four years. This is especially the case for lower chambers. Upper chambers sometimes display elements of constitutional design that attempt to make them distinct from the lower houses. This can be seen, firstly, in electoral formulas, which may differ between the two houses as for example in the Czech Republic and Slovenia. The members of the lower house in the Czech Republic are elected by a PR electoral system based on party lists, while the senators contest elections in single-member districts; in Slovenia, the members of the National Assembly are elected by a PR system in multimember districts, while the members of the National Council are indirectly elected by an electoral college. But it can also be seen, secondly, in the length of upper second chamber terms. For example, the National Council in Slovenia is elected for five years, in contrast to the National Assembly's four-year term. The Czech Senate is elected for the period of six years, in contrast to the Chamber of Deputies' four-year term; moreover, a third of senatorial places are subject to electoral contest every second year.

Two further observations that we can make on the basis of Table 8.1 concern changes in the names of parliamentary chambers and, in many cases, shorter initial terms. Both relate to the institutional origins of Central and Eastern European legislatures. The postcommunist parliaments have not been built from scratch, but rather originated in the old communist legislatures. As we shall see later, this has had several repercussions for the internal life of these parliaments. But it also accounts for changes in the names of various chambers in the early 1990s, as the new MPs and political elites tried to disassociate legislatures from their communist past.

Thus, for example, the Grand National Assembly in Bulgaria became the National Assembly. In addition, countries like the Czech Republic and Slovakia, as well as the Baltic states, which all emerged as new independent states after the breakdown of communist federal systems, elevated previously provincial level parliaments to the status of sovereign and supreme bodies. There, too, renaming of legislatures was part and parcel of the creation of a new constitutional framework.

The short term of the first democratically elected parliaments relates to the major task these bodies faced after the demise of the communist regimes – writing and ratifying new constitutions. As we can see in Table 8.1, the first freely elected Czech and Slovak legislatures had their term deliberately shortened to two years, in which they were supposed to draft a new constitution, a process which was then to be followed by elections under a newly designed constitutional order. This was the case also in many other states, like Estonia, Lithuania or Romania, where parliaments basically disbanded themselves before serving a full term, after they ratified new constitutions. In Romania, for example, the first free elections took place in 1990. The new constitution was agreed upon and ratified (by a referendum) in December 1991. The constitution stipulated that both presidential and parliamentary elections had to take place a year after the ratification of the basic law and, indeed, the president and parliament were elected in the second free elections in 1992.

The shorter terms of the first postcommunist parliaments can therefore be explained by the fact that they were entrusted with the important task of drafting and agreeing new constitutions. It should be noted here that this has had major consequences for the institutional structure in Central and East Europe in general, and the position of parliaments in particular. Since parliaments were the prime constitution-makers, rather extraordinary powers have been vested in the legislatures, at least in comparison with the position of parliaments in Western European countries that changed their constitutions, like France in 1958 or Spain in 1978 (see Lane and Ersson, 2000). Moreover, communist constitutions had usually endowed parliaments with supreme powers, even if this was on paper rather than in reality. The strong constitutional position of parliaments thus happened to be the starting point of all negotiations on new constitutions in the early 1990s. This strong constitutional position was most unlikely to be removed given that the same parliaments also became constituent assemblies.

Parliaments and Representation

Parliaments are, perhaps above any other thing, symbols of representation. They are sometimes deliberately set up to reflect the socio-cultural diversity of their respective societies. Indeed, communist legislatures generally made a determined effort to secure the equal representation of women, peasants, workers, and national minorities, even if this was based on a distortion of the competitive electoral process. In democracy, the citizens elect their representatives to parliament, and these representatives, accountable to the citizens through the electoral process, then check upon the government. In most European democracies, such representation operates through political parties, which select, campaign for, and provide list of representatives that sit on parliamentary benches. However, links between parliaments and the electorate are also provided, especially between elections, by constituency representation, whereby individual MPs may choose to promote the interests of certain geographical areas, sectors of society or even individual constituents. The particular form in which models and modes of representation develop in any political system depend also on many informal practices. Moreover, it also depends on a range of formal political institutions, most importantly the electoral system and the nature of political parties and party systems. The parliaments in Central and Eastern Europe are no exception to this: their links with society have been greatly influenced by both the nature of parties, elections and electoral systems, as well as the structure of their membership.

Parties and Elections

Today, multiparty elections and multiparty systems are a norm across the Central and East European region. However, organized political parties have emerged relatively slowly and, indeed, the parties were not the most prominent actors in the early years of democratization. Partly because of strong anti-party sentiments among the population and new political leaders alike, and partly because of the authoritarian nature of the communist regimes, the early transition period was dominated by broadly based anti-communist movements and umbrella organizations like the Civic Forum and Public Against Violence in the former Czechoslovakia, the National

Salvation Front in Romania, Sajudis in Lithuania and Demos in Slovenia. With a few exceptions, like in Bulgaria, these movements also won the first freely contested parliamentary elections. Parties began to emerge only as these broad movements started to disintegrate in the parliament during their first term in office. In that sense, parliaments performed one very important function in the early stages of postcommunist politics: they became the arenas in which new political alliances were forged and new political parties were established. Given that most of the newly established parties were formed from above and consequently lacked links with wider society, their survival would have been unimaginable without the institutional, logistical and often also financial support that was provided to them by parliaments. In addition, parliaments provided a means by which former communist parties could redefine themselves, allowing them to make spectacular comebacks to political prominence in many countries of the region including Hungary, Poland and Albania.

However, the rapid and somewhat disorderly process of party formation also had negative consequences for the links between parliaments and the electorate. Many political parties disappeared during the parliamentary term and other parties were formed instead. For example, as against the initial eight parliamentary parties in the Federal Assembly in the former Czechoslovak Federal parliament in 1990, MPs were organized in no fewer than 16 parliamentary parties by the end of 1991. In Slovakia, the 18 parties and coalitions that registered for the elections in 1994 in fact represented 31 parties and movements. This party and party system fragmentation caused great confusion among the voters, and effectively prevented the formation of stable ties between representatives and the represented.

The links between parliaments and the electorate, as indicated above, were also shaped by the electoral system. PR systems based on party lists combined with large constituencies generally favour representation by parties, rather than the emergence of strong links between individual MPs and their constituencies. In contrast, majoritarian systems with single-member districts, such as the British first-past-the post, are more favourable to the formation of such links. The countries of Central and Eastern Europe show a great variety of electoral systems, but most have adopted, for lower-house elections, either a PR electoral system (such as Bulgaria, Croatia, Czech Republic and Moldova) or a mixed electoral system, where part of the house is elected on the basis of a PR system and another part by single-member constituencies (such as Hungary, Lithuania and Ukraine).

However, the key problem with electoral systems in the region has always been their relatively frequent changes. The manipulation of electoral system has been most visible with respect to legal thresholds to enter parliament (see Shvetsova, 1999). For example, Latvia, Lithuania, Moldova and Poland have all raised such barriers in order to reduce the number of parties in parliament. The Czech Republic has done so for coalitions of parties. The result of these changes has been not only a reduction in the number of represented parties, but also a large share of 'wasted votes', because sizeable proportions of electorates vote for small parties that fail to secure representation. Slovakia has also manipulated the size of its electoral districts, actually making the whole country one electoral district. Thus, together with the generally high organizational fragmentation of individual political parties, the frequent tinkering with electoral rules had one major effect: it made it difficult to establish stable and predictable patterns of representation or, to put it differently, clear and transparent links between members of parliament and the electorate.

In spite of such elements of fluidity and change, a number of patterns are now emerging across the region, in reaction to both the relative stabilization of parties and party systems, as well as the increasingly settled institutional framework of these new democracies. Firstly, political parties generally provide a key anchor for parliamentarians, not least because MPs now owe their career to political parties rather than to their own individual qualities and personalities. Voters too vote primarily for political parties, rather than for persons. Parties are thus the key agencies of representation, similarly to most countries in Western Europe. Consequently, the various forms of constituency representation tend also to be, at least as yet, relatively underdeveloped in the region, even though research in this area suggests that some form of territorial and sectoral representation is taking part of MPs' working routines in, for example, Slovakia (Malova and Sivakova, 1996) and Poland (van der Meer Krok-Paszkowska, 2000).

The crucial role played by political parties in organizing the links between parliaments and the electorate are of course most advanced in areas where party system stabilization has reached the highest level, like in the countries of Central Europe, Slovenia or the Baltic republics. Interestingly, it may also strongly relate to the design of electoral systems. And this is the second important point to note. As Sarah Birch (2001) has argued, while no independent candidates were elected through PR systems (in Central Europe), the situation in some of the mixed systems, like in Ukraine, suggests otherwise. In the 1998 elections in that country, for example, 116 independent candidates – a quarter of the whole parliament – were elected through single-member electoral districts.

Members

Not surprisingly, a large number of deputies in the first postcommunist parliaments of Eastern Europe were drawn from the ranks of opposition movements. These movements themselves were largely composed of intellectual elites, independent professions and artists, who constituted the backbone of anti-communist dissent. As a consequences, the early parliaments gained significant legitimacy in the eyes of the population, as the former dissidents replaced the communist-era deputies and apparatchiks. In some cases, like in the former Czechoslovakia, the replacement took place before the first democratic elections, as a result of agreements between the outgoing communist regime and the opposition during the Round Table negotiations. Thus, the Federal Assembly and the Czech and Slovak National Councils engaged in a self-cleansing process, whereby between one-third and one-half of the sitting federal and national council MPs were replaced by candidates supported by the anti-communist opposition.

However, the gains in terms of democratic legitimacy were offset by the inexperience of these new members in operating in a large-scale organization. Moreover, former dissidents were elected alongside a sizeable group of prominent actors and musicians, which boosted the electoral lists of newly formed and thus largely unknown parties to lend them extra popularity. Although dissidents and artists often displayed considerable rhetorical talents in parliamentary debates, both their organizational skills and their loyalties to bodies like parliamentary parties or parliamentary committees were poor. Ironically, it was the MPs of the (ex)communist parties that often turned out to be the more effective parliamentarians, since they had learned the necessary skills of negotiation, deal-making and constituency representation under the previous regime.

Partly because of the composition of the first democratic parliaments in Eastern Europe, the turnover of MPs has been high in comparative terms. Put simply, members of each successive parliament in the region are largely different persons, a fact which undermines deputies' long-term specialization and legislative continuity and stability. Many of the former dissidents, as well as the majority of artists and intellectuals, did not conceive of their position as deputies as a life-long career and consequently did not seek re-election. Moreover, the organizational instability of political parties as well as a relatively high level of electoral volatility has meant that incumbency rates among the Eastern European parliamentarians remain relatively low, though perhaps not as low as in the early years of postcommunist transformation.

Quotas for representation of various sectors of society are largely missing in the new parliaments of the region. The exceptions are several countries, for example Poland, Hungary and Romania, which introduced measures to either guarantee or encourage representation of their respective ethnic minority groups (see Juberias, 1998). However, representation of women has suffered in comparison with the communist period, even though the numbers of women deputies are not uniformly low as the European average. As of June 2002, European countries, including the Nordic states, had an average of 17 per cent of women MPs in (both houses of) parliament (see *www.ipu.org*). In Eastern Europe this number was, in the same period, easily exceeded by, for example, Bulgaria (26 per cent), Poland (22 per cent) and Croatia (21 per cent); it is also matched by both Latvia (17 per cent) and Estonia (18 per cent). However, both Albania (6 per cent) and Macedonia (7 per cent) are well below the European average, as are Hungary (9 per cent) and Lithuania (11 per cent).

This all said, the position of individual members of Eastern European parliaments are increasingly affected by a general tendency towards political professionalism. A move towards the creation of professional deputies and politicians has been promoted in the region by significant increases in deputies' salaries, introduction of travel and accommodation allowances, and by general improvements in MPs' working conditions – for instance, the creation of new parliamentary buildings. Croatia is a good example of such a dramatic development, as the professional full-time status for MPs, including full salaries, was introduced in 1992, shortly before the election to the second postcommunist parliament. Until then, the deputies were entitled only to per diem payments and other small compensations of costs.

This all means that being a deputy is now a lucrative job, which increases the dependence of parliamentarians on their party organizations, and thus also makes them less likely to defect from the party or vote against it. In addition, professionalism also empowers parliamentarians in the region to perform their representative duties on a more consistent and enduring basis. It thus improves conditions for serving both the non-geographical interests of various social, religious, professional and sectoral organizations, and the territorial interests of the MP's constituency.

Executive–Legislative Relations

The relationships between parliaments on the one hand, and the government and the president on the other hand, are central to any democracy, let alone a new one. At the same time, these relationships are complex, depending on a range of formal and informal practices. The constitutional prerogatives vested in legislatures and the executive are of course most important because they define the broad framework for interactions between the two powers. However, numerous informal rules and conventions, such as the customs concerning the nomination of prime ministers following an election, are equally important, especially given that formal documents like constitutions cannot legislate for every conceivable political situation. Indeed, the lack of established customs and informal norms has arguably been behind many conflicts between the region's prime ministers and presidents (see Baylis, 1996).

Formally, the parliamentary system of government, with a weak formal position of presidents (heads of state) and government's dependence on the confidence of the legislature, is a dominant model of executive–legislative relations in the region. Romania and Ukraine are exceptions, in that both countries adopted a semi-presidential system of government in which the head of state possesses significant powers vis-à-vis both the government and the parliament. Several states in the region, like Poland and Croatia, had initially also chosen a semi-presidential system, modelled on the French Fifth Republic, but eventually adopted constitutional reforms (Poland in 1997 and Croatia in 2000) that also provide for a parliamentary system.

The new parliaments of Central and Eastern Europe enjoyed significant advantages over their governments in the early years of transition. This made legislatures appear stronger and more powerful in the matrix of executive–legislative relations than the same bodies in the established parliamentary democracies of Western Europe. Firstly, the parties that formed governing coalitions in the region were seldom able to achieve or impose party loyalty among their MPs. In addition, because of the high degree of political polarization, the coalition partners often quarrelled among each other, sometimes to the extent that part of the government voted with the opposition in parliament. In some countries, like the Czech Republic (up to 1996) or Hungary, this has not led into a significant degree of governmental instability, but perhaps only because parties in the opposition suffered even greater splits and flux than the parties of the government. However, in countries like Estonia, Latvia, Poland and Albania, governments lasted on average less than one year, a figure well below the European average of 1.9 years (see Blondel and Müller-Rommel, 2001).

Second, the frequent conflicts between governments (prime ministers) and presidents undermined executive cohesion. The highly charged relationship between the former Polish president Lech Walesa and several of the Polish governments between 1990 and 1995 is a good example (see van der Meer Krok-Paskowska, 2000). Arguably, these conflicts led the Polish political elite to return to the drawing board and change the so-called Little Constitution in a manner substantially reducing the powers of the president. Disagreements over political issues, personnel questions and executive powers had also been behind destabilizing conflicts between presidents Zhelev, Iliescu and Goncz and prime ministers Dimitrov, Roman and Antall in (respectively) Bulgaria, Romania and Hungary in the first half of the 1990s. The conflicts between the former president Kovac and the former prime minister Meciar in Slovakia between 1994 and 1998 led not only to a change of constitutional framework, but also to the implication of government in the kidnapping of president's son (see Kopecky, 2001). Parliaments were of course the main beneficiary of these conflicts, because in the absence of cohesive executive leadership they were less vulnerable to ceding powers to either presidents or governments.

Third, state bureaucracies were in a state of disarray and thus did not provide the executives with sufficient support to draft and implement policies. The performance of state bureaucracies, and thus of the government, was also negatively influenced by frequent changes in all levels of state administration. Mainly for political reasons, whoever won the elections changed personnel in all key administrative positions, precluding continuity and stability in policy formation. Unfortunately, the parliaments as a whole, and the individual MPs in particular, were not endowed with administrative resources any greater than those of the executive (see Olson, 1997). This all meant not only that the governments were initially unable to create and maintain executive dominance typical for the established democracies of Western Europe, but also that the overall quality of legislation has been poor, as exemplified by the frequent amendments and changes that are typical of the legislative process in the region.

The politicization of the civil service prevails to a large extent in all the countries of Central and Eastern Europe. Nevertheless, the position of governments has in general improved in the region, to the extent that the balance of power between the executives and legislatures has increasingly been tipped in favour of the former. There are several elements involved here. Firstly, parties and party systems have stabilized somewhat in comparison with the early years of transition, as indicated above. This has enabled political leaders to organize the relationship between the executive and legislative branches much better and to impose a degree of party discipline and cohesion. It is not unusual now to read accounts of parliaments in the region in which observers will point to the existence of disciplined parties and strong government majorities, as for example in Hungary and in Slovakia (e.g. Agh, 1995; Malova and Sivakova, 1996).

The stronger position of governments also relates to a general improvement in 'the art of coalition formation' across the region. Compared to the early years of transition, for example, the parties now tend to sign coalition agreements. Moreover, these documents contain far more detailed understandings about policies and other issues than similar documents written and signed a few years ago, which helps to reduce the scope for quarrelling among the coalition partners. One such agreement had been signed between the right-of-centre Civic Democrats and the Social Democrats in the Czech Republic following the 1998 elections, enabling the latter party to form the minority government in exchange for support of several constitutional amendments advocated by the former party. The government stayed in office for the entire four-year term.

Last but not least, the position of governments in the region has been significantly strengthened vis-à-vis parliaments by the introduction of fast-track legislative procedures. This relates to the fact that most countries in the region seek speedy accession to the EU and, as a result, have to comply with a set of conditions specified by the European Commission (see Chapter 14). Adoption of the corpus of EU legislation contained in the so-called *acquis communautaire* is a precondition for joining the club. The absorption of such a vast amount of laws would of course be unimaginable if normal legislative procedures, notably those inherited from the past, were used. Therefore, the countries in the region aspiring to the EU membership have amended their rules of procedure and treat EU-related laws as a priority, as for example in Bulgaria, or even use extraordinary parliamentary sessions to speed up the adoption of such laws, as in Slovenia. Needless to say, these procedures are foremost government procedures and they have reduced the capacity of parliaments to challenge the legislation emanating from the executive.

Internal Structures and Procedures

Standing orders represent for parliament what a constitution represents for the country's political system. They are the basic rules regulating the internal functioning of parliaments. As with many constitutions in the region, the standing orders of new Central and Eastern European parliaments were inherited from the legislatures of the communist period. These provided some basic rules to regulate political conflict and to offer rudimentary internal organization, but because they both lacked legitimacy and were designed for a different political system, standing orders have been subject to even more frequent changes than the constitutions. The capacity of parliaments to organize themselves and to react to the policy demands placed upon them was thus limited, at least for the period immediate after the end of communist rule.

Parliamentary Committees

Specialized parliamentary committees, consisting of a small group of deputies, are critical to the deliberative powers of parliaments.

Parliamentary committees also condition effective parliamentary influence in the policy-making process because they enable parliamentarians to develop specialization in particular policy areas and to acquire the necessary information to challenge government. Parliaments in the region have all developed such systems, although the precise number of committees, as well as their internal structure and procedures, vary considerably across the region. However, since most communist-era legislatures had some type of committee system, the internal organization of parliaments was, in this particular aspect, generally less problematic than the organization and functioning of parliamentary parties (see below), the organization of parliamentary support staff, or even the reform of presiding chairmanship of parliaments.

In common with practice in continental European countries, there has been an attempt in the region to establish a system of permanent legislative committees whereby their structure parallels that of the corresponding ministries with a view to ensuring the supervisory and controlling powers of parliament over the executive. However, parliaments in the region have also offered some innovation in parliamentary institutional design, for example, by establishing so-called legislative committees. These committees, variously named in different legislatures, have been charged with the responsibility of ensuring the compatibility of laws with the constitution, and to coordinate the work of different committees. They consider all bills, and have thus become very powerful and prestigious. Their existence is a direct result of the complexity of the legislative process in the postcommunist countries and, still more so, of the sheer volume of legislation that the parliaments in the region have had to process within a short period of time. The Macedonian parliament, for instance, held 123 sessions between 1991 and the first half of 1996, during which it dealt with 1,820 topics on the agenda and adopted 1,133 laws (Mircev and Spirovski, 1998)!

The number of bills that has gone through Central and Eastern European parliaments since the fall of communism partly explains why committees did not quite develop a strong position from which to challenge their respective governments. Indeed, committees in the region initially enjoyed a relatively powerful position, free of much of the external control experienced by the committees of West European parliaments. Again, this was mainly because political parties were unable to control their own members on committees.

As a result, committees frequently introduced substantive amendments to government legislation, even though they were also obviously limited in their action by a shortage of time for deliberation, and pressure from governments that they consider the bills urgently. In Romania, for example, the demands on an already highly fragmented parliament were such that, in the late 1990s, the government began to rule by extraordinary decrees in order to circumvent a lengthy legislative process (Malova and Haughton, 2002). Needless to say, the pressures on committees, in Romania or elsewhere in the region, have increased further with the introduction of fast-track legislative procedures related to the EU legislation, as already discussed.

Committee membership in the region also usually reflects the party composition of parliament, in that both members of committees and the committee chair positions are distributed among parties according to their share of seats. Committees thus can hardly renounce their party political character and, as parties themselves began to reassert themselves over individual MPs, conflicts began to be structured along party lines, rather than within the parties themselves. In addition, some countries have seen attempts to curtail the power of committees by changes in their institutional status. In the Czech Republic, for example, committees now consider bills only on their second reading, after the broad principles of the bill have been agreed upon during a first reading on the floor of the house. This still leaves committees with considerable scope to amend the details of the bill, but it is certainly more difficult to do so than when committees were considering bills before they reached the chamber itself.

Parliamentary Parties

Parliamentary parties or party groups in the parliaments of established democracies of Western Europe are the key means by which the parliamentarians organize themselves to manage the collective affairs of the legislature (e.g. Heidar and Koole, 2000). This has not always been the case in Central and Eastern Europe. As Olson (1994b, p. 45) pointed out with regard to the Czechoslovak Federal Republic, the Federal Assembly 'had more in common with the American Congress than with any European parliament', largely because of the weakness of parliamentary parties. Indeed, like elsewhere in the region, parliamentary parties frequently changed in composition: members defected to another parliamentary group, or became independent. In Slovakia, for example, 44 parliamentary seats (out of 150) changed hands from one parliamentary party to another between the elections of 1990 and 1992; between 1992 and 1994 elections the number of seats changing hands was 28 (Malova and Krause, 2000). The parties themselves often fractured into several subgroupings, or disappeared altogether (e.g. Gillespie *et al.*, 1995; Karasimeonov, 1996; Kask, 1996). In the wake of such instability, parliamentary party leaders struggled to enforce a common line on parliamentary party members. The instances of individual MPs introducing their own legislation, often against the wishes of their own party or the government coalition they represented, were thus more common than in better-established parliaments elsewhere.

Much of this has to do with the generally slow process of party formation in the region (see Chapter 9), where 'party' has been a dirty word, associated with the disciplined and corrupt hierarchy of the communist party. Moreover, political parties in general, and parliamentary parties in particular, had initially functioned in an unclear legal framework, most notably because parties as institutions were new to both political elites and the electorate and the rules governing their functioning were highly contentious. Under these circumstances, parliamentary party groups acted more like 'clubs' of individual deputies, who met each other to discuss issues and make decisions, but were often unable to agree upon common action.

However, as with many other areas of parliamentary life in the region, things have been settling into certain patterns in the past few years. Firstly, the number of parties that actually enter the parliament has been decreasing, as a result of both the effect of (many times) increased thresholds to enter parliament, as well as a degree of stabilization of voting behaviour at the mass level. The internal organization of parliament has thus gradually become more stable, especially given the fact that parliamentary parties themselves dominate the party as a whole. Indeed, the leadership of political parties often consists of a large group of members of the parliament, which means that conflicts between parliamentary party factions and the party itself are often less apparent than in established democracies.

Secondly, the institutional context in which parliamentary parties operate has firmed up, so that it is increasingly difficult for individual deputies to defect from their party and/or to set up wholly new parties. In Hungary, for example, the number of MPs needed to form a parliamentary party, and thus to receive a financial subsidy and administrative support from the parliamentary budget, has been increased from ten to fifteen in recent years (Ilonszki, 2000). Similar measures have been introduced in the Czech Republic where, in addition, parliamentary parties that are formed anew during the legislative term do not receive financial subsidies (Kopecky, 2001).

In the Polish Sejm – the parliament with perhaps the most notorious fragmentation of parliamentary parties anywhere in the region – the minimum number of MPs for the formation of a parliamentary party (*klub*) has also been increased, from the previous three to fifteen deputies. It was also in Poland, during the second legislative term, that several MPs from all but one parliamentary party were expelled, for example for breaking voting discipline (van der Meer Krok-Paszkowska, 2000). Indeed, expulsions of MPs have similarly occurred in all countries of the region and indicate that parliamentary parties and their leaderships have found at least some leverage in controlling the behaviour of their own members. Consequently, the picture of flux and instability that had dominated most accounts of the first postcommunist parliaments in the region (e.g. Remington, 1994; Agh, 1994; Longley and Zajc, 1998) has now given way to accounts that stress the emergence of distinct parliamentary cultures, settled institutional structures and parliamentary routines.

Conclusion

The postcommunist parliaments in the early years of transition experienced a paradox between high opportunity and low capacity (Olson, 1998). Compared with the legislatures of established democracies, they were significantly less subject to the control of well-established political parties and powerful interest groups, or under the dominance of strong executives. At the same time, they were constrained in their action by their own unsettled internal procedures, the presence of inexperienced members, and the fragmented nature of parliamentary parties. In addition, all parliaments in the region had initially to function within a provisional or highly disputed constitutional framework. The vast majority of the region's parliaments were, in fact, charged with responsibility to write and ratify new constitutions. Moreover, the emergence of independent statehood in the states of former Yugoslavia or Czechoslovakia had extended the process of constitution-making, and thus the period of institutional uncertainty, well into the mid-1990s.

The parliaments that are in operation at the beginning of the second postcommunist decade are different. Their capacity to act has significantly improved as the process of institutionalization has progressed. Their internal structures and procedures are now more defined and settled. Legislative tasks are increasingly performed on a routine basis. A system of parliamentary committees is in place. Large groups of MPs have now served for one or more parliamentary terms, which, together with generally improved conditions for their work, has enhanced stability and continuity in the legislative process. Parliamentary parties too have become more accepted means by which parliament in general, and individual MPs in particular, organize the functioning of the legislature. Although changes of institutional structure still occur, major constitutional conflicts seem by now to have been resolved. Indeed, with the exception of Romania and Ukraine, all states in the region have now settled into some form of parliamentary system of government, with formally weak presidents. Parliamentary rules which regulate interactions within legislatures have also been established and consolidated.

However, the increased institutional capacity of parliaments should be seen in the changed external context in which legislative bodies now function, most notably in the context of increasingly powerful governments and better organized political parties. The overarching goal of Central and Eastern European states to join the EU has also led to the adoption of fast-track legislative procedures, further reducing parliaments' independent input into the policy-making process. This means neither that parliaments are completely impotent in contemporary postcommunist Europe, nor that these institutional developments have worked uniformly. It rather means that parliaments throughout the region have begun to resemble their sister institutions in established democracies, both in terms of their internal organization and procedures and in terms of the external constraints that are normally placed upon such institutions in modern democracy.

9

Political Parties

PAUL G. LEWIS

Political parties are an indispensable component of modern liberal democracy. They make a critical contribution to the political life of emerging or consolidating democracies in Central and Eastern Europe (CEE). As in other pluralist systems, parties help to define and express competing political interests. They also serve to integrate them within the institutions that represent the entire community and legislate for the country as a whole. Such competitive parties are quite different from the organizations that sustained one-party communist rule. They represent a central part of the liberal-democratic formula that seeks to synthesize social diversity and political competition within a framework of common values and constitutional order. It is not difficult to understand the testing character of these different tasks and the conflicting demands they make under conditions of postcommunist transformation. The outcome in terms of democratic development and party activity in CEE has, nevertheless, so far been a positive one overall. The achievements of the new democratic parties generally augur well for the future political development of the region.

At the start of the new century, of the region's eighteen states, eleven were identified as being free in terms of their ranking for political liberties and civil freedom, six were partially free, and only Belarus was placed in the unfree category. Further, sixteen were classed as electoral democracies, with Bosnia as well as Belarus being excluded from this well-populated category (Karatnycky, 2001, p. 649). The region as whole thus provides extensive scope for competitive party activity. Its strengthening democratic identity suggests that the actual role of such parties has become increasingly prominent and that fertile ground exists for their further growth. That is not to say that party development in CEE has not encountered

153

major obstacles since the end of communist rule. The new institutions show considerable weaknesses in terms of structure and operation. Membership is low, organizational structures are weak, party systems fragile and the behaviour of party leaders is often unpromising in terms of the evolution of a solid, party-based democracy. But such problems are also prominent in the established democracies. The weaknesses of parties in CEE are not just those of inexperience but also signs of the problematic nature of contemporary party democracy as a whole.

Functions and Origins of Political Parties

The nature and activity of individual parties in CEE vary widely, but some generalizations can be made about the kind of activity they undertake and the nature of their overall contribution to the democratic process. At the very least, in democratic systems parties serve to: structure the vote for reasonably freely elected legislatures; act as the prime agents of formal political representation in parliamentary institutions; and, provide the basis of or prime building blocks for government formation and the policies they implement. Somewhat more debatably, parties also: provide channels for political participation and present themselves as major agencies of political mobilization; act as agencies for the recruitment of political leaders; serve as major fora for political debate, programme drafting and policy formation; aggregate interests and define group objectives for their articulation in the political arena; and facilitate the integration of citizens within the political system as a whole.

Whatever the character of the actual institutions and the range of functions they are able to perform in CEE, it is generally the case that parties of some kind play a prominent part in the reasonably free elections that are held in nearly all the countries of the region. The case of Belarus, the authoritarian characteristics of whose regime actually strengthened through the 1990s, is a singular one. Conditions there have provided little opportunity for the development and activity of democratic competitive parties. Elections were nevertheless held in 1995, with 48 per cent of seats being filled by candidates with no party affiliation. A further round, whose validity was yet further questioned, was held in 2000 and 'independents' (all loyal to President Lukashenka) then took 74 per cent of parliamentary seats. In Ukraine, another former Soviet republic, two-thirds of the vote also went to independent candidates in 1994. In the next elections, held in 1998 and after changes in the electoral mechanism, 74 per cent of the seats were won by candidates with some party affiliation. A still higher proportion, 79 per cent, received mandates in the elections of March 2002. In all other CEE countries parties fully dominate the electoral process and now act as the primary agents of parliamentary representation.

Parties now play the overwhelmingly dominant role in government formation and the conduct of government throughout the region. In terms of the basic party functions identified above, the main questions at issue are how solid parties are as the main components of government formation, and how effectively they perform their role as agents of political representation. In the first case, the situation in CEE is different from that in some established democracies – and certainly from established Anglo-American practice – in that governments are rarely formed by a single party. Coalition governments are the rule, a natural consequence of the relatively large number of parties elected to many parliaments and the lack of capacity on the part of any one organization to secure a parliamentary majority.

While this is not a particular CEE characteristic (and is seen in many West European democracies), it does reflect the specific conditions of postcommunist change and the weakness of many of the new parties that have been established or brought back to active political life since 1989. The early parliaments in postcommunist CEE were often fragmented and subject to major flux as numerous new and old parties battled for representation. In the early years highly proportional electoral mechanisms that lacked any threshold for entry to parliament were sometimes introduced. This gave a wide range of political forces their own seats in the legislature. General conditions for party development and institutional growth in the early postcommunist period were not at all favourable, either. Little organized political opposition to communist rule in CEE was able to develop prior to its collapse, and even a powerful independent social movement like that organized by the Solidarity trade union in Poland during 1980–1 was effectively neutralized for much of the following decade. Only in Hungary was there a pattern of evolutionary regime change. Proto-parties came into being well before the end of communist rule, with the Hungarian Democratic Forum being established in September 1987 and registered as a party the following year.

The Emergence of Parties in CEE

As a rule, parties were established after or during the first democratic elections. They had not been prominent in the early stages of regime change, and they did not channel the pressures that helped bring about the end of communist rule. It was generally within a social movement or under an umbrella organization sheltering a number of diverse political groups and orientations that the newly formed opposition groups and infant democratic forces entered the newly liberated CEE political arena. If parties as institutions are not popular in Western democracies and are little trusted, such suspicions are more prominent in CEE where parties command even less public confidence (Wyman *et al.*, 1995).

Apart from Solidarity, which gained the upper hand after the semi-free Polish elections of June 1989, a prominent role was also played, and early elections won, by movements like Civic Forum and Public Against Violence in a still-unified Czechoslovakia, by Popular Fronts in Moldova, Estonia and Latvia, by a Democratic Opposition in Slovenia, and even by an inaccurately named National Salvation Front in Romania (which was more a cover for forces associated with the communist establishment). In other countries, where social forces were generally weak and opposition movements largely absent, established communist forces also won in rapidly organized and hardly fully competitive – if formally free – elections. This was the case with the Socialist Parties of Bulgaria and Serbia, the League of Communists in Montenegro, and the Party of Labour in Albania. The process of democratic party formation was accordingly even slower in these countries. It was particularly delayed in Ukraine and Belarus where competitive elections were not held until 1994 and 1995 respectively.

Even in the more rapidly democratizing countries of Central Europe, where the early anti-communist movements broke up quite rapidly, it took some time for the different political tendencies to become identified and for separate political parties to be formed. Patterns of party development were, therefore, quite complex and differed considerably both among the countries of the CEE region and between the contrasting sectors of the newly expanded political arena of each postcommunist state (Lewis, 2000, pp. 32–48). Groups on the anti-communist right in Poland found it particularly difficult to organize effectively and act within a common institutional framework. A number of them regrouped under the Solidarity banner in 1996 and won the election held the following year. The coalition government it formed ran into increasing difficulties, however, and in 2001 (as we saw in Chapter 2) the Solidarity group failed to gain any parliamentary seats at all.

The Civic Democratic Party formed in 1990 by Vaclav Klaus on the basis of the Czech Civic Forum, on the other hand, has played a prominent role in the country's political life since that date. Right-wing forces have also been strong in Hungary, although FIDESZ (the Alliance of Young Democrats) has replaced the Hungarian Democratic Forum as the main party on that side of the spectrum. The main centre-right organizations in Romania and Bulgaria took several years to gain effective power and also failed to sustain their role as the main competitor to leftist parties for more than one parliamentary term. The Democratic Convention of Romania lost power to a social-democratic alliance in 2000 and was eclipsed by the nationalist Party of Greater Romania as the main party of opposition. The coalition headed by the Christian-Democratic Union of Democratic Forces lost power in Bulgaria in 2001, and was succeeded by a diffuse nationalist movement headed by Simeon II as the last occupant of the Bulgarian throne.

Alongside socio-political movements like Solidarity in Poland and Civic Forum in Czechoslovakia that acted as birthplace and nursery for one group of new parties, there was also a major evolution of former ruling communist parties. But not all on the left moved in the same direction. Those in Poland and Hungary transformed quite rapidly and with considerable success into a fair approximation of Western social-democratic parties and maintained a strong electoral presence. These new socialists won elections in Poland in both 1993 and 2001, and achieved an equivalent success in Hungary in 1994 and 2002 (see Chapter 4). A similar path was followed by the Lithuanian Democratic Labour Party, which won a striking electoral victory in 1992 and made a strong showing in 2000. The Communist Party of Bohemia and Moravia in the Czech Republic has retained its traditional identity and remained a marginal political force in a number of elections, although it performed rather better in 2002. The Slovak Party of the Democratic Left has suffered another fate (see Chapter 3) and showed that extensive reform of a former ruling party is no guarantee of subsequent electoral success.

A further group of parties has emerged and followed a path of development related to but still distinct from both these models. Poland's United Peasant Party enjoyed a legal though marginal existence throughout the communist period as a junior partner of the ruling party. In 1990 it aligned itself with groups emanating from the pre- and immediate post-war period and established itself as a significant postcommunist political force. Other parties of an 'historic' character trace their roots directly to parties of the pre-communist period, and have developed separately from both communist and active anti-communist forces. The Czech Social Democratic Party is the most striking example of such an organization, while an agrarian party, the Independent Party of Smallholders, built with some success on pre-war foundations in Hungary. These differentiated patterns of development must also be set against the generally unpromising social and political conditions inherited from the communist period. These meant that the period of party formation and early democratic development was in some cases tumultuous and in others relatively sluggish.

The Evolution of Party Politics

One sign of such early problems was the relatively large number of weak parties elected to the newly democratized parliaments, which then showed a high degree of fragmentation. Such problems should not be over-emphasized as the divisions within many early CEE parliaments were not that pronounced, but fragmentation has nevertheless declined over time as a number of major parties have became established and electoral mechanisms have been progressively refined. Indicators of this process are often expressed in terms of the effective number of parties engaged in the electoral process. This is not just a count of all those participating but expresses a statistically derived index of the overall pattern formed by the organizations taking part. The preponderance of a few reasonably large parties is thus balanced against the overall number of different organizations active in the process. It is generally assumed that a smaller number of 'effective' parties leads to better government. In many countries (Poland, Estonia, Slovenia, Romania, Hungary, Bulgaria and the Czech Republic) the effective number of parties indeed declined between 1992 and 2000, although it is a trend not seen in others like Slovakia, Latvia and Lithuania (Bielasiak, 2002, p. 201).

In terms of democratic performance, however, overcoming problems of parliamentary fragmentation is linked with the need to achieve adequate representation for most of the electorate. There is often a distinct trade-off between securing a reasonably low effective number of electoral parties and making sure that not too many voters are left without representatives in parliament. The problems of a highly fragmented electoral process like that of Poland, nevertheless, diminished considerably through the 1990s while the system succeeded in maintaining a high degree of voter representation. While the effective number of parties fell from 14.7 to 4.6 per cent between 1992 and 2000, the proportion of voters left unrepresented (i.e. those whose vote was 'wasted' because their favoured party did not enter parliament) rose only from 10.3 to 11.8 per cent. In Estonia, Slovenia, Romania, Hungary, Bulgaria and the Czech Republic, on the other hand, there was a fall both in the effective number of parties and in the proportion of voters whose party choices were not reflected in the legislature. The trade-off between the formation of a less crowded electoral arena and adequate voter representation thus developed positively through the first postcommunist decade.

A fuller understanding of the role of parties in CEE politics and their contribution to the political system as a whole requires a more detailed investigation of the structure of party representation. One way to determine whether individual parties have established themselves in parliament and the political system as a whole is to look at the pattern of parliamentary representation over time. The capacity of parties to assume a major political role and sustain it through several parliaments is one major index of party development and a reflection of the role parties have been able to sustain under the newly democratized regimes. The picture an overview presents in terms of parliamentary representation in the more democratically advanced countries of Central Europe is one of increasing stability for much of the postcommunist period. Hungary and the Czech Republic had only one new parliamentary entrant in the second and third parliaments elected since the end of communist rule. Poland, Slovakia and Slovenia generally had two new entrants in each successive parliament of this period (Lewis, 2000, p. 131).

This record shows a substantial degree of stability in terms of political representation and party development in the leading democratic countries of CEE. It is certainly greater in Hungary and the Czech Republic, but there also seems to be more stability in Poland, Slovakia and Slovenia. In no case, however, has a single party been able to maintain an independent governing role, and even the Central European states have generally been governed by two or more parties in coalition. The position of the Czech Social Democrats after 1998 was rather different – although in line with the general principle – in that they governed with the acquiescence of the Civic Democrats, who would otherwise have been the main opposition party. A different note was also struck by the 2001 elections in Poland, where both parties that had formed part of the governing coalition lost all parliamentary representation and four new political organizations entered the Sejm. At this juncture, the record of party stability and patterns of development as reflected in patterns of parliamentary representation is a mixed one.

The Nature of the CEE Party Spectrum

Another perspective on party development is provided by examination of the precise nature of the parties that have developed in CEE. How far, for example, do they fit into the framework of the established party families evident in Western Europe? By and large, similar kinds of parties in terms of ideological orientation and family identity have developed in CEE as in Western Europe and a brief list would include seven variants: communist successor organizations, social democrats, liberals (and market-oriented conservatives), ethnic groupings, agrarians, traditional conservatives (sometimes including organizations with a Christian Democratic orientation), and nationalists. All contemporary parties of any parliamentary significance are covered by this list, although some parties that are prominent in Western Europe do not make an appearance. Green parties, for example, were initially thought likely to be prominent actors in the new postcommunist politics of CEE, but ten years later they occupied a very minor role in the party spectrum. Only in the Ukrainian parliament of 1998 were they represented in their own right, although elsewhere they have played some part in broader electoral associations (like the Slovak Democratic Coalition).

One distinctive influence on the development of CEE party identity is the requirement of democratic conditionality for the ten countries applying for membership of the European Union. Another important feature is membership of the transnational party internationals as well as links with EU-based party federations. Confirmation of the democratic credentials and institutional identity of a post-1989 party by one of the major internationals or federations has often been a major advantage in stabilizing the position of a new party and enhancing its status over competitors in the same area of the political spectrum – as well as rewarding it with financial and other material advantages. The major transnational groupings are the Socialist International, Liberal International, and the Christian Democratic and People's Parties International, as well as federations like the conservative European Democratic Union and Christian Democratic European People's Party (EPP) based on the party groups of the European Parliament and the Parliamentary Assembly of the Council of Europe. Members of these groups from CEE countries are listed in Table 9.1. In terms both of its resemblance to the range of political families seen in Western Europe and the association of individual organizations with transnational party groups, the CEE party spectrum thus suggests a substantial degree of development in terms of identity formation and ideological correspondence with established political norms.

Several broad categories of CEE party are not affiliated with any of the international or pan-European federations. One obvious group consists of the parties that trace their history back to the ruling institutions of the communist period and have undergone little change in the intervening period. Apart from the Communist Party of Bohemia and Moravia in the Czech Republic it also includes similar parties in the former Soviet republics of Moldova, Ukraine and Belarus. Not allied with any of the West European groups are also the more nationalist parties that have often played a central role in the political systems of several countries (although not generally those in the forefront of democratic change) like the Movement for Democratic Slovakia, the Party of Greater Romania, the People's Movement Rukh in the Ukraine, and the Slovenian People's Party, as well as the more recently formed – and still ill-defined in terms of its political identity – National Movement of Simeon in Bulgaria. Having transformed itself into a party in April 2002 the movement was not accepted as a valid candidate by the European People's Party, whose chairman criticized it for the nature of its policies, lack of internal democracy and cooperation with former communists. Agrarian organizations like the Polish Peasant Party no longer have a West European equivalent, either.

Many of these parties just seem to be *sui generis* in CEE terms and do not fit well the West European patterns for this reason. This is an aspect often referred to in terms of parties that are standard or

TABLE 9.1   *Membership of party internationals*

Socialist International	Liberal International	Christian Democratic International	European Democratic Union
Social Democratic Party of Albania/ Socialist Party of Albania, cons.		Christian Democratic Party of Albania	Democratic Party of Albania
Belarussian Social Democratic Party, obs.		Belarussian Popular Front, Christian Democratic Party, obs.	United Civil Party, obs.
Social Democratic Party of Bosnia and Herzegovina	(Bosnian) Liberal Party, obs.	(Bosnian) New Croatian Initiative	
Bulgarian Social Democratic Party/ Europe Left, obs.	(Bulgarian) Liberal Democratic Union, obs.	Union of Democratic Forces/Democratic Party, obs./ Bulgarian National Peasant Union, obs.	United Christian Democratic Centre/ Union of Democratic Forces/Democratic Party
(Croatian) Social Democratic Party	Croatian Social Liberal Party/ Liberal Party	(Croatian Democratic Union member of EPP)	
Czech Social Democratic Party		(Czech) Christian Democratic Union	(Czech) Civic Democratic Party/ Civic Democratic Alliance
(Estonian) Moderates	Estonian Reform Party/ Estonian Coalition Party	(Estonian) Fatherland and Union	(Estonian) Fatherland Union
Hungarian Socialist Party/ Hungarian Social Democratic Party, cons.	(Hungarian) Alliance of Free Democrats	Hungarian Democratic Forum/FIDESZ – Hungarian Civic Party	Independent Smallholders' Party/Hungarian Democratic Forum/FIDESZ – Hungarian Civic Party
Latvian Social Democratic Workers' Party	Latvia's Way	(People's Party member of EPP)	
Lithuanian Social Democratic Party	Lithuanian Liberal Union/New Union-Social	Lithuanian Christian Democratic Party	Fatherland Union – Lithuania Conservatives

TABLE 9.1   *(continued)*

Socialist International	*Liberal International*	*Christian Democratic International*	*European Democratic Union*
	Liberals/ Lithuanian Centre Union, obs.		
Social Democratic Union of Macedonia, obs.	(Macedonian) Liberal Democratic Party		IMRO – Democratic Party, obs./ Party of Albanians, obs.
Social Democratic Party of Moldova, obs.		(Moldovan) Popular Christian Democratic Front	
Social Democratic Party of Montenegro, cons.	Liberal Alliance of Montenegro		
(Polish) Democratic Left Alliance/ Labour Union		(Solidarity Social Movement member of EPP)	(Polish) Freedom Union
Democratic Party of Romania	(Romanian) National Liberal Party	Hungarian Christian Democratic Party/ National Peasant Christian Democratic Party/Democratic Alliance of Hungarians in Romania, obs.	National Peasant Christian Democratic Party/Democratic Alliance of Hungarians in Romania
Social Democratic Party of Slovakia/ Party of Democratic Left	(Slovakian) Democratic Union	Christian Democratic Movement of Slovakia, obs./ Party of Hungarian Coalition, obs.	Christian Democratic Movement of Slovakia/Party of Hungarian Coalition
(Slovenian) United List of Social Democrats	Liberal Democracy of Slovenia	New Slovenia	Slovenian People's Party – Christian Democrats
	(Ukrainian) Liberal Party, obs.	(Ukrainian) Christian People's Union, obs.	

cons. and obs. = consultative and observer status only.
Sources: derived from different organizations' websites.

non-standard (in terms of fitting into established West European categories), a category first developed in the Slovak context where Meciar's Movement for a Democratic Slovakia (MDS) has provided a prime example of 'non-standardness' (Wightman, 1998, pp. 157–8). It refers to a party that, characteristically, has strong roots in the communist regime but is also leader-dominated and populist, with nationalist leanings and a confrontational style. The existence of such parties, and their prominence in some countries (generally those that have made limited progress towards a Western-style democracy), can partly be explained by the continuing legacy of the communist regimes and delays in the development of a modern, European party identity. But the existence of such parties may also be accounted for on less historical grounds. By no means all parties are best defined by their programme or ideological heritage. Some parties are most appropriately characterized by their charismatic or clientilistic characteristics, features that clearly apply to parties like that headed by Meciar in Slovakia.

Generally speaking, empirical research has shown a relatively high level of programmatic crystallization of parties and party systems in Central Europe and a lower one in more problematic democracies like those of the Balkans, typified in this instance by Bulgaria (Kitschelt *et al.*, 1999). But there is no guarantee that existing regional characteristics in terms of the path and character of party development will all disappear and that a uniform model based on West European patterns emerge. The survival of leader-dominated parties like that of Meciar's MDS, a model replicated in several Balkan countries and former Soviet republics, has been facilitated by control over state resources and the capacity for patronage, conditions that have clearly been more prevalent in the less democratized CEE countries. Elements of clientelism can certainly help sustain the position of a party leader under such conditions, and have often been linked with diffuse appeals to nationalism as a cover for more sectional interests. Such features were present in Croatia until Tudjman's death in 1999 as well as in some other Balkan states. The relatively nationalist and clientelist path taken by the traditionally dominant parties in the FSU also distinguish them sharply from the distinctively postcommunist line of development followed by the old socialist and workers' parties in Hungary and Poland. Elements of corruption and financial abuse of formally democratic office have not been absent in Central Europe, but they have been marginal to the primary identity of the communist successor parties rather than providing the basic means of their survival in postcommunist political life.

Overall, then, the party spectrum of contemporary CEE is sufficiently complex and fluid to resist easy definition and effective analysis through the prism of any single classification system – although a clearer view of the party landscape can be gained by distinguishing between the different parts of the region. The post-Soviet republics of Ukraine, Moldova and Belarus continue to be strongly influenced by the character of the former regime. If they are no longer actually dominated by the institutions of communist rule, then they are certainly still strongly influenced by their style and the procedures through which they operated. Central Europe, on the other hand, has seen a rapid evolution from the Soviet model, with party systems characterized by extensive and effective competition, distinctive arenas of programmatic competition and relatively frequent alternation of party government.

Party arrangements in the Balkans have lain somewhat between these two models, and seen either the lengthy dominance of a partially reformed communist establishment with relatively weak democratic party opposition (Romania and Bulgaria) or the rule of authoritarian right-wing parties whose democratic credentials were no more convincing than those of their neighbours (Croatia). The rump Yugoslavia under Milosevic managed to combine elements of both these models in a distinctive form of authoritarian and aggressive rule. In the Baltic states, on the other hand, a shorter period of communist rule and stronger nationalist opposition helped create the conditions under which communist supremacy could be overcome more rapidly and with greater success than in other republics of the FSU with corresponding advantages for the development of more democratic party systems. Such developments confirm the importance of a clean break from the former regime as a major condition for democratic and effective party development (Bunce, 2000, pp. 706–19).

Party Structure and Organization

The problems involved in developing effective democratic parties in postcommunist CEE have generally been associated with their thin membership base and weak organizational structure, and with the slender resources at their disposal. The resources available to CEE parties can be analysed under several headings.

Membership

By the end of the 1990s this was still highest in the old communist parties of the region or their successors. The Czech Communist Party retained 140 thousand members and Democratic Left Alliance in Poland some 80 thousand. The rejuvenated Polish Peasant Party, which also had strong roots in the former regime, claimed 120 thousand members. Other agrarian parties also have high levels of membership support and, with 60 thousand, the Independent Smallholders' Party is the largest in Hungary. Some of the prominent governing parties have had far fewer members. The Czech Social Democratic and Civic Democratic Parties had enrolled 18 and 19 thousand people respectively, while in Hungary FIDESZ had even fewer with 16 thousand. In comparative terms CEE party membership levels remained low. Central European parties were estimated to have enrolled between 1 and 4 per cent of the adult population by the mid-1990s in contrast to 15–16 per cent in countries like Austria and Sweden. But membership in UK and the Netherlands, at 2.5 and 2.1 per cent, was in the same range and, while levels in Central Europe were relatively low, they were not regarded as being markedly out of line with those of some countries of Western Europe (Lewis, 1996, pp. 14–15).

More recent research presents another different perspective on membership issues. A further survey confirms not just the low – and generally declining – membership levels in Central Europe but also points to a more dramatic fall in party membership in Western Europe in the context of substantial and consistent aggregate evidence of growing disengagement from established parties (Mair and van Biezen, 2001, p. 14). The main point emphasized here is not so much that Central European parties have few members but that this is not a surprising state of affairs in the light of broader European experience. The conclusion to be drawn from this comparison is that party membership is often low and declining in many European countries – but that the fall has been more pronounced in some Western countries than in the east, and that some Western party membership levels were low at the outset. Austrian membership totals as a percentage of the electorate dropped by four points during the 1990s, for example, but Swedish levels (at least by some accounts) fell by considerably more. French totals also nearly halved over the ten-year period. Indeed levels of party membership are now higher in Slovakia, Hungary and the Czech

Republic than in either France or UK. Whether these changes had any influence on the effectiveness of party activity or on the quality of democratic practice overall is by no means clear, but it does seem reasonable to conclude that low membership levels in CEE does not necessarily have direct implications for party strength or weakness, or for the consolidation of democratic party systems.

Structure

The conditions of contemporary party activity, the elitist attitudes held by many CEE party leaders and the reluctance of the public to join them have all combined to give the members the parties did enrol a relatively marginal role in the organization as a whole. This has also been reflected in the restricted institutional development shown by many parties and the relative weakness of party structure. In many cases there seems to have been little conception of how a rank-and-file membership could be organized or what it was actually for in the first place. And there has been little correlation between the development of organizational structure and party success at the polls. It was one of the paradoxes of the Polish election of 2001 that the party which had paid most attention to questions of institutional development and put most effort into organizing a national structure – the Freedom Union – failed to reach the electoral threshold and lost the parliamentary representation it had maintained since its formation in 1990. Questions of inner-party democracy have also often been ignored and rarely perceived to be much of an issue in party life at all. Postcommunist politics and the practice of liberal democracy are generally understood to operate most effectively at national level and within the narrow confines of the political elite. This often involves a very limited conception of the political party, and provides few incentives for developing a party's organizational network or much of a sub-national structure.

In line with patterns of party membership it has been possible to identify some national differences in party structure and organizational development. With more members on the ground, for example, Czech party organizations have shown a greater capacity for development as autonomous units. They have had some power to manage their own affairs, settle management and leadership issues on their own account, and control their own finances. In Hungary, on the other hand, the resemblance of the new parties' structures to

HUNGARIAN
PARTY
ELITE

those of the former ruling communist party was remarked on at an early stage, the growth of a professional staff and bureaucratization only leading to the emergence of a sharply restricted and elitist democracy, contributing yet further to an established 'representation deficit' (Ilonszki, 1998, pp. 157–70). In Poland it was once again the parties like the Social Democracy and the Peasant Party, institutions with roots in the former regime, that had stronger local networks and were better represented at the grass roots. In other cases, local party structures were very weak and in keeping with the low level of party membership nationally.

The organizational assets inherited from the communist regime by successor parties have also diminished. As membership of the once all-powerful Communist Party of Bohemia and Moravia dropped away – falling by over half between 1992 and 1999 – a similar decline could be seen in the party's network of local organizations. Such tendencies are not always identified as a problem or a sign of institutional weakness. The body established by the National Movement of Simeon II in Bulgaria in 2002 was explicitly conceived as an electoral party and did not seek to maintain a local network between elections. The Civic Platform that emerged after the 2000 presidential election in Poland and scored a reasonable success in the 2001 parliamentary elections, to take another example, fell prey to internal dissension when the development of its organizational structure was discussed. Some were fearful of excessive dominance by the parliamentary faction and argued for strong grassroots democracy; others favoured a 'light' organizational touch and saw the party as an electoral organization.

Funding

 # POL
PARTIES

The weak membership base of many CEE parties and the emphasis on national and parliamentary leadership in their organizational structures is also reflected in their funding patterns. Membership dues, naturally enough, played a considerably larger role in the finances of communist and successor social democratic parties than in most liberal and right-wing organizations. In the early to mid-1990s the Czech communists and Hungarian socialists drew, respectively, 41 and 20 per cent of their income from their members, and the Polish social democrats (in 1998) 43 per cent. None of the other main Hungarian parties drew more than 10 per cent of their income from members, and patterns of funding were little different for the leading Polish organizations (with the exception of Solidarity Electoral Action, which had little official income on its own account and was dependent on the resources of the trade union for much of its activity). Precisely where the rest of the funds used to fund party activity came from is not always very clear, although national legislation generally provides for the regular publication of party accounts and full transparency of the parties' financial dealings.

The distribution of state property and other assets at the end of the communist period has given some parties substantial material assets and left them with major advantages over their competitors. Such resources provide parties with more than 80 per cent of annual income in some cases. Diverse forms of 'economic activity', for instance, were a category that provided 88 per cent of the Polish Peasant Party's income in 1998 and 91 per cent in 1999. Direct state funding for parties in Hungary and the Czech Republic was already quite generous, and the Hungarian Free Democrats obtained 91 per cent of their funds from this source in 1995. The Hungarian Socialists also drew on substantial state funds to supplement the sizeable income it already derived from its members. The situation in Poland, however, was rather different, as there was no direct funding of party activity (apart from the reimbursement of election expenses) until 1997. The provision of salaries to members of parliament, payment of substantial expenses and the funding of party group activity to some extent made up for the absence of direct state funding, although this did not help parties without parliamentary representation and tended to feed the popular suspicion that such support was just another means by which professional politicians were able to line their pockets at the public's expense.

The issue of how party activity should be best financed – as well as the overall means of how party politicians' relations to financial resources should be regulated in general – remains a live and contentious issue in many countries of the region (and outside them). Finance is clearly an important condition of effective party activity, although it is not particularly clear what role it has played in the political trajectory of individual parties or how important it is for the large numbers of new parties that continue to break through and gain entry to the parliamentary arena in a number of CEE countries. It has been argued that the relationship between, in particular, campaign finance laws and party system development has not received sufficient attention (Roper, 2002, pp. 175–6). This observation is certainly accurate, but the precise relationship will be a difficult one to establish. A general impression is that finance is not a prime condition for political success, and that the continuing fluidity of the political constellation offers diverse opportunities and various points of access to the political arena. There are also, however, some indications that the pattern of state funding in new CEE democracies is rather different from that in recently democratized Southern European regimes, and that the tendency for funds to flow more strongly to the parties' central offices than to their parliamentary leadership may have major consequences for their patterns of development.

The Media

The importance of the media in party competition in modern democracies and the substantial costs they involve suggest that access to the media may be a significant link between a party's material status and its chances of political success. The Polish record shows, however, that expenditure on the media has been a limited element in party outgoings in election campaigns – little more than 20 per cent as a rule (although they may be more substantial in the personalized competition seen in presidential contests). That, of course, is not to argue that media and television resources are not of great importance in new democracies where many parties are competing to construct and project a distinctive political identity, where members are thin on the ground and unable to spread the parties' message by word of mouth, and where party organizational networks fail to penetrate many local communities.

Television in particular plays a major role in projecting party leaders and securing critical shifts in a party's image as a condition for electoral success. TV presentation during the 2001 election campaign in Poland projected Self-Defence leader Andrzej Lepper from the margins of political life, where he played a lively but limited role as organizer of peasant blockades, to a central position by developing a more statesmanlike image that appealed to far broader sectors of the electorate. Similar examples could be drawn from most countries of the region. The interplay of media and party politics takes other forms than politicians simply exploiting the opportunities that television offers. Those controlling major media outlets can use the position to launch their own political careers, as

Berlusconi has done so successfully in Italy. The influence of the owner of Poland's major TV satellite channel, Zygmunt Solarz, has been reported to extend to control over thirty parliamentary deputies who helped promote his interests. Supporters of the Polish Catholic station, Radio Maryja, equally helped ensure the strong showing of the League of Polish Families in the 2001 elections. Slovak media magnate Pavol Rusko founded his own political party, ANO (Alliance of the New Citizen), in April 2001 and clearly had hopes of winning over a substantial segment of the 40 per cent of Slovaks who watched the news programme broadcast by his station.

Television has, not surprisingly then, been the most politically sensitive medium in postcommunist CEE. The 'media war' that flared up with particular ferocity in Hungary during 1992 was one of the major conflicts of the first postcommunist administration as the government attempted to strengthen its position by imposing strict control over media budget allocations. Dominant parties were often very closely involved in the reorganization and daily administration of the main TV channels. The development of a relatively pluralist framework in this area was a gradual process, and by the mid-1990s, only in Poland, Slovenia and the Czech Republic were the electronic media not described as still functioning as 'direct extensions of the power structure' and viewed primarily as government mouthpieces (Jakubowicz, 1996, p. 21).

The position with regard to the press and print media is rather different, and more rapid progress was made towards the emergence of what could be described as a pluralistic system of party-oriented newspapers. The print media are less important politically – and correspondingly less vulnerable to the restrictions of state control. This has mixed consequences for the development of a free and varied press in CEE. While state agencies and major power-holders have been less concerned to maintain control and exclude competing interests, both public and political parties soon began to lose interest in the press and were less likely to buy political publications or subsidize their production. The circulation of newly founded papers declined as the novelty of press freedom began to fade and costs began to rise. The normal processes of market competition and the intervention of foreign entrepreneurs exert their not unexpected influence. British press baron Robert Maxwell showed an early interest in the Hungarian press and exercised close control over editorial appointments in the papers he acquired. Following his death the government daily was acquired by Swiss proprietors, while other publications changed hands with equal rapidity. Yet others reverted to state ownership as the prospect of a healthy profit diminished and private companies lost their earlier interest. By the time a socialist government was elected in Hungary in 1994 there was no clear outlet for left-wing opinion among any of the surviving newspapers.

Conclusion

Much of the discussion of the trajectory of democratic change in CEE, as elsewhere, now focuses on issues of consolidation and the institutionalization of political parties and the systems they form (Randall and Svåsand, 2002; Bielasiak, 2002; von Beyme, 2001b). A number of complex issues have been raised in this discussion, and any conclusions reached are necessarily tentative and often ambiguous. As a very broad generalization, however, parties have developed quite successfully in most countries of the region, steps have been taken towards the emergence of viable party systems, and a growing Europeanization of the party political processes in many CEE countries can be identified. Granted, the degree of progress in some of the former Soviet republics and levels of political stability in some Balkan (and especially former Yugoslav) countries is not striking. Party turnover and volatility in voting patterns are also high elsewhere. Even amongst the democratic leaders membership levels are low (or have even declined) and party organization is often rudimentary. But many of the characteristics and apparent defects are increasingly evident in Western Europe too, and CEE party development certainly appears to be adequate to sustain continuing democratic development. Whether this will continue to be case with the continuing prevalence of 'flash' parties that suddenly erupt on the political scene, in the light of the 2001 elections in Poland (which saw the removal from parliaments of both wings of the former governing coalition and the entry of four new bodies that were hardly parties at all in any normal sense), and the continuing strength of extremist and highly diffuse political forces in the Balkans, remains to be seen. It might, however, also be argued that these features reflect processes increasingly seen in Western Europe and that they are evidence that the Europeanization of CEE party structures and systems is continuing – if sometimes in unexpected ways.

10

Elections and Voting Behaviour

KRZYSZTOF JASIEWICZ

It is conventional wisdom that the Central and East European revolution was won on the streets of Prague and Leipzig, Timisoara and Bucharest, in the shipyards of Gdansk and steel mills of Krakow. This point of view hardly can be disputed, but it is also true that this revolution was won in voting booths across the region. Street demonstrations and strikes usually initiated the change and often delivered the ultimate blow to the old regimes, but with almost no exception competitive elections were the real turning point in the process of political transition. Ever since this breakthrough, the (usually) free and the fair elections have been a focal point in the Central and East European democratic consolidations. And even in those countries that stumbled on their road to democracy, elections never became irrelevant. For instance, the spectacular street demonstrations that led to the collapse of the Milosevic regime in Yugoslavia in 2000 came about as an expression of the will of the people who, unlike their rulers, were determined to treat the presidential election and its real outcome seriously.

In the late 1980s all Central and East European communist regimes faced – although most of them failed to recognize it – crises of legitimization (Rigby and Feher, 1982; Rychard, 1992). Since their rise to power after World War II, the communists of Central and Eastern Europe legitimized their rule through two mechanisms. The first may be called 'legitimization through utopia': a promise to create an ideal system of social, political, and economic institutions, guaranteeing all citizens equal rights and equal access to the benefits of the welfare state; a system that would eventually generate an affluent society, free of exploitation and conflict. The second was legitimization through 'the Soviet tanks factor': the adoption of the Brezhnev doctrine (well before the term was invented) to convince the potentially rebellious populations that the Soviet Union would not tolerate other than communist regimes in the region, and that the only alternative to a national communist government and limited sovereignty would be a direct Soviet occupation. The technically democratic procedures, such as elections, sessions of parliaments, and nomination of cabinets, served only as a rubber-stamp for the legitimization achieved through the above-mentioned mechanisms. Nonetheless, these rubber-stamps were perceived by the communists as very important devices. Very seldom would they implement any decisions without subjecting them to a process of such a formal legalization; very often they would prosecute oppositionists for alleged violations of law and 'constitutional order'.

By the late 1980s both mechanism of legitimization had exhausted their potential. The promise of a better, more just political system and society was never fulfilled, and even the communist leaders occasionally had to admit this. But above all, the countries of Central and Eastern Europe experienced economic crisis, or, at the very best, stagnation. The gap between their 'economies of shortage' (Kornai, 1980) and the affluent market economies of Western Europe in North America became wider than ever. The people responded with disbelief to the official statistics on economic growth, which were themselves much less impressive than in the 1950s or 1960s. In recognition of these facts the communist leaders in Hungary and Poland launched programmes of economic reforms, but the ultimate failure of these programmes contributed to the further delegitimization of the system.

The election of Mikhail Gorbachev as the Soviet leader originally did not place in question the validity of the Brezhnev doctrine. But in 1987 and 1988 he and his aides began to encourage the communist leaders of Central and Eastern Europe to experiment with their economic and political institutions – within, it should be remembered, the framework of a 'socialist choice'. These friendly suggestions received a very mixed response from those to whom they were directed. Only the reformist factions of the Polish and Hungarian communist parties understood them as a backing against their own hardliners and pursued cautious policies of liberalization. Nonetheless, the hardline leaders of Czechoslovakia or the GDR could not any longer present their conservative positions as congruent with the Soviet line. The window of opportunity for the opposition and dissatisfied populations had been opened. Still, it was not until the formation of a Solidarity-based government in Poland and the breaching of the Berlin Wall in 1989 that the Brezhnev doctrine could be pronounced dead.

The communist reformers of Poland in Hungary were the first to recognize an urgent need for renewed legitimization of their rule. They did not plan to transfer power to the opposition. Rather, they were hoping to co-opt moderate opposition groupings to the system and share with them responsibility for the implementation of further economic reforms, which would carry necessary austerity measures, in all likelihood extremely unpopular among the populace. Despite the different strength of opposition forces in Hungary and Poland (in Poland strong, since 1980 united in the political movement of Solidarity; in Hungary weak and isolated) the communists of both countries applied very similar strategies. They opened up a process of negotiations, legitimizing the opposition but also forcing it to recognize as legitimate the institutions of the system. Among the major items on the negotiation table were the terms for new general elections – elections that would broaden the legitimization base of the renewed institutions of political representation. The Hungarian and Polish communist reformers were undoubtedly hoping to win these elections. With such an outcome, they would have regained unquestioned legitimacy, in exchange for granting the leaders of opposition a limited access to power (which would also mean joint accountability). Neither in Poland nor in Hungary were the communists able to achieve their goals, and were swept out of power in elections of 1989 (Poland) and 1990 (Hungary). The Czechoslovak hardliners did not do any better: they were first forced to enter power-sharing arrangements with the opposition (1989), and subsequently were defeated in elections (1990).

In Bulgaria and Albania the communists, facing the rapidly growing popular unrest, decided to have an early election and legitimize their rule in the eyes of the international community and the domestic population. This decision originally seemed to pay off, as the communists faced a rather poorly organized opposition and were able to intimidate and misinform the electorate. Yet the communist victory in both countries only reinforced the unrest and consolidated the opposition. In both cases, the new elections were called within a year, this time generating a victory of the opposition.

The course of events in Romania varied significantly from the patterns of developments elsewhere in East-Central Europe. There were no organized opposition, no reform-minded communist leaders, no roundtable talks; there was violence. The communist party vanished from the Romanian political scene after the December 1989 revolution, but the National Salvation Front (NSF), a seemingly *ad hoc* outcome of this revolt, in many ways substituted for a post-communist party. It won legislative elections in 1990 and 1992, and its leader, Ion Iliescu, was each time elected as president.

In Yugoslavia, the communists faced the challenge not from a democratic opposition, but from the republican nationalist movements. In elections held in various republics between April and December 1990, the nationalists and their allies won in Slovenia, Croatia, and Macedonia, while the communists prevailed in Serbia and Montenegro. In consequence, the three former republics left the federation and received international recognition as sovereign states, while the two latter remained within the rump Yugoslav federation.

In the former Soviet Union, the winds of political change were reflected in electoral outcomes as early as 1989 and 1990. In March 1989 (three months before the historic Polish election – a fact often overlooked by analysts) in the elections to the newly established Congress of People's Deputies, voters for the first time in the history of the USSR were given a choice among several candidates. In each of the three Baltic republics, Lithuania, Latvia, and Estonia, as many as three-quarters of the seats were won by candidates endorsed by the republic's national liberation movement. This development had no direct political consequences, as the Congress was a largely ceremonial body and, in any case, Baltic deputies were greatly outnumbered by those from other Soviet republics. Yet just a year later, the Baltic liberation movements emerged victorious in elections to the republican-level Supreme Soviets, which accelerated the drive toward full independence of each nation. Their goal was ultimately achieved after the failed August 1991 coup in Moscow and the dissolution of the Soviet Union in December 1991. Also in Moldova, Ukraine, and Belarus, the 1989 and 1990 elections, although they did not remove communists from power, nonetheless gave substantial momentum to the national liberation movements there.

Looking at the process of regime transition in Central and Eastern Europe from a comparative perspective, one can observe that it passed through several distinct phases:

Phase zero: The communist regimes either resist pressure to reform from a more or less organized opposition, or rule practically uncontested.

Phase one: The communist regimes come under pressure from the opposition, the public, and/or the international environment to open up the process of negotiations. The opposition enters this process represented by an umbrella organization, which covers groupings with various ideological and political orientations. The process of negotiations, usually called a roundtable, provides a mutual legitimization for the opposition (recognized by the regime as a partner) and the institutions of the old regime, in particular the government and parliament. The roundtables as such obviously exceeded the constitutional framework of the communist state; the state institutions make necessary provisions to legalize the outcome of the negotiations (including the adoption of a new electoral law and constitutional amendments). The institutional role of the communist party diminishes during this process (while its leaders play an insignificant political role), and in most cases the 'leading role of the [communist] party' is dropped from the constitution. Developments in the former Soviet Union and Yugoslavia, unlike elsewhere in East-Central Europe, are in this phase marked not so much by the communist–anticommunist cleavage as by the conflict between the peripheral republics seeking sovereignty and the centre, desperately trying to salvage the federation's integrity.

Phase two: Both regime and opposition claim they represent the interests of the people, although against each partner in the roundtable negotiations a claim could be made that it represented nobody's interests but its own. These claims had to be weighed through the process of (more or less) contested elections. Elections provided also a broader legitimization of the roundtable accords, and, ultimately, led to the creation of indisputably legitimized institutions of political representation. Typically, the opposition entered the electoral process under the protective umbrella of one organization, with only minor groupings running independently. Also the communist party usually participated in the elections as a united force, often under a changed name.

Phase three: Developments in this phase differ within the region. In the Northern Tier (Poland, Czechoslovakia, Hungary, Slovenia, Croatia, and the Baltic states) the elections bring about a landslide victory for the opposition. The defeat of the communists leads to a disintegration of this party and/or profound turnover in its leadership. But the victorious former opposition also disintegrates (Croatia is the only exception here), the umbrella organizations either lose their popular support or simply cease to exist, and the political scene becomes highly fragmented. This fragmentation was usually reflected in the outcome of the second set of general elections.

In the Southern Tier the postcommunist organizations win the first elections – the opposition is too weak and the population too intimidated to overcome the resistance of communists, entrenched in the state bureaucracy and mass media. But after the elections the opposition – still unified under a protective umbrella, and now a legitimate actor on the political scene – gains momentum and challenges the postcommunist governments. In Bulgaria and Albania this challenge leads, within about a year, to new elections, which tip the balance of power toward the opposition. In Romania, a united and better (compared with 1990) organized opposition still loses to the Democratic Front of National Salvation in the 1992 elections, only to win decisively in 1996. Developments in Ukraine, Moldova, and Macedonia differ, for specific reasons, from this pattern (as does the situation in Yugoslavia and worn-torn Bosnia).

Despite local variations, the process of political change in all the Central and East European countries followed the same general pattern, from polarization to fragmentation: a united opposition faced the old regime in a stand-off (at a roundtable and/or during elections) and remained united until the apparent defeat of the communists.

It is often stressed (see, for instance, O'Donnell *et al.*, 1986) that the first free elections after a prolonged period of totalitarian or authoritarian rule play the role of 'founding elections': they lead to the establishment of a relatively stable configuration of actors on the political scene, although not necessarily a stable government. In the case of Central and Eastern Europe the definition of founding elections should be extended to encompass the first, the second, and sometimes also the third and perhaps further electoral acts. The first elections were, as a rule, a plebiscite against communism; not until after the defeat of the communists did the party system begin to take shape in an unrestricted way.

Seats and Votes: The Politics of Electoral Reform

When in 1909 universal male suffrage was introduced in Sweden by a Conservative government, the same reform act substituted proportional representation for the existing winner-take-all system. The Conservatives, whose electoral base was in the Swedish nobility, spread more or less evenly throughout the country, would suddenly become relatively narrow, wanting to assure for themselves at least a minimal level of representation in parliament (Pontusson, 1992, p. 433). Similar decisions were made at that time elsewhere in continental Europe, leaving Great Britain as the last European bastion of first-past-the-post elections and Westminster-type democracy. Many theorists believe that choosing the proportional representation (PR) voting system was a very unfortunate decision, since plurality voting (first-past-the-post in single-member constituencies) seems conducive to two-party systems and stable, majoritarian governments, while PR, on the other hand, tends to generate multiparty systems and coalition or even minority governments, vulnerable to challenges and therefore unstable (Duverger, 1963 and 1986; Riker, 1986). This relationship between the type of voting system and political stability has been recently questioned (Lijphart, 1991), and the problem remains open to further inquiry. Central and Eastern Europe provides here several very interesting cases (for a summary overview, see Table 10.1).

TABLE 10.1 *Electoral systems in Central and Eastern Europe (as of September 2002)*

Country	Date of most recent election	Electoral system[*]
Albania	June 2001	Mixed. 100 deputies elected in single-member districts by majority vote (with runoff). A make-up distribution of seats from national list to achieve full proportionality (party list PR, 4% threshold), for the total of 140 seats.
Bosnia-Herzegovina	November 2000	Party list PR in two separate compartments: the Muslim-Croat Federation and the Bosnian Serb Republic.
Bulgaria	June 2001	Party list PR in districts, 4% threshold.
Croatia	January 2000	Party list PR in districts, with 5% threshold.
Czech Republic	June 2002	Party list PR in districts, 5% threshold.
Estonia	March 1999 (*March 2003*)	Party list PR in districts, 5% threshold.

(cont. overleaf)

TABLE 10.1   *(continued)*

Country	Date of most recent election	Electoral system*
Hungary	May 2002	Mixed. 176 seats distributed by majority-plurality vote (two rounds) in single-member districts,152 by party list PR in multi-member districts (4% threshold), 58 compensation seats by party list PR nationwide (4% threshold)
Latvia	October 2002	Party list PR in districts, 4% threshold.
Lithuania	October 2000	Mixed. 71 deputies elected in single-member districts by majority vote (with runoff), 70 deputies by party list PR nationwide (4% threshold).
Macedonia	September 2002	Mixed. 85 members elected by majority vote in single-member districts, with runoff; 35 deputies elected by party list PR nationwide.
Moldova	February 2001	Party list PR nationwide, 6% threshold.
Poland	September 2001	Party list PR in districts, 5% threshold
Romania	November 2000	Party list PR in districts, 5% threshold.
Slovakia	September 2002	Party list PR in districts, 5% threshold.
Slovenia	October 2000	Party list PR in districts, modified to allow nationwide compensatory distribution of seats.
Ukraine	March 2002	Mixed. 225 deputies elected in single-member districts by majority vote (with runoff), 225 deputies elected by party list PR in districts (4% threshold).
Yugoslavia	September 2000	Party list PR in two separate compartments: Serbia and Montenegro.

* Electoral system used in the most recent election.
PR = proportional representation.

The mechanisms of choosing electoral systems in Central and Eastern Europe were in many instances remarkably similar to those in Sweden eighty years earlier. The elections that have taken place in the region since 1989 may indeed be regarded as a case study in the introduction of universal suffrage. True, the people of the region did vote in communist times, and 99.9 per cent turnouts did not come exclusively from the stuffing of electoral boxes. But in reality these people were disfranchized: the act of voting was reduced to a ritual, with no real political meaning. The communist masters had no reason to worry about the outcome of the voting – it had been known even before the elections began.

In 1989–90 this was no longer the case. Just like the Swedish Conservatives, the communists in power, still having the legislative process under their control, opted for solutions they perceived as advantageous. Interestingly, for the first election in a given country their typical choice was a plurality (or majority) vote. The communists were hoping to gain in this system of voting because of at least three factors: (i) they were better organized than the opposition; (ii) their local bosses believed they could still intimidate voters, particularly in rural areas; (iii) they enjoyed name recognition, while the leaders of opposition were in most cases practically unknown to the public. In some instances these calculations were correct; in others they proved fatal.

In the June 1989 elections in Poland, the communists, according to a very peculiar electoral law designed at the roundtable, were ensured 173 of the 460 seats in the Sejm, with an additional 126 allocated to their allies and 161 open to contest by anybody else. However, all 100 seats in the Senate were open to unrestricted contest, by majority vote in multi- (two- or three-) member constituencies, and 99 of them were won by Solidarity. The communists, who under a PR system would have won 25–30 seats in the Senate, were left empty-handed.

Unlike in Poland, in Bulgaria and Albania the communists profited from majority voting in the first contested elections (1990 and 1991, respectively). In Bulgaria, where a mixed system was used, the postcommunist BSP fared better in the majority vote than in PR, and eventually won a majority of seats. In Albania, where all seats where allocated by majority vote, the victory of the communists was even more spectacular. In Ukraine, similarly, the postcommunists were able to assure their victory in a majoritarian vote.

For the 1990 elections in Hungary, a highly complicated mixed system was adopted – again a compromise between the communists (who insisted on single-member constituencies) and the opposition. The hopes of the postcommunists that they would profit from a majority vote proved overly optimistic: they won only one seat by this mode, while in the PR vote collected 11 per cent of the votes and 14 seats (plus an additional 18 after the make-up distribution on the national level). Similar was the fate of communists in the first multi-party elections in Croatia, Slovenia, and Macedonia, which used majoritarian systems. In Czechoslovakia the communists, wisely, did not object to the Civic Forum/Public Against Violence proposal to return in the June 1990 election to the traditional system of proportional representation (with a 5 per cent cutoff). They finished as the second strongest party. Romania and Moldova also adopted PR systems for their first and subsequent elections.

The transition to proportional representation systems in new Central and East European democracies was advanced further when Poland, Bulgaria, and Albania adopted such systems for their second parliamentary elections. This time the communists, so badly defeated in majority voting in Poland and losing popular support in Bulgaria and Albania, opted – like the Swedish Conservatives of 1909 – for a PR solution, and because of their strong representation in parliaments were able to secure the desired legislation. PR or mixed systems were adopted also in Croatia, Slovenia, the Baltic states, and in Ukraine (since 1998). Finally, Macedonia, the last country in the region still using a fully majoritarian mode of elections, introduced a mixed system for the 1998 election.

By the late 1990s, all umbrella organizations of democratic opposition and national liberation movements in the region had disintegrated, giving way to political fragmentation. Was the PR-based electoral law to be blamed? As indicated above, when the electoral regulations were chosen, the effectively available options were very limited: <u>from a certain point onwards the former communists were interested in adopting a PR system, and usually had enough control over the legislative to secure such a regulation. But perhaps more important, they were supported in this bid by many of their foes: new and renewed small parties, which could not afford the risks associated with a winner-take-all system. Political fragmentation usually preceded the adoption of a PR-based voting system, not vice versa.</u> This does not mean that a well-designed electoral law would not have curtailed the number of parties represented in parliament (as evidenced by the 1993 and subsequent elections in Poland). But it could not prevent or even reduce political factionalism and fragmentation, because their major sources were outside the political and legislative process: in the peculiarities of social structure of a society undergoing rapid economic, social, and political change.

The political polarization of the 1980s and early 1990s reflected sociological features of communist societies: petrified social

[margin annotation: PR / FRAGMENTN *]*

structures, low levels of social mobility, and dichotomized visions of social order – vanguard versus masses, *nomenklatura* versus people, them versus us. The current fragmentation (the actual levels of which differ, obviously, from country to country) reflects the ongoing change of this order, the disintegration of old structures and the emergence of new ones. The group loyalties and group interests of the past dissolve (some of them die hard, as is true of the provincial *nomenklatura* or workers in the mammoth enterprises of socialist industry). What emerges to replace them is not yet new solid structures, but a state of *anomie* (normlessness) and a fragmented society. In the opinion of many, such a society is likely to be haunted for a long time by the spectres of the past.

Patterns of Voting Behaviour

In his essay *Reflections on the Revolution in Europe*, Ralf Dahrendorf made the following prediction about the course of reforms in the region: 'I suspect that... in East Central Europe... the pendulum of normal politics will have to swing once in the liberal and once in the social direction before you feel that you have made it. The liberal direction... involves the jump start of economies... Opposition to this process is bound to arise, and it will be about the social cost of economic growth. At some point, in four or even eight years' time... other groups will take over. They may even be called Social Democrats' (Dahrendorf, 1990, pp. 71–2). In at least eight countries of the region (Lithuania, Poland, Hungary, Albania, Bulgaria, Romania, Moldova, and Macedonia) the electoral pendulum swung in the social direction, often earlier than the four or eight years Dahrendorf had predicted. The victorious parties were called social democrats, socialist, or 'democratic left'. With only one exception (the Czech Social Democrats), they were reformed (more or less) communists.

   The electoral resurgence of former communists constitutes one of the most fascinating aspects of democratic consolidation in East-Central Europe. The 'Dahrendorf hypothesis' has been commonly accepted as the main explanation of the pendulum effect in Central European electoral politics (Brown, 1994; Mason, 1996; Holmes, 1997). This point of view is based on the presumption that societies undergoing a rapid social and economic change bifurcate into the winners and the losers, the haves and the have-nots, causing massive feelings of relative deprivation, which in turn generates political populism. The hardships of transition feed retroactive sentiments – longings for the times of full employment and a reliable, if merely minimal, social safety net. Such reasoning hardly defies common sense and seems at least reasonable. As Mateju, Rehakova and Evans (1999) point out, there are at least four processes in post-communist societies undergoing transition to the market that reinforce class interests (and, by implication, class, that is economically based, voting):

1. The emergence of a class of proprietors and entrepreneurs.
2. The increase in class consciousness of the workers, deprived of the special position given to them by communist ideology and threatened by rationalization of industrial production and employment.
3. Growing economic inequality.
4. The strengthening of materialist (as opposed to post-materialist) values, due to a rapid transition from an economy of shortage to an economy of abundance.

In the authors' view, this analysis applies to all postcommunist polities in Central Europe. The authors recognize the initial role of other (that is, cultural) factors, but predict that the outlined processes 'create conditions for the strengthening of class-based voting behaviour and the crystallization of the "traditional" left-right political spectrum' (ibid., p. 235). They find empirical evidence to support these predictions for the Czech Republic.

Many other authors have accepted similar point of view, while trying to incorporate to their analytical schemes those other, ideological and/or cultural factors. Herbert Kitschelt (1992) expected that the party competition space in the early stages of transition to market economy would be defined by two cross-cutting cleavages, between market versus distributive and libertarian/cosmopolitan versus authoritarian/particularist political strategies (or, to put it differently: the first cleavage would pit the supporters of the free market against those preferring state protectionism, the second would reflect the opposition between pro-Western, inclusive, open attitudes on the one hand and the ones that are more exclusive and focused on protection of a given group's ethnic, religious, and/or cultural identity on the other). With the progress of transition, the orthogonal relationship between these two dimensions should be supplanted by a parallel one, with the ends of political continuum defined, as in Western Europe, by a libertarian and distributive left and an authoritarian and pro-market right. Evans and Whitefield (1993), accepting the central premises of Kitschelt's analysis, have pointed out that the actual patterns of party competition may be country specific, involving at least three dimensions: socio-economic, ethnic (in multi-ethnic states), and valence (like the issue of nation-building in breakaway states). For most states in the region they predicted that socio-economic cleavages should become (in the absence of sizeable ethnic minorities or the break-away factor) the main basis for party competition. Unlike Kitschelt, they expected that economic and cultural liberalism would remain associated with each other in East-Central Europe, hence specific issue dimensions would be defined by redistributive, authoritarian, anti-Western attitudes vying with pro-market, liberal, cosmopolitan ones. Szelenyi, Fodor and Hanley (1997) observed that many intellectuals have interpreted the political developments of the 1980s and 1990s in Central Europe in terms of a conflict between conservative and liberal values, dismissing the role of the socio-economic or left–right dimension. On the basis of empirical evidence from Hungary and Poland in the early 1990s, they suggested instead a 'theory of two axes', pointing out that '[w]hile the Liberal/Conservative cleavage is created by differences in values, the Left/Right axis is based on economic interests' (ibid., p. 205). All the cited authors agree that, as the transition to market economy progresses, economic cleavages of this kind will gain more a prominent role in determining the actual choice the voter makes in the voting booth.

This hypothesis, obviously, can be (and has been) tested empirically. However, its testing has been limited to those cases for which a body of reliable empirical data on voting behaviour exists. Such data are rather scarce for the East and the South, but quite abundant for Central Europe, in particular for Poland, Hungary, and the Czech Republic (see Markowski and Toka, 1995; Toka, 1997; Kitschelt *et al.*, 1999; Mateju, Rehakova and Evans, 1999). The available data seem to confirm that two major cleavages are particularly relevant for voting behaviour in postcommunist Europe: the socio-economic cleavage between the supporters of a free-market economy and those preferring welfare-oriented state interventionism, and a cultural cleavage between particularism and universalism. The latter may at specific times and places express itself as a conflict between the traditional and the modern, the confessional and the secular, or between exclusive nationalism and a more inclusive, pan-European orientation. It may also still reflect attitudes toward the communist past of a given country. Contrary to predictions, however, the data suggest that the role of this value-based cleavage is not diminishing with the progress of transition. The constituencies of the post-Solidarity parties and the postcommunist Democratic Left Alliance in Poland do not differ from one another in terms of their views on the economy and social welfare programmes (which is hardly surprising given the strong trade union component of both movements); what sets them apart are views on such issues as abortion or the public role of the Roman Catholic church (Jasiewicz, 1999). Similarly, religiosity is the best predictor of voting preferences in Hungary (Szelenyi, Fodor and Hanley, 1997). These attitudes are also reflected in the actions of political elites. It is not coincidence that after the 2002 Czech elections the Social Democrats rejected the option of a coalition with another left-wing party, the Communists. This coalition would have enjoyed a comfortable majority in the parliament, yet the Social Democrats preferred to form a much weaker coalition with centrist parties rather than to break the isolation of the unapologetic Communists. Ethnic issues (such as policies towards ethnic minorities) still greatly influence patterns of voting behaviour in the Baltics (the Russian minority in Latvia and Estonia) and the Balkans (Albanians in Macedonia, Turks in Bulgaria, Hungarians in Romania, not to mention the situation in Bosnia or Kosovo). In Slovakia, the three major parties of ethnic Hungarians managed to overcome their differences regarding social and economic policy issues to form a coalition and enhance their chances vis-à-vis parties of the Slovak majority for the 1998 election. Across the region, political parties based on ethnicity are much more common than those based on social class (such as the Polish Peasant Party).

Still, the cases of successful resurgence by the former communists in the mid-1990s may be attributed, at least in part, to the social costs of economic growth. The hardships of the transition (which often reached the point of absolute pauperization), whether caused by the ultimately successful 'shock therapy' (as in Poland), or by a 'shock without therapy' (as in Lithuania or Bulgaria), caused widespread popular dissatisfaction and gave a competitive advantage to political actors promising quick and easy solutions. The former communists were as eager as anyone else to make such promises. Having also the additional advantage of control over the assets of their predecessors (from material resources to connections in the media), they were able to mobilize electoral support sufficient to win, either as a single actor, or as a senior partner in a coalition.

They could be prevented from scoring such a victory by some idiosyncratic factors, falling into three general patterns (see Jasiewicz, 1998): a relatively smooth economic transition without a dramatic decline in standards of living (Slovenia, the Czech Republic), the presence of an external threat associated with the communist past (Latvia, Estonia), or an effective non-liberal alternative (the semi-authoritarian regimes in Croatia and Slovakia).

But there were no quick and easy fixes for the ills of transition, and the victorious reformed communists were either forced to continue the reform policies of their predecessors (Poland, Hungary, Lithuania), or simply waste time and national resources (Bulgaria). As in any democracy, the scrutiny of unfulfilled and fulfilled promises came at the next free and fair elections, in which the postcommunists were defeated. As the vicissitudes of transition continued, the failures of political elites to resolve important problems, coupled with incompetence, corruption, and cronyism, brought about the general disillusionment and apathy of the electorate. The turnout in elections declined, sometimes dramatically (for instance in the Czech Republic from 98 per cent in 1990 to 58 per cent in 2002), while voter volatility remained high, with many voters choosing, often at the very last moment, to cast a vote for the 'highest bidder': a party or a candidate that was the most critical of the current government and promised the easiest solutions for the future. The postcommunists, who were among the first to use populism as a tool to enhance their chances in elections, after their tenure in government have become perceived as the part of the establishment, as rascals that must be thrown out.

Consequently, at the turn of the century, the electoral pendulum began to swing neither to the left nor to the right, but altogether away from the left–right dimension. Various anti-establishment and even anti-system parties and movements began to score well in elections. Perhaps the most spectacular was the victory of the National Movement for Simeon II in the 2001 general election in Bulgaria. The former king/tsar Simeon II (from the House of Saxe-Coburg-Gotha), who assumed the throne as a child during World War II and soon was forced to abdicate and emigrate by the communists, became the last hope of the Bulgarian people, disappointed with alternating governments of both the postcommunists and the Union of Democratic Forces. The movement was institutionalized just a few months before the election, yet it managed to win 42 per cent of the vote and 50 per cent of seats in the National Assembly. Simeon II returned from his exile and became prime minister under the name of Simeon Saxecoburggotski. Nonetheless in its policies Simeon's government has continued, by and large, the moderate course of reforms initiated by previous democratic governments.

Also in Poland an anti-system party, Self-Defence, has become a major player on the political arena. It was established in the early 1990s as a movement of farmers demanding more protective policies from the government. It was better known for its (often illegal) protest actions, such as road blockades, than for its electoral prowess. In the 1997 general election it won a fraction of one per cent of the vote; its charismatic and autocratic leader, Andrzej Lepper, fared only a little better in the 1995 and 2000 presidential elections. Yet in the 2001 general election Self-Defence mustered 10 per cent of the vote and 53 seats in the Sejm, becoming the third strongest party in parliament. Its constituency tends to be indifferent to the great postcommunist/post-Solidarity cleavage, or sometimes even openly hostile to both parties of this divide. It is composed mostly of people who may or may not be truly poor, but who in either case see themselves as the losers in the process of transition.

Populist slogans featured also prominently in the campaign of Young Democrats and allied parties in Hungary in 2002. The coalition led by the Young Democrats won the plurality of seats, but had to yield control of the government to the coalition of the postcommunist Socialists and the Free Democrats.

Political populism – understood here as an ideology that calls for protection of the 'man in the street' from economic misfortunes (allegedly caused by reforms introduced for the benefit of narrow elites), usually coupled with ethnic or religious particularism or even xenophobia (again, in the name of protection of the in-group against alien/forces and foreign schemes) – has been present in East-Central European politics ever since the beginning of the transition, and before. As early as 1990, Poland saw the bizarre presidential candidacy of an émigré entrepreneur, Stanislaw Tyminski. In Slovakia, Meciar was elected – not once – on such a populist–xenophobic ticket, and his popularity is still high (as evidenced by the strong showing of his party in the September 2002 election). Nor did the postcommunists cease to employ populist slogans in their campaigns. The rise of Lukashenko, a former kolkhoz director, to dictatorial power in Belarus is on an extreme example of the vulnerability of a young electoral democracy to populist demagoguery. In early 2001 populism played a significant role in the electoral resurgence of communists in Moldova. It is also omnipresent, along with ethnic xenophobia, in the slogans of the Czech Communists, who in the 2002 election collected many votes from the ranks of the former supporters of the Republicans, a far-right party (Pehe, 2002).

Almost all East-Central European countries aspire to join the European Union; eight (the Czech Republic, Estonia, Hungary, Latvia, Lithuania, Poland, Slovakia, and Slovenia) are slated for admission as early as 2004. Central European populists see in the European Union the epitome of their fears: free markets, open borders, supranational political institutions. The already ongoing public debate on the EU membership (which in many countries will include a referendum) brings to the forefront the cleavage between the particularistic and redistributive (in their extreme xenophobic–populist version) attitudes and the universalistic, liberal, pro-European ones. This cleavage typically combines an economic dimension (losers versus winners in the process of transition) with one that stems from differences in values, and runs roughly along the lines predicted by Evans and Whitefield. It may supersede other cleavages: the re-emerging traditional left/right, or the liberal/conservative. The electoral resurgence of political populism has recently taken place also in several current member states of the EU (to mention only Jean-Marie Le Pen in France or Jörg Haider and his Freedom Party in Austria). This obviously opens up avenues for most odd political alliances and configurations. At the very beginning of the new millennium, politics in Europe (not only East-Central Europe) seem to have entered a new (but not quite unexplored) territory.

11

Constitutional Engineering in Central and Eastern Europe

KLAUS VON BEYME

The study of constitutional practice and the processes through which constitutions are drawn up and applied was a major focus of political science in its early years, although it was one that tended to attract less attention as behavioural studies became more dominant. The end of orthodox communist rule in Central and Eastern Europe and the establishment of democratic regimes in many countries of the region was one of a range of factors that have brought constitutional issues and the process of constitutional engineering to the forefront of the political agenda. Constitutional arrangements play a large part in determining the relative importance of the different institutions that make up the new democratic order and deciding the 'rules of the game' by which they operate, while in some contexts the constitution-making process itself became an object of political struggle. To the extent that democratization in Central and Eastern Europe has involved basic questions of statehood, identity and citizenship as well as the very status of 'the political', constitutional engineering has been a particularly important part of the process of democratic transition in the region.

Aspects of Constitutional Engineering in Central and Eastern Europe

From a normative perspective the constitution-making process is often expected to meet certain requirements. These include a range

190

of features such as that constitutions ought, firstly, to be written by specially convened assemblies and not by institutions that are already in existence (Elster, 1998, p. 117). Not all the East European constitutions met this condition in the first round of democratization. Sometimes for good reasons: systems that chose a slow path of transition because a certain liberalization had already been achieved under the old regime, such as Hungary or Poland, kept the old institutions and constitutional texts and only amended them according to the needs of the process of transition. The idea behind this demand was that constituent assemblies should not be dominated by special interests, a view that reflected abstract and rather optimistic assumptions. Constitutions, in fact, are normally produced by the power of dominant groups with some compromises for minorities (von Beyme, 1968).

Elections to the constituent assembly ought, secondly, to involve the proportional system rather than follow majority principles. This rule did not always work in situations where postcommunist forces remained dominant, as they often hoped to preserve their power by keeping the old majority system – until they discovered that a proportional electoral law was more likely to assist their efforts to retain power. There is often a demand, thirdly, that a constituent assembly should not meet in the capital or a big city, which may apply to systems in upheaval – such as the 'Weimar Republic' in Germany which had to meet in Weimar because Berlin was unsafe. It was a certain proof of maturity that most East European constitution-makers did not need these precautions because no illegitimate veto players were threatening the fairness of the constitution-making process. It is also generally regarded to be a necessary democratic condition, fourthly, that the constitution should be ratified by the people. But in situations where constitutional engineering takes place on the basis of a political 'pact', this was not always feasible. Referendums can sometimes – as in Russia or Romania – be a means of concealing the shortcomings of the constitution-making process.

The process of institution-building normally began with the drafting of a new constitution. Constitutions contain the meta-rules of a system which are accepted by most of the groups supporting the new regime. The third wave of democratization in Europe after 1989 led to a paradoxical situation, however: the meta-rules had to be fixed while their foundations were not yet consolidated or agreed upon by many relevant political forces of the transitional regimes. More than in former transitions, the written constitution – which represented a return to democracy after an episode of dictatorship – was a promise for the future. What Philippe Schmitter (1992, p. 161) called the 'partial regimes' of the constitutional systems were barely developed: there were parties, but hardly a true 'party system', and the system of interest groups remained underdeveloped. The problems of constitution-making under conditions of non-consolidation were nevertheless less difficult because many constitution-makers oriented themselves towards Western models (Schweissfurth and Alleweldt, 1997, p. 54) – most frequently those of France and Germany. But the final result was remarkably coherent – mainly because of many systemic legacies from the socialist constitutions of the *ancien regime*. One exception was the introduction of a concept of human rights – in contrast to positive social rights. Most constitutions now recognized 'inalienable' rights that had been unknown in the communist period (see, for instance, Bulgaria, Art. 6.1; Lithuania, Art. 18; Poland, Art. 30; and Hungary, Art. 8).

There were two roads to constitutionalism in Central and Eastern Europe: pluralist bargaining or the imposition of ideas by a dominant group; and two kinds of outcome, in terms of reform of the old constitution or the introduction of a new one (see Figure 11.1). The figure shows little correlation between the nature of transformation and the road taken to constitutionalism. There were countries whose transition was characterized by pluralist bargaining but which did not manage to produce a new constitution and had to

	Pluralist bargaining	Dominant political group imposes its ideas
Reform of the old constitution	Hungary, Albania, Poland	Many CIS states
New constitution	Russia (1993) Czech Republic (1992)	Lithuania (1992) Yugoslavia (1992) Romania (1991) Croatia (1990) Bulgaria (1991) Slovenia (1991) Slovakia (1992)

FIGURE 11.1   *Institution-building and constitutional order*

amend the old one. But there were also many autocratic regimes, such as those of the CIS states, in this group. Countries which saw a clear rupture from the old regime in Schmitter's sense were in a position to impose constitutional ideas, either on the basis of a democratic forum (Czech Republic, Slovakia, Lithuania) or through the activities of reform communists who managed to stay in power in the first period of transition (Romania, Bulgaria, Albania, Serbia). But a new constitution in the second case did not necessary mean a new constitutional system. There was an intervening variable in the constitution-making game: where new states were created because of the disintegration of multi-ethnic communist regimes, such as in the Baltic states or in the successor states of Yugoslavia, the incentives to create a new constitution were stronger. The new democracies wanted to emphasize their old tradition, not only in resounding preambles such as those devised in Slovakia or Croatia. Only in two Baltic states, Estonia and Latvia, did the search for continuity lead to the alternative option. They amended the pre-Soviet constitution – abolished following the Soviet annexation in 1940 – in order to demonstrate the continuity of their democratic statehood.

Hungary and Poland demonstrated a further paradox: the more democratic the majority of citizens who pushed the system into early concessions to the opposition, the less radical was the degree of constitutional innovation during the first phase of transition. This paradox can be extended to encompass later attempts to construct whole new constitutions: Poland finally managed to produce a constitution in 1997, but it was not very well received. The new Polish constitution was endorsed by national referendum on 25 May 1997, but it was only accepted by a narrow margin (53:46 under conditions of a low voter turnout of about 43 per cent). The rightwing parties, Solidarity trade union and the Catholic Church had proclaimed a boycott of the referendum. The level of support for the constitution of the 'Third Polish Republic' did not promise much for its future success, and it placed the pragmatism of Hungary's constitutional inactivity in a more positive light.

Hungary embarked on a 'constitution-making endgame' (Arato, 1996, p. 31). A parliamentary drafting committee was established in 1995, on which opposition parties ended up with more representation than originally intended. The final draft of Hungary's new basic law was submitted to parliament in May 1996. Although the basic features of the system in operation since 1989 were changed only moderately, the amendments provoked a boycott of the sessions by numerous members of the Independent Smallholders' Party, the Christian Democrats and some members of the Hungarian Democratic Forum. A decision on the draft was postponed – most groups were able to live with the old patchwork that hardly embodied a constitution at all. Furthermore, the more clumsy the constitution-making process, the greater the advantages for the institution of the constitutional court which thus acquired quasi-constituent powers and channelled processes of constitutional change (Arato, 1995, p. 48).

These particular roads to constitution-making placed a strain on the constitutional myths that influenced the new democrats in Central and Eastern Europe: effective 'institutional engineering' was generally meant to be dependent on success in the transformation of the former planned economies into market systems. In the light of quantitative studies (Hellman, 1996, p. 56) there is little evidence for the validity of this assumption. In a comparative context 'stopgap constitutionalism', or simple postponement of the constitution-making process, had no discernible positive effects on the adoption of economic reform. Hungary and Poland are the high scorers in terms of economic achievement in spite of being constitutional latecomers. The Czech Republic, on the other hand, with the rapid consolidation of a coherent constitution and having stronger market economy traditions between the two world wars, did less well in the area of economic reform.

The continuity of elites and ideas has led in many countries of Central and Eastern Europe to a strong emphasis on plebiscitarian elements which had only existed on paper in the old communist regimes. In formal terms, the people can be involved in constitution-making in two ways:

- in the election of a constitutional assembly,
- in deciding on the draft of the constitution by a referendum.

This double involvement of citizens in exercising their constituent power has not been feasible in all cases. The fourth French Republic had shown in 1946/47 that ultra-democratic procedures do not guarantee a smooth bargaining process with good final results. On that occasion French citizens rejected the first draft for the constitutional assembly, and a second – more conservative – draft had to be elaborated. Even this shaky consensus lasted only a decade until the

	Parliamentary constitution-making	Plebiscitarian constitution-making	
		Assembly (ex ante)	Referendum (ex post)
Bargained institution-building	Germany (1949) Hungary (1989) Poland (1992)	France (1947) Italy (1948)	Spain (1978)
Leadership of a dominant group	Czech Republic (1992) Slovakia (1992) Latvia (1992)		France (1958) Lithuania (1992) Romania (1992) Estonia (1992) Russia (1993)

FIGURE 11.2   *Institution-building and democratization*

regime's collapse in 1958. Due to their urgent economic and social problems the former communist countries were under even greater pressure than France had been, with the result that many of them had no time for double consultation of the people. They opted for either parliamentary or plebiscitarian constitution-making (see Figure 11.2). Either path could be followed in a context of fairly pluralist bargaining by democratic forces or by the leadership of a dominant group that was largely democratic-minded. However, only a minority of cases followed the parliamentary path to institution-building.

The Efficient Parts of the Constitution: Regime-Building in Central and Eastern Europe

Constitutions normally contain four parts. Two shorter sections – concerning the 'dignified parts' of the constitution – outline the foundations of the regime in a *preamble* and sometimes add *state goals*. Neither type of declaration can really be enforced by law or 'constitutional complaint'. Two longer – more 'efficient' – parts of the constitution contain the *organization of powers* and declare *human and citizens' rights*. The latter have frequently also been counted among the 'dignified parts', and this is also the case with the social rights which many new democracies inherited from the former socialist ideology. On this basis two major decisions have to be taken in the process of regime building:

• the appropriate mix for accommodating regional and ethnic interests;
• the choice of an executive which combines both fair representation and government effectiveness in executive–legislative relations.

The search for the right institutional mix was most difficult in former federations like Czechoslovakia, Yugoslavia and the Soviet Union. All three federations collapsed – Czechoslovakia rather late in the process of consolidation. But even in non-federal systems some form of autonomy for the subsystems in combination with a fair proportional electoral system was inevitable.

The decision about an appropriate system of legislative–executive relations seemed to be less difficult. But the struggle in the Hungarian parliament to establish a popularly elected president in the constitutional draft of 1996 showed that even this decision could cause never-ending conflict. In the second round of democratization of former monarchies after World War I, in countries such as Finland and the Weimar Republic, the semi-presidential system represented an attempt to devise the republican version of a constitutional monarchy. But in the third round, after 1989, the practice of semi-presidentialism was dominated by a search for the 'strong government' to which politicians were accustomed under communist regimes. *Semi-presidentialism* can thus suffer from an inborn conflict of two potential majorities – that for the president and another for parliament. This does not mean that ultra-sceptics such as Juan Linz are right in maintaining that only parliamentary systems guarantee a reliable path to democracy. Poland has shown that a semi-presidential system, which under Walesa regularly humiliated the legislative branch with minor constitutional changes, could be transformed into just another variant of the parliamentary system in which Kwasniewski does not act very differently from a popularly elected president as in Finland, Portugal or Austria.

Least contradictory have been the constitutions of pure parliamentary systems existing in Hungary and Czechoslovakia. *Pure parliamentarism* with a president elected by the legislature has not, however, guaranteed a relationship free of tension between prime minister and president, as the relations between Havel and Klaus in the Czech Republic, or Goncz and Antall in Hungary have shown. Goncz did not accept the weak position assigned to him by the constitution, and the conflict between Goncz and Antall articulated the conflict between the social forces that maintained the operation of the system. In 1991 the Constitutional Court began limiting the president's powers. The conflicts seemed to be ridiculous and were reminiscent of the struggle for prestige in France between President Chirac and Prime Minister Jospin under conditions of 'cohabitation': who had the right, for example, to represent his country at international conferences? The compromise in Hungary thus resembled the typical solution of semi-presidential systems: both went to the conference of Visegrad.

In most Central and East European systems a kind of '*rationalized parliamentarism*' was developed in order to stabilize the executive branch, which includes institutions such as:

- the *popular election* of the president,
- *limitations on the vote of non-confidence* according to French or German provisions (a pure parliamentary system such as Hungary adopted – as had Belgium and Spain – the German 'constructive vote of non-confidence' – an apparent terminological contradiction in itself),
- *collective responsibility of ministers*: only Poland in its Small Constitution (superseded by the full Constitution of 1997) maintained the contradictory principle that ministerial solidarity (Art. 53.3) was accompanied by a provision for individual ministers to be dismissed by vote of censure. This contradiction served to strengthen President Walesa who could get rid of ministers who lost his confidence by mobilizing the parliamentary groups that supported him. The president could thus destabilize his government and impose himself as an arbiter. When Prime Minister Hanna Suchocka was toppled, the president – even before a formal vote of censure – negotiated with the Solidarity group and other foes of the prime minister. Solidarity then threatened strikes. This did not go as far as the mobilization of the miners by the first Romanian president, who was trying to put pressure on his prime minister. But in neither case did presidential actions serve the consolidation of parliamentary democracy.

Before 1989 the reintroduction of a *second chamber* was not on anybody's mind in Central and Eastern Europe. But when the president exercised czar-like powers that threatened to bring about political stalemate in Poland, the idea of a strengthened second counter-balance in the form of the Senate gained strength (*EECR*, Fall 1992, p. 13). Nevertheless, as in other semi-presidential systems, the second chamber was not really in a position to perform a function that is feasible mainly in terms of the operation of a federalist second house (as in Russia, Yugoslavia and Bosnia-Herzegovina). Second chambers continue to exist in Poland, Romania and the Czech Republic, however. Slovenia has also established a corporate chamber in the form of a 'State Council', which represents a combination of regional and functional interests. It was no accident that the Czech Republic had problems in establishing its bicameral parliament. Due to protracted struggles over details of the electoral mechanism the first elections to the Senate did not take place until November 1996 (Elster *et al.*, 1998, p. 95). The Hungarian parliament comes closest to the old British concept of 'parliamentary sovereignty'.

The real function of parliament is normally, however, dependent on the party system and its ability to guarantee quick and effective cabinet formation after elections. On the whole this has been achieved in a satisfactory way. The new democracies in Central and East Europe are different from those of 1945 which installed the long-lasting dominance of a single party leader in the West (De Gasperi, Adenauer, De Gaulle after 1958) and in providing even for the effective possibility of *alternative government*. This was facilitated by a unique constellation: as representatives of continuity the postcommunists had the chance to make a rapid comeback even in the countries considered most anti-communist (Lithuania 1992, Poland 1993, Hungary 1994) – a possibility which was excluded in Western Europe for the *ancien regime* conservatives after fascism. On the whole, *executive–legislative relations* in Central Europe developed much better than in Russia or even in Belarus with their overwhelming dominance of presidential powers. The more mature systems – with minor exceptions – chose the pure parliamentary system. Semi-presidentialism has not so far threatened the process of consolidation in any of the countries concerned. The hope of most of these countries to enter both NATO and the European Union contributed to moderation in most cases. But even in the parliamentary system of Slovakia, a president like Meciar could endanger this process of accommodation in Europe.

The Dignified Parts of the Constitution:
Human and Civil Rights

There is no consensus in any country on how elaborate a constitution should be. Mainstream views are determined by the fashions of constitutional mythology. Three waves developed three distinct generations of understandings. The first generation – represented by the Basic Law of the Federal Republic of Germany – wanted to stick to the conventional 'negative' liberal civil and political liberties. The second generation tried to include positive rights on the protection of human welfare, social security, leisure and housing. Even under the impact of East German constitutional ideology, the majority in Germany in 1994 was ready to accept such demands only as declarations among general 'state goals' in order to emphasize that they were not enforceable. The third generation of rights includes economic development, environmental protection and peace. It was not by chance that such attractive preambles and state goal declarations were more frequently used in the new democracies that had been accustomed to a propagandistic approach to citizens under communism.

Where the constitution was meant to be valid only for a transitional period it was normally kept short, as in Hungary. The Hungarian preamble thus emphasizes the commitment to facilitate the peaceful transition to a constitutional state while establishing parliamentary democracy and a 'social market economy'. The more coherent Czech constitution of 1992 was much more demanding and included '*civic society*', as part of the family of European and world democracies in its preamble. The most exuberant example of such a preamble was the Polish constitution of 1997. It demonstrated the stalemate between the forces in the country in such terms: 'Both those who believe in God as the source of truth, justice, good and beauty, as well as those not sharing such faith but respecting those universal values as arising from other sources' were invoked in the preamble. The reference to God did not pacify the conservative Catholic fundamentalists. The bishops found ironically that: 'God was defined in the Preamble as the source of truth, justice, good, and beauty. God so understood is a god of philosophers, and possibly masons, but not of Christians for whom God is, first of all, a God of love' (quoted in Spiewak, 1997, p. 92). True believers among the Catholics resented the presentation of materialism in the constitution as being no longer embedded in Marxism but one sneaked in by means of Western consumerism and hedonism.

In many constitutions (for instance Bulgaria, Art. 22, and Slovakia, Art. 31) *political pluralism* and/or the competition of parties has been codified. Hungary even mentioned that 'no party should exercise exclusive control of a government body'. The East European concept of a constitution was also different from that in the West insofar as it did not distinguish so strictly between the *public and the private sphere*, emphasized *social rights* with more enthusiasm than liberal negative rights, and incorporated many of the duties to which the citizens were accustomed under communism. The Czech Republic in certain respects is different. Its preamble is more liberal and directed toward a 'civil society'. It contains the anomaly (Sunstein, 1995) that no itemization of such civil rights is to be found in the constitution. The historical reason for this was the Charter of Fundamental Rights and Freedoms passed in 1991 by the Federal Assembly of the Czech and Slovak Republics. The Charter contained an ample set of rights, but also certain social and economic privileges in favour of the handicapped, women, adolescents, and parents raising children. Barely enforceable were provisions like those of Art. 28: 'Employees are entitled to fair remuneration for work and to satisfactory working conditions'.

Conflict between the two republics threw the status of the Charter into doubt. The Slovak Republic included the Charter with some modifications. In the Czech Constitution of December 1992 only a hint of the protection of such rights was included in Art. 3: 'Part of the constitutional order of the Czech Republic is the Charter of Fundamental Rights and Freedoms'. Czech nationalists had some doubts whether the Charter was really part of the Constitution. It was suspected that Arts. 3 and 4 were the product of pressure from the Council of Europe, requiring the guarantees of basic rights. The real pressure, however, came from traditional postcommunist forces who wanted the social and economic rights of the Charter included in the constitution. Whatever the doubts as to the legal status of the Charter, the effectiveness of the legal protection depended on the Constitutional Court established as the 'judicial body for the protection of constitutionality'. Since the Constitutional Court – unlike in other countries, such as Bulgaria – was included under the judiciary, Art. 4 must also apply to the Czech Constitutional Court. In many budding democracies – developing into 'defective democracies', normally emphasizing democratic participation more than legal protection – the status of constitutional guarantees remained unclear or unenforceable, but this was hardly the case in the Czech Republic.

Amongst the dignified formula that of the '*market economy*' – and most frequently the German version 'social market economy' and the combined form of the 'social and democratic legal state' – was part of many constitutions. All the other constitutions adopted some variation of the 'constitutionally legalized state'. The Anglo-Saxon influence was more perceptible in the formula of the '*civil society*' found in the preambles of the Czech Republic, Lithuania and Slovenia. The more the credentials of the nation-state might be doubted, the more the continuity was emphasized by lengthy references to history. Lithuania remained vague: 'many centuries ago', Slovakia, hardly ever an independent state, invoked the 'cultural heritage of Cyril and Methodius' and the 'historical legacy of the Great Moravian Empire'. Croatia even inserted a historical list of all the decisions made by the Croatian estates operating within foreign empires.

The *separation of state and church* has been emphasized in many constitutions. According to the predominant interpretation this is no longer an attack on the free exercise of religion. The privileged mention of a 'traditional religion of the Republic' in the Bulgarian constitution (Art. 13.3) is unique. It has no equivalent even in a dominantly Muslim state as in Albania (Art. 10 of the 1998 draft). Unique, too, were the good intentions devoted to the prevention of systems falling back into totalitarianism. Most *abuses of communist systems* were enumerated and forbidden, such as forced labour, censorship (Slovenia, Art. 1), and the death penalty (Romania, Art. 22.3; Slovakia, Art. 15.3; Slovenia, Art. 17; Czech Republic, Charter Art. 6.3). The right to life logically entailed the outlawing of death penalties (Bulgaria, Art. 28; Estonia, Art. 16). The right to life was limited by the addition that the death penalty is permissible 'until its abolition by a federal law'. The counter-reaction against totalitarian dangers led to a frequent tendency to include well-meaning provisions such as outlawing regulations that limit emigration (Poland, Art. 52; Russia, Art. 27; Slovakia, Art. 23), or forbidding deportation, torture, and medical experiments on human beings (Estonia, Art. 18).

In Eastern Europe the idea of 'civil society' was an important vehicle for opposing the bureaucratic communist system. Civil society is intimately linked to the notion of '*citizenship*', which is no longer understood as a question of who gets a national passport.

Citizenship in many of the new constitutions is linked to duties as much as to rights. In some countries the deprivation of citizenship was outlawed. Only in Poland did the provision that the president could deprive a citizen of Polish citizenship exist (Art. 41 of the old constitution, Art. 144 of the constitution of 1997), although it was expressed in terms of 'granting and giving consent for renunciation of Polish citizenship'. Following the example of the German Basic Law, the *constitutionality of parties* appeared in some of the constitutions of the new democracies (Bulgaria, Art. 149.5; Estonia, Art. 48.3; Poland, Little Constitution, Art. 5). In Estonia social organizations were also included. In most countries a Constitutional Court was established. But only in a few cases – such as in Bulgaria – was the Court directly entrusted with the responsibility for deciding whether the constitutionality of parties should be endorsed or not.

In most new constitutions the *protection of private property* was new. Poland (1997, Art. 20) emphasizes not only private ownership and cooperation between the social partners, but even creates privileges for small farmers: 'The basis of the agricultural system of the State shall be the family farm' (Art. 23). This statement was true even under communism – but this was precisely the problem. Poland was the exception: a country where communism did not do what communists normally did first, namely collectivize agriculture. Poland did not succeed in creating large and modernized estates. The surviving family farms are now endangered and can hardly maintain their existence under international conditions of growing market openness, while militant parties of small farmers create a problem for coalition-building in the Polish parliament. Perhaps the Polish provision should not ridiculed too much. After all, even Switzerland only recently got rid of a typical interest group article (23 bis) which promised to promote 'agriculture in the mountains'.

In countries with a certain continuity, such as in Yugoslavia (Art. 73), Bulgaria (Art. 18) and Slovakia (Art. 20.2), *state ownership* was protected in certain areas like mining. This provision was even applied to agricultural land in some of the succession states of the former Yugoslavia. Expropriation was usually excluded or placed under strict parliamentary control: 'The law will specify which property other than property listed in Article 4 that is essential to meet the needs of society, the development of the national economy, and public interest can be owned only by the state' (Slovakia,

Art. 20.2). Three vague general clauses raise misgivings that a wide range of possibilities for state property remains open. The Central and East European conception of property rights has been correctly described as 'trans-liberal' (Elster *et al.*, 1998, p. 84). The boundaries between individual right and institutional guarantees are frequently blurred in the new democracies. Rationalized parliamentary systems have been concerned with *governmental stability*, and the president has often been subject to clear rules of consultation in order to avoid giving too much discretion to the head of state (Hungary, Art. 33.3; Bulgaria, Art. 99). It was the Swedish constitutional reform of 1971 that first introduced this kind of provision. Although many new constitutions have preserved some *plebiscitarian elements* of the former socialist constitutions, the manipulative excesses of communist democracy in terms of recall (Poland, Little Constitution, Art. 6) or the imperative mandate for deputies (Bulgaria, Art. 67.1) were forbidden.

The most important test of the democratic convictions of constitution-makers in the new regimes was the treatment of *ethnic minorities*. There were declarations of the 'multinational people' (Russia, Preamble) or invocations of the 'democratic tradition of nation-building' (Yugoslavia, Art. 4) which recalled the rhetoric of the old regime. The treatment of different languages was the most important part of the ethnic relations. Sometimes an official state language was fixed (Bulgaria, Art. 3; Lithuania, Art. 14). Regulations were most illiberal in Bulgaria: Art. 36.2 and 36.3 stipulated that the 'study and use of the Bulgarian language is a right and obligation of every Bulgarian citizen'. In certain situations the sole use of the official language was a legal requirement. This was very much in the tradition of the Bulgarization of Turkish names in the 1980s, which did not stop at the cemeteries of the Muslims in Bulgaria. Less emphatic was the Slovakian formulation (Art. 34.2) which did not impose a duty but only mentioned the 'right of the ethnic minorities to learn the official language'. This did not rule out the possibility of conflict with the Hungarian minority, where tensions were as severe as those in the case of the Turks in Bulgaria. The Council of Europe even had to intervene because of an aggressive Slovakization of names. The most curious provision was found in the rump Yugoslavia. After forty years of propaganda for an integrated Serbo-Croatian language under Tito, the constitution under Serbian dominance restricted the notion 'Serbian' to two dialects written with Cyrillic characters. It was apparently those countries that were fairly homogeneous in ethnic respects that could afford to be most liberal – like Hungary.

Nobody can deduce the social reality of ethnic politics from constitutional texts. Ethnic relations can only be studied in practice. The Czech Republic and Hungary were most generous in granting affirmative action and offering financial and organizational help – also emphasized in the abstract in Romania (Art. 6) and Slovakia (Art. 34.1). But constitutional provisions are just an indicator of deficiencies in the protection of rights of ethnic minorities in those countries. Even a country like Estonia, which was the most developed in the Soviet Union and is considered in many respects as being mature enough for membership of the European Union, showed so many illiberal practices in its treatment of the Russian minority that European institutions had to intervene. Surveys have suggested that, while institutions and policies can quickly be adapted to European standards, the civic society that has to give life to such formal provisions is still underdeveloped. Asked who should be a citizen of the Baltic countries, 34 per cent of the Estonians and 43 per cent of the Latvians were willing to accept only pre-1940 residents of the country – thus excluding all Russians. Only Lithuanians (12 per cent) were more generous in this respect (Rose, 1997, p. 43) – but conditions are different in that country, and there is no Russian minority that often forms a majority in major cities.

The legacies of the old regimes have been most visible in the *declaration of social rights and citizens' duties* in the Constitution. Poland (Little Constitution, Art. 77) promised to support the 'creative intelligentsia'. Under early communism in East Germany, the constitution of the Land Saxony-Anhalt in 1946 stipulated the 'right of youth to pleasure' – a fairly ridiculous variation of the old principle of 'pursuit of happiness'. One could ask why only young people have this right? Most constitutions after 1989 therefore generalized and neutralized the same idea, mentioning just a 'right to pleasure'. Under communism many citizens had abused this right even during working hours.

Environmental policy has also been a feature of constitutions in the West, but mainly as the declarations of a state goal. When postcommunist countries accepted the 'right to an auspicious environment' in their constitutions, they transformed it immediately into a duty: 'Everyone is obliged to protect and enhance the environment and the cultural heritage' (Slovakia, Art. 44.2). Duties like military service were normal, though rarely mentioned in Western constitutions.

But a duty to pay taxes was discovered under the new market conditions (Romania, Art. 53). The combination of social rights and political duties can develop coercive aspects if the system develops in the direction of illiberal democracy. Some constitution-makers, as in the Czech Republic (Charter 41.1) and in Slovakia (Art. 51), were aware of the fact that the social rights 'can be claimed only within the limits of the law that execute these provisions'.

There is an old constitutional debate surrounding the idea that such rights should not therefore be mentioned in the constitution (the Basic Law in Germany), and that those reformers who emphasize the necessity of such declarations do so mostly as a reminder for legislators. Under conditions of democratic non-consolidation such positive rights tend to shift the centre of activity for implementation from the courts to the executive. The excessive enumeration of these duties was an *ancien regime* legacy, although military service and tax-paying seem to be normal obligations. But Poland in 1997 not only added environmental protection – as many former postcommunist constitutions did – but also 'loyalty to the Republic of Poland and concern for the common good' (Art. 84).

Protection of Rights and Constitutional Courts

The protection of rights was a major issue after the collapse of communism. It has been said (Posner, 1995, p. 72) that we romanticize rights and that there is a good deal of 'rights fetishism'. This ideological approach to a 'civic religion' of rights was unavoidable in postcommunist regimes. Austria was the torchbearer for introducing constitutional courts into the constitution. There was a similar tradition in the old German Empire and a codification for such an institution featured in the revolutionary constitution of Frankfurt in 1848. The German model created in 1949 established a wider range of 'judicial review' than the Supreme Court in the USA, and this was widely adopted by new democracies from Spain to Russia. In Central and Eastern Europe the 'Austrian model' was popular in because it was better equipped than the US version to supervise the separation of powers and relations between the public agencies. The only drawback was that the US judicial review systems seemed to be more appropriate to oversee the defence of individual rights. The Supreme Court was no special constitutional court. In Central and East Europe it was agreed from the outset that the constitutional courts should be separated from the ordinary court system. Sometimes – as in Bulgaria and Albania – it became part of the constitutional arrangements further to the chapters on the judiciary.

There are two options for the protection of human and civil rights: judicial review, and the more patrimonial way that developed from an established 'right to petition' in the Scandinavian countries, expressed in the person of the *ombudsman*. Poland has combined the two traditions, which had frequently been considered incompatible, and had already created an ombudsman (Art. 208) besides the Constitutional Court in the closing months of the communist regime. The outgoing regime did not anticipate how effective such an office could be even under authoritarian conditions, as the first ombudsman for 1988–92, Ewa Letowska (1995, p. 63), stated in the first evaluation of the new office. The cooperation of the two institutions, the ombudsman and the Constitutional Court – as well as the High Administrative Court – was also better than expected. The ombudsman was the most active agency in submitting complaints to the Tribunal. The office has pushed Polish courts to apply international human rights standards by looking for precedents in legal decision-making at the Strasbourg Court. The ombudsman, moreover, contributed to the instruction of the public on the rule of law and the principles of a civil society. This is especially important in dealing with the bureaucracies, which mostly worked in the spirit of the old regime. The cooperation was, however, not always marked by full harmony, and clashes occurred between the ombudsman and public prosecutor (Jaster, 1994, pp. 113ff, 144f). There are also ombudsmen as a parliamentary auxiliary institution in Romania (Arts. 55–7), Slovenia (Art. 159), Ukraine (Art. 55.3) and Hungary (Art. 32B), where ombudsmen are also provided for national and ethnic minorities.

The principle of *judicial review* by constitutional courts was introduced in some Central and East European countries before the end of communism, although the principle was obviously not compatible with the hegemonic claims of the party. In Poland the constitution was amended as early as 1982, and the Constitutional Court began to work in 1986. In the first year of its existence it issued seven sentences (Garlicki in Landfried, 1988, p. 208). The Hungarian Constitutional Court earned the highest marks for its activities, although the possibility of the public raising cases for its jurisdiction placed an unusual burden on the shoulders of the judges. Most of them were theoreticians and not used to serving as judges, because most of those with judicial experience had been compromised in the communist period. Therefore, even in Hungary a further professionalization of judges will have to take place for democracy to be further consolidated (Brunner, 1993; Majoros, 1993). The recruitment problem was, however, a problem that faced just one country. Judges are generally badly trained and courts have an overload of cases. Most of the lawyers have a rather passive perception of their role. The *dominance of the procuracy*, which monopolized the procedure under communist conditions, has yet to be fully overcome (Petrova, 1996, pp. 67, 70). Poles have increasingly turned, therefore, to the European Tribunal of Human Rights because the courts in Poland are overburdened with cases (Spiewak, 1997, p. 95).

Traditions of arbitration and the 'outsourcing' of issues have to be learned in the process of consolidating civil society in Central and East Europe. If the Constitutional Court is mentioned in the constitution outside the context of the judiciary – as in Bulgaria Art. 147 – this could mean that it is considered more as a political institution. But in no Central and East European country has the Court pretended to a rule that was comparable with that of the Russian Constitutional Court under Valerii Zorkin until 1993 (see von Beyme, 2001a, pp. 111ff). Consequently most constitutional courts – with the exception of Albania, Yugoslavia and partly Belarus – do not act on their own initiative. Most constitutional courts are competent to intervene in conflicts above the jurisdiction of other state institutions. In most systems only state organs have the right of complaint, and only in Hungary has the institution of a popular right to complain (*Popularklage*) been institutionalized.

An important contribution to the development of civil society has been the introduction of the '*constitutional complaint*', first developed in Germany. Half of the new democracies inserted procedures for constitutional complaint into the Constitution (Albania, 1998, 174i; Croatia, Art. 125; Poland, Art. 79.1; Slovakia, Art. 127 – although not in this case against court decisions; Slovenia, Art. 160; and the Czech Republic, Art. 87.1d). In Poland Art. 79 introduced the possibility that 'everyone whose constitutional rights and freedoms have been infringed shall have the right of appeal to the Constitutional Tribunal for its judgment on the conformity to the Constitution of a statute or another normative act.' Wisely enough, this possibility did not apply to the imputed infringement of citizens' social rights (Arts. 80, 81). When the new constitution was passed the first ombudswoman of Poland had some doubts about this important mechanism. She expected a large number of complaints – accompanied by growing social impatience because of lengthy deliberations, and even aggressive responses from citizens when complaints were not accepted by the Constitutional Tribunal (Letowska, 1997, p. 81). All these misgivings were justified in the light of German experience. But there was some comfort from its base in Karlsruhe: in spite of all these shortcomings in the process of constitutional complaint it did not undermine the position of the prime court when public trust is evaluated by opinion surveys.

The old elites – who still constituted a majority in the 1990s amongst staff in the middle ranges of the institutional network – in the long run will discover that Constitutional Courts have certain advantages. In democratic systems they perform important functions in the area of 'blame-sharing'. Government alone is not responsible for certain unavoidable but unpopular measures which have to be taken in order to consolidate democracy. *Fairness* is an important principle on the road of democratic institution-building. *Efficiency* is another one – which is normally underrated in the first period of democratization. In the first instance new democracies normally pay most attention to the legitimacy of the new order and only in the second place direct their attention to the principle of efficiency. This does not only apply to the first two branches of government in new democracies. All branches have to develop a sense for the '*costs of liberty*', and recognition of the negative liberties implies a public machinery for the protection of rights and means for their enforcement. This involves the activities of the police, prosecutors, judges and lawyers. The costs of positive liberties in terms of social benefits have been studied extensively, but little is known about the costs of protecting and enforcing negative liberties, which were safeguarded under communism by the provisions of a generally repressive system (Posner, 1995, p. 72).

Conclusion

'Transitology' has sharpened our perspectives on a certain trade-off between constitutionalism and democracy, between the protection of rights and the possibilities for participation. The communist legacy has emphasized participation rather than the protection of rights, although communist constitutions contained an impressive list of rights on paper – which is where they mostly remained. Weak constitutionalism may complement democracy by maintaining a high level of stability in social decision-making. Strong constitutionalism may correspondingly conflict with democracy because there can be too many immunities and too much inertia for social decision-making to be effective (Lane, 1996, p. 264). The necessary balance between constitutionalism and democracy has not yet been found in most of the new democracies in Central and Eastern Europe. Some sceptics thought at the outset that positive guarantees of rights in participatory democracy could never fully be reconciled with negative guarantees of rights under liberal constitutionalism. Liberal democracy tends to be rational, limiting the possibilities of participatory democracy. By autonomous decision liberal democracy thus fetters itself – like Ulysses – in order to prevent the self-destruction of the system (Merkel, 1999, p. 370).

According to Freedom House statistics, 56 countries can be classified as illiberal democracies – lying between consolidated democracy and autocracy. Most of them emphasize political participation more than the protection of civil rights. Russia (and most CIS member states) and Slovakia were classified as '*illiberal democracies*' at the end of the century (Merkel, 1999). Most of the Central and East European countries had already achieved the level of '*liberal democracy*' by this stage, however. Only Albania, Bulgaria, Yugoslavia, Romania, and Ukraine remained '*defective democracies*', a sub-type of the 'illiberal' category. Russia was also mentioned among the delegative democracies in the first years of its existence. Estonia and Latvia – because of their treatment of the Russian minority – originally received the label of '*exclusive democracy*'. Belarus, alone among European states, was clearly '*autocratic*'. In most of these negative cases not even basic democratic rights are fully guaranteed, and elections are generally 'free but not fair'. In an early classification which puts '*anocracy*' at the centre of attention – a mixture of anarchy and autocracy (Gurr, 1991) – there are various intermediate stages between illiberal autocracy and liberal democracy. A classification by von Beyme (1996, p. 167) has also shown that regimes change. Romania and Bulgaria in the new century seem to have improved their position and moved towards democracy (Merkel *et al.*, 2002, p. 182);

the same holds true for Slovakia and Bulgaria. The aim of integration within the EU provides an important degree of momentum for these rapid changes. As a broad outcome, the development of a balance between the principles of democracy and constitutionalism in Central and Eastern Europe is already quite impressive.

PART THREE

Issues of Public Policy

12

Managing Transition Economies

GEORGE BLAZYCA

The sudden collapse of communism in Central and Eastern Europe in 1989 took most observers, and many local political activists, by surprise. It was a surprise mingled with excitement and, for the most part, joy. The newly emerging political elites in Central European countries quickly asserted that after their unwilling participation in the failed experiment of communism it was time to put things right, to 'return to Europe' and to Western values in political and economic life. Western living standards also had considerable allure and the idea that the market would quickly deliver that better life appeared to be compelling.

General commitments on policy direction, of course, were easy to make. The more thorny question was how transition should be achieved. At that time a greatly self-assured West, its confidence boosted by the collapse of 'actually existing socialism', the only competitor system on the globe, provided ready recipes. In the economic sphere the transition had to be from plan to market. It should be achieved quickly for fear of slippage and a return to a species of communism and central planning or something worse. The route map was elaborated in what became known as the 'Washington Consensus'. To a greater or lesser extent that package set the scene for economic policy in East-Central Europe until the late 1990s. But by the end of the decade, as it became apparent that most postcommunist economies were still far from the transition destination (whatever that was), the usefulness of the earlier consensus was increasingly questioned.

In this chapter we begin with a review of the Washington Consensus before moving to a more detailed account of the transition experience, focusing on some striking and perhaps unexpected outcomes, before concluding with a brief discussion of some issues likely to be important for the future.

The Washington Consensus

Transition begins with collapse. The Soviet-style centrally planned economy, whose weaknesses had been dissected for decades both in and outside the region, a system that had been extensively patched up by economic reformers, finally stopped working. In the 1980s economic growth decelerated sharply in the USSR. Elsewhere it was grinding to a halt. In explaining that collapse some authors emphasized mainly economic factors, like system complexity and lack of adaptability (Nove, 1977; Ellman, 1989; Csaba, 1995); others identified more political aspects, especially the failures associated with a lack of genuine democratization (Dobb, 1970; Ticktin, 1993); and others still combined the two in a thesis of sheer systemic exhaustion (Wiles, 1982).

It is worth focusing for a moment on the late 1980s where hindsight perhaps encourages us to slip too easily into something of a *fin de siècle* mood. Nevertheless deepening chaos was a reality throughout much of the region – whether in the USSR as the unintended result of Gorbachev's *perestroika* and *glasnost*, in the GDR whose 'tourists' were massed in Hungary waiting for the border with Austria to be opened, or in Poland where the shelves in the shops were even emptier than usual. By November 1989 the Berlin Wall was breached and the long postwar division of Europe was ended. Although Western governments and institutions, especially international financial and economic institutions, were momentarily caught off guard, they quickly found a response. There was some talk of a 'new Marshall plan' for postcommunist reconstruction in Europe to be supported by the resources liberated by the 'peace dividend' – the reduction in arms expenditure that was expected to accompany the end of the Cold War. There was also some talk (although in Brussels not much) of quickly extending the European Union's umbrella over East-Central Europe.

But in the end no Marshall plan appeared and by the mid-1990s the 'peace dividend' seemed to have vanished. For most of the EU, preoccupied with its own internal structure, its single market and the difficult tasks associated with the introduction of a common currency, extending membership eastwards was the last thing it needed or wanted. A *Financial Times* editorial from late 1994 captures the mood. Commenting on the first of the European Bank for Reconstruction and Development's (EBRD) annual *Transition Reports*, the FT noted that the Bank was

> right to call on wealthy states, which already have functioning market economies, to help the re-integration of the transitional economies into the network of global trade and investment … the record of the EU in this respect leaves much to be desired. Mired in recession for the past three years and still digesting the Maastricht treaty, the EU has approached trade negotiations with nit-picking narrowness. It has also been far too ready to impose anti-dumping and other restraints on trade in 'sensitive' products, such as steel, textiles, and processed foods, which make up the bulk of exports from central Europe.

Instead of the big resources needed to kick-start modernization in the postcommunist economies, what the West offered was advice, advice by the bucketful. The Washington institutions, especially the IMF, took the lead, but most Western governments became involved in a variety of bilateral initiatives aimed at educating East-Central Europeans into the ways of the market. The early 1990s was a happy time for the 'travelling market and democracy consultants', many of whom quickly earned a poor reputation as they dispensed advice from international hotels in short stopovers in capital cities. Indeed, even the only new international economic institution specifically set up to foster development in postcommunist economies, the EBRD, was quickly embroiled in a scandal over the expensive marble cladding (imported from Italy) for its new London headquarters.

But what did the advice add up to? What was the Washington *Wash. Consensus* Consensus all about? The package as usually described had four elements: *stabilization, liberalization, privatization* and *restructuring*.

It was argued first and rightly that in those economies where inflationary pressures were strong, indeed so strong in some cases as to threaten hyperinflation, there could be no progress to building market mechanisms unless those pressures were extinguished. Hence the need for *stabilization*.

At the same time it was argued that postcommunist economies had to *liberalize* across almost all dimensions of economic life.

*(Contras of
Wash.
Consensus*

Prices had to be freed (notwithstanding inflationary pressures) because otherwise the market mechanism could not function. Wages, on the other hand, had to be tightly controlled to break the inflationary spiral. Economic activity in a wider sense had also to be liberalized, permitting the emergence of new small businesses, and of takeovers and mergers of those that continued to exist. There should also be a speedy move from the previously closed economy to an internationally open and free trade regime. This had profound implications for the domestic currency where convertibility was urged as another decisive break with the past, ending forty or more years of economic isolation. Liberalization had much to commend it and seemed in many respects a healthy tonic following the failures of excessive state intervention. While many of its aspects were essential (freeing prices, permitting economic initiative), others were more controversial (tight wage restraint, the complete and sudden opening-up to the world economy) as they were bound to impose costs on certain sections of society and sectors of the economy.

Privatization was a central element of the 'Washington package'. It was justified as an essential ingredient of the market economy, important in shaping 'correct' economic incentives, but it was also crucial in confirming the state's withdrawal from economic life. In due course it became the most controversial component of the Washington Consensus, highly contested and, as we will see below, errors were made.

The structural defects of the 'command economy' were well known: wasteful and anti-environmental processes producing goods not much desired but always snapped up; overblown industrial sectors and grossly underdeveloped services; top-heavy industrial organization with giant vertically integrated firms locked into a 'do-it-yourself' manufacturing culture a million miles from contemporary capitalism's 'just-in-time' or 'lean production'; the almost total lack of any small- and medium-sized (SME) business sector and so on. The need for *structural* change was clear, but unlike stabilization, liberalization and privatization, all of which could in theory be completed almost overnight, it would take time and money.

Because of its one-sidedly free market emphasis the Washington Consensus came to epitomize the 'neo-liberal' approach to postcommunist economic reconstruction. It set broad parameters on policy choice even if the detailed experiences of countries across the region showed particular solutions could vary a great deal, a feature especially noticeable in privatization. But what it did most forcibly was to foreclose any more 'statist' approach to postcommunist reconstruction. Indeed one of the most severe weaknesses of the Washington Consensus was that it excluded the state from playing any substantial role in either promoting economic recovery or in market building. In this context a 'Marshall Plan' for postcommunist reconstruction would indeed have been difficult to implement. The deliberate downplaying of the role of the state was at once understandable and, as a policy element, immediately popular in most postcommunist economies. The mood of neo-liberal ascendancy, in the early 1990s, was pervasive and difficult to resist.

The first and most developed application of the Washington *Balcerowicz* Consensus took place in Poland in 1990 when the famous 'Balcerowicz plan' was launched to stabilize the economy and switch on the market mechanism. Other countries had later experiences with what came to be known as 'shock therapy'. But in all cases implementation sooner or later ran up against political barriers and economic results were rarely of the kind that had been anticipated. In the Polish case, for example, where the authorities predicted a short, sharp recession before better times, what they got was a much longer and deeper downturn. It was not long before political reaction forced policy adjustment. Difficulties in policy implementation highlighted the importance of political and social factors in postcommunist transition. Soon the notion became popular that transition was in fact 'path-dependent' (Hausner *et al.*, 1995) – that is, that the room for manoeuvre was much less than the neo-liberal approach assumed, and that it depended on the specifics of recent history, especially, in East-Central Europe on the reform history of the 1970s and 1980s.

The initial certainties of 1989–90 were wrapped up eloquently in political and social terms in Francis Fukuyama's famous article (later book), *The End of History*, and technically in what seemed an unassailable economic neo-liberalism. However the sheer diversity of real experiences across postcommunist economies soon opened up a much wider discussion on transition.

Transition Experiences

Two Striking Output Trajectories: East-Central Europe versus the CIS

One of the most striking aspects of the postcommunist experience is how a monolithic economic system which displayed strong systemic features regardless of nationality (the shortage economy existed wherever there was central planning) shattered into more than 25 pieces that soon revealed very different characteristics. Explaining such enormous variety is a major challenge. Many factors combine to play a part. First, 'starting points' are important. Despite the common features of the planned economy it is plain that the reform experience of the 1970s and 1980s must have been important in shaping subsequent developments. Second, the precise nature and mix of policies implemented after 1989 must also have shaped performance. Third, geography was another key factor; in particular, countries closer to Berlin tended to be energized by the warm glow that came from being close to the economic powerhouse of the EU (although the positive effects were less apparent in the former GDR, which became a part of Germany itself).

Before exploring the underlying diversity in postcommunist economic experience in greater detail we offer a stylized picture based on performance across countries and across the principal macroeconomic dimensions – output, (un)employment and inflation. First a word of caution: many other aspects also deserve consideration and some key socio-economic indicators, particularly relating to distribution and inequality, are reviewed elsewhere in this book. It is important too not to become 'mesmerized' by bald output figures. They overlook informal activities, not adequately captured by national statistical authorities, as well as considerations relating to the quality of output (important since output quality is generally assumed to have improved since 1989). Moreover there is much more to transition than simply recapturing the lost output 'height' of 1989.

Despite these qualifications, Figure 12.1 shows clearly that two postcommunist transition experiences exist: the Commonwealth of Independent States (CIS) experience, with an initially more muted reaction to system collapse but then a much steeper and more prolonged decline with the first signs of recovery appearing only in 1999–2000, and the 'East European' experience, with a steeper initial reaction followed by much earlier but slow recovery from 1994. 'Eastern Europe' is considered here to be the 'EE11' (see Table 12.1 for details), a group of countries with its own internal diversity, but on average, postcommunist transition implied a steep recession, bottoming out in 1993 when collective output was 21 per cent below its level of 1989. It was not until 2001, when the group recovered from 'transition shock', that its GDP was 2.1 per cent greater than in 1989. For CIS, however, output continued to decline

TABLE 12.1 *Postcommunist economies: output performance (1989–2001)*

	Output – real GDP (1989 = 100)											
	1990	*1991*	*1992*	*1993*	*1994*	*1995*	*1996*	*1997*	*1998*	*1999*	*2000*	*2001*
Eastern Europe	*93.2*	*82.9*	*79.3*	*79.0*	*82.1*	*86.9*	*90.2*	*92.1*	*94.0*	*95.6*	*99.1*	*102.1*
Albania	90.0	64.8	60.1	65.9	71.4	80.9	88.2	88.2	88.6	95.0	102.4	109.5
Bulgaria	92.9	73.3	64.7	59.5	63.0	67.3	71.3	76.2	78.1	77.8	80.7	84.2
Croatia	92.9	73.3	64.7	59.5	63.0	67.3	71.3	76.2	78.1	77.8	80.7	84.2
Czech Republic	98.8	87.3	86.9	86.9	88.9	94.1	98.2	97.4	96.3	95.9	98.7	102.2
Hungary	96.5	85.0	82.4	81.9	84.4	85.6	86.8	90.7	95.1	99.1	104.3	108.3
Macedonia	89.8	84.3	78.7	72.8	71.6	70.8	71.6	72.6	75.1	78.4	82.0	78.2
Poland	88.4	82.2	84.4	87.6	92.1	98.6	104.5	111.7	117.1	121.8	126.7	128.1
Romania	94.4	82.2	75.0	76.2	79.2	84.8	88.2	82.8	78.8	77.9	79.3	83.5
Slovakia	97.5	83.3	77.9	75.1	78.7	84.0	89.3	94.8	98.7	100.6	102.8	106.2
Slovenia	91.9	83.7	79.1	81.4	85.7	89.3	92.4	96.6	100.3	105.5	110.4	113.7
Yugoslavia	92.1	81.4	58.7	40.6	41.7	44.2	46.8	50.3	51.5	42.4	45.1	47.9
CIS	*96.8*	*90.9*	*78.0*	*70.4*	*60.3*	*56.9*	*55.0*	*55.6*	*54.0*	*56.4*	*61.1*	*64.9*
Belarus	98.1	96.9	87.6	81.0	70.8	63.4	65.2	72.6	78.7	81.4	86.1	89.6
Moldova	97.6	80.5	57.2	56.5	39.0	38.5	36.2	36.8	34.4	33.2	34.0	36.0
Russia	97.0	92.2	78.8	71.9	62.8	60.2	58.2	58.7	55.8	58.8	64.1	67.3
Ukraine	96.4	88.0	79.3	68.0	52.4	46.0	41.4	40.2	39.4	39.3	41.6	45.4
Baltics	*97.8*	*89.9*	*67.9*	*58.2*	*55.2*	*56.5*	*58.8*	*63.7*	*66.7*	*65.6*	*69.2*	*73.4*
Estonia	91.9	82.7	71.0	65.0	63.7	66.6	69.2	76.5	80.3	79.8	85.3	89.8
Latvia	102.9	92.2	60.1	51.1	51.5	51.0	52.7	57.3	59.5	60.1	64.3	69.1
Lithuania	96.7	91.2	71.8	60.2	54.3	56.1	58.7	63.0	66.2	63.6	66.1	69.9

Note: CIS total includes all members, not just the European four itemized.
Source: UNECE (2002).

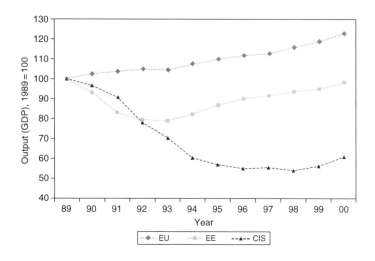

FIGURE 12.1   *Output trajectories after 1989*

until 1998 when it was 46 per cent below its 1989 level, and even in 2001 the region was a long way from any recovery.

Perhaps the most obvious lesson here is that notwithstanding various IMF packages applied at different times throughout the region, market-induced recovery, even in Eastern Europe, did not happen quickly. This was certainly not the anticipated outcome and the longer economies stayed stuck in recession, the more tarnished the Washington Consensus became. While one response was (and always will be) that the packages were not 'properly' implemented, another was that the policies themselves were flawed, and in particular that they overlooked the importance of institutional factors, including the various institutions – rule of law, effective corporate governance, financial transparency – that are needed for markets to work effectively.

Diversity within East-Central Europe – Output Paths

Leaders (Poland, Hungary and the Czech Republic) and laggards (Ukraine and Moldova) on the transition highway are frequently identified. Poland, Hungary and the Czech Republic started to come out of recession by 1993–4. By 1996 Poland had recovered ~~GDP~~ its 1989 output and was the first postcommunist economy to do so, ~~GROWTH~~ although it should be noted that Polish output in 1989 was still below its 1978 peak. The Czech Republic looked to be close behind, but a currency crisis in 1997 triggered a renewed downturn setting back recovery and the country only made good its 1989 GDP in 2001. Hungary did better, nearly getting there by 1999. At the start of the new millennium all three countries had at least some cause for celebration. The economic situation of Ukraine was however completely different – recession deepened in the mid-1990s with only the faintest sign of recovery even in 2001 when GDP was still almost 55 per cent below the level of 1989. Moldova's performance was worse still, the decline so steep that in 2001 its GDP was 64 per cent below its 1989 level. The difference in performance between leaders and laggards reflects a situation in which a market mechanism (of some type) is being fairly successfully installed in the first group but sheer hopelessness appears to prevail in the second, where whatever policies are adopted seem to be incapable of restoring economic dynamism. Indeed, in that second group of countries there is a well-documented retreat from the market, a 'primitivization' of the economy, and a step backwards in time to pre-market forms of exchange based on barter.

Diversity within East-Central Europe – Unemployment Paths

The 'transition' experience can also easily be captured in changes on the labour market and in particular in unemployment. Here the broad picture that emerges across countries is at first sight a great surprise. Those economies with steepest and longest lasting output contraction have, until very recently, the lowest unemployment. Moldova, according to the data, lost two-thirds of its GDP over the first transition decade but enjoys full employment (with an unemployment rate of only 1.7 per cent in 2001). Even Ukraine, despite its one-third output decline, had an unemployment rate (3.7 per cent) that would easily pass for full employment in contemporary Western economies. Any economic studies we might have undertaken in the past would not have prepared us for this, which can only mean that whatever economic mechanism exists in Moldova or Ukraine it is not a recognizable market species. But there is another surprise that has also attracted much attention.

Until 1998 the Czech unemployment experience tracked much more closely that of Ukraine than the group of reforming countries with which it is more commonly associated. In terms of output trajectory there is little difference between the Czech Republic and Hungary, but what happened in the labour market is a world apart. Hungarian unemployment, like Polish, rose rapidly as transition recession hit. In Hungary unemployment stabilized at a high rate (over 10 per cent) during most of the 1990s. Poland's faster recovery helped pull down its exceptionally high unemployment until the end of the decade, when it started to creep back up. Against the Polish or Hungarian pattern, which does make some sense in conventional economic terms, the Czech experience is very strange. Despite a significant output decline similar to its neighbours, it managed to retain full employment (with less than 4 per cent out of work) until it ran into the currency crisis of 1997. If a market mechanism was operating in the Czech Republic in the 1990s, here too it must have had peculiar characteristics. This is the more surprising when we recall that the Czech prime minister through most of the period, Vaclav Klaus, liked to present himself as the 'Thatcher' of the region.

In reality, despite his market rhetoric, Klaus presided over a system that until 1997 had successfully insulated itself from the need to adjust to output decline. But this could not for long be hidden from 'the market', especially foreign investors, in an economy so close and of so much interest to those investors. Limited economic restructuring in the Czech Republic meant that productivity growth was lower and competitiveness declining. Yet the exchange rate had appreciated strongly in the early 1990s, making matters difficult in export sectors. By 1996 the current account deficit had risen to a dangerous 8.6 per cent of GDP (a rule of thumb is that if it exceeds 5 per cent trouble is looming). This could not long be sustained and in May 1997 investors withdrew their support, sending the currency spiralling downwards. It was a significant development as the first occasion when a postcommunist transition economy had been disciplined by the market.

Diversity within East-Central Europe –
Market-Building Success and Failure

By the mid-1990s the 'emerging market' economies of East and Central Europe displayed a sufficiently great diversity to make it possible to identify those where the market-building process had gone furthest and fastest. This, alongside the Czech crisis (soon to be followed by the Russian devaluation of August 1998), drew the attention of the economic policy community to new concerns, much more to do with institutions and institution-building than with public or private ownership. Issues that had not commanded great interest in the early days of transition, such as corporate governance, transparency and corruption, became more fashionable. We return to them below. Perhaps here however, as we continue to try to assess transition 'progress', we should note the next momentous event in the economic transformation of the region – the selective invitation, from the European Commission in Brussels in 1998, to begin negotiations on EU accession.

EU membership was a strategic goal of almost all countries in the region, with Belarus, seeking union with Russia, a lonely exception. EU accession became the dominant medium-term policy concern and East and Central European countries were desperately keen to be viewed as *EU-converging* rather than as *emerging markets*. The European Commission made annual assessments of the candidate countries, in a process that was drawing to a close in 2002, according to how successfully they met the so-called 'Copenhagen criteria' for membership (see Chapter 14). Those criteria were partly political and partly economic but in their economic aspects they offered wide scope for interpretation, making them eminently useful to EU gatekeepers. One well-known expert, Marie Lavigne, summed up the view of many on the Copenhagen criteria when she wrote, 'in the end, the transition economies will be admitted to the EU once the present EU membership for political reasons deems such an expansion to be desirable' (Lavigne, 1999b, p. 60). Although the EC shied away from rankings and league tables a strong sense existed in 2002 that a first-wave EU enlargement would take place in 2004, as had been promised, embracing at least Poland, Hungary, the Czech and Slovak Republics, Estonia and Slovenia.

Quite apart from the elasticity or otherwise of the Copenhagen criteria most measures of transition progress across the region would probably select a similar group of 'front-running' reformers. If we look, for example, at success in finding economic recovery alongside stability we can fairly easily identify a group of countries (Poland, Slovenia, Hungary, Slovakia, Czech Republic) that by the year 2000 had achieved recovery (in the sense of getting very close to or exceeding 1989 GDP levels) and stabilized their economies (bringing inflation in most cases down to single figures). A second group (Estonia, Croatia, Bulgaria, Lithuania, Latvia) had significant stabilization achievements but still large output gaps, and a third group (Romania, Ukraine, Moldova) was far from stable and also in a weak situation with respect to output recovery. A two-dimensional summary of a complex transition process has severe limitations, but stability and recovery are certainly important accession considerations. Too great instability in the inflation sense and the European single market will not function effectively nor will there be much chance of bringing more countries into the single currency, a commitment that all new members must make. Too far behind along the recovery axis and the income gap becomes too wide, implying the need for transfer payments from the richer to the poorer, that are not easy to imagine on a large scale where bigger countries (Romania for example as an existing EU candidate or, perhaps one day in the future, Ukraine) are involved.

The vacuum left by the sudden collapse of communism would obviously quickly be filled with something. The conviction that lay behind the Washington Consensus was that 'the market', alongside liberalization and privatization, would not only fill the gap but also quickly produce results. To the extent that it transpired the process was much slower and more costly than most had expected, and it occurred only in one group of postcommunist economies, those Central European economies that were closest to the West and with the longest reform histories. Yet even in that group there were many 'transition surprises'. Elsewhere, in the CIS, the evidence shows that the post-planning vacuum was filled by other forms of economic relationships, mainly pre-market (barter) and pathological market forms (Mafia).

Transition Surprises

It became apparent at an early stage that implementation of the Washington Consensus was no simple technical exercise in economics. Most important, the political conditions had to be 'right', the central will to act strong, and parliament and major political parties won over (or at least promising not to rock the boat). Imposing stabilization shocks on any society is a highly dangerous activity risking political backlash. Poland became the Washington Consensus role model for shock therapy in the early 1990s only because of an uncommon configuration of circumstances. The new Solidarity government ceded an unusual degree of authority to its deputy prime minister and finance minister, Leszek Balcerowicz, an economist with an unshakeable conviction in neo-liberal solutions. With strong support from the Washington institutions the 'Balcerowicz plan' emerged, its key element price liberalization but stiff wage control, currency convertibility with sharp zloty devaluation, and a tight fiscal squeeze. This, the first well-developed shock therapy programme for postcommunism, was launched on 1 January 1990.

The effect was devastating: the Polish output decline was immediate and sharp (later, other countries imposed varying degrees of shock). As Balcerowicz has on numerous occasions affirmed, he operated in an exceptional political situation, in an 'extraordinary politics' where the Solidarity movement outside government placed the government under its protective 'parasol', at least for a few crucial months. Without that guarantee, and given that the Balcerowicz plan overshot most of its critical 'targets' (it was thought that in 1990 GDP would fall by 3.5 per cent and growth resume strongly in 1991 – in fact, GDP fell by 11.4 per cent in 1990 and by a further 7.4 per cent in 1991), it is hard to believe that the programme would have lasted for as long as it did (the eighteen months before political pressures forced a softening of wage control). The sociologist, Zygmunt Bauman (1994, p. 22), observed 'Neither the workers of the communist-built industrial dinosaurs, nor the state-tied farmers, got what they bargained for, but they got much which they did not bargain for (including mass unemployment and the cancellation of state credits).'

Why had Solidarity, a basically syndicalist movement, strongly attached, until almost the day before the plan was launched, to a 'social market economy', to social justice, and firmly opposed to unemployment and the unfettered market, suddenly have a change of heart? Why was the neo-liberal route to modernization so uncritically adopted? Why were the alternatives (some variant of the European social market) so abruptly swept aside? What was the allure of a market-dominated Anglo-Saxon economic model over the 'relationship capitalism' much more commonly found in continental Europe and, in Poland's situation, only across the frontier in Germany? *Good Question*

For some the answer lay in the self-assuredness with which the neo-liberals spoke at a peculiar moment in history when the global advantages were theirs. The recent memory of what state intervention in the economy looked like was also fresh enough to cast doubt on all economic policy projects that gave a role to central institutions. For others it was to do with the unevenness in the power relationships between the international (Western) financial community and new and weak governments in Central Europe. Others saw less reason for surprise. One view is that during the post-martial law period in the 1980s General Jaruzelski succeeded in so neutralizing and demobilizing Solidarity that the intellectual elite had a free hand after it was invited to share power in 1989. In this light 'extraordinary politics' was simply a different variant of authoritarianism. Poland in 1990 was a strange place. It had what seemed to be postcommunism's strongest and best organized workers' movement, but Solidarity-in-government soon became distanced from Solidarity-in-society. The government immediately adopted a technocratic posture, developing and promoting policies reflecting interests that had the shallowest of roots in society. It had, as Bauman (1994) puts it, the programmes but not the constituencies, while the constituencies that did exist expected quite different programmes. It was an odd situation. It would have been easier to understand the emergence of highly technocratic Balcerowicz-type programmes in other countries, those that lacked the strong elements of civil society that existed in Poland. Although it distanced Solidarity-in-society, without Solidarity and its parasol the Balcerowicz plan could not in fact have been implemented.

Why Solidarity split of its constituency.

Shocks, Therapies, Fraud and Corruption

The Balcerowicz plan soon acquired a broader significance, becoming the touchstone of what was needed in initial stages of the shift from plan to market. Its 'shock' aspects were evident enough and keenly felt in fast falling real incomes. Its 'therapy' aspects were supposed to lay the basis for an irreversible marketization of the economy, for entrepreneurship, growth, development and a better life for the great majority. Its 'model' qualities limited the economic policy debate, in those early days, to a discussion between the merits of 'shock versus gradualism' in stabilizing economies and embracing the market.

Shock therapy programmes wherever they were applied rested on fairly heroic assumptions, the most important of which was that economic agents (especially those we call 'firms') would respond to an economic medicine used before only in capitalist economies with well-established private ownership and functioning market mechanisms. But would state-owned enterprises react to the squeeze that was about to be imposed? Could new economic policy-makers succeed where generations of reformers before them had failed to impose on state-owned enterprises Kornai's famous 'hard budget constraint' (the idea that firms could not spend in any period more than revenue and borrowing permitted)? Could privatization be pushed through quickly enough to ensure that a range of new private owners (shareholders) were conjured into existence, a group that could better be relied on to respond to market signals and make the required adjustments at the level of the enterprise? Shock therapy programmes, reflecting the best of sophisticated (mainstream) economic thinking, were, for postcommunist societies, rather like autopilots without aeroplanes.

Early experience also suggested that 'therapy' might easily become dislodged from 'shock', especially if the former centrally planned economies did not respond in quite the way the policy-makers had expected. For example, the traditional 'soft-budget constraint' might have gone, but what replaced it in most countries was a huge growth in inter-enterprise debt that took most of the early 1990s to work out. It became clear that without reliable intermediate institutions in the financial sector shock therapy was likely to be seriously impaired. The surge, on the other hand, in (very) small-scale private enterprise to which we return below, must have been one of transition's more welcome surprises and the growth in informal economic activity a considerable relief given how difficult it was proving to achieve improvements in performance elsewhere. Many observers also noted that a flaw with shock therapy was that it failed to appreciate the importance of institutions to the working of the modern capitalist economy (Kozul-Wright and Rayment, 1997; Kolodko, 2000).

If stabilization and shock therapy, where it was needed, was difficult enough to manage, privatization created more intractable and certainly more long-drawn-out problems. Privatization at first looked fairly straightforward. Indeed the idea that the postcommunist state had something that could be simply freely given away to the people was a tempting prospect for politicians searching for constituencies and eager to demonstrate that transition had some clear benefits. The privatization experience across the region was hugely diverse and it, more than any other aspect of economic transition, created room for group interests to shape and reveal themselves. In many cases it was a highly contested activity.

After a false start in Poland in 1991, with privatizations following the British style (initial public offerings – IPOs – on a newly reopened stock exchange, too slow and inappropriate to local conditions where few people had savings to invest), the favoured Polish approach to asset sales became the worker–management buy-out (WMBO). It had the merit that the state could facilitate credits to smooth the buy-out process. It was also faster than the IPO route. But it was something of a transition surprise, this time as it turned out a welcome one, that in Poland, the lead reformer in the region with the leading regional reformer at the helm, privatization turned out not to be a speedy process at all.

Superficially attractive schemes for 'mass privatization' (a share give-away to the population – in principle the easiest and the fastest route to creating a private economy) were implemented in Russia and the Czech Republic long before a limited mass privatization experiment was launched in Poland in 1996. Between October 1992 and June 1994 some 22,000 Russian firms were privatized and 144 million citizens received their privatization vouchers, most of which were quickly disposed of for cash. As might have been expected, the immediate assessment of the architects of the scheme was that 'the ownership structure of Russian firms ha[d] taken a great leap towards efficiency' (Boycko *et al.*, 1995, p. 116). But by the end of the decade the prevailing view was quite different. Privatization had become mired in corruption, and the authors of the reform had themselves been found guilty of accepting huge sums in the form of advances on a book that had not yet been written from dubious business sources.

In Czechoslovakia an ingenious voucher privatization scheme commanded near universal approval especially for its speed (it was launched in 1992 and completed by 1995), until the crisis of May 1997 prompted a re-examination and Czech privatization began to be referred to in the Western financial press as 'botched' (Wagstyl, 1999). Its essential flaw was that it allowed shares in privatized firms to be accumulated by investment trusts that were in fact the puppets of the banks which were themselves still state-owned entities. Ownership was far from simple and clear and the incentives supposed to operate as part of the market mechanism were seriously impaired. In Hungary, in the early transition years, the state

[margin, handwritten, rotated] PRIVITIZATION EXPERIENCES

privatization agency sold off state firms quickly on a case-by-case basis mainly directly to foreign investors, its economy becoming one of the first to experience a significant increase in foreign ownership, but avoiding Russian and Czech type problems.

Privatization was clearly an essential component in managing economic transition. For shrewd operators it provided a once in a lifetime route to unimaginable wealth. In the fog of transition much scope existed to pick up valuable state assets at bargain basement prices. One interest group already to some extent practised in this was the *nomenklatura* of the communist period (the *kleptoklatura* as it became known in Poland and elsewhere). Russian mass privatization allowed a new elite, the oligarchs, to buy up the country's most valuable enterprises. In Poland, with its strong tradition of worker activism, privatization could only proceed by institutionalizing a significant share for the employees themselves. Indeed in the early 1990s some Polish observers noted that within the state enterprise adjustments were sometimes frozen by a 'Bermuda triangle' of managers, unions and workers' councils. But the triangle of interests was not going to last for long: the workers' councils were bought out with more tempting privatization rewards in return for self-liquidation; trades unions were everywhere on the defensive; and managers (or managers/politicians) were fast becoming the ascendant group in making the relevant decisions.

Throughout the region emerging business elites began to shape a significant new interest group, sometimes wielding political power almost directly (as did the oligarchs in Yeltsin's Russia) but always likely to have some influence over politicians. Indeed, with the passage of time, the murky nexus between business and politics, between legality, sharp practice and corruption, began to be viewed as one of the most serious and unanticipated barriers in getting to transition's market economy destination (at least before the Enron scandal in the USA reminded us that mature market economies can also generate high degrees of corruption). By 2002 no one doubted that privatization and especially 'mass privatization' had created massive opportunities for larceny. The apologist view is that all this was regrettable but there was no other way at the time and now things are settling down; a business climate much like that typical of Western economies is emerging and laying the basis for solid economic development. The alternative view is that those transition economies worst affected remain a long way from economic 'take-off'. There seems little doubt that privatization was in some cases rushed through with not enough thought for the wider institutions that were needed to mould emerging market economies into tolerable systems, meeting society's material needs and expectations, laying the basis for growth and development and doing it all in an equitable and transparent way.

Perhaps another, though welcome, transition surprise lay in the explosion of entrepreneurialism in many postcommunist economies. Again, this was more evident in Central Europe than in eastern parts of the region, the result of the interaction of a number of factors including transition starting points, whether or not a small-scale private sector already existed, the degree of genuine liberalization of economic life, and, perhaps crucially, the extent of pressure on the 'obsolete' sector to restructure. In this context it may not be surprising that a late 1990s survey across 23 countries found that in Poland almost 80 per cent of adults professed a preference for self-employment. This was greater even than in the USA (71 per cent), Hungary (50 per cent), Great Britain (45 per cent), the Czech Republic (37 per cent) or Russia (33 per cent) (Blanchflower and Oswald, 2000). Sometimes intentions are one thing, actions another, but the phenomenal development of the new private sector in Poland has been frequently noted: where Poland had 350,000 sole-proprietor firms in 1989, by 1998 their number reached 2.1 million (Rapacki, 2001). Given that remarkable development it seems odd that emerging business interests seemed unable to find a clear or distinct voice on Poland's political scene. There was, for instance, no Polish *poujadism* – the political movement of small shopkeepers in France in the 1950s. The group that espoused the market, and the need to build a new middle class, most consistently and directly was Leszek Balcerowicz's own Freedom Union (*Unia Wolnosci*) party, but in the September 2001 general election it failed to reach the 5 per cent threshold.

Returning to broad policy choices, after more than ten years of transition experience, the neo-liberal camp still asserts that it had good sense on its side. If postcommunist society had a choice it was, as it is sometimes crudely put, between 'Poland and Ukraine' – between 'shock therapy' and 'no shock–no therapy'. One problem with this view is that it fails to recognize how quickly Poland moved from shock therapy to a sensible pragmatism once it became clear just how frail Solidarity's parasol was. It should be possible in the light of experience to design much more effective transition strategies for those countries that have so far, and at great cost, postponed serious adjustment to new economic conditions. We know much more, for example, about privatization pitfalls. Moreover, the weaknesses displayed at the heart of the private enterprise system in the USA in the recent period, with deep-rooted fraudulent practices leading to the dramatic collapse of giant firms like Enron and WorldCom, underscore some of the flaws in the Anglo-Saxon model that was so enthusiastically embraced across East and Central Europe after 1989.

Unresolved Issues: Policy Dilemmas

After more than ten years of postcommunist transition the division of East and Central Europe into two country groups ('EU-converging' and 'others') was a clear feature of the landscape; but in general, the postcommunist experience, as captured in indicators of economic performance, was one of great diversity. The 'transition' has in all cases been longer and more costly than anticipated, with serious and unexpected setbacks especially in the Czech Republic and Russia where poor policy choices, at least with respect to privatization, were partly to blame. Nevertheless, by the end of the 1990s the best-performing transition economies seemed to be moving ahead at a good pace in GDP growth-rate terms. Then disaster struck. As the world economy turned down from the year 2000, Central and Eastern Europe was dragged into its first market-induced recession since the 1930s. It was unfortunate to have gone through 'transition recession' in the early 1990s only to meet 'cyclical recession' so soon afterwards in 2001–2.

Our brief overview has tried to capture transition across a number of simple macroeconomic dimensions with a few words on the underlying microeconomic mechanisms without which a market economy cannot function effectively. We should not overlook the fact that embracing the market has generated sharp internal differentiation within postcommunist societies, and this distributional aspect may be a strong influence on future developments. Spatial as well as social inequalities have been increasing. Material inequality is much greater than before 1989, and income, in 2002 and beyond, matters much more since access to important services such as health and education (at least in the 'leading' reformer group) is increasingly market determined. Unemployment hits society unevenly too, a transition cost disproportionately forced on the less well educated, older workers, those unlucky enough to be locked into heavy industry and those who live in smaller towns. Capital cities have acted as powerful magnets for foreign investment with other regions lagging behind. But the region as a whole, including Russia, attracts paltry sums of foreign investment – only $27bn from a world total of $1,300bn in 2000 according to the UN Committee on Trade and Development (UNCTAD) – much less than serious modernization requires. Across the region, within each country, there are winners and losers. The winners – the better-educated, the better-connected, usually city-dwellers – have often done spectacularly well out of transition, but the losers – typically farmers, pensioners, workers in declining state industries – have reason to be resentful.

If the first transition decade is judged to be broadly successful this is only so for one group of countries (those that are rapidly EU-converging) and even they display deep internal unevenness. One of the major problems for the future will be how, even in that country group, to prevent already existing divisions from deepening, either from a sense of social justice or because growing inequalities may ultimately threaten stability and become a barrier to further development. Reducing inequality should become a principal policy concern in the future and there are signs that the Washington Consensus is evolving to give it greater emphasis.

EU accession will in turn have a profound impact on the future of Central and Eastern Europe. Given the still steep downward gradient in income as well as huge differences in economic structures across Europe from West to East it is very hard to imagine a single currency 'Euroland' stretching from Glasgow to Bialystok, from Galway Bay to the Gulf of Riga, but that, nevertheless, is the medium-term objective. There may be a danger here that the rapidly EU-converging economies may be tempted to move too quickly into Euroland forcing the next severe deflation on already relatively weak economies when 'catch-up' in real terms is what is most needed. Existing Euroland members survived the pressures imposed by the Euro corset during the 1990s but in some cases it was a close call: Central Europe is incomparably weaker and it might be a mistake to be dazzled by the glitter of the € when *real* convergence between economies is far from complete. On the other hand if enlargement forces a greater flexibility and adaptability on the EU there may be some hope of accelerated economic development in Central Europe in the years ahead. There is certainly reason to believe that multinational investment in the region will accelerate, but whether this will lead to the 'screwdriver plant' (low value-added assembly operations only) or a deeper integration into the global economy remains to be seen. In an optimistic scenario Central Europe's delayed third modernization will take off and all 15+ EU members will benefit, although to varying degrees.

By the early years of the new century it seemed almost certain that an impending EU enlargement would be the main challenge facing transition economies as well as the Union itself. At one level EU membership might be taken to indicate that postcommunist transition was, for some countries, over or nearly so. On the other hand, the sheer disparity in almost all socio-economic indicators between the EU 15 and aspiring members in Central Europe suggests that the Union of the future will be very different from the EU of 2002. Whatever problems may arise will be compounded and indeed may be overshadowed by the consequences of the new frontier that will cut East-Central Europe, dividing EU from non-EU members. It would be a great pity if the Iron Curtain comes to be displaced by 'a thick glass screen' a few hundred kilometres to the east through which 'former Soviet satellites gaze wistfully at the promised land' (Stephens, 1997).

13

Changing Societies: Class and Inequality in Central and Eastern Europe

TERRY COX

Compared with political and economic changes, social structural changes tend to be slower and to take place over a longer time span. This means that the outcome of the changes is less clear than with political change, and that some current changes are not simply the result of the end of communist rule, but must be traced over a longer span of time. In examining social change in contemporary Central and Eastern Europe, we must distinguish between different types of changes. On the one hand there are the long-term changes. Some of these are common to modern societies in general and are the consequences of long-term modernizing processes such as industrialization, urbanization and the development of communications. For any particular country or region these changes are intertwined with the more specific effects of political and institutional legacies. For Central and Eastern Europe 'late development' and the 'transition to communist rule' have left significant legacies that separate their history from that of the West. On the other hand there are the more immediate consequences of the 'second transition' from communist rule. To a large extent these changes in postcommunist social structures are still unfolding. As Eyal *et al.* have commented, the societies of Central and Eastern Europe are still in a state of flux:

> Which groups of actors will be able to act collectively, where social cleavages will stabilize, where the boundaries around classes or other social actors will form, and what kinds of actions will be taken are all still being negotiated and struggled over. (Eyal *et al.*, 1998, p. 164)

Long-Term Social Structural Changes: Stratification and Mobility

As far as long-term 'modernizing' trends are concerned, Central and Eastern Europe has experienced similar processes of industrialization, urbanization, globalization and trends towards greater social and cultural differentiation to those undergone in the West. By the late twentieth century the societies of Central and Eastern Europe contained large urban populations; they had experienced considerable economic growth based on industrial development; standards of public health, literacy and education had risen dramatically during the century, and the vast majority of the population had access to basic incomes and employment.

At the same time Central and Eastern Europe has been shaped by its own specific history as a 'late developing' region in relation to Western Europe. Initially modernization in Western Europe trapped its eastern neighbours in a dependent economic relationship that limited industrial development to a few areas such as parts of the Czech lands, and cities such as Budapest, Warsaw and Kyiv. The population of the region was predominantly rural with large proportions engaged in peasant farming. The middle class remained small in numbers and lacking in influence, and was engaged mainly in administrative activity rather than commerce and entrepreneurship. Instead, the intelligentsia took on a distinctive position in society, either as part of the establishment in clerical, military or state bureaucratic positions, or in the formation of modernizing nationalist or revolutionary elites (Janos, 1982; Chirot, 1989).

Central and Eastern Europe only broke away from its dependent relations and developed a more autonomous and divergent path of development as a result of its transitions to state-managed economies, for some countries as part of the Soviet experience, or, for others, following the export of the Soviet model in the 1940s. The older historical legacies became mixed with the political and economic institutional arrangements of communist regimes to produce new and distinctive patterns of social structure, social stratification and mobility. These in turn influenced the paths of development taken as part of the transition from communist regimes after 1989 and subsequent attempts to establish liberal democratic institutions and market economies (Cox and Mason, 1999).

The influence of these different trends can be seen in patterns of social stratification and mobility. Central and East European societies have undergone some of the same patterns of changes in their socio-occupational structures, and display similar patterns of social mobility between generations to those of other industrial societies. However, at the same time we can also see some features that are distinctive for Central and East Europe, producing patterns of stratification and mobility that diverge from the experience of their Western neighbours.

The key patterns of development in the socio-occupational structures which seem to be common in the history of most industrial societies include declining proportions of the population in agriculture; a dramatic growth in numbers of manual production workers, followed by a gradual decline; a steady increase in the proportion of non-manual workers and professionals; and a decline in the numbers of owners of small and medium businesses. An evaluation of how far Central and Eastern Europe has followed these patterns has been provided in a recent study by Domanski. Based on large-scale survey data from Bulgaria, the Czech Republic, Hungary, Poland and Slovakia (and also covering Russia), the study traces changes in the membership of different occupational groups within families over three generations, from father's father through to father, to the adult grandson's first job and current post. For each country, by tracing changes in the relative size of occupational groups at different points in time, and the mobility of individuals between occupational groups compared with their father's and grandfather's positions and their own earlier careers, Domanski is able to show that Central and Eastern Europe has followed very similar broad patterns of change in socio-occupational group structure to those of Western Europe, although in some cases these are modified by specific historical legacies (Domanski, 2000, pp. 14–21):

- In each country there was a decline in the agricultural workforce as a whole, and, after an initial increase in the numbers of farm worker/employees following the introduction of collective and state farms, a subsequent fall in the numbers of agricultural workers during the later years of communist rule and across the period of the postcommunist transition. (This general trend applied even in Poland where the proportion of independent peasant farmers remained higher than in neighbouring countries.)
- At the same time there was a steady increase in the proportion of manual workers (including skilled and unskilled workers and technicians) followed by the beginnings of a decline in recent years.

- There was also a steady increase in the proportions of routine non-manual workers and of professionals and managers, although these groups decreased slightly in numbers in the 1990s.
- Finally there was a decline in the numbers of private business owners and the self-employed, followed by a new growth as part of the postcommunist transition.

According to Domanski, these trends reflect the emergence, first, of industrial societies in Central and Eastern Europe under communist rule, and then the beginnings of a shift to 'postindustrial systems', displaying very similar patterns of change to those of Western Europe. However, there are aspects of the specific Central and East European experience that affect this general pattern. First, the slight increase in the proportion of farmers since 1988 diverges from the Western pattern, reflecting the transition from communist rule and a change in policy direction towards the commercialization and privatization of farming under postcommunist governments. Secondly, the trends in the proportions of business owners and the self-employed, although superficially similar to the Western experience in some ways, have also been shaped by successive regime changes in Central and Eastern Europe. Rather than reflecting business concentration as in the West, the decline of the two 'owner' categories in Central and Eastern Europe was the result of deliberate decisions to eradicate them under communist rule. The recent increase in these groups reflects the new pro-business policies of the postcommunist governments. Finally, and perhaps most difficult to interpret, is the relative decline in the professional and managerial categories since the late 1980s. For Domanski, this is a temporary outcome of the political transition associated with the retirement of a section of the communist elite and an ensuing 'circulation of elites', which 'would have brought about a reduction in the relative size of the intelligentsia and managerial cadres' (Domanski, 2000, pp. 21–2).

Interconnected with trends in the socio-occupational structure, comparative studies of different industrial societies have also discovered cross-national similarities in patterns of social mobility and the extent of barriers to mobility. These have been identified especially between agricultural and non-agricultural sectors, manual and non-manual workers, and to entry into occupational elites of higher government officials, managers and professionals (Erikson and Goldthorpe, 1992). According to Domanski, 'the structure of intergenerational movements in East Central Europe strongly resembles the general shape of basic distances and rigidities in the West which we know from previous studies' (2000, p. 62). The social distance is clearest between the agricultural and non-agricultural sectors. Comparing data from Bulgaria, the Czech Republic, Hungary, Poland and Slovakia, low levels of mobility between generations were found in all of them. In Bulgaria and Poland more than three-quarters of all those working in agriculture were recruited from farming families, while in the other three countries, probably reflecting the greater modernization of their farming sectors under communist rule, the corresponding figure was between 40 and 50 per cent. The next biggest barrier is between manual and non-manual workers, with the most distinct divisions occurring in Bulgaria, the Czech Republic, and Poland, while the lines are rather more blurred in Hungary and Slovakia. However, a more divergent picture emerges in the case of elite recruitment. Here, only Hungary clearly resembles the Western levels of social distance, followed by Bulgaria, while in the Czech Republic, Poland and Slovakia 'access to the occupational elite … seems relatively open' (Domanski, 2000, pp. 62–5).

Social Change in the Postcommunist Transition

While the long-term trends in socio-occupational structure and social mobility highlight the changes currently taking place in the societies of Central and Eastern Europe that they share with industrial societies in general, research based on classifying populations by occupational groups may also obscure some highly significant lines of division that are currently emerging. In particular they may blur differences between classes and social groups defined in terms of competing economic interests, power relations and social outlooks. While some aspects of social structure are clearly influenced by long-term modernizing trends, competing social interests and political cleavages in Central and Eastern Europe may be more influenced by postcommunist economic and political transformations. For such questions, first we need to examine trends since the end of communist rule in patterns of inequality, and then to explore whether such inequality may provide a basis for class divisions and cleavages. In particular we will address such questions as whether new elite groups are emerging in dominant positions in the economy and the state, and whether the growing inequalities associated with a market economy are leading to the creation of an 'underclass' in chronic poverty and long-term unemployment.

Income Distribution and Inequality

As George Blazyca shows in the previous chapter, growing differences are emerging especially between the 'EU-converging countries' of Central Europe and the Baltic area and the rest of Eastern Europe. During the first half of the 1990s, all the countries of Central and Eastern Europe shared similar experiences of the 'transition recession' that resulted from the development of a market economy. However, the duration and depth of that crisis varied considerably from country to country, with differing consequences for changing social patterns. While the Central European economies experienced shorter recessions and began to recover in the mid-1990s, the decline continued in the CIS countries until later in the decade. The decline in output had severe consequences for the income of the population. This can be seen in Table 13.1,

TABLE 13.1 *Percentage changes in per capita income during economic transition*

	National accounts data	Household budget data
Eastern Europe		
Bulgaria (1989–93)	n.a.	−45
Czech Republic (1988–93)	−7	−12
Hungary (1987–93)	+1	−26
Poland (1987–93)	−11	−26
Romania (1989–94)	−18	−43
Slovakia (1988–93)	−29	−29
Slovenia (1987–93)	+20	+8
Baltic states		
Estonia (1988–94)	n.a.	−37
Latvia (1988–95)	n.a.	−45
Lithuania (1988–94)	−44	−42
CIS		
Belarus (1988–95)	−30	−44
Moldova (1988–93)	−67	−67
Ukraine (1988–95)	−64	−62

Source: adapted from Milanovich (1998, p. 34).

which shows changes in income per head according to two main measures, using national accounts and household budget surveys. Reflecting their longer period of declining growth, the former Soviet states show greater declines in income per capita than in the former Eastern Europe, with only Slovenia experiencing a rise in average incomes during the transition period.

These different experiences of transformation have had different consequences for patterns of social stratification and inequality. Declines in output and per capita income have affected different sections of the population in different ways, with the result that the transition has been accompanied by increasing income inequality. A widely accepted method of measuring income distribution is the Gini coefficient, which indicates the degree of income inequality, in this case between individuals, on a scale ranging from the hypothetical extremes of 0, representing perfect equality, to 1, representing the complete monopolization of all income by one person.

According to the data in Table 13.2, changes in levels of inequality were already becoming apparent in the first half of the 1990s, but with different patterns emerging in different countries. On the

TABLE 13.2   *Changes in Gini coefficients for per capita income*

	1987–90	*1993–4*	*1996–8*
East Central Europe and Baltic	*0.23*	*0.29*	*0.33*
Bulgaria	0.23	0.38	0.41
Croatia	0.36	–	0.35
Czech Republic	0.19	0.23	0.25
Estonia	0.24	0.35	0.37
Hungary	0.21	0.23	0.25
Latvia	0.24	0.31	0.32
Lithuania	0.23	0.37	0.34
Poland	0.28	0.28	0.33
Romania	0.23	0.29	0.30
Slovenia	0.22	0.25	0.30
CIS	*0.28*	*0.36*	*0.46*
Armenia	0.27	–	0.61
Belarus	0.23	0.28	0.26
Georgia	0.29	–	0.43
Moldova	0.27	–	0.42
Ukraine	0.24	–	0.47

Source: adapted from World Bank (2002, p. 9).

one hand, East Central Europe registered lower levels and only small increases of inequality. On the other hand, a group mainly consisting of countries further to the east, including Bulgaria and the former Soviet republics, experienced a dramatic growth and much higher levels of inequality. In the second half of the 1990s East Central Europe, now joined by the Baltic countries, experienced only small further increases in inequality, while the former Soviet republics of the Commonwealth of Independent States (CIS) underwent further significant increases. (The exception here was Belarus which had a relatively low increase in inequality, mainly because it advanced less far in introducing the measures of economic restructuring adopted by other countries in the region.)

Such changes in income inequality had different consequences in terms of patterns of income distribution within each country. According to Milanovich (1998, pp. 44–5) there were three main different experiences of transition in the way it affected different strata within each society. Using household budget data to divide each population into five quintiles, he found that between 1987/8 and 1993/4:

(a) in Hungary, Slovakia and Slovenia there was barely any redistribution of income between the five different strata;
(b) in the Czech Republic, Latvia, Poland and Romania, and also in Belarus, the main losses were experienced by the bottom three quintiles, while the second highest group experienced a small decrease, and the top 20 per cent was the only group that had clearly gained in its share of total income;
(c) in the remaining countries for which were was relevant data, including Bulgaria, Estonia, Lithuania, Moldova and Ukraine, the top 20 per cent gained a much larger increase over the rest of society; while the bottom quintile lost between 4 and 5 per cent of total income the top quintile gained much more, especially in Ukraine and Lithuania, where they gained 14 per cent and 11 per cent respectively.

New Elites and Emergent Capitalism

Looking beyond income inequality we need to examine whether new patterns of inequality are emerging in terms of decision-making power in both economic life and politics. With the end of the communist parties' monopoly on power and the liberalization of the economy the '*nomenklatura*' elites of the old communist regimes lost most of the power and privileges they had enjoyed through their political positions. At the same time the emerging market economy led to a widening of inequalities of wealth and income. At the end of the 1980s there was much speculation about who would be the main beneficiaries of these changes. On the one hand it seemed possible that people who had become self-employed or had started small businesses in the last decade of communist rule would be in a good position to build on their experience of operating in a market economy and becoming a new postcommunist bourgeoisie. On the other hand the predominant view was that the new entrepreneurs of the 'second economy' had insufficient capital and resources to expand into large-scale businesses, and a more likely development was that of 'political capitalism' in which the former communist *nomenklatura* would translate their political power into private wealth. The former bureaucrats of the communist party/state would be able to use their political power to transfer state-owned assets to their own new private companies. This would result in the coalescence of a new power elite or 'grand coalition' of the higher and middle levels of the bureaucracies of the old state and ruling party with managers of large- and middle-sized companies and entrepreneurial groups (Hankiss, 1990; Staniszkis, 1991).

During the early 1990s this view came under challenge, at least as far as the countries of Central Europe were concerned. Drawing on data from Hungary (Szalai, 1999) and the Czech Republic, Hungary and Poland (Eyal *et al.*, 1998), it was argued that although the intentions of the communist *nomenklatura* might have been accurately described by writers such as Hankiss, in practice they were not very successful in turning themselves into a propertied ruling elite. The evidence suggested instead that those best able to build on their positions under the old regime were, more narrowly, the younger generation of state and party officials and technocratically oriented managers of state companies who were in middle-ranking positions in the 1980s. By 1993, 'former technocrats were prominent among the new political elite of post-communism, while former socialist managers and deputy managers occupied top economic positions'. However, this 'successor' elite had not turned themselves into a new property-owning class, but exercised decision-making power on the basis of the cultural capital they

[margin note, handwritten:] CONTRA ARG of ELITE COMME GRAB DURING PRIVATISATION

possessed in the form of their specialist knowledge and networks of contacts (Eyal *et al.*, 1998, p. 116).

While this new managerial economic elite was forming, the democratization process created opportunities for new political and cultural elites to emerge. These comprised the leaders of the newly formed political parties and a new 'opinion forming intelligentsia', drawn mainly from people who had been in professional and intelligentsia positions under the old regime, or from former dissident intellectuals. For writers such as Szalai and Eyal *et al.*, in post-communist Central Europe these three elite groups have coalesced into an uneasy but peaceful relationship, to form a new power elite. For Higley and Lengyel (2000, pp. 9–10) on the other hand, rather than a power elite, there remain basic distinctions between economic and political elites. Different countries in Eastern Europe have developed varying degrees of unity and consensus among their elites. In Central Europe, despite substantial elite turnover and sharp policy differences, the turnover has been peaceful and there has been inter-elite consensus on the rules and institutions of the new democratic system.

However, in South-Eastern Europe and the former Soviet republics of Eastern Europe a different picture seems to be emerging. In contrast to the institutionalization of elite competition in Central Europe, countries such as Serbia, Bulgaria and former Soviet republics have experienced more open power struggles between elites, oscillating between authoritarian and democratic tendencies (Higley *et al.*, 1998). For Eyal *et al.* this may be connected with different patterns of transition and elite formation. In Eastern Europe, they suggest, an economic transition to capitalism is less clear-cut and members of the former *nomenklatura* have been more successful in maintaining their elite positions in both the economy and in politics. At the same time, trends towards democratization and the freedom of the media are weaker, with the result that 'the opinion-making intelligentsia is much more marginal and ... it is also intimidated' (1998, p. 166).

Poverty

At the other end of the social scale there are questions about the changing character of poverty, and whether the poor are forming an increasingly distinct group in postcommunist society. According to one recent study, 'the increase in poverty – and its persistence during the past decade – alone would probably suffice to distinguish the experience of the transition countries ... from other regions' (World Bank, 2000, p. 2). The experience of suffering a decline in their share of a national income that was itself contracting, resulted for many people in Central and Eastern Europe, in a slide into poverty. A wide range of factors influenced the incidence of poverty and determined which groups within societies were most vulnerable to it. Particularly important were employment status and income from employment. In general, according to Milanovich, 'the unemployed and farmers are, in all countries, more likely to be poor than the average person; pensioners' likelihood to be poor is about average; and workers' households are slightly less likely. No regularity emerges regarding the position of the self-employed.' While unemployment in general is a cause of poverty, long-term unemployment of over a year is particularly significant since it usually involves not only loss of earned income but also loss of unemployment benefits. World Bank data for the mid-1990s in Central and Eastern Europe suggest that poverty rates were higher than average in households containing someone who was long-term unemployed, and higher still if more than one member or the head of household was long-term unemployed (Milanovich, 1998, pp. 94–5).

Other factors affecting poverty include family size, age, gender and education. Larger households are more likely to be poor than smaller families: over the region as a whole the poverty rates for five-member households is between 1.5 and 2.5 times higher than for average-sized households. Households with larger than average numbers of children are particularly vulnerable, as are households where the income earners have only primary or vocational education. Some groups of pensioners face particular problems. Although pension levels in many countries are set to be above, or at least equivalent to the poverty line, this often applies only to the full pension entitlement, and some pensions, for example for disabilities or early retirement, are set at a lower level. Women are more vulnerable to poverty in two ways, in that they are more likely to be single-parent heads of households, and in that women's pensions are often lower than men's. There are also strong regional disparities within countries, with much higher risk of poverty in rural areas and declining areas of rustbelt industries, and a much lower risk of poverty in capital cities (Milanovich, 1998, pp. 101–7; World Bank, 2000, pp. 68–90).

In some countries a vicious circle sets in when people's employment situation is interconnected with questions of whether they have connections to informal kin or friendship networks of support, and the extent to which they can make a political case to receive state benefits. In Hungary, according to Szalai, among those most vulnerable to poverty in the 1990s were people who gave up their rural roots and moved to become wageworkers in single industry towns as part of the 'socialist' industrialization process. As a consequence of their migration this group had lost effective support networks based on family or work colleagues, and in the course of the economic transformation they came to depend particularly on their low state incomes at the same time as the level of social service provision was cut back. Their situation was undermined further as a result of their lack of connection to new forms of pressure group politics, which sought to influence the direction of increasingly selective forms of state welfare support (Szalai, 1996).

There is much debate among researchers about the best way to measure poverty, and about the common definitions that might be used so that international comparisons are possible. A common method is to estimate the absolute amount of money needed per day for subsistence in each country, including food and other necessary expenditure such as housing or clothing. To enable comparisons 'a poverty line is fixed in U.S. dollars and then converted into national currency units using purchasing power parity (PPP) exchange rates [which] measure the relative purchasing power of different currencies over equivalent goods and services'. This avoids the problem that goods have different prices in different countries, and is able to take into account different patterns of consumption between countries. Two measures of such 'absolute poverty' are commonly used: $2.15 per day, representing the absolute minimum for European climates, and $4.30 per day, which also takes minimal costs of clothing, housing and local transport into account. This latter rate approximates more closely to the official poverty lines adopted by several governments in the region (World Bank, 2000, p. 370).

Assuming the higher of these two poverty lines, Milanovich has estimated that across the former Soviet Union and Eastern Europe as a whole between the late 1980s and 1995 the numbers of the population in poverty rose from just under 14 million, or 4 per cent of the population, to 168 million, or 45 per cent of the population. Within this overall increase, however, different countries experienced very different rates of increase. While there was only a slight

Class and Inequality

increase in the incidence of poverty, of between less than 1 per cent and 2 per cent, in the countries of Central Europe (the Czech Republic, Hungary, Slovakia and Slovenia), other countries experienced much greater increases, ranging for example from an increase from 2 to 15 per cent in Bulgaria, to a rise from 2 to 63 per cent in Ukraine (Milanovich, 1998, p. 69). Table 13.3 provides more recent figures showing the proportion of the population in each country during the late 1990s that fell below each poverty line.

Differences between countries have emerged not only in the extent of poverty, but also in terms of its main characteristics. The character of poverty in different societies is in turn closely related to changing patterns of employment and unemployment. In Central Europe between 1989 and 1992 there was a sharp decline in employment with negligible job creation, resulting in a sharp rise in unemployment. From 1993 the decline in employment slowed down and job creation rates rose slightly to between 3 and 4 per cent per annum. In these countries unemployment is closely related to

TABLE 13.3 *Absolute poverty in selected years, 1995–9*

Country	Survey year	% below poverty line: $2.15 per day	% below poverty line: $4.30 per day
Albania	1996	11.5	58.6
Armenia	1999	43.5	86.2
Azerbaijan	1999	23.5	64.2
Belarus	1999	1.0	10.4
Bulgaria	1995	3.1	18.2
Croatia	1998	0.2	4.0
Czech Republic	1996	0.0	0.8
Estonia	1998	2.1	19.3
Georgia	1999	18.9	54.2
Hungary	1997	1.3	15.4
Latvia	1998	6.6	34.8
Lithuania	1999	3.1	22.5
Macedonia	1996	6.7	43.9
Moldova	1999	55.4	84.6
Poland	1998	1.2	18.4
Romania	1998	6.8	44.5
Slovakia	1997	2.6	8.6
Slovenia	1997/8	0.0	0.7
Ukraine	1999	3.0	29.4

Source: adapted from World Bank (2000, p. 35).

poverty and there are large gaps between the incomes of the employed and the unemployed. In the CIS countries, on the other hand, the more sustained decline in GDP during the 1990s was accompanied by less restructuring of enterprises and a less pronounced decline in formal employment. Employers retained workers but paid them less and allowed large arrears of wage payments to develop. More people have had to survive by turning to unofficial self-employment and subsistence production. In these countries unemployment is less closely related to poverty and there are smaller gaps between the standards of living of the employed and unemployed. This is reflected in the following comparison: in the CIS countries the mean expenditure of households with unemployed heads is 85 per cent of the mean income of households with employed heads, whereas in the countries of Central Europe the corresponding figure is 68 per cent (World Bank, 2000, pp. 67, 123–5).

Thus, a specific feature of the new kinds of poverty that have emerged in some countries in Central and Eastern Europe, and especially in the CIS countries, is poverty in the working population. As noted above, this applies to farm workers in all countries in the region, but other vulnerable groups include industrial manual workers in the declining formerly state-owned heavy industries, and low-skilled clerical workers who formerly worked in the lower levels of the communist state bureaucracies. Employment in these categories was particularly badly hit by the transition recession and, where jobs are still available, wages have fallen well below price levels so that many people in employment are earning less than the average wage.

For people in this situation their income from a main job is clearly inadequate to meet their subsistence needs. According to the 2001 New Europe Barometer (NEB) survey, only 34 per cent of employed people in the ten EU candidate countries of Central and Eastern Europe report that 'they earn enough to buy what they need'. This group ranges in size from 16 per cent in Slovakia to 58 per cent in Slovenia (the only country where a majority of the workforce had sufficient income from one job). However, very few people whose job does not provide sufficient income have fallen into complete destitution. For the majority of the population throughout the region economic transformation has resulted in people achieving subsistence through a range of different kinds of work including growing their own food and various kinds of unregistered casual work in the 'grey economy'. The same NEB survey found that 70 per cent of all respondents (employed, unemployed and pensioners) reported they could cope by drawing on a range of different resources. For individual countries this ranged from 59 per cent in Poland to 82 per cent in Slovenia (Rose, 2002, pp. 13–15).

Declining Standards of Health and Quality of Life

Although the majority of people in Central and Eastern Europe have been able to cope somehow in generating the means of their subsistence, they have done so at the expense of their quality of life and, in some cases, their physical and mental health. Engaging in a range of different activities to earn a sufficient income for themselves and their families has required people to work long hours in conditions of considerable insecurity. While subsistence food production is very vulnerable to the vagaries of the climate, casual work is by definition not always available, and therefore both are likely to increase levels of anxiety among those engaged in them.

Thus, a further consequence of the economic transformation and the growth in poverty is an increase in the vulnerability of some sections of society to further problems of poor health for themselves and their families. This may be reflected increasingly in the future in higher incidence of certain illnesses, higher infant mortality and decreased life expectancy. So far, the legacy of the comprehensive state health care systems developed under communist rule has been effective in maintaining much higher levels of welfare than exist in many countries with high rates of absolute poverty in other parts of the world. However, some serious problems are beginning to emerge, especially in CIS countries. Male life expectancy declined by more than five years in Ukraine between 1989 and 1994, and by an average of over four years in the Baltic countries. High rates of infant mortality have also been recorded in some CIS countries and parts of South-Eastern Europe. For example infant mortality per one thousand live births was 24 in Albania, 19 in Romania and 18 in Moldova, compared with rates as low as 6 in the Czech Republic and Slovenia. New health problems have also arisen where further factors such as civil war and unrest have intervened to disrupt and undermine public services. For example, while child malnutrition is not a general problem in Central and Eastern Europe, rates as high as 6, 8 and 10 per cent of children under five years have been recorded in the 1990s respectively for Macedonia,

Albania and Azerbaijan. Drug use is on the increase, especially among unemployed young people in a number of CIS countries, and the incidence of sexually transmitted diseases increased three-fold in Ukraine and Belarus between 1989 and 1997 (World Bank, 2000, pp. 41–3; World Bank: *http://www.worldbank.org/data/*). A further factor affecting public health has been a deterioration in the provision of social welfare and health services. Under the communist regimes these were often provided through the workplace. However, as a result of privatization and commercialization, enterprises and organizations have had to focus their activities on profit-making and to cut back on the provision of clinics, nurseries and welfare support. More generally, many governments have found themselves unable to maintain previous levels of support for social and health services, although, as with other changes discussed above, there are signs of growing differences between countries in the region. For example there was a decline during the 1990s in the average annual real expenditure on public health in most countries in Central and Eastern Europe, from under 5 per cent a year in Hungary, Slovakia and Romania to over 10 per cent in Ukraine and Bulgaria. On the other hand, some countries in Central Europe and the Baltic area actually increased their real expenditure during the same period, and in the case of Slovenia by more than 5 per cent (World Bank, 2000, p. 270).

The worsening situation in health and social welfare has been exacerbated by the decline in the real income of public employees working in these areas and the increased pressure on patients to make extra unofficial payments to them. While under communist rule it was usual to offer a bribe to doctors and other care workers to ensure good treatment, such extra payments have increased further in some countries. For example it has been estimated that the proportion of patients making extra payments for their treatment ranges from 91 per cent in Armenia to 78 per cent in Poland, 60 per cent in Slovakia and 21 per cent in Bulgaria. At the same time as such payments have become a more important part of the income of health workers, the poorer sections of the population have become less able to afford them. It has been estimated that around 30 per cent of hospital patients in Georgia and Ukraine have had to borrow money to pay for their treatment. Many others probably forgo treatment because they cannot afford it (World Bank, 2000, p. 264).

In addition to its consequences for physical health, economic transformation has had an equally serious impact on the psychological well-being and morale of the populations of Central and Eastern Europe. While the legacy of the old social welfare system may have lessened the immediate impact of economic hardship on physical health, it can also be argued that the past access to such benefits now accentuates the feelings of humiliation and despair at their decline. One possible reflection of this may be the rising suicide rates that some countries have experienced during the 1990s. The highest rates were reported for Lithuania where they rose from around 30 per 100,000 of the population in 1991 to over 45 in 1996, before falling to just over 40 per 100,000 in 1998. Estonia also experienced a similar pattern with an increase in the mid-1990s followed by a slight fall by 1998. Other former Soviet republics have experienced a levelling off after a mid-1990s peak, such as Ukraine, or a continuing rise, such as Latvia and Belarus. Some Central European countries experienced a different pattern however: the Czech Republic experienced a high of around 30 per 100,000 in 1991, followed by a decline. Hungary, which previously had the highest rates of suicide in Europe, actually experienced a decline in the 1990s, from a peak of over 45 per 100,000 in 1987 to just over 35 per 100,000 in the mid-1990s (Elekes and Paksi, 1999, p. 141; World Bank, 2000, p. 50).

More generally, an impression of the state of 'post-transition morale' can be gained from opinion polls and sociological survey research. To begin with, a significant proportion of the population seemed prepared to accept a deterioration in their standards of living in the interests of transforming the economy. According to the Eurobarometer surveys carried out on behalf of the European Commission in 1991, favourable evaluations of the new market economy outweighed unfavourable responses in all countries in the region except Romania, by proportions ranging from 52 per cent in Hungary to 9 per cent in Lithuania, with the Slovak sample recording an equal balance between the two. By 1994, however, although Romania now showed a positive balance, public belief in the benefits of a market economy had declined by an average of 22 per cent across the region (European Commission, 1994).

More recent figures seem to suggest a growing divergence between the economically more successful and the less successful countries. According to survey data from the 2001 Candidate Countries Eurobarometer, carried out on behalf of the European Commission, large majorities in Slovenia (85 per cent) and the Czech Republic (74 per cent), and narrower majorities in Poland,

Hungary, Latvia and Slovakia, considered themselves either satisfied or very satisfied with life in general (compared with an average for EU member countries of 83 per cent). This contrasted with only a third of respondents in Bulgaria and 40 per cent in Romania and Lithuania. (The overall figures were amalgamated from questions covering respondents' feelings about their personal happiness, health, family situation, and the economy and society in general.) Within different societies, at the same time, more satisfaction was expressed by groups that were more successful in economic or educational terms. For the ten EU candidate countries as a whole, 65 per cent of managers and 61 per cent of those who completed their education at 20 years or older were satisfied or very satisfied, compared with only 39 per cent of the unemployed and 41 per cent of those who left school at 15 years or under.

However, when asked to reflect on whether life had improved during the transformation years of the 1990s a rather more negative picture emerged. Only a minority thought the quality of life had improved in the previous five years. The highest proportion responding positively was 38 per cent in Slovenia, and only Latvia, Estonia and the Czech Republic also recorded positive replies of more than one-third of the sample. In Bulgaria, Lithuania and Slovakia more than half thought the quality of life had deteriorated. Furthermore, people in the ten candidate countries were not very optimistic about improvements during the five years from 2001 onwards. Only Romania recorded a majority (53 per cent) of respondents who thought life would improve, and in some countries where people had been most positive about the past five years, such as Slovenia and the Czech Republic, only around a third of the respondents thought life would improve (European Commission, 2002, pp. 12–16).

Conclusion

In some aspects of social change, especially in socio-occupational structure and patterns of social mobility between generations, the countries of Central and Eastern Europe have been converging with their western neighbours since the middle of the twentieth century. While some differences in the detail of these patterns were attributable to the specific historical experience of Central and Eastern Europe, these may become weaker as a result of the transition to a market economy in the eastern half of the continent. However, in other respects, social change in Central and Eastern Europe has been very different and more dramatic than that experienced in Western Europe in recent years. In particular there have been rapid and far-reaching changes in the social character and, in many cases, the composition of both elite groups and those in long-term poverty. As a result the structure of the societies of Central and Eastern Europe has become based on much wider social divisions than in the past. There are also signs that the experience of poverty, or the threat of it and the need to undertake a range of employment to achieve sufficient income, is seriously affecting the health and morale of the population in the region.

We have also seen how, in terms of the extent of social inequality, the social and political character of the new elites, the extent and character of poverty, and in the worsening situation of public health and the quality of life, a widening gap is emerging between different groups of countries in the wider region. If these disparities are reinforced by the redrawing of the boundaries of the EU eastwards, the current divergences in types of political regime may also become wider with unpredictable consequences for political disaffection and unrest. These issues are likely to form the backdrop to any study of the politics of Central and Eastern Europe over the early years of the new century, and may call into question whether we will any longer be able to regard the countries of the region as a meaningful unit.

14

The Implications of EU Enlargement

HEATHER GRABBE

The European Union has had a profound transformative impact on Central and Eastern European (CEE) politics over the past decade. Ten CEE countries have so far applied for membership – Bulgaria, Czech Republic, Estonia, Hungary, Latvia, Lithuania, Poland, Romania, Slovakia and Slovenia – and more are likely to join the list in future. Eight of these countries are set to be admitted in 2004, along with Malta and Cyprus, while Bulgaria and Romania have set themselves the target date of 2007. However, the EU has influenced these countries' domestic policy-making and many aspects of their political development long before accession. The EU also has a role in the region beyond the current candidates, because of the attractions of membership and because the enlargement process will have a range of economic, political and security implications for the countries that are left outside it.

This chapter investigates how the EU enlargement process has worked so far in the candidate countries, and its effects on the surrounding region. It starts with a discussion of the conditions for accession. The second section considers the effects on domestic politics in the candidate countries. The third section discusses the likely impact of enlargement on surrounding countries, while the fourth section looks specifically at the export of the EU's border control policies. The chapter concludes that the EU must begin to develop a strategy that takes into account the effects of enlargement on its new CEE neighbours.

The Accession Process So Far: Travelling in Hope

The evolving relationship between the EU and the CEE applicants for membership has had three broad phases so far. After 1989, the EU offered more aid through the Phare programme and signed 'Europe Agreements' giving trade concessions to the would-be members. In 1993, it set conditions for membership and began a 'pre-accession strategy' that led to the publication of the Commission's 'opinions' on the applicants' readiness for membership in 1997. In 1998, substantive negotiations began with five of the countries (Czech Republic, Estonia, Hungary, Poland and Slovenia), while the other five candidates (Bulgaria, Latvia, Lithuania, Romania and Slovakia) joined negotiations in 2000. Cyprus and Malta completed in December 2002, along with eight of the CEE candidates negotiations. The EU has promised to reconsider Turkey's ambition to start negotiations in December 2004.

The EU as a Moving Target: What Exactly Do Applicants Have to Do Before They Can Join?

The EU set four conditions for membership at the Copenhagen European Council in 1993:

> Membership requires that the candidate country has achieved [1] stability of institutions guaranteeing democracy, the rule of law, human rights and respect for and protection of minorities, [2] the existence of a functioning market economy as well as the capacity to cope with competitive pressure and market forces within the Union. [3] Membership presupposes the candidate's ability to take on the obligations of membership including adherence to the aims of political, economic and monetary union. [4] The Union's capacity to absorb new members, while maintaining the momentum of European integration, is also an important consideration in the general interest of both the Union and the candidate countries.

These conditions were designed to minimize the risk of new entrants becoming politically unstable and economically burdensome to the existing EU. They were thus formulated as much to reassure reluctant member-states as to guide the candidates, and this dual purpose of the conditionality has continued to play an important role in the politics of accession within the EU.

(COPENHAGEN AGREEMENTS)

The fourth condition reflects member-state anxieties about the impact that enlargement might have on EU institutions and policies because of the increase in numbers and diversity, apart from the specific problems that CEE members might bring in. It is a condition for enlargement, whereas the others are conditions for entry. All of the accession conditions are general and vague, leaving a lot of room for the EU to interpret them. Elaboration of what constitutes meeting the accession conditions has progressively widened the detailed criteria for membership, as new conditions can be added and old ones redefined. Moreover, new issues of concern arise, so the EU has added specific requirements for individual countries such as the closing down of nuclear power plants in Bulgaria, Lithuania, Slovakia, and improving the treatment of children in state care in Romania. It is also very difficult to pinpoint exactly when each of the accession conditions has been met, giving the European Commission a degree of discretion in reporting on the candidates' progress. The Copenhagen conditions do not provide a check-list of clear objectives; nor do they specify the means to achieve stated goals. They are not like the conditions set by the IMF, where there are quantitative targets for macroeconomic performance.

The first two Copenhagen conditions require definitions of what constitutes a 'democracy', a 'market economy' and 'the capacity to cope with competitive pressure and market forces', all highly debatable and slippery concepts. The EU has never provided an explicit definition of any of them, although there are implicit assumptions about their content in the Commission's opinions on the candidates' readiness for membership (published in 1997) and the annual reports it has published on the candidates' progress since 1998.

The third condition is concerned with the '*acquis communautaire*', which is the whole body of EU rules, political principles and judicial decisions. These 'obligations of membership' are also open to interpretation. In previous enlargements, they were held to lie solely in implementation of the EU's 80,000 pages of legislative texts – which keep growing as the EU develops new policies and issues new directives, declarations and jurisprudence. For this enlargement, the *acquis* has been defined more broadly as 'all the real and potential rights and obligations of the EU system and its institutional framework' (Gialdino, 1995).

Such a formulation is also open to minimalist and maximalist interpretations, and these in turn affect the demands made on CEE applicants. So far, the EU has generally presented a maximalist interpretation to the applicants. Moreover, the conditions are a moving target as the EU's agenda gets more detailed and more demanding, because the Union itself develops new policies and responsibilities during the period while the candidates are preparing themselves for membership. Since 1993, the EU has added new policy areas to its activities, such as justice and home affairs, and the Schengen area of passport-free travel; a common foreign and security policy, with a defence identity; and a common currency. All of these developments add to the requirements that the candidates have to meet before accession. The CEE countries have no possibility of negotiating opt-outs like those applying to some member-states on Schengen and monetary union. The candidates also have to take on the EU's 'soft law' of non-binding resolutions and recommendations.

The *acquis* is divided into 31 different 'chapters' for the purpose of negotiations. Because progress in closing the chapters is one of the few clearly measurable parts of the process, candidate countries concentrated their efforts on getting chapters provisionally closed, and opening new ones, in order to demonstrate their progress. But closing chapters does not guarantee an earlier date for accession, and provisionally closed chapters can be reopened later in negotiations, so the deal is not final until the accession treaty is signed.

When is a Country Ready to Join?

By 1999, the EU had decided that all ten central European candidates had met the political conditions for accession – which are an explicit prerequisite for starting negotiations. Some of the candidate countries had also made quick progress towards meeting the economic and *acquis* conditions. By 2000, all of the five countries that started negotiations in 1998 had become functioning market economies and were close to becoming competitive in the single market.

The EU concluded negotiations with ten candidates in December 2002. Of the five Central European countries that started negotiations in February 2000, Latvia, Lithuania and Slovakia caught up with the front-runners relatively quickly, having opened most of the chapters in negotiations and made rapid progress in preparations. However, Bulgaria and Romania continued to lag behind the other candidates, and in its 2001 progress reports, the Commission assessed them to be insufficiently close to meeting the accession conditions to join the first group of CEE members of the EU.

For several years after the conditions were first set, it was not clear exactly which elements of the political and economic conditions had to be fulfilled for an applicant to be admitted to which benefits. But by the end of the 1990s, a rough progression had emerged of stages in the accession process:

- Privileged trade access and additional aid.
- Signing and implementing an enhanced form of association agreement (Europe Agreements for the current candidates, Stabilization and Association Agreements for South-Eastern European countries).
- Opening of negotiations (explicitly dependent on meeting the democracy and human rights conditions since 1999).
- Opening and closing of the 31 chapters.
- Signing of an accession treaty.
- Ratification of the accession treaty by national parliaments and the European Parliament.
- Entry as a full member.

Aspirant members have to become like the EU in certain areas viewed as essential to the future functioning of the EU. Regulatory alignment with the Single Market – which involves the removal of all trade barriers and meeting EU product and process standards – is non-negotiable, and it was the first set of priorities presented to the candidates by the EU (Sedelmeier and Wallace, 2000). Similarly, the candidates cannot have opt-outs on monetary union, Schengen or the emerging European security and defence identity, even though member-states like Britain, Ireland and Denmark have them.

Ultimately, an applicant is ready to join when member-states are convinced that the new member will behave like a good citizen in the EU. A potential member-state has to show a certain style of operation – in its public policy-making and state administration – that looks familiar to member-states if it is to be acceptable. The capacity to implement and enforce EU-inspired legislation effectively is vital to meeting the conditions.

What Impact on Domestic Politics?

Joining the EU requires a profound transformation of a country's laws, institutions, policies and orientations. Gaining entry to the Union is much more difficult and complex than is joining NATO, which essentially requires political commitment and changes to the armed forces. It is also much more difficult to join the EU now than it was for poor countries like Greece, Ireland, Portugal and Spain in the 1970s and 1980s. The EU itself was less complex before the creation of the Single Market and the establishment of a common currency, so membership then required fewer adjustments. Moreover, in past enlargements, the EU allowed the candidates to negotiate long transitional periods and it provided much more aid to them after accession than it has offered to the current applicants. It was partly the experience of relatively expensive previous enlargements and very slow adaptation by poorer countries like Greece that led to such tight conditions for the CEE countries.

EU membership now requires changes to a huge range of policies, and the reshaping of many of a country's political institutions. The EU's members have developed some form of coordination, harmonization or common rules in almost every area of public policy – although the extent of harmonization varies greatly. Its effects range very widely, from the creation of market regulators to civil service reform, from border controls to hygiene standards in abattoirs. Moreover, the political and economic conditions are new in this enlargement, so the EU has an influence in CEE domestic politics that goes beyond the Union's remit for its current member-states (see Grabbe, 1999).

The EU and its member-states are already involved in shaping political institutions too, through the creation of new agencies and new coordination procedures within and between government agencies, as well as in transferring policies. The EU has had an impact on the reform of the civil service, public procurement, budgetary procedures, and regional self-government. The accession process puts direct pressure on three sets of relations between different parts of the state: the relationship between the executive and legislature; the emergence of a privileged accession team in the executive; and the relationship between central and regional governments (see Grabbe, 2001a).

The stability of democratic institutions is one of the three general conditions for accession, and the EU has promoted the involvement of political institutions beyond the executive to implement and enforce the *acquis*. Yet, at the same time, the incentives and constraints created by the accession process support the emergence of a core national executive at the expense of other branches and levels of government – including the legislature and regional actors. The accession process encourages the emergence of a strong, central team to manage the accession process, because the conditionality is based on implementing a vast array of legislation and procedural rules in order to comply with EU standards, which in turn depend on reporting from the centre of government to Brussels. This creates an 'executive bias' in the accession process, because of the structure of negotiations and the fact that EU actors mostly see the process of adopting EU norms as an administrative exercise. This bias in turn exacerbates statist tendencies in CEE, which were already evident owing to the previous decades of state socialism. If the EU continues with this approach, it could erode public support and involvement in European integration. Negotiations between bureaucracies do not necessarily contribute to the development of shared values as a basis for new structures of government. This has implications for the future behaviour of the applicants as member-states: 'EU standards' are frequently invoked as a means of legitimizing institutional frameworks in CEE, but the administrative bias of the accession process can have the effect of impeding the development of a wider debate on forms of governance.

The EU has become yet another actor in party competition. Pressures from the EU interact with domestic debates about both policies and governance. The interaction between EU pressures and domestic processes can be seen clearly in centre–regional relations as well, where there is 'triadic engagement' between the EU, national governments and sub-national administration (Hughes *et al.*, 2001). An appeal to 'Europe' is a constant feature of the domestic debate (see Fowler, 2001, on Hungary). All sides and all political parties make this appeal, yet the EU is a confusing model, as political actors can point to the very different examples of how different member-states run their affairs and implement EU policies. The EU's own diversity thus undermines its effort to export a single model of governance, and the accession process itself presents conflicting demands. This provides ammunition for many different sides in domestic political battles.

Finally, the EU has been unable to provide models in some of the areas where the candidate countries needed them most. When it comes to the most sensitive and difficult issues in the region, such as the status and treatment of minorities, human rights, corruption, organized crime, the EU is agnostic. Although new members have to meet the political conditions, the EU has no democratic *acquis* on which to draw to provide guidance to the candidates. The member-states are themselves diverse in their policies on issues like provision of bilingual education for the children of ethnic minorities, or on tackling corruption in the public sector. Although they form part of a community of nations and share norms on what is and is not acceptable behaviour on the part of the state, the trickiest dilemmas of democracy cannot be solved by drawing on codified guidance set down in EU law.

The Differential Impact of Enlargement Across Central and Eastern Europe

The candidate countries have become increasingly similar to EU member-states through the accession process, and also by their integration into the single market through trade and investment driven by the single market. Once they join the EU, most of them will be active players in the Union's internal politics. Several of the new members will also be concerned to intensify the EU's engagement with their neighbours that remain outside it.

EU enlargement will have significant economic and political implications for the East European countries that will be excluded from the process into the medium term. These countries differ markedly in the extent and likely duration of their exclusion. At one end of the spectrum is Bulgaria – an EU candidate country which already enjoys a high degree of economic integration with the EU and which might join the EU just a few years after the first round of expansion. At the opposite end of the spectrum are the European CIS countries, which have low levels of integration with the EU and for which exclusion from EU membership could be permanent. The left-outs thus comprise three distinct groups:

- The candidate countries Bulgaria and Romania, for which the main problem is a possible lengthy delay to EU entry.
- The 'Western Balkans' of Albania, Bosnia and Herzegovina, Croatia, Macedonia and Yugoslavia, for which the EU has devised the special instrument of Stabilization and Association Agreements (SAAs). The SAAs offer trade access, political dialogue and cooperation in many areas – like the Europe

Agreements signed with the accession candidates – but the SAAs mention only the possibility of evolving towards full candidate status. Among these countries, Croatia is the closest to joining the EU, having applied for membership in 2003.

• The European CIS countries of Belarus, Moldova and Ukraine. These countries are the most distant from Brussels in geographic as well as political, institutional and economic terms. Exclusion from EU membership could be permanent. Relations with the EU are governed by Partnership and Cooperation Agreements (which also apply to relations with non-European CIS countries), which offer political dialogue and the prospect of a free trade area.

The differences between the 'ins' and the 'outs' are already significant in terms of average income per head, output and progress in reform. EU enlargement risks solidifying and deepening further this divergence through several different effects, which are explored in what follows.

The Economic Effects: Trade, Investment and Aid

The costs of exclusion from EU membership in terms of trade and aid flows are likely to be fairly low for the Balkan countries, but could be more substantial for the CIS countries, mainly because of the adverse impact of EU visa and border regimes (discussed below). Patterns of trade have already changed because of liberalization, not membership. That means that any trade diversion affecting the left-outs has already occurred, and full membership for the ins will have little further impact. The main area where trade remains highly controlled is agricultural products, because of the protection of EU agricultural markets.

Accession could have a much more significant impact on the geographical distribution of foreign direct investment (FDI). EU accession had a significant impact on FDI inflows in previous enlargements. Six countries joined the EU between 1973 and 1986, and entry to the EU generally brought an increase in capital inflows for Portugal and Spain, although Greece was an exception (Baldwin, François and Portes, 1997). EU entry will make the East European countries more attractive as a production location because it will guarantee unfettered access to a huge market and protect investors against any sudden changes in trade policy. Furthermore, the process of preparing for accession in itself attracts more inward investment (Bevan and Estrin, 2000).

Although financial transfers are not the primary motivating factor for countries to seek EU membership, accession will bring immediate financial rewards. Once they join, new member-states will gain increasing aid from the EU's agriculture and regional policies. The EU has increased its aid to South-Eastern Europe in recent years, but these flows will be small relative to the transfers to new member-states after they join.

The Impact on Domestic Reforms

Perhaps the main effect of the prospect of EU membership has been its role as an anchor to the reform process. The drive to join the EU has been one of the most powerful incentives for undertaking major reforms in the region. Through the tasks set annually by the European Commission, the EU ensures consistent external pressure on successive governments, helping to ensure continuity of reform efforts. The reform anchor role offered by the credible prospect of membership has been reinforced by tangible benefits linked to progress in reforms, such as additional aid, trade access and political support.

When prospects for EU membership recede, it is more difficult to overcome domestic political opposition to difficult reforms by justifying hard choices in the name of EU requirements. For Bulgaria and Romania, the first wave of EU enlargement will be a stark reminder of their exclusion, which will make it harder for politicians in these countries to argue for more EU-inspired policy changes that are painful to implement. Slower reform has a direct negative impact on performance, and it also has an adverse impact on foreign direct investment. Investors feel more confident about putting their money into a country if it has been given the EU's seal of approval.

When other CEE countries apply to join, they are also likely to find that progress towards EU membership helps to encourage reforms, while loss of support for the reform process is detrimental to FDI inflows. Consequently, a loss of reform momentum seems likely to damage FDI receipts, and may well exacerbate a vicious circle of reduced investment and slower reform. So putting in an application may not be a good idea if there are likely to be many disappointments and long years before membership.

Accession Requirements versus Development Needs

For future aspirants, it is also important to recognize the opportunity costs of EU accession preparations. For countries that are unlikely to join the EU within the next ten to twenty years, it is unlikely to be optimal to expend enormous efforts in meeting EU standards and harmonizing with EU policies designed for established market economies, if this is at the cost of more immediate policies to establish sustainable economic growth. EU policies are often cumbersome to administer and implement. For countries that are likely to join soon, the overall benefits of EU membership certainly outweigh the short-term costs of sub-optimal policies and regulatory regimes. But countries that have little hope of meeting the conditions in full for many years might be better advised to use the eventual prospect of membership as an incentive to undertake basic reforms, rather than concentrating on the detail of EU policy models.

The EU accession process is based on the model for previous enlargements, rather than being designed specifically to assist and encourage transition economies. As a result, the structure of incentives and constraints that it imposes on economic and regulatory policies may be inappropriate for countries facing acute development and/or reconstruction problems. EU policy-makers tend to assume that accession and transition require the same policies. However, although many accession-related policies are also required for successful economic transformation, applicants have to take on numerous EU policies that were developed for advanced, industrialized economies. They were not designed for countries in transition, and they often require a complex institutional structure for implementation that is little developed in Eastern Europe.

The experience of Bulgaria and Romania over the past decade carries important lessons for the rest of the region. The accession process does not guarantee economic success, nor does it underwrite governmental programmes. It can help to anchor reforms, but there are other prerequisites that the EU cannot provide: particularly important are the institutional capacity to implement laws and regulations, and a political consensus that provides continuity across changes of government. The EU helps governments to overcome opposition to unpopular measures, but EU has few sanctions that can be applied to unwilling governments: it can only encourage, not coerce. Future aspirants will find that they can only use an application to join the EU as a route to economic success if they already have both widespread political support for the necessary reforms and also adequate institutional resources to implement the measures demanded by the EU. The EU is no panacea for weak institutions and a lack of political consensus.

New Dividing Lines in Europe: The Impact of EU Border Policies

Until the end of the Cold War the EU was largely an economic club, with little harmonization of its members' foreign policies. But since the early 1990s, the Union has been establishing a major foreign policy role for itself. The EU's size and weight as a regional player will grow further after enlargement: it will be a weightier trade bloc with a bigger market, and so a stronger economic power. Meanwhile, its foreign and security dimensions are growing – slowly but surely – and it is developing military capabilities that might eventually be used independently of NATO.

What does this new foreign and security policy capacity mean for the rest of the region? For countries in the Balkans, Moldova and Ukraine, a bigger foreign policy dimension increases the attraction of the EU as a club to join. For Russia, it will increase wariness about the EU's security and military dimensions, and worries about access to Kaliningrad, the Russian enclave that will soon be surrounded by EU members. It will also have concrete effects in causing greater isolation for Russia's border regions. Eastward enlargement will also have some negative unintended consequences because of the ripple effects of its border and visa policies in the 'Schengen' area.

For ordinary people living in the region surrounding the EU, the main effects of enlargement will be felt through the visa and border control policies that the EU is developing and already starting to export to the applicants through the conditions for accession. Securing the applicants' borders against illegal migrants and cross-border crime is an important part of the EU's accession strategy because of the political sensitivity of these issues among current member-states. The enlargement process has coincided with the rapid development of a new policy area for the EU in justice and home affairs. New members have to comply fully with the EU's emerging policies for border management, asylum, immigration, and police and judicial cooperation. Not only do EU border policies go to the heart of the CEE countries' new-found sovereignty, but their foreign relations are affected as well.

The result for the CEE countries joining the EU will be greater integration with Western Europe at the price of cutting ties with their eastern neighbours. Applying EU visa policies will inevitably inhibit economic integration and bilateral cooperation between countries that are 'ins' and 'outs' in the EU accession process. More stringent controls on the movement of people and goods across the borders of the applicant countries are expensive to implement and are disruptive to trade and investment. The applicant countries provide markets for goods from the surrounding region and jobs for migrant workers. Replacing the Iron Curtain with a visa wall further east also has security implications for the whole of Europe if unstable, poor states are isolated on the fringes of an enlarged 'Fortress Europe'.

The EU has not yet developed a policy for dealing with the gaps between the main candidates for EU membership and the left-outs. Nor does it yet have a strategy for integrating the wider Europe into its zone of stability and prosperity. But the EU is increasingly feeling responsible for the countries on its new borders, and 'proximity policy' is beginning to be recognized as necessary in Brussels and EU capitals. The Union will have to reconsider its role as a development agency after enlargement, as the countries on its periphery are likely to experience widening gaps with their neighbours. The EU will have to consider additional measures to help countries that cannot join for many years. It will have to start with Bulgaria and Romania, as these countries are currently falling between two stools, neither included fully in the group of countries moving rapidly towards EU accession, nor in EU policies for the Balkans. In the longer term, a more comprehensive development policy will be needed if the EU is to be effective in stabilizing the region surrounding its enlarged borders.

Conclusion

The aspiration to join the EU has driven rapid and profound changes to both policies and institutions in the candidate CEE countries. The EU's influence in these countries is wider than in its current member-states owing to the additional political and economic conditions set for this enlargement. The wide margin left for interpretation of the conditions has allowed the EU to play a role in many aspects of political life in CEE. In particular, the EU has shaped many areas of public policy, especially market regulation and control of borders. It has also affected the development of governance by requiring a high degree of centralization of many aspects of domestic policy-making to meet its requirements. But the accession process has also become a political football in party competition, and the diversity of the current member-states provides many different examples for politicians from across the spectrum to draw on in support of their positions.

Eastward enlargement of the EU will have a range of effects on the wider Europe beyond the current applicants. Some of these are already evident: visa policies and Schengen border controls are drawing new lines of exclusion between applicants and their neighbours, and FDI has been concentrated in the front-runner countries. This will widen gaps in economic performance between the CEE countries.

For the countries that have no hope of joining for many years, the EU is offering greater aid and trade access, as well as association and partnership agreements of various kinds. However, unless there is a marked change in EU policy, enlargement will also have negative implications for the wider region. In particular, the EU's visa policies and external border controls are already drawing new lines of division within the East European region. Enlargement is also likely to reinforce the geographical concentration of foreign investment, which has been one of the keys of successful transition. In addition, the EU's preferences tend to overlap with those of NATO, causing double exclusion for some countries.

The net effect on CEE as a whole is likely to be positive, not negative. But the unwanted consequences of enlargement mean that the EU will have to engage – in its own interest – with the countries lying on its new frontiers. There is no longer a well-guarded Iron Curtain protecting the EU-15 against would-be migrants and other consequences of poverty and political unrest in neighbouring countries. In future, the EU will have to engage much more closely with the rest of the region, knitting the enlargement process together with its nascent foreign policies.

PART FOUR

Central and Eastern Europe in Comparative Perspective

15

Democratization in Central and Eastern Europe: A Comparative Perspective

GEOFFREY PRIDHAM

Postcommunist politics in Central and Eastern Europe, as a new field of scholarship, has advanced considerably since regime change began with the contemporaneous collapse of communist systems at the end of the 1980s. Previously contained within communist studies, which now suddenly ended as it was, Central and Eastern Europe (CEE) has now become a familiar presence on the map of comparative politics. Nevertheless, it remains within its relatively new postcommunist format; and, for this reason, has essentially to be viewed from the perspective of the democratization process. It is this that still provides the most dynamic focus for viable comparisons.

This burgeoning of work on CEE has inevitably had its focal points, some of them obvious. As previously occurred in relation to the Southern European new democracies, electoral studies were first in line simply because the onset of free elections offered immediately usable data for psephologists and other interested scholars. Linked to this, the study of political parties and party systems has been another growth area, although systematic comparative studies are fewer than might be expected given the richness of empirical material from so many countries that have in one form or another embraced competitive politics (Lewis, 2000). A special area offering much potential for cross-national analysis is coalitional behaviour within the context of this wide range of multiparty systems (Pridham, 2002).

Other familiar comparative themes have emerged in a more uneven fashion. Institutional engineering and development have begun to attract more attention (Zielonka, 2001), although governance in general is a still neglected area, just as is public policy – with the very major exception of political economy, simply because postcommunist economic transformation has stimulated a virtual subfield in the literature involving economists and political scientists alike. Another exception is the selective focus on international relations, with a clear priority given to security matters as well as European integration and the prospects here for CEE countries.

Of some concern, however, is an asymmetry in the adoption of comparative approaches and problems already tested and refined in Western contexts. This was convenient at first, with available comparative texts and theories either read in the original English (now widespread as the language of political science in CEE) or translated into the languages of these countries. But we are still talking about a comparative politics that was originally based on the study of developed Western states and, while adapted to accommodate for instance developing countries, nevertheless has so far taken little account of the distinctive features of postcommunist systems. A common phenomenon of the 1990s in Western Europe, the United States and elsewhere was the influx of comparativists working alongside established scholars from what had previously been communist studies. While dialogue between both sides has taken place, this has not led to any significant challenge to established comparative concerns in the light of new experiences as well as old legacies in postcommunist Europe. But there are various signs of present and future change; and these include some rethinking of approaches in the field of democratization.

One basic feature helps to put these advances and their limitations into perspective. We are still confronting countries that are undergoing regime change. Some of them have progressed a long way in institutionalizing their new democracies and in becoming fully fledged market economies as well as achieving viability as new states. Certain others have still much ground to cover for they are either fragile or questionable new democracies though not necessarily on the degenerated scale found in some Central Asian new republics. As a whole, the change that has occurred belies the more pessimistic predictions at the start of the 1990s about the democratic regimes that had just replaced communist rule, made with the admittedly easier transitions in Southern Europe in mind. But we cannot yet say the CEE countries may safely be counted among the established democracies of the world. In this sense, the first decade of the twenty-first century is likely to be decisive.

This transitional nature of Central and Eastern Europe is suggested by the very term 'postcommunism', which highlights both the persistent legacy of the old regime but also the continuing process of transformation (Sakwa, 1999, p. 127). Probably, its active use will cease when no longer relevant and only then will these countries be fully accommodated within the broad field of comparative politics. But for that to be effective, comparative politics itself will have to change and adapt. The very diversity of regime change outcomes so far, commonly noted when making cross-national comparisons of CEE countries let alone of former Soviet republics, is an indication that this change might be under way.

Regime Change Trajectories and the Prospects for Democratic Consolidation

Conventionally, the process of democratization is divided into its transition and consolidation stages – the latter being usually broader and deeper (involving society much more directly) and taking longer to be achieved. In reality, however, both consist of different operative levels which may indeed change their dynamics once uncertainties of the earlier stage are resolved. Above all, it is important not to make too sharp a distinction between transition and consolidation, but to focus on the gathering momentum of regime change and establish whether this has a more positive or negative thrust (Pridham, 2000).

In this chapter, various comparative exercises are utilized that together provide a composite overview of regime change developments before drawing conclusions about their advance towards achieving consolidation. The main purpose of this approach is to facilitate the measurement of democratic consolidation and to accommodate the emerging diversity of regime change trajectories. These six democratization tests are in order:

1. the diachronic, focusing on the evolution of regime change in a country-based fashion and on the positive and negative outcomes so far;
2. regional classification, where new democracies are examined in terms of geographical groupings and their commonalities;

3. cross-national variation, where – alternatively – differences between individual countries are examined more closely;
4. the quantitative or checklist approach, whereby these countries are accorded gradings in terms of progress made towards (most often) the liberal democratic model;
5. the qualitative, where criteria of substantive democracy are introduced and evaluated, this being seen as tantamount to testing their merits as prospective consolidated democracies; and,
6. the dynamic, assessing movement, or the lack of it, in the direction of democratic consolidation and the probability of arriving there.

While there may be some material or marginal overlap between these tests, they combine comparative perspectives in a way that give us a better grasp on postcommunist democratizations in Central and Eastern Europe than is usually offered by a bland discussion of consolidation. As a whole, democratic consolidation is in sight when a new democracy becomes institutionalized, its rules and procedures are being internalized, and democratic values are being disseminated through the activation of civil society and a process of 'remaking' of the political culture (Pridham, 2000, p. 20).

The Diachronic Development of Democratization

The diachronic test concerns regime change trajectories as initially determined by the different types of revolutions from 1989 and then, subsequently, by the predominance of reformist forces or alternatively old-regime elements and the emergence to a greater or lesser degree of civil society. At the same time, this political transformation has been affected by the radical or gradualist strategies adopted by different countries to implement economic system change from state-run to market economies. And, in some cases, new state formations and national questions associated with these have monopolized the attention of political elites at times and distracted from the tasks of democratization. It may be said that economic pluralization and modernization have significant effects in underpinning and rooting new democracies. This bodes well for their achieving democratic consolidation; just as the resolution of national questions or failure to do so, especially with ethnic polarization, is likely to have respectively positive or negative consequences. However, theoretical work on democratization has been slow to confront such arguments.

By these criteria, particular countries are evidently in the lead – notably, Slovenia, Hungary and Poland. It is no coincidence that these countries underwent forms of liberalization, if not incipient democratization, while still formally under communist rule in the later 1980s, thus giving them an early advantage when regime change began in earnest at the end of that decade (Bebler, 2002). Poland had a relatively strong civil society at the outset and embarked on a 'big bang' economic transformation that eventually helped to act as a consolidating influence on politics. Poland too has not had to face the national question with new state formation and difficult minority problems, although the slowness in the crystallization of the party system is one qualifying point in that country's regime change progress.

At the other end of the scale, there are countries like Ukraine with its largely formal democracy and weakly planted rule of law; Macedonia – a new state with a fragile ethnic balance; and also Albania whose backward socio-economic development acts as an obstacle to any ready democratic consolidation. Then, we have in Belarus the one obvious case of democratic inversion – that is, initial democratization becomes checked and regime change redirected back to an authoritarian solution, in this instance a personal dictatorship rather than the former regime (albeit with a distinct nostalgia for former communist times). Both Croatia and Serbia were during the 1990s in a hybrid regime category of formal democratic features but authoritarian practices, but since the end of the rule of both Tudjman and Milosevic in 1999–2000 these two countries have reverted to the path of democratization that they had embarked on briefly and unsuccessfully at the start of the 1990s.

This kind of diachronic narrative has various novel comparative uses, although it is already detailed in the available literature especially on individual countries. In particular, it casts light on cross-national diversity which has tended to become more and more evident with time. This will presumably increase further as we move through the new decade and some postcommunist democracies take their place among established democracies while others possibly fail to consolidate. At the same time, the examples of Croatia and Serbia remind us that regime change is not necessarily a linear process. Will therefore cases like Belarus redirect once more their trajectories or harden further their authoritarian tendencies?

Another use is to note descriptively when key stages or critical junctures in the course of democratization are accomplished. These should include: a new democratic constitution in place; the legitimation of alternations in power (that is, their full acceptance by the losers); the stabilization of party systems, consisting of regime loyal actors and thus enhancing elite consensus on democratic rules, procedures and values; the opening of negotiations for EU membership as having a gradual consolidating potential for new democracies with the implementation of political and economic conditions and of European legislation; and, finally, evidence of progress in the shaping of a post-authoritarian political culture.

Judged in this light, nearly all CEE countries achieved the first stage by 1992 (though Poland sits awkwardly in not having a full constitution until 1997), while they have a perhaps surprisingly strong record for regular alternations in power over the past decade (with, admittedly, public concern over the pace of economic reform playing a vital part in this pattern). Party system stabilization has, however, been slow in most cases with the exception of Hungary and the Czech Republic. Even recent elections, as in Bulgaria and Poland in 2001, have shown a remarkable rise in the fortunes of new political forces and decline in those of older ones. In Slovakia, this instability is very much evident if not on the increase with the successful emergence of a series of new parties; while systemic factors are still present with the failure to establish a full elite consensus on democratic rules. Clearly, in this and some cases in the Balkans, the continuing impacts of economic change and national questions affect party development. The opening of EU negotiations in 1998 with some CEE countries (Poland, the Czech Republic, Hungary, Slovenia and Estonia) together with NATO accession of the first three in 1999 differentiated among postcommunist new democracies, although later EU entry talks from 2000 with others (Slovakia, Latvia, Lithuania, Bulgaria and Romania) have since reduced this difference, especially with the first three of the latter closing the gap with the first group of candidate countries. Change in political culture remains as yet incomplete, no surprise given the normal time lag involved, but the limited evidence so far available suggests again some significant cross-national variation, with countries in East-Central Europe more advanced than elsewhere in the region (Ulram and Plasser, 2001).

The Regional Classification of Democratization

Cross-national comparisons of CEE countries often start with regional groupings. These are said to have various commonalities with a bearing on the prospects for democratization. Such groupings are usually East-Central Europe (ECE), comprising as its core the Visegrad states of Poland, Hungary and the Czech and Slovak Republics; and South-East Europe (SEE), more popularly called the Balkans, with all the historical and image connotations this term arouses. That leaves ex-Soviet republics which, while often less convincingly democratic, are sufficiently diverse to suggest the need for further distinctions. Most obviously among the countries considered here are the Baltic states which may also, in some ways, be grouped alongside those from East-Central Europe. Countries like Belarus, Ukraine and Moldova may, for our purposes, be functionally grouped together as 'outsider' European states, although as noted above they vary among themselves.

The purpose in such groupings is essentially heuristic, using their commonalities to explore similarities in democratization fortunes, although falling well short of any determinism. Cultural factors, always difficult to operationalize, are nevertheless important as background. There is the difference between Catholic and Orthodox countries as a basic dividing line between ECE and SEE, but this cannot explain all that has distinguished these two regions since 1990. Looking back over time, religion has proved not to be an immutable impediment to regime change and its progress (Karatnycky, 2002, p. 107). But this should be no surprise seeing that culturalist assumptions about Catholic countries being unfit for liberal democracy, heard in the days before Franco and other dictators departed, were later disproved.

In applying these groupings, it should not be forgotten, it is a matter here of geography mixed with history and recent political patterns. Thus, ECE has a compelling sense of 'returning to Europe' given location, traditional if interrupted links with other core European states, and through these an association with European political values, especially those pertaining to liberal democracy. This was shown by informal multilateral and bilateral links growing readily after the Iron Curtain disappeared, such as in the fields of transnational party cooperation and local twinning arrangements across frontiers. The former developed more easily than, say, with Balkan countries because of commonalities like Catholicism, which helped to establish such cooperation among Christian Democratic parties. Town twinning has advanced most intensively between Germany and Poland, of all new democracies, for historical and geographical reasons. With SEE countries, the embracing of 'Europe' has been more complicated since this has to some degree been motivated by a desire to 'escape from the Balkans', meaning its complicated historical legacies and the region's unfavourable reputation but also present instabilities. Furthermore, these countries have not generally had such traditional links with core European countries, which therefore took longer to develop in the 1990s – not to mention the slowness with which the EU itself took to engage seriously with this region.

Some historical legacies have been a major impediment to democratization. Of these the most important has been the state tradition which in its patrimonialist form in the Balkans left deeper legacy problems for eventual democratization than in ECE (Diamandouros and Larrabee, 2000, pp. 29–35). This was expressed in a number of ways such as the greater state role in the economy and in society, reinforced in later times by either 'sultanistic' forms of communist rule (as in Albania and Romania) or particularly 'thorough' versions of that rule, as notably in Bulgaria. Somewhat by contrast, the state in ECE countries played a part in furthering the entrepreneurial spirit in economic relations, which came to flourish notably in Czechoslovakia in the inter-war period (this in turn providing an historical reference point for economic marketization in the postcommunist period, especially in the Czech Republic). Similarly, civil society has, albeit to a limited degree, emerged more easily in ECE countries than those of the Balkans, where traditional state/society relations long discouraged the organizational capacity of social actors (ibid., p. 31). Thus, the ECE countries had a rather better starting-point for postcommunist socio-economic modernization than those located in other parts of the former Eastern bloc.

Such legacies may be modified in their relevance for regime change by political variables. For instance, the two regions have differed in the extent to which they have experienced the collapse of former communist federations, with consequent state-building problems including those involving the regulation of ethnic relations. In ECE, the major example of this was the division of Czechoslovakia which was conducted so bloodlessly it became known as the 'velvet divorce', despite some momentary increase in tensions between Czechs and Slovaks. By contrast, the collapse of Yugoslavia was followed by a series of horrific Balkan wars over the 1990s. There, it soon became clear, political leaders were not so committed to making the new democratic politics work as in ECE; and nationalist politics dominated for a time. Despite complications over large Russian minorities in the Baltic states, and official antagonism towards the Hungarian minority in Slovakia in the mid-1990s, nothing comparable to the tragedy of the former Yugoslavia occurred in ECE.

Cross-national Variation in Democratization Paths

Comparing the two regions, it is obvious that regime change has faced more arduous problems in the SEE than in the ECE countries. However, there are limits to the extent to which one may argue on the basis of regional groupings. For as time has passed, cross-national diversity has come more apparent; and this has tended to modify conclusions based on commonalities related largely to the past. But this has not always occurred in a linear fashion, in the sense of each region becoming uniformly more diverse.

For instance, as Croatia and Serbia have demonstrated, democratization may proceed in a zig-zag fashion – a term that has also been applied to the case of Slovakia in summarizing the successive stages of regime change there in the 1990s, with initial democratization in the final years of the Czechoslovak federation, then the authoritarian tendencies of Meciar's government of 1994–8, followed by the more sustained period of democratic change since the alternation in power of 1998. Debate some years ago about Slovakia's possible 'special path' – even including a supposedly divergent political culture – revolved around its divergence from 'Central European' patterns. Also at play was some element of national images, that of Slovakia continuing to suffer from the impact of the Meciar years. By contrast, the reputation of the young Czech Republic as a whole benefited considerably from its dynamic record in introducing a market economy, but it was also exaggerated and this began to be noticed only when the economic miracle turned sour in the later 1990s (Fawn, 2000, pp. 83–5 and 119ff.).

It is possible to apply this kind of analysis to the Balkan countries. Cross-national diversity there has been evident in looking at the former Yugoslav republics, such as in contrasting Slovenia and

Macedonia on grounds of democratic stability. Clearly, involvement in the Balkan wars demarcated Croatia, Serbia and Bosnia-Herzegovina from the others (Slovenia was only briefly engaged in the first, rather swift, war of independence from Yugoslavia). For these wars froze progress in democratization and, in Serbia's case in particular, helped to allow for a brutal repressive regime under Milosevic. Undoubtedly, restored democratization in Serbia and Croatia with the onset of the new century makes for less diversity now within this regional grouping. Croatia's new rulers are determined their country should catch up with more advanced postcommunist democracies, while legacy problems from the Milosevic years are severe in Serbia and will not make for easy democratic consolidation there. Among the Balkan countries, Bulgaria and Romania are officially designated as transformation frontrunners by virtue of being selected for EU membership talks, which entail meeting the necessary political and economic conditions. However, Romania is usually viewed as the 'laggard' among all the candidate countries presently negotiating entry.

The Baltic states and the 'outsider' grouping come across differently in this light. While some years back, Estonia was given preference over the other Baltic republics as an EU candidate country, on mainly economic reform grounds, the success of Latvia and Lithuania in their negotiations with Brussels has brought them almost level with Estonia. Latvia and Estonia have been distinguished for their much larger Russian minorities than Lithuania, with early problems pointing to complicated democratizations, but pressure from the EU has been significant in helping to alleviate such tensions. The tendency now to consider these three countries as a grouping on their own is now reinforced by their common acceptance as future NATO member states. However, the 'outsider' countries have, as indicated above, followed rather different patterns of regime change, so, clearly, diversity has remained among them. Their main commonality is the fragility, if not disappearance, of democratic procedures and the weakness of the rule of law.

An alternative way to identify cross-national variation is to apply again the series of critical junctures (listed above under diachronic development) freely without recourse to regional groupings. This does in some cases cut across preconceptions about the different regions, especially ECE and the Balkans. The early finalization of constitutions makes no noticeable distinction among postcommunist states except for Belarus and Moldova (both 1994) and also Poland (1997). But while a constitution is the centrepiece of regime transition this late full constitution in Poland's case cannot be treated as problematic for that country's democratic consolidation. In general, while obviously crucial in itself, the timing of a constitution is not as such a sure indicator of democratization's progress on other levels. Some of the as-of-now least consolidated new democracies inaugurated early constitutions, such as Albania and Macedonia both in 1991.

Alternation in power patterns does not greatly distinguish between the various countries. Those like Poland, Hungary and Slovakia and also Bulgaria as well as the Baltic republics have experienced fairly regular alternation. However, the Czech Republic had several centre-right governments led by Klaus before alternation in 1998 brought to power the Social Democrats for the first time, their place in government being confirmed in 2002. The relative lateness of this change followed developments in the party system, such as the rather gradual rise to competitive strength of the CSSD, but that in no way reflected negatively on consolidation in that country. In Romania's case, the delay of alternation until 1996 was more serious because until then the ruling Party of Social Democracy in Romania showed signs of not having convincingly reconstructed itself from communist times. But changes in this party during opposition have, with return alternation in 2000, brought a new momentum to regime change (and EU accession prospects) following disappointment with the reformist governments of 1996–2000.

In only a few cases has alternation in power been linked to systemic considerations. This was true of the 1997 election in Albania which saw the defeat of Sali Berisha, whose tenure as president had been increasingly marked by authoritarian practices. The return to office of the Socialists has not, however, led to stabilization of the political scene; and Berisha in any case sought to contest the outcome of alternation. In Slovakia, the 1998 election was regarded as systemically significant because of Meciar; just as the 2002 election in that country was similarly seen in these terms, especially abroad, despite much progress meanwhile in Slovakias progress towards democratic consolidation. In Macedonia, broad coalitions comprising parties from both ethnic communities act as a barrier to alternation, for this would indeed disturb the fragile relationship between them. Belarus is obviously a case apart, for there

Lukashenka uses his powers of office to suppress the rights and activities of the opposition.

Party system stabilization is not an absolute precondition for democratic consolidation. However, there is an ongoing dynamic between the two, so that any high degree of instability in what is still an unsettled party system is likely to have wider systemic repercussions. By this criterion, Poland and Slovakia do not rate well among ECE countries just as Bulgaria since the 2001 election now counts as another example. Instabilities in these countries are likely to point to extended consolidation of the regimes in question rather than to any system threat or reversal. Only in Slovakia is Meciar's continuing popularity seen by some as a sign of democratic uncertainty, although his defeat in 2002 points towards his political demise. By and large, systemically disloyal parties are not in great abundance in CEE countries. This applies in the Czech Republic to the Communist Party of Bohemia and Moravia, whose isolation in the party system has now been somewhat reduced by its grudging debate about future strategy and, recently, by its increased electoral support. In Hungary, the racist Justice and Life Party (MIEP) has been more of an embarrassing nuisance than a serious threat. Rumours that it might be considered as a possible coalition partner for Fidesz were ended by MIEP's failure to be re-elected to parliament in 2002. In Albania, Berisha has as opposition leader been accused of fomenting unrest in the country and has in the past even been suspected of planning a coup.

EU membership negotiations now place many of these postcommunist democracies on an equal footing in formal terms. However, there are various points of distinction that make for cross-national diversity. Firstly, other postcommunist countries have not (yet) been invited to negotiate, while further ones have few if any prospects for membership of the EU, although some form of intermediary status may be possible. In the first instance, we mainly have in mind other Balkan countries which continue to fail the Copenhagen conditions. Some like Serbia and Croatia had until recently regimes that were not liberal democratic, although Croatia begins to look like a reasonable prospect for eventual membership negotiations (it has recently signed a stabilization and association agreement). It is the 'outsiders' – here literally proving their description as such – for whom the chances of EU accession are dim indeed, although there are some differences. Belarus has non-existent relations with Brussels, for its type of regime excludes serious consideration of a link. There are some relations between the EU and Moldova but not much chance of these developing given concern on Brussels' part over human and democratic rights in that country. Of the three, Ukraine has the greatest ambitions with regard to the EU (Kuchma has declared a wish for his country to join by 2011). But the EU continues to exert pressure for democratic reforms, thus indicating caution.

These different degrees of relations with the EU on the part of postcommunist countries reflect on the extent of their individual integration in Europe, which may also be measured by the depth of commercial and other economic forms of integration that precede or develop in parallel with membership negotiations. This cross-national variation in integration carries a message about its consolidation effects, given the need by candidate countries to satisfy the political and economic conditions, including their implementation, to a satisfactory degree. The pressure here becomes intense with the advance of negotiations, the increasing policy 'bite' from carrying through the *acquis communautaire* and the sheer impatience to succeed and be given a final date for admission. Evidently, the four Visegrad states together with the Baltic republics and Slovenia are more or less at a comparable stage, although some differences may be noted as between Slovenia and Slovakia over the achievement of economic modernization. At the other end of the scale are those countries whose prospects for EU membership are not strong – which, in turn, reduces the EU leverage on them for deepening their democratic reforms.

Progress in remaking post-authoritarian political culture is less easy to answer because it is the critical juncture last in line. The dozen years since the fall of communism are not by normal standards long enough for this to be advanced to any great degree. That may, however, be qualified where an earlier liberalization allowed restricted pluralization to take place, and here Poland, Hungary and Slovenia are again highlighted together. Survey research indeed suggests that some ECE countries – Slovakia included – compare quite well with West European democracies in terms of diffuse support for democracy. This is, however, accompanied by high levels of dissatisfaction with the policy output and the functioning of new democracies in these countries. People with authoritarian inclinations are more numerous in Balkan countries like Bulgaria. However, Ukraine and Russia have by comparison a weaker base of confident democrats to balance this factor (Ulram and Plasser, 2001).

The Quantitative Approach to Democratization

Quantitative tests of new democracies involve gradings according to set criteria, allowing for another, more formal, means of assessing cross-national variation. Such tests are the favoured means of international organizations or agencies, concerned with democracy monitoring or promotion. They are sometimes called the checklist approach because these criteria are tested separately and in turn without reference to an overall conceptual framework. In the case of the 2001 Freedom House Survey (Karatnycky, 2002), ratings are on a scale of 1 to 7 for respectively the most or least free with respect to political rights and civil liberties. Countries are also given a general freedom rating and typed as electoral democracies or not. Altogether, this evidence highlights some basic differences among the countries examined in this chapter, which tend to confirm the broad picture so far established by the first three tests but now in a numerical form.

Thus, all are described as electoral democracies except for Belarus and Bosnia-Herzegovina. Three freedom ratings are given: only one (Belarus) is 'not free'; six are 'partly free' (Albania, Bosnia-Herzegovina, Macedonia, Moldova, Ukraine and Yugoslavia); while the rest are 'free'. This includes the Baltic republics, the Visegrad countries, Slovenia and the three Balkan countries of Bulgaria, Romania and Croatia. The ratings for political rights and civil liberties do, however, make some distinction among the third category. For instance, those given a 1 for political rights and 2 for civil liberties (here on a par with the UK) include the following: the four Visegrad countries, the Baltic states and Slovenia. The two remaining EU candidate countries are seen as not far behind: Romania is given respectively 2 and 2, while Bulgaria is given 1 (showing an improvement over political rights) and 3. The two recent return cases of democratization, Croatia and Yugoslavia (Serbia and Montenegro), are given ratings respectively of 2 and 2 (with an improvement in civil liberties) and 3 and 3 (with an improvement in both cases). Improvement involves comparison with the previous year's Freedom House survey and therefore significant movement in democratization. Hence, among the Balkan countries, we have a picture that confirms differentiation but also change. The three 'outsiders' come across as an altogether different set of countries although with some variation. Their ratings are: Belarus 6 and 6; Ukraine 4 and 4; and, Moldova 2 and 4 (by comparison, Russia is rated 5 and 5).

The Qualitative Approach to Democratization

A qualitative assessment of new democracies is complementary to previous tests as it requires focusing more on substantive criteria of democracy and using qualitative analysis. This is the preferred approach in academic work on democratization but it is also adopted by some monitoring agencies as well as international organizations, most notably the European Commission in its annual progress reports on candidate countries. In general, progress with substantive criteria is regarded as evidence of movement towards democratic consolidation.

We consider this approach by comparing sources of these different kinds: the overview essay on formal and substantive democracy in CEE countries by Kaldor and Vejvoda (Kaldor and Vejvoda, 1999); the official opinions of the European Commission on applicant states (European Commission, 1997); the latest in the series of European Commission reports, i.e. those for 2001 (European Commission, 2001); and the reports of the EU Accession Monitoring Programme of the Open Society Institute on both judicial independence and minority protection (Open Society Institute, 2001a,b). Given the dates of these publications, we are able to make specific comparisons of individual countries across time in the past half-decade utilizing two sources for both starting and end points. However, the material available concentrates on the ten candidate countries and therefore does not include the 'outsiders' as well as Balkan countries other than Bulgaria and Romania.

In ECE, the situation as defined by the European Commission in 1997 was one of fairly stable democratic institutions though with significant cross-national variation. By 2001 there had continued to be much progress, but with problems that had still to be addressed. Hungary was already in 1997 seen in the institutional procedural sense as a fully democratic country, with new institutions functioning properly and respecting the limits on their competences and cooperating with each other (a standard description applied to other cases indicating a significant degree of institutional consolidation). By 2001, Hungary had shown very significant progress in creating a truly independent judiciary but without this task being completed. The judgements on Poland were similar. In 1997, the Czech Republic had recently undergone the split with Slovakia, raising some questions about democratic progress, but there was now constitutional stability and political institutions were seen as consolidated; by 2001, the main problem appeared to be court reform.

Slovakia was in 1997 a major exception to the picture of consolidation of political institutions across the region, but by 2001 there had been considerable progress although there was still a need for further judicial reform. Slovenia in 1997 was seen in similar terms to those of Hungary and Poland, with significant progress reported four years later in establishing a truly independent judiciary. In other words, ECE did not present a uniform picture although by the early years of the new century a high degree of institutional consolidation was evident throughout the region.

The Baltic states were all recognized in 1997 for their high degree of institutional consolidation (using the standard description). But there were some qualifications: a weak judiciary and problems with implementing the rule of law in Lithuania, and a lack of effective law enforcement in Latvia and Estonia, while the latter also needed a better functioning judicial system. By 2001, all were thought to have made important progress in creating an independent judiciary but this was especially so in Estonia. Thus, these three countries showed much more uniformity than was the case in the ECE region. The two Balkan countries were in a similar position in 1997 in having stable democratic institutions, but this was especially true of Bulgaria, while Romania had undergone a dispute over the constitutional interpretation of the presidential mandate. Both countries needed to improve their practice of the rule of law, although by 2001, Bulgaria had advanced more than Romania in developing an independent judiciary. Despite this, both were seen as having made progress in institutional consolidation.

Across the region, both Hungary and Slovenia stood out as having a positive record in both 1997 and 2001 so far as human and minority rights were concerned. There are still problems over the position of the Roma minority, but these are common to all CEE countries. So, altogether, this situation bodes well for the democratic consolidation of both countries. Poland is in a similar position, assisted by its position as the only country in the region without a significant ethnic minority. The Czech Republic, on the other hand, was criticized in 1997 for lacking an active human rights policy and for persistent latent racism. By 2001, there had been a government response to this, but from the perspective of the European Commission there was still a need for further legislation and better implementation of existing policies. Slovakia was noted in 1997 for disputes and tensions over both the sizeable Hungarian minority and the Roma; but a considerable change had occurred by

2001 with significant measures to protect minorities although there were still some problems of implementation.

The Baltic republics showed a difference between Lithuania and Latvia and Estonia, for the latter two had large Russian minorities. While Lithuania was known in 1997 for a liberal citizenship law, substantial measures to protect minorities and no problems over respect for human rights, the other two states were criticized for limited access to citizenship for ethnic minorities and the question of minorities was a sensitive and controversial issue. However, there was no problem in these countries in respect of human rights. By 2001, Lithuania was regarded as satisfactory concerning minorities while in Latvia and Estonia there had been progress in integrating their minorities although there was much that had still to be done.

In the two Balkan countries there were various problems, with Bulgaria more advanced than Romania in 1997. The Turkish minority was well integrated in Bulgaria but at the same time there were deficiencies in respect for human rights. By 2001, some specific human rights problems were still evident (such as police violence and trafficking in human beings) and a problem of enforcement in minority legislation especially in the face of discrimination against the Roma. Romania had shown some improvement by 2001, although there still shortcomings in respect for human rights and in securing the rights of minorities.

Overall, some postcommunist countries were even in 1997 comparable with those of Western Europe, and all the countries of the ECE region had made significant advances towards democratic consolidation by the early years of the new century.

The Dynamic Approach to Democratization

This test attempts to capture movement in democratization, meaning not so much speed along its path as the dynamics of the process. This occurs at different levels, but with a positive impetus in their interactions. It may be through voting momentum over successive elections favouring parties committed to democracy; or different party elites deciding it is in their interests to go along with the new democratic politics despite initial doubts which may be ideological or related to the prospect of democratization as they perceive it. Quite often in regime change there may appear turning points when political choice can waver between options; and, it may take some event or influence (such as international pressure) to tip the balance. Here, passing critical junctures may be decisive as described above. Agreement on a constitution, while usually failing to meet all expectations and party interests, may help to deepen the sense of underlying consensus and willingness to engage in unfamiliar political compromise. The reaction of losers from alternation in power may be a crucial moment which, if overcome satisfactorily, may set a precedent for subsequent elite behaviour. And the gathering pace of EU negotiations may well have a reinforcing effect on democratization, especially if ultimate success looks increasingly likely, and finally persuade some reluctant political actors to cast their lot with the democratic game.

Seen in this light, regime change in Central and Eastern Europe comes across as showing reasonable progress. Rarely have constitutional arrangements been a matter of controversy, although this happened in Poland with Walesa's ambitions for presidential powers and in Slovakia where constitutional issues during the Meciar years reflected political polarization and tensions. Again, in Albania, Berisha's draft constitution was in 1994 rejected because of growing concern over his authoritarian intentions. But in recent years such issues have evaporated, except currently in Romania, even though EU accession has required various constitutional amendments. A measure of elite commitment to democratization has been the conversion of former communist regime parties to centre-left politics. There have been some exceptions but in recent years the Romanian and Bulgarian parties have moved down the social democratic road. And there are many signs that EU accession has developed a wider domestic momentum in accession countries (by the same token, any stalling of this process would have momentous effects on their consolidation prospects).

Central to regime change dynamics in CEE have been parallel transformations and their interactions with democratization. It is too complicated a situation to judge whether a radical or gradualist approach to economic change has been better for democratization because of different national circumstances; but one trend is apparent. Economic discontent or concern over the pace of economic change has invariably been a major reason for alternation in power, but this has been regime-reinforcing because of the preponderance of democracy-loyal parties. In no CEE country has the economy resulted in regime change reversal, and it was not a major factor behind developments in Belarus. It may, on the other hand, help to influence the fairly widespread distrust towards political institutions, but this has not been channelled in an anti-system direction. What is more likely, therefore, is a slowing effect on democratic consolidation. Only in countries such as Ukraine, not to mention the Central Asian republics, is persistently poor economic performance detrimental to the development of democratic institutions and practices, but that is because it combines with other factors such as deeply corrupt elite behaviour and a weak civic culture.

State- and nation-building has produced quite contrasting outcomes: detrimental through war to democratization in Croatia, Serbia and Bosnia-Herzegovina; but peaceful in the Czech and Slovak Republics. While the Czechs were able to take advantage of Prague's government infrastructure and the new country's association with the former Czechoslovakia (and also had no strong minority problems), it is possible in Slovakia's case to establish a link between initial national uncertainties, tensions over the strong Hungarian minority and problems of the Meciar government between 1994 and 1998. But the inclusion of the Hungarian party in the government there since then has helped to reduce ethnic difficulties. Croatia and Serbia have recently changed regime course again, although the war legacies may continue for some time to cause problems especially in Serbia. This is even more true for ethnically war-torn Bosnia-Herzegovina.

Altogether, the prospects for democratic consolidation across the region look better than half a decade ago. Conceivably, the most difficult decade is behind the countries we have considered in this volume, although this does not mean the path of democratization will not face challenges and problems in the years to come. But, relatively speaking, the situation is now moving ahead towards consolidation; and this tends to demarcate this part of the post-communist world from most parts of the former Soviet Union.

Looking to the Future: A New Comparative Politics of Europe?

In short, therefore, democratic consolidation is very largely on track in Central and Eastern Europe, although as we have seen there is significant cross-national variation. In the simplest terms, we are talking about regimes that are now mostly recognizable as liberal democratic, at least in their construction and potential if not actual achivement so far. Hybrid regimes like Croatia and Serbia have disappeared and their replacements look like additions to the pattern elsewhere in CEE. Bosnia-Herzegovina is undoubtedly weak especially at the civil society level, and international support will remain an important factor there. Ukraine has serious difficulties which may or may not prove systemically problematic in the future. Belarus remains the one exception, as not a hybrid regime but a straightforward despotic one – for the present.

Democratizations in CEE, initially inviting comparisons with earlier regime change in Southern Europe, have tended over time to demonstrate more differences than similarities, not least because they have formed part, simultaneously, of a multiple transformation process. This has acquired its own dynamic which has eventually helped to carry forward political change or has, in some cases, complicated it. Undoubtedly, this frame of reference merits greater attention in developing and broadening the concerns of democratization theory. For it helps us to understand why, despite severe legacies from communism and many obstacles facing democratic consolidation, progress towards the latter has outstripped expectations. In addition, factors like a more supportive international environment in Europe – one which has also goaded these new democracies along the path to liberal democracy – do much to explain why democratizations, so far at least, have been rather more successful than those in Latin America.

If this relatively optimistic conclusion proves enduring, subject to further developments in the first decade of the new century, then we are looking to established democracies eventually throughout the region. This tendency is likely to be reinforced by EU enlargement during this very decade just as, it seems, the worst problems of both economic transformation and state- and nation-building may be behind rather than ahead. When reflected at the academic level, this settling down of postcommunist democracies means a broadening of comparative politics with respect to Europe. But it will also entail some adaptation. At the official level, pressure has been asymmetrical in the sense of these democracies having to conform to European (that is, West European) standards. But that will begin to change, for instance, once they start acquiring full membership of the EU and begin to assert more freely their own political, economic and socio-cultural concerns.

These countries will bring their own histories with them and that must include their legacies from the communist period, which obviously distinguishes their experience from that of Western Europe. Different cultural norms and policy demands will appear on the European agenda, such as ethnicity, which has usually been banished in post-Fascist Western Europe. The study of political parties and party systems is now showing some signs of unfamiliar challenges. In particular, we are talking about a considerable addition of small states (apart from Poland and Romania) to the new concert of Europe; and this may well modify the role enjoyed so far by big country players on the European stage. Above all, the term 'postcommunist' will probably disappear from common usage. Moreover, with ever closer relations at all levels – commercial and touristic as well as political – there is likely to emerge elsewhere greater interest in and awareness of the countries of Central and Eastern Europe. If comparative politics responds to all these developments and the newly consolidated democracies join the agenda of mainstream political science, the general outcome should be one of enriching engagement.

Further Reading

An excellent general history of the whole region is Andrew Janos (2000). Richard and Ben Crampton (1996) have produced a useful historical atlas that illustrates the shifting nature of borders that has been a hallmark of that history. Mark Mazower (1998) sets out the wider pan-European context, and his later book on the Balkans (2000) helps to counter Western prejudices about that region. The introduction to Norman Davies's magisterial survey of Europe (1996) forcefully redresses the tendency of Western historians of 'Europe' to ignore the whole region. Milan Kundera's deliberately provocative essay (1984) sparked off a wide-ranging debate about the identity of 'Central Europe' as a distinctive region, and outstanding contributions to this debate are gathered in Schöpflin and Wood (1989). An illuminating perspective on national and ethnic issues by one of the leading historians working on the region is Charles Ingrao (1999). Inter-war history is well covered in Joseph Rothschild (1974), as is the communist period by the same author and Nancy Wingfield (2000). The meaning of the 1989 Revolutions is discussed in a most engaging way by Kumar (2001), and the practical issues raised by the 'return to Europe' are presented in Mayhew (1998) and Henderson (1999).

There are a number of good general monographs on *Poland*, the most up-to-date of which is George Sanford (2002), focusing on the constitution and the adaptation of political institutions. Also valuable are Taras (1995), Millard (1999), Schleifer (1997) and Brzezinski (1998). Two worthwhile edited collections are Staar (1998) and Wojtaszczyk (1997). The historical dimension of Poland's break with communism is analysed with distinctive interpretations by Kaminski (1991) and Tittenbrun (1993). Tworzecki (1996) provides an effective discussion of the regional and ideological dimensions of political parties in the early stages of their development, which may be supplemented by Szczerbiak's (2001a) detailed treatment of party organization. Ekiert and Kubiak (1999) discuss the continued turmoil of Poland's civil society. Prizel (1998) provides the best treatment of foreign policy, including its wider sources and implications.

There are excellent overviews of the *Czech Republic and Slovakia* in Skalnik Leff (1996), Fawn (2000), Shepherd (2000) and Henderson (2002). The revolution of 1989 is analysed by Wheaton and Kavan (1992), Calda (1996) and Saxonberg (2001). The break-up of Czechoslovakia can best be approached from the legal perspective of Stein (1997) combined with the economic insight of Dedek *et al.* (1996). Innes (2001) examines the particular contribution that was made by the party system. Kopecky (2001) offers an outstanding comparison of the legislatures and party systems.

The best overall introduction to the institutions of government in *Hungary* in English is Korosenyi (1999), and the most useful introduction to political developments during the 1990s is Andor (2000). Swain (1992) examines the late communist period, and Tokes (1996) provides a full and authoritative account of Hungary's 'velvet revolution'. Several useful contributions consider the subsequent period, including Cox and Furlong (1994) and Braun and Barany (1999).

On the *Balkans* during and after the communist era, see Crampton (2002) for an accessible survey and Gallagher (2001) for a study that gives more attention to the international dimension of the conflict. It is supplemented by a companion volume (Gallagher, 2003a), which examines the international response to postcommunism and war in Yugoslavia during the 1990s. Ramet (1992) examines Tito's flawed experiment in communist federalism, and can usefully be compared with Allcock (2000), which analyses communist Yugoslavia and its break-up from the standpoint of a political sociologist. Among the most rewarding of the single country studies are Popov (2000), Collin (2001), Vickers and Pettifer (1997) and Bell (1998). On Romania, see Gallagher (2003b).

The two standard histories of *Ukraine* are Magocsi (1996) and Subtelny (2000). For an analysis of the drive to independence, see Kuzio and Wilson (1994), and in more detail Nahaylo (1999). Accessible short studies of recent politics include Motyl (1993), Garnett (1997) and Lieven (1999). Wilson (2002) covers both history and the period since independence. On the Ukrainian economy there is Aslund and de Ménil (2000), and on foreign policy Moroney *et al.* (2002) and Wolczuk (2002). Good books on *Belarus and Moldova* are harder to find; but the standard work on Moldova is King (2000), and on Belarus try Garnett and Legvold (1999), Marples (1999), and more recently Korosteleva, Lawson and Marsh (2003) and White, Korosteleva and Löwenhardt (forthcoming).

The *constitutions* of the region are conveniently collected in International Institute for Democracy (1996, 1997). There is a thoughtful study of institutional change in Elster, Offe and Preuss (1998), and current developments are fully covered in the *East European Constitutional Review*. A particularly detailed study of constitutional change in Ukraine is available in Wolczuk (2001). On the important issue of corruption, see Miller *et al.* (2001). The study of *elite politics* under communism was a well-developed field but it *was* literally 'kremlinological,' focusing primarily on the Soviet elite. Linden and Rockman (1984) offered methodological reflections about studying elites in communist East Europe, while Rush (1974), McCauley and Carter (1986), and Taras (1989) focused on communist succession. The specific role of political leadership in and after the 1989 revolutions is theoretically addressed in Przeworski (1992) and Colton and Tucker (1995). Articles by Tokes (1990), Zubek (1991) and O'Neil (1996a) conceptualize leadership transition in Hungary and Poland. Higley *et al.* (1996, 1997) examine the formation of postcommunist elites, while Hanley *et al.* (1998) and Eyal *et al.* (2000) provide data on recruitment and types of elites. Rose, Mishler and Haerpfer (1998) consider popular attitudes to leadership. Baylis (1996), Ishiyama and Velten (1998) and Taras (1998) examine presidents in postcommunist states. Biographies of the three presidents best known in the West include Kurski (1993) on Walesa, Keane (2001) on Havel, and Cohen (2000) on Milosevic.

Comparative studies of *parliaments*, focused especially on the 1990s, include Agh (1994), Remington (1994), Olson and Norton (1996) and Longley and Zajc (1998). Specific aspects of legislative behaviour and institutional development are covered in Agh (1996) and Olson and Crowther (2002). Studies focused on individual countries include Kopecky (2001) and Van der Meer Krok-Paszkowska (2000).

The fullest studies of *party and party system development* in the region are provided by Lewis (2000) and Kitschelt *et al.* (1999), the former of which is shorter and more accessible to the non-specialist reader. A good recent overview of the subject is that by von Beyme (2001b) as well as, for those with the appropriate language skills, de Waele (2002). The origins and role of political parties are also usefully introduced in general texts such as those of Agh (1998, ch. 5) and Nagle and Mahr (1999, ch. 7). Bielasiak (2002) provides an up-to-date discussion of questions of party system institutionalization. The different chapters in Lewis (1996) offer an early account of party structure and organizational development in some of the countries of the region. A more recent study of trends in membership levels is given by Mair and van Biezen (2001) and a comprehensive, though early, account of the postcommunist media with useful information about their party links was that of O'Neil (1996b). Contributions to an edited book by Lewis (2001) discuss recent developments in a number of different countries as well as covering topics raised here such as Europeanization and trans-national party cooperation, organizational development and the professionalization of party activities, and party funding.

Authors of several books published in recent years have attempted to present comparative analyses of *elections and electoral behaviour* in Central and East Europe, often in connection to the development of party systems and/or more general issues of postcommunist political development. Among the most successful endeavours of this sort are Birch *et al.* (2002), Holmes (1997), Kitschelt *et al.* (1999), Lewis (2000, 2001) and Tworzecki (2002). There are also some fine analyses of elections and related developments in particular countries, such as Tokes (1996), Tworzecki (1996) and Szczerbiak (2001a). Election results and copies of the relevant legislation for Bulgaria, Czechoslovakia, Estonia, Hungary, Latvia, Lithuania, Moldova, Poland, Romania, Russia, Slovakia and Ukraine may be consulted at *www.essex.ac.uk/elections*.

On the politics of *economic reform*, see the story of the 'Balcerowicz plan' by one of its principal architects, in Sachs (1993). The theory behind privatization is very clearly set out by Frydman and Rapaczynski (1994), who also give a lucid account of experiences in the early 1990s. A thorough review of the impact of transition on the labour market during the 1990s is that of Mickiewicz and Bell (2000). Martin's article (1998) on Central Europe and globalization neatly sets out many of the key issues, and his book (1999) gives an excellent overview of enterprise, including foreign firms' role, in transition. The former chief economist of the World Bank offers his trenchant criticisms of the Washington Consensus in Stiglitz (2002), while a Polish finance minister gives his in a wide-ranging work, covering all postcommunist economies, in Kolodko (2000). Some of those works beginning to probe EU enlargement to the east include Ingham and Ingham (2002) and Dawson and Fawn (2002). For those interested in the logic of central planning, the classic work is the two-volume work by the Hungarian economist, Janos Kornai (1980); a more accessible account is Winiecki (1988). Among the best sources of up-to-date economic data on the region are the European Bank for Reconstruction and Development (EBRD) and the United Nations Economic Commission for Europe (UNECE). The EBRD annual *Transition Report* is invaluable, as is the UNECE *Economic Survey of Europe*; both organizations have extremely useful websites. The quarterly Country Reports of the Economist Intelligence Unit provide one of the best ways of picking up a snapshot of current economic and political conditions in Central Europe. Another useful handbook to the region is provided in *Central and South-Eastern Europe* (2003), which is regularly updated. The website of the United Nations Economic Commission for Europe is at *www.unece.org* and that of the United Nations Committee for Trade and Development is at *www.unctad.org*, while the European Bank for Reconstruction and Development is at *www.ebrd.com*.

On long-term changes in *social stratification and social mobility*, Domanski (2000) provides a thorough discussion. Eyal *et al.* (1998) provide analysis and discussion of the new postcommunist elites and develop their theory that Central Europe has developed a new form of managerial capitalism, all based on their own extensive survey research. Alternative approaches to elites and circulation and competition between them are provided in edited volumes by Higley, Pakulski and Wesolowski (1998) and Higley and Lengyel (2000). While it mainly deals with Russia, the volume edited by Shlapentokh, Vanderpool and Doktorov (1999) also provides useful discussion of elites in other former Soviet republics. For detailed analysis and information on poverty and inequality, see the publications of the World Bank (2000, 2002), and especially Milanovich (1998). On the sociology of postcommunist transformations, see Stark and Bruszt (1998), and Cox and Mason (1999).

On the impact of *EU enlargement* on the region, see Grabbe (2001a) on the impact on governance, and also Goetz and Wollmann (2001). An overview of effects on specific countries is available in Henderson (1999). On the impact on democratization, see Whitehead (1997). For a comprehensive view of EU policy towards the region, see Mayhew (1998), Sedelmeier and Wallace (2000) and Grabbe (2001b). An overview of the costs and benefits of enlargement is available in Boeri *et al.* (2002).

There are now several theoretical or comparative studies on *post-communist democratization* in Central and Eastern Europe. They notably include Plasser, Ulram and Waldrauch (1998), while both Linz and Stepan (1996) and Pridham (2000) provide substantial coverage of CEE – the former by means of country case studies in part IV, the latter as part of a cross-regional comparative discussion which questions and adapts traditional theoretical concerns based on Southern European and Latin American experiences. There are several collections of sub-area studies within CEE, some with comparative insights. Pridham and Gallagher (2000) and Pridham and Agh (2001) contain both thematic and country chapters; while Agh (1998) also concentrates in comparative fashion on the latter sub-area. Earlier country case-study treatment of CEE countries is found in the volumes edited by Dawisha and Parrott (1997). Two combined edited volumes have appeared recently that focus thematically and through case studies on institutional and international aspects of democratization in CEE: see Zielonka (2001) and Zielonka and Pravda (2001). Institutional and international factors are also considered in Elster, Offe and Preuss (1998) and Pridham, Herring and Sanford (1997).

A comprehensive reader on the 'politics of the postcommunist world' is available in White and Nelson (2001), which reprints about fifty articles with a predominantly crossnational approach. In a rapidly changing situation, current developments and changing theoretical perspectives must be followed through the scholarly and more popular literature. There are several periodicals that deal specifically with Central and Eastern Europe, among them *Communist and Post-Communist Studies*, *East European Politics and Societies*, *Europe-Asia Studies* (formerly *Soviet Studies*), the *Journal of Communist Studies and Transition Politics*, and *Problems of Post-Communism*. Daily access to developments in the region is available through a variety of on-line services, particularly those of the Open Media Research Institute (*www.refrl.org/newsline*).

Bibliography

Agh, Attila (ed.) (1994) *The Emergence of East Central European Parliaments: The First Steps.* Budapest: Hungarian Centre of Democracy Studies Foundation.

Agh, Attila (1995) 'The Experience of the First Democratic Parliaments in East Central Europe', *Communist and Post-Communist Studies*, vol. 28, no. 2, pp. 203–14.

Agh, Attila (1996) 'Political Culture and System Change in Hungary,' in Fritz Plasser and Andreas Pribersky (eds), *Political Culture in East Central Europe.* Aldershot: Avebury, pp. 127–48.

Agh, Attila (1998) *The Politics of Central Europe.* London: Sage.

Agh, Attila and Gabriela Ilonszki (eds) (1996) *Parliaments and Organized Interests: The Second Steps.* Budapest: Hungarian Centre of Democracy Studies Foundation.

Allcock, John (2000) *Explaining Yugoslavia.* London: Hurst.

Almond, Gabriel and G. Bingham Powell (eds) (1983) *Comparative Politics Today.* Boston, MA: Little, Brown.

Andor, Laszlo (2000) *Hungary on the Road to the European Union. Transition in Blue.* Westport, CT, and London: Praeger.

Andorka, R. (1999) 'Dissatisfaction and Alienation', in R. Andorka, T. Kolosi, R. Rose and G. Vukovich (eds), *A Society Transformed.* Budapest: Central European University Press.

Arato, Andrew (1995) 'Parliamentary Constitution Making in Hungary', *East European Constitutional Review*, vol. 4, no. 4 (Fall), pp. 45–51.

Arato, Andrew (1996) 'The Constitution-Making Endgame in Hungary', *East European Constitutional Review*, vol. 5, no. 4 (Fall), pp. 31–9.

Arriagada, G. (1992) 'Reflections on Recent Elections in Latin America and Eastern and Central Europe', in L. Garber and E. Bjornlund (eds), *The New Democratic Frontier.* Washington, DC: National Democratic Institute for International Affairs.

Aslund, Anders and Georges de Ménil (eds) (2000) *Economic Reform in Ukraine: The Unfinished Agenda.* Armonk, NY and London: M.E. Sharpe.

Baldwin, Richard E., Joseph F. François and Richard Portes (1997) 'The Costs and Benefits of Eastern Enlargement', *Economic Policy*, vol. 12, no. 24 (April), pp. 125–76.

Bauman, Zygmunt (1994) 'After the Patronage State: A Model in Search of Class Interests', in Christopher G. A. Bryant and Edmund Mokrzycki (eds), *The New Great Transformation? Change and Continuity in East-Central Europe.* London: Routledge.

Baylis, Thomas A. (1996) 'Presidents Versus Prime Ministers: Shaping Executive Authority in Eastern Europe', *World Politics*, vol. 48, no. 3 (April), pp. 297–323.

Bebler, Anton (2002) 'Slovenia's Smooth Transition', *Journal of Democracy*, vol. 13, no. 1 (January), pp. 127–40.

Bell, John D. (1997) 'Democratization and Political Participation in "Post-Communist" Bulgaria', in Karen Dawisha and Bruce Parrott (eds), *Politics, Power, and the Struggle for Democracy in South-East Europe*. Cambridge and New York: Cambridge University Press.

Bell, John D. (ed.) (1998) *Bulgaria in Transition: Politics, Economics, Society and Culture after Communism*. Boulder, CO and Oxford: Westview Press.

Bevan, Alan and Saul Estrin (2000), 'The Determinants of Foreign Direct Investment in Transition Economies', Centre for New and Emerging Markets Discussion Paper 9, London: London Business School.

Bielasiak, Jack (1997) 'Substance and Process in the Development of Party Systems in East Central Europe', *Communist and Post-Communist Studies*, vol. 30, no. 1 (March), pp. 23–44.

Bielasiak, Jack (2002) 'The Institutionalization of Electoral and Party Systems in Postcommunist States', *Comparative Politics*, vol. 34, no. 2 (January), pp. 189–210.

Birch, Sarah (2001) 'Electoral Systems and Party Systems East and West', *Perspectives on European Politics and Society*, vol. 2, no. 3, pp. 355–77.

Birch, Sarah, Frances Millard, Marina Popescu and Kieran Williams (2002) *Embodying Democracy: Electoral System Design in Post-Communist Europe*. Basingstoke: Palgrave.

Blanchard, Olivier *et al.* (1991) *Reform in Eastern Europe*. Cambridge, MA: MIT Press.

Blanchflower, David and Andrew Oswald (2000) 'Entrepreneurship: A World of Contenders', *Financial Times*, 17 February, p. 19.

Blazyca, George (1995) 'Monitoring Economic Transformation', in G. Blazyca and Janusz M. Dąbrowski (eds), *Monitoring Economic Transition: The Polish Case*. Avebury: Aldershot.

Blondel, Jean and Ferdinand Müller-Rommel (eds) (2001) *Cabinets in Eastern Europe*. Basingstoke: Palgrave.

Boeri, Tito *et al.* (2002) *Who's Afraid of the Big Enlargement? Economic and Social Implications of the European Union's Prospective Eastern Expansion*. CEPR Policy Paper No. 7, London: Centre for Economic Policy Research.

Boycko, Maxim *et al.* (1995) *Privatizing Russia*. Cambridge, MA: MIT Press.

Braun, A. and Z. Barany (eds) (1999) *Dilemmas of Transition: The Hungarian Experience*. Lanham, MD: Rowman & Littlefield.

Brown, J.F. (1994) *Hopes and Shadows: Eastern Europe after Communism*. Durham, NC: Duke University Press.

Brubaker, Rogers (1996) *Nationalism Reframed: Nationhood and the National Question in the New Europe*. Cambridge and New York: Cambridge University Press.

Brunner, Georg (1993) 'Zweieinhalb Jahre ungarische Verfassungsgerichtsbarkeit', *Der Staat*, no. 2, pp. 287–315.

Brzezinski, Matthew (1998) *The Struggle for Constitutionalism in Poland*. Basingstoke: Macmillan.

298

Bunce, Valerie (2000) 'Comparative Democratization: Big and Bounded Generalizations', *Comparative Political Studies*, vol. 33, no. 6/7 (August–September), pp. 703–34.

Calda, Milos (1996) 'The Roundtable Talks in Czechoslovakia', in Jon Elster (ed.), *The Round-Table Talks and the Breakdown of Communism*. Chicago: University of Chicago Press, pp. 135–77.

Carothers, Thomas (1995) 'Democratic Promotion Under Clinton', *Washington Quarterly*, vol. 18, no. 4 (Autumn), pp. 13–28.

Central and South-Eastern Europe 2003 (3rd edn, 2002) London: Europa.

Chehabi, H.E. and Juan J. Linz (eds) (1998) *Sultanistic Regimes*. Baltimore, MD: Johns Hopkins University Press.

Chirot, Daniel (1989) *The Origins of Backwardness in Eastern Europe: Economics and Politics from the Middle Ages until the Early Twentieth Century*. Berkeley: University of California Press.

Cohen, Lenard J. (2000) *Serpent in the Bosom: The Rise and Fall of Slobodan Milosevic*. Boulder, CO: Westview Press.

Collier, David and Steven Levitsky (1997) 'Democracy with Adjectives: Conceptual Innovation in Comparative Research', *World Politics*, vol. 49, no. 3 (April), pp. 430–51.

Collin, Matthew (2001) *This is Serbia Calling*. London: Serpent's Tail.

Colton, Timothy J. and Robert C. Tucker (eds) (1995) *Patterns in Post-Soviet Leadership*. Boulder, CO: Westview Press.

Cox, Terry and Andy Furlong (eds) (1994) *Hungary: The Politics of Transition*. London: Cass.

Cox, Terry and Bob Mason (1999) *Social and Economic Transformation in East Central Europe*. Cheltenham: Edward Elgar.

Crampton, R.J. (2002) *The Balkans Since the Second World War*. London: Longman.

Crampton, R. and B. Crampton (1996) *Atlas of East European History in the Twentieth Century*. London: Routledge.

Csaba, Laszlo (1995) *The Capitalist Revolution in Eastern Europe: A Contribution to the Economic Theory of Systemic Change*. Cheltenham: Edward Elgar.

Dahrendorf, Ralf (1990) *Reflections on the Revolution in Europe*. New York: Random House.

Davies, Norman (1996) *Europe: A History*. Oxford: Oxford University Press.

Dawisha, Karen and Bruce Parrott (1997) *Democratization and Authoritarianism in Postcommunist Societies*, 4 vols. Cambridge and New York: Cambridge University Press.

Dawson, Andrew H. and Fawn, Rick (eds) (2002) *The Changing Geopolitics of Eastern Europe*. London: Frank Cass.

Dedek, Oldrich *et al.* (1996) *The Break-up of Czechoslovakia: An In-Depth Economic Analysis*. Aldershot: Avebury.

Diamandouros, N. and S. Larrabee (2000) 'Democratisation in South-Eastern Europe: Theoretical Considerations and Evolving Trends', in Geoffrey Pridham and Tom Gallagher (eds), *Experimenting with Democracy: Regime Change in the Balkans*. London: Routledge, pp. 24–64.

Dobb, Maurice (1970) *Socialist Planning: Some Problems*. London: Lawrence & Wishart.

Doder, Dusko and Louise Branson (1999) *Milošević: Portrait of a Tyrant*. New York: Free Press.

Domanski, H. (2000) *On the Verge of Convergence: Social Stratification in Eastern Europe*. Budapest: Central European University Press.

Done, K. (1998) 'Pace Quickens on the Long Hard Road', *Financial Times*, 8 May (supplement).

Duverger, Maurice (1963) *Political Parties*. New York: Wiley.

Duverger, Maurice (1986) 'Duverger's Law: Forty Years Later', in Bernard Grofman and Arend Lijphart (eds), *Electoral Laws and Their Political Consequences*. New York: Agathon Press.

EBRD (1996) *Transition Report*. London: European Bank for Reconstruction and Development.

Ekiert, Grzegorz and Jan Kubiak (1999) *Rebellious Civil Society: Popular Protest and Democratic Consolidation in Poland, 1989–1993*. Ann Arbor: University of Michigan Press.

Elekes Z. and B. Paksi (1999) 'Are Politics Getting People Down? Changing Trends in Suicide and Alcoholism', in Z. Speder (ed.), *Hungary in Flux*. Hamburg: Kramer.

Ellman, Michael (1989) *Socialist Planning*, 2nd edn. Cambridge: Cambridge University Press.

Elster, Jon (ed.) (1996) *The Round Table Talks and the Breakdown of Communism*. Chicago: University of Chicago Press.

Elster, Jon (1998) 'Deliberation and Constitution Making', in J. Elster (ed.), *Deliberative Democracy*. Cambridge and New York: Cambridge University Press, pp. 97–122.

Elster, Jon, Claus Offe and Ulrich K. Preuss (1998) *Institutional Design in Post-Communist Societies: Rebuilding the Ship at Sea*. Cambridge and New York: Cambridge University Press.

Erikson, R. and J. Goldthorpe (1992) *The Constant Flux: A Study of Class Mobility in Industrial Societies*. Oxford: Clarendon Press.

European Commission (1994) *Central and Eastern Eurobarometer Survey*. Brussels: European Commission.

European Commission (1997) *Agenda 2000: 3. The Opinions of the European Commission on the Applications for Accession*. Brussels.

European Commission (2001) *Enlargement: 2001 Regular Reports on Progress towards Accession*. Brussels.

European Commission (2002) *Candidate Countries Eurobarometer 2001*. Brussels: European Commission.

Evans, Geoffrey and Stephen Whitefield (1993) 'Identifying the Bases of Party Competition in Eastern Europe', *British Journal of Political Science* vol. 23, no. 4 (October), pp. 521–48.

Eyal, Gil, Ivan Szelenyi and Eleanor Townsley (1998) *Making Capitalism Without Capitalists: The New Ruling Elites in Eastern Europe*. London: Verso.

Fawn, Rick (2000) *The Czech Republic: A Nation of Velvet*. London: Routledge.

Feature (1997), 'The 1997 Polish Constitution', *East European Constitutional Review* (Spring-Summer), pp. 64–96.

Fish, M. Steven (2000) 'The Executive Deception: Superpresidentialism and the Degradation of Russian Politics', in Valerie Sperling (ed.), *Building the Russian State: Institutional Crisis and the Quest for Democratic Governance*. Boulder, CO: Westview Press, pp. 177–92.

Foldes, Gyorgy (1993) 'A Kadar-rendszer es a munkassag', *Eszmelet*, no. 18–19, pp. 57–93.

Foldes, Gyorgy (1995) *Az eladosodas politikatortenete, 1957–1986.* Budapest: Maecenas Konyvkiado.

Fowler, Brigid (2001) 'Debating Sub-State Reform on Hungary's "Road to Europe"', ESRC 'One Europe or Several?' Programme Working Paper 21/01, Sussex: Sussex European Institute.

Franck, Thomas M. (ed.) (1968) *Why Federations Fail: An Inquiry into the Requisites for Successful Federalism.* New York: New York University Press.

Frydman, Roman and Andrzej Rapaczynski (1994) *Privatization in Eastern Europe: Is the State Withering Away?*. Budapest: Central European University Press.

Fukuyama, Francis (1992) *The End of History and the Last Man.* New York: Free Press.

Gallagher, Tom (2001) *Outcast Europe: The Balkans from the Ottomans To Milosević, 1789–1989.* London: Routledge.

Gallagher, Tom (2003a) *From Tyranny to Tragedy: The Balkans After the Cold War.* London: Routledge.

Gallagher, Tom (2003b) *Distrusting Democracy: Romania Since 1989.* London: Hurst.

Garnett, Sherman (1997) *Keystone in the Arch: Ukraine in the Emerging Security Architecture of Central and Eastern Europe.* Washington, DC: Carnegie Endowment.

Garnett, Sherman and Robert Legvold (eds) (1999) *Belarus at the Crossroads.* Washington, DC: Carnegie Endowment.

Garton Ash, T. (1989) 'Does Central Europe Exist?', in George Schöpflin and Nancy Wood (eds), *In Search of Central Europe.* Oxford: Polity, pp. 191–215.

Gialdino, Carlo Curti (1995) 'Some Reflections on the *Acquis Communautaire*', *Common Market Law Review*, vol. 32, no. 5, pp. 1089–121.

Gillespie, Richard, Lourdes Lopez Nieto and Michael Waller (eds) (1995) 'Factional Politics and Democratization', special issue of *Democratization*, vol. 2, no. 1 (Spring).

Goetz, Klaus H. (2000) 'European Integration and National Executives: A Cause in Search of an Effect?', *West European Politics*, vol. 23, no. 4 (October), pp. 211–31.

Goetz, Klaus H. and Hellmut Wollmann (2001) 'Governmentalising Central Executives in Post-Communist Europe: A Four-Country Comparison', *Journal of European Public Policy*, vol. 8, no. 6 (December), pp. 864–87.

Gortat, Radzislawa (1993) 'The Feud within Solidarity's Offspring', *Journal of Communist Studies*, vol. 9, no. 4 (December), pp. 116–24.

Grabbe, Heather (1999) 'A Partnership for Accession? The Implications of EU Conditionality for the Central and East European Applicants', EUI Working Paper RSC No. 99/12, San Domenico di Fiesole (FI): European University Institute.

Grabbe, Heather (2001a) 'How does Europeanisation Affect CEE Governance? Conditionality, Diffusion and Diversity', *Journal of European Public Policy*, vol. 8, no. 6 (December), pp. 1013–31.

Grabbe, Heather (2001b) *Profiting from EU Enlargement*. London: Centre for European Reform.

Gurr, Ted (1991) 'The Transformation of the Western State: The Growth of Democracy, Autocracy and State Power since 1800', in Alex Inkeles (ed.), *On Measuring Democracy*. New Brunswick: Transaction, pp. 69–104.

Hankiss, Elemer (1990) *East European Alternatives*. Oxford: Clarendon Press.

Hanley, Eric, Petr Mateju, Klara Vlachova and Jindrich Krejci (1998) 'The Making of Post-Communist Elites in Eastern Europe', *Social Trends*, Working Paper No. 4.

Hanley, Sean (1999) 'The New Right in the New Europe? Unravelling the Ideology of "Czech Thatcherism"', *Journal of Political Ideologies*, vol. 4, no. 2 (June), pp. 163–90.

Hanley, Sean (2001) 'Towards Breakthrough or Breakdown? The Consolidation of KSCM as a Neo-Communist Successor Party in the Czech Republic', *Journal of Communist Studies and Transition Politics*, vol. 17, no. 3 (September), pp. 96–116.

Haughton, Tim (2001) 'HZDS: The Ideology, Organisation and Support Base of Slovakia's Most Successful Party', *Europe-Asia Studies*, vol. 53, no. 5 (July), pp. 745–69.

Haughton, Tim (2002) 'Slovakia's Robert Fico: A Man to be Trusted or Feared?', *East European Perspectives*, vol. 4, no. 11.

Hausner, Jerzy *et al.* (eds) (1995) *Strategic Choice and Path-Dependency in Post-Socialism*. Cheltenham: Edward Elgar.

Hayden, Jacqueline (2001) 'Explaining the Collapse of Communism in Poland: Strategic Misperceptions and Unanticipated Outcomes', *The Journal of Communist Studies and Transition Politics*, vol. 17, no. 2 (June), pp. 108–29.

Heidar, Knut and Ruud Koole (eds) (2000) *Parliamentary Party Groups in European Democracies. Political Parties Behind Closed Doors.* London: Routledge.

Hellman, Joel (1996) 'Constitutions and Economic Reform in the Postcommunist Transitions', *East European Constitutional Review*, vol. 5, no. 1 (Winter), pp. 46–56.

Henderson, Karen (1995) 'Czechoslovakia: The Failure of Consensus Politics and the Break-Up of the Federation', *Regional and Federal Studies*, vol. 5, no. 2 (Summer), pp. 111–33.

Henderson, Karen (ed.) (1999) *Back to Europe: Central and Eastern Europe and the European Union*. London: UCL Press.

Henderson, Karen (2002) *Slovakia*. London: Routledge.

Henn, Matt (2001) 'Opinion Polls, Political Elites and Party Competition in Post-Communist Bulgaria', *Journal of Communist Studies and Transition Politics*, vol.17, no. 3 (September), pp. 52–70.

Higley, John and G. Lengyel (eds) (2000) *Elites After State Socialism*. Lanham, MD: Rowman & Littlefield.

Higley, John and Michael G. Burton (1997) 'Types of Political Elites in Postcommunist Eastern Europe', *International Politics*, vol. 34, no. 2 (June), pp. 153–68.

Higley, John, Judith Kullberg and Jan Pakulski (1996) 'The Persistence of Postcommunist Elites', *Journal of Democracy*, vol. 7, no. 2 (April), pp. 133–47.

Higley, John, Jan Pakulski and Wlodzimierz Wesolowski (eds) (1998) *Postcommunist Elites and Democracy in Eastern Europe*. London: Macmillan.

Holmes, Leslie (1997) *Post-Communism: An Introduction*. Durham, NC: Duke University Press.

Horejsi, Tomas (2002) 'CSSD posili Bezpecnostni radu statu', *Lidove noviny*, 24 July.

Howard, Dick (ed.) (1993) *Constitution Making in Eastern Europe*. Baltimore, MD: Johns Hopkins University Press.

Hughes, James, Gwendolyn Sasse and Claire Gordon (2001), 'Enlargement and Regionalization: The Europeanization of Local and Regional Governance in CEE States', in Helen Wallace (ed.), *Interlocking Dimensions of European Integration*. Basingstoke: Palgrave.

Ilonszki, Gabriella (1998) 'Representation Deficit in a New Democracy: Theoretical Considerations and the Hungarian Case', *Communist and Post-Communist Studies*, vol. 31, no. 2 (June), pp. 157–70.

Ilonszki, Gabriella (2000) 'Parties and Parliamentary Party Groups in the Making: Hungary, 1989–1997', in Knut Heidar and Ruud Koole (eds), *Parliamentary Party Groups in European Democracies: Political Parties Behind Closed Doors*. London: Routledge, pp. 214–30.

Ingham, Hilary and Mike Ingham (eds) (2002) *EU Expansion to the East: Prospects and Problems*. Cheltenham: Edward Elgar.

Ingrao, C. (1999) 'Understanding Ethnic Conflict in Central Europe: An Historical Perspective', *Nationalities Papers*, vol. 27, no. 2 (9 June), pp. 291–318.

Innes, Abby (2001) *Czechoslovakia: The Short Goodbye*. New Haven and London: Yale University Press.

International Crisis Group (1999) *Is Dayton Failing?*. Brussels: International Crisis Group.

International Crisis Group (2002) *Macedonia's Public Secret: How Corruption Drags the Country Down*. Brussels: International Crisis Group.

International Institute for Democracy (1996) *The Rebirth of Democracy: 12 Constitutions of Central and Eastern Europe*, 2nd edn. Strasbourg: Council of Europe Press.

International Institute for Democracy (1997) *Transition to Democracy: Constitutions of the New Independent States and Mongolia*. Strasbourg: Council of Europe Press.

Ishiyama, John T. and Matthew Velten (1998) 'Presidential Power and Democratic Development in Post-Communist Politics', *Communist and Post-Communist Studies*, vol. 31, no. 3 (September), pp. 217–33.

Jakubowicz, Karol (1996) 'Media Legislation as a Mirror of Democracy', *Transitions*, vol. 2, no. 21, p. 21.

Janos, Andrew (1982) *The Politics of Backwardness in Hungary 1825–1945*. Princeton, NJ: Princeton University Press.

Janos, Andrew (2000) *East Central Europe in the Modern World. The Politics of the Borderlands from Pre- to Post-Communism*. Stanford, CA: Stanford University Press.

Jasiewicz, Krzysztof (1997) 'Poland: Walesa's Legacy to the Presidency', in Ray Taras (ed.), *Postcommunist Presidents*. Cambridge: Cambridge University Press, pp. 130–68.

Jasiewicz, Krzysztof (1998) 'Elections and Voting Behaviour', in Stephen White, Judy Batt and Paul G. Lewis (eds), *Developments in Central and East European Politics 2*. Basingstoke: Macmillan; and Durham, NC: Duke University Press, pp.166–87.

Jasiewicz, Krzysztof (1999) 'Polish Politics after the 1997 Election: Polarization or Pluralism?', *Soviet and Post-Soviet Review*, vol. 26, no. 1–2, pp. 93–114.

Jaster, Georg (1994) *Der polnische Beauftragte für Bürgerrechte*. Baden-Baden: Nomos.

Jaszi, Oszkar (1923) 'Dismembered Hungary and Peace in Central Europe', *Foreign Affairs*, vol. 2, no. 2 (December), pp. 270–81.

Juberías, Carlos Flores (1998) 'Electoral Legislation and Ethnic Minorities in Eastern Europe: For or Against?', in Lawrence D. Longley and Drago Zajc (eds), *The New Democratic Parliaments: The First Years*. Appleton: Research Committee of Legislative Specialists, IPSA, pp. 297–318.

Kaldor, M. and I. Vejvoda (1999) *Democratization in Central and Eastern Europe*. London: Pinter.

Kaliska, Gabriela (2002). 'V nedelu sa dozvieme, aky bude novy parlament', *Pravda*, 20 September.

Kaminski, Bartlomiej (1991) *The Collapse of State Socialism: The Case of Poland*. Princeton, NJ: Princeton University Press.

Karasimeonov, Georgi (1996) 'The Legislature in Post-Communist Bulgaria', *The Journal of Legislative Studies*, vol. 2, no. 1 (Spring), pp. 40–59.

Karatnycky, Adrian (ed.) (2001) *Freedom in the World: The Annual Survey of Political Rights and Civil Liberties*. New York: Freedom House.

Karatnycky, Adrian (2002) 'The 2001 Freedom House Survey', *Journal of Democracy*, vol. 13, no. 1 (January), pp. 99–112.

Kask, Peet (1996) 'Institutional Development of the Parliament in Estonia', *The Journal of Legislative Studies*, vol. 2, no. 1 (Spring), pp. 193–212.

Bibliography

)hn (2001) *Vaclav Havel: A Political Tragedy in Six Acts.*
rk: Basic Books.

_____ nos (1996) *Kis Allambiztonsagi Olvasokonyv. Oktober 23.–Marcius 15–Junius 16 a Kadar korszakban.* Budapest: Magveto.

King, Charles (2000) *The Moldovans: Romania, Russia, and the Politics of Culture.* Stanford, CA: Hoover Institution Press.

Kitschelt, Herbert (1992) 'The Formation of Party Systems in East Central Europe', *Politics and Society*, vol. 20, no. 1 (March), pp. 7–50.

Kitschelt, Herbert, Zdenka Mansfeldova, Radoslaw Markowski and Gabor Toka (1999) *Post-Communist Party Systems: Competition, Representation, and Inter-Party Cooperation.* Cambridge and New York: Cambridge University Press.

Kolodko, Grzegorz (2000) *From Shock to Therapy: The Political Economy of Postsocialist Transformation.* Oxford: Oxford University Press.

Kopecky, Petr (2001) *Parliaments in the Czech and Slovak Republics: Party Competition and Parliamentary Institutionalization.* Aldershot: Ashgate.

Kopecky, Petr and Cas Mudde (2000) 'Explaining Different Paths of Democratization: The Czech and Slovak Republics', *Journal of Communist Studies and Transition Politics*, vol. 16, no. 3 (September), pp. 63–84.

Korecky, Miroslav and Ondrej Bilek (2002) 'Snemovna byla tovarnou na zakony', *Lidove noviny*, 10 May.

Kornai, Janos (1980) *The Economics of Shortage.* Amsterdam: North-Holland.

Korosenyi, Andras (1999) *Government and Politics in Hungary*, trans. Alan Renwick. Budapest: CEU-Osiris.

Korosteleva, Elena A., Colin W. Lawson and Rosalind J. Marsh (eds) (2003) *Contemporary Belarus: Between Democracy and Dictatorship.* London and New York: RoutledgeCurzon.

Kosovo Report (2000) Oxford: Independent International Commission on Kosovo.

Koudelka, Frantisek (2000) 'Husakuv pad 1987', *Soudobe dejiny*, vol. 7, no. 3, pp. 473–525.

Kowalik, Tadeusz (2001) 'The Ugly Face of Polish Success: Social Aspects of Transformation', in George Blazyca and Ryszard Rapacki (eds), *Poland into the New Millennium.* Cheltenham: Edward Elgar.

Kozul-Wright, Richard and Paul Rayment (1997) 'The Institutional Hiatus in Economies in Transition and its Policy Consequences', *Cambridge Journal of Economics*, vol. 21, no. 5 (September), pp. 641–66.

Kramer, M. (1997) 'Social Protection Policies and Safety Nets in East Central Europe: Dilemmas of the Postcommunist Transformation', in E. Kapstein and M. Mandelbaum (eds), *Sustaining the Transition: The Social Safety Net in Postcommunist Europe.* New York: Council on Foreign Relations.

Kraus, Michael and Alison Stanger (eds) (2000) *Irreconcilable Differences? Explaining Czechoslovakia's Dissolution.* Lanham, MD: Rowman & Littlefield.

Kumar, K. (2001) *1989: Revolutionary Ideas and Ideals.* Minneapolis, MN: University of Minnesota Press.

Kundera, Milan (1984) 'The Tragedy of Central Europe', *New York Review of Books*, 26 April, pp. 33–8.

Kurski, Jaroslaw (1993) *Lech Walesa: Democrat or Dictator?*. Boulder, CO: Westview Press.

Kuzio, Taras and Andrew Wilson (1994) *Ukraine: Perestroika to Independence.* London: Macmillan.

Landfried, Christine (ed.) (1988) *Constitutional Review and Legislation. An International Comparison.* Baden-Baden: Nomos.

Lane, Jan-Erik (1996) *Constitutions and Political Theory.* Manchester: Manchester University Press.

Lane, Jan-Erik and Svante Ersson (2000) *The New Institutional Politics: Performances and Outcomes.* London: Routledge.

Lasswell, Harold D. (1986) 'Democratic Leadership', in Barbara Kellerman (ed.), *Political Leadership.* Pittsburgh, PA: University of Pittsburgh Press.

Lavigne, Marie (1999a) *The Economics of Transition: From Socialist Economy to Market Economy*, 2nd edn. Basingstoke: Palgrave.

Lavigne, Marie (1999b) 'Conditions for EU Entry: The Transition Economies', in Jozef M. van Brabant (ed.), *Remaking Europe: The European Union and the Transition Economies.* Lanham, MD: Rowman & Littlefield.

Lehmbruch, Gerhard and Philippe Schmitter (eds) (1982) *Patterns of Corporatist Policy-Making.* London: Sage.

Lesko, Marian (2000) *Masky a tvare novej elity. Citanie o dvanastich politikoch z piatich vladnych stran.* Bratislava: Institut pre verejne otazky.

Letowska, Ewa (1995) 'The Ombudsman and Basic Rights', *East European Constitutional Review*, vol. 4, no. 1 (Winter), pp. 63–5.

Letowska, Ewa (1997) 'A Constitution of Possibilities', *East European Constitutional Review*, vol. 6, no. 2/3 (Spring/Summer), pp. 76–81.

Lewis, Paul G. (1990) 'Non-Competitive Elections and Regime Change: Poland 1989', *Parliamentary Affairs*, vol. 43, no. 1 (January), pp. 90–107.

Lewis, Paul G. (ed.) (1996) *Party Structure and Organization in East-Central Europe.* Cheltenham: Edward Elgar.

Lewis, Paul G. (1999) 'Parties and Parliaments in East Central Europe: Poland as a Trend-Setter', Paper presented at the Conference 'Ten Years After: Democratic Transition and Consolidation in East Central Europe', Budapest, 17–20 June.

Lewis, Paul G. (2000) *Political Parties in Post-Communist Eastern Europe.* London: Routledge.

Lewis, Paul G. (ed.) (2001) *Party Development and Democratic Change in Post-Communist Europe: The First Decade.* London: Frank Cass.

Liebich, Andre (1997) 'The Communists Reincarnated: Their Return in Russia and Eastern Europe', *World Affairs*, vol. 1, no. 1 (January–March), pp. 66–78.

Lieven, Anatol (1999) *Ukraine and Russia: A Fraternal Rivalry.* Washington, DC: Institute of Peace Press.

Lijphart, Arend (1991) 'Constitutional Choices for New Democracies', *Journal of Democracy*, vol. 2, no. 1 (Winter), pp. 72–84.

Linden, Ronald H. and Bert A. Rockman (eds) (1984) *Elite Studies and Communist Politics*. Pittsburgh, PA: University of Pittsburgh Press.

Linz, Juan J. and Alfred Stepan (1996) *Problems of Democratic Transition and Consolidation: Southern Europe, South America, and Post-Communist Europe*. Baltimore, MD: Johns Hopkins University Press.

Longley, Lawrence D. and Drago Zajc (eds) (1998) *The New Democratic Parliaments: The First Years*. Appleton: Research Committee of Legislative Specialists, IPSA.

Macmillan, Margaret (2001) *Peacemakers: The Paris Conference of 1919 and its Aftermath*. London: John Murray.

Magocsi, Paul Robert (1996) *A History of Ukraine*. Toronto: University of Toronto Press.

Mair, Peter and Ingrid van Biezen (2001) 'Party Membership in Twenty European Democracies', *Party Politics*, vol. 7, no. 1 (January), pp. 5–21.

Majoros, F. (1993) 'Ungarische Verfassungsgerichtsbarkeit seit 1990', *Berichte des Instituts für Osteuropa-Studien* No. 15.

Malova, Darina and Danica Sivakova (1996) 'The National Council of the Slovak Republic: Between Democratic Transition and National State-Building', *The Journal of Legislative Studies*, vol. 2, no. 1 (Spring), pp. 108–32.

Malova, Darina and Kevin Krause (2000) 'Parliamentary Party Groups in Slovakia', in Knut Heidar and Ruud Koole (eds), *Parliamentary Party Groups in European Democracies: Political Parties Behind Closed Doors*. London: Routledge, pp. 195–213.

Malova, Darina and Tim Haughton (2002) 'Making Institutions in Central and Eastern Europe, and the Impact of Europe', *West European Politics*, vol. 25, no. 2 (April), pp. 101–20.

Markowski, R. and G. Toka (1995) 'Left Turn in Poland and Hungary Five Years After the Collapse of Communism', *Sisyphus: Sociological Studies*, vol. 1(9), pp. 77–99.

Marples, David (1999) *Belarus. A Denationalised Nation*. London: Routledge.

Martin, Roderick (1998) 'Central and Eastern Europe and the International Economy: The Limits to Globalisation', *Europe-Asia Studies*, vol. 50, no. 1 (January), pp. 7–26.

Martin, Roderick (1999) *Transforming Management in Central and Eastern Europe*. Oxford: Oxford University Press.

Martin, Terry (2001) *The Affirmative Action Empire: Nations and Nationalism in the Soviet Union, 1923–1939*. Ithaca, NY: Cornell University Press.

Mason, David S. (1996) *Revolution and Transition in East-Central Europe*, 2nd edn. Boulder, CO: Westview Press.

Mateju, P., B. Rehakova and G. Evans (1999) 'The Politics of Interests and Class Realignment in the Czech Republic, 1992–96', in Geoffrey Evans (ed.), *The End of Class Politics? Class Voting in Comparative Context*. Oxford: Oxford University Press.

Mayhew, Alan (1998) *Recreating Europe: The European Union's Policy toward Central and Eastern Europe*. Cambridge: Cambridge University Press.

Mazower, Mark (1998) *Dark Continent. Europe's Twentieth Century*. London: Penguin.

Mazower, Mark (2000) *The Balkans*. London: Weidenfeld & Nicolson.

McCauley, Martin and Stephen Carter (eds) (1986) *Leadership and Succession in the Soviet Union, Eastern Europe and China*. Armonk, NY: Sharpe.

Merkel, Wolfgang (1999) 'Defekte Demokratien', in Merkel and Andreas Busch (eds), *Demokratie in Ost und West*. Frankfurt: Suhrkamp, pp. 361–81.

Merkel, Wolfgang, Hans-Jurgen Puhle *et al.* (2002) *Defekte Demokratien. Theorien und Analysen*. Opladen: Leske und Budrich.

Mickiewicz, Tomasz and Janice Bell (2000) *Unemployment in Transition: Restructuring and Labour Markets in Central Europe*. Amsterdam: Harwood Academic Publishers.

Milanovich, B. (1998) *Income, Inequality and Poverty during the Transition from Planned to Market Economy*. Washington, DC: World Bank.

Millard, Frances (1999) *Polish Politics and Society*. London: Routledge.

Millard, Frances (2000) 'Presidents and Democratization in Poland: The Roles of Lech Walesa and Aleksander Kwasniewski in Building a New Polity', *The Journal of Communist Studies and Transition Politics*, vol. 16, no. 2 (June), pp. 39–62.

Millard, Frances (2003) 'Elections in Poland 2001: Electoral Manipulation and Party Upheaval', *Communist and Post-Communist Studies* (March 2003).

Miller, William L., Ase B. Grodeland and Tatyana Y. Koshechkina (2001) *A Culture of Corruption? Coping with Government in Post-Communist Europe*. Budapest: Central European University Press.

Mirčev, Dimitar and Igor Spirovski (1998) 'The Role and Early Experiences of the Macedonia Parliament in the Process of Transition', in Lawrence D. Longley and Drago Zajc (eds), *The New Democratic Parliaments: The First Years*. Appleton: Research Committee of Legislative Specialists, IPSA, pp. 111–24.

Moroney, Jennifer, Taras Kuzio and Mikhail Molchanov (eds) (2002) *Ukrainian Foreign and Security Policy: Theoretical and Comparative Perspectives*. Westport, CT: Praeger.

Motyl, Alexander (1993) *Dilemmas of Independence: Ukraine After Totalitarianism*. New York: Council on Foreign Relations.

Müller-Rommel, Ferdinand and Darina Malova (2001) 'Slovakia', in Jean Blondel and Müller-Rommel (eds), *Cabinets in Eastern Europe*. Basingstoke: Palgrave, pp. 73–83.

Müller-Rommel, Ferdinand and Zdenka Mansfeldova (2001) 'Czech Republic', in Jean Blondel and Müller-Rommel (eds), *Cabinets in Eastern Europe*. Basingstoke: Palgrave, pp. 62–72.

Musil, Jiri (1995) 'Czech and Slovak Society', in J. Musil (ed.), *The End of Czechoslovakia*. Budapest: Central European University Press, pp. 77–94.

Nagle, John D. and Alison Mahr (1999) *Democracy and Democratization: Post-Communist Europe in Comparative Perspective.* London: Sage.

Nahaylo, Bohdan (1999) *The Ukrainian Resurgence.* London: Hurst.

Nelson, Daniel and Stephen White (eds) (1982) *Communist Legislatures in Comparative Perspective.* London: Macmillan; and Albany, NY: SUNY Press.

North, Douglass C. (1992) *Institutions, Institutional Change, and Economic Performance.* Cambridge and New York: Cambridge University Press.

Norton, Philip (1990) 'General Introduction', in Norton (ed.), *Legislatures.* Oxford: Oxford University Press, pp. 1–16.

Nove, Alec (1977) *The Soviet Economic System.* London: George Allen & Unwin.

O'Donnell, Guillermo (1979) *Modernization and Bureaucratic-Authoritarianism.* Berkeley: University of California Press.

O'Donnell, Guillermo, Philippe C. Schmitter and Laurence Whitehead (eds) (1986) *Transitions From Authoritarian Rule: Tentative Conclusions about Uncertain Democracies.* Baltimore, MD: Johns Hopkins University Press.

OECD (1998) *Poverty and Targeting of Social Assistance in Eastern Europe and the Former Soviet Union.* Paris: OECD.

Olson, David (1994a) 'The Sundered State: Federalism and Parliament in Czechoslovakia', in Thomas F. Remington (ed.), *Parliaments in Transition: The New Legislative Politics in the Former USSR and Eastern Europe.* Boulder, CO: Westview Press, pp. 97–123.

Olson, David M. (1994b) 'The New Parliaments of New Democracies: The Experience of the Federal Assembly of the Czech and Slovak Federal Republic', in Attila Agh (ed.), *The Emergence of East Central European Parliaments: The First Steps.* Budapest: Hungarian Centre of Democracy Studies Foundation, pp. 35–47.

Olson, David M. (1997) 'Paradoxes of Institutional Development: The New Democratic Parliaments of Central Europe', *International Political Science Review*, vol. 18, no. 4 (October), pp. 401–16.

Olson, David M. (1998) 'The Parliaments of New Democracies and the Politics of Representation', in Stephen White, Judy Batt and Paul G. Lewis (eds), *Developments in Central and East European Politics 2.* Basingstoke: Macmillan; and Durham, NC: Duke University Press, pp. 126–46.

Olson, David M. and Philip Norton (eds) (1996) *The New Parliaments of Central and Eastern Europe.* London: Frank Cass.

Olson, David M. and William E. Crowther (eds) (2002) *Committees in Post-Communist Democratic Parliaments. Comparative Institutionalization.* Columbus: Ohio State University Press.

O'Neil, Patrick H. (1996a) 'Revolution from Within: Institutional Analysis, Transitions from Authoritarianism, and the Case of Hungary', *World Politics*, vol. 48, no. 4 (July), pp. 579–603.

O'Neil, Patrick H. (ed.) (1996b) 'Post-Communism and the Media in Eastern Europe', special issue of the *Journal of Communist Studies and Transition Politics*, vol. 12, no. 4 (December).

O'Neil, Patrick (1998) *Revolution from Within. The Hungarian Socialist Workers' Party and the Collapse of Communism.* Cheltenham, and Northampton, MA: Edward Elgar.

Open Society Institute/EU Accession Monitoring Programme (2001a) *Monitoring the EU Accession Process: Judicial Independence.* Budapest: Central European University Press.

Open Society Institute/EU Accession Monitoring Programme (2001b) *Monitoring the EU Accession Process: Minority Protection.* Budapest: Central European University Press.

Pehe, Jiri (2002) 'Czech Elections: Victory for a New Generation', *East European Perspectives*, vol. 4, no. 17, 21 August.

Petrova, Dimitrina (1996) 'Political and Legal Obstacles to the Development of Public Interest Law', *East European Constitutional Review*, vol. 5, no. 4 (Fall), pp. 62–70.

Plasser, Fritz, Harald Waldrauch and Peter Ulram (1998) *Democratic Consolidation in East-Central Europe.* Basingstoke: Macmillan.

Pontusson, Jonas (1992) 'Sweden', in Mark Kesselman and Joel Krieger (eds), *European Politics in Transition.* Lexington, MA and Toronto: Heath.

Popov, Nebojsa (2000) *The Road to War in Serbia: Trauma and Catharsis.* Budapest: Central European University Press.

Posner, Richard A. (1995) 'The Costs of Enforcing Legal Rights', *East European Constitutional Review*, vol. 4, no. 3 (Summer), pp. 71–83.

Priban, Jiri (2001) *Disidenti prava. O revolucich roku 1989, fikcich legality a soudobe verzi spolecenske smlouvy.* Prague: Sociologicke nakladatelstvi.

Pridham, Geoffrey (2000) *The Dynamics of Democratization: A Comparative Approach.* London: Continuum.

Pridham, Geoffrey (2002) 'Coalition Behaviour in New Democracies of Central and Eastern Europe: The Case of Slovakia', *Journal of Communist Studies and Transition Politics*, vol. 18, no. 2 (June), pp. 75–102.

Pridham, Geoffrey and Attila Agh (eds) (2001) *Prospects for Democratic Consolidation in East-Central Europe.* Manchester: Manchester University Press.

Pridham, Geoffrey and Tom Gallagher (eds) (2000) *Experimenting with Democracy: Regime Change in the Balkans.* London: Routledge.

Pridham, Geoffrey, Eric Herring and George Sanford (eds) (1997) *Building Democracy? The International Dimension of Democratisation in Eastern Europe.* London: Leicester University Press.

Prizel, I. (1998) *National Identity and Foreign Policy: Nationalism and Leadership in Poland, Russia and Ukraine.* Cambridge and New York: Cambridge University Press.

Przeworski, Adam (1992) *Democracy and the Market.* Cambridge and New York: Cambridge University Press.

Racz, Barnabas (1993) 'The Socialist-Left Opposition in Post-Communist Hungary', *Europe-Asia Studies*, vol. 45, no. 4, pp. 647–70.

Ragaru, Nadege (2001) 'Islam in Post-Communist Bulgaria: An Aborted "Clash of Civilizations"', *Nationalities Papers*, vol. 29, no. 2 (June), pp. 293–324.

Ramet, Sabrina Petra (1992) *Nationalism and Federalism in Yugoslavia, 1962–1991*, 2nd edn. Bloomington: Indiana University Press.

Randall, Vicky and Lars Svåsand (2002) 'Party Institutionalization in New Democracies', *Party Politics*, vol. 8, no. 1 (January), pp. 5–29.

Rapacki, Ryszard (2001) 'Economic Performance 1989–99 and Prospects for the Future', in George Blazyca and Rapacki (eds), *Poland into the New Millennium*. Cheltenham: Edward Elgar.

Remington, Thomas (ed.) (1994) *Parliaments in Transition*. Boulder, CO: Westview Press.

Rigby, T.H. and Ferenc Feher (eds) (1982) *Political Legitimation in Communist States*. New York: St. Martin's Press.

Riker, W. H. (1986) 'Duverger's Law Revisited', in Bernard Grofman and Arend Lijphart (eds), *Electoral Laws and Their Political Consequences*. New York: Agathon Press.

Romsics, Ignac (1999) *Hungary in the Twentieth Century*, translated by Tim Wilkinson. Budapest: Corvina and Osiris.

Ronnas, Per (1995) 'Romania: Transition to Underdevelopment', in Ian Jeffries (ed.), *Problems of Economic and Political Transformation in the Balkans*. London: Pinter.

Roper, Steven D. (2002) 'The Influence of Romanian Campaign Finance Laws on Party System Development and Corruption', *Party Politics*, vol. 8, no. 2 (April), pp. 175–92.

Rose, Richard (1997) 'Rights and Obligations of Individuals in the Baltic States', *East European Constitutional Review*, vol. 6, no. 4 (Winter), pp. 35–43.

Rose, Richard (2002) 'A Bottom Up Evaluation of Enlargement Countries: New Europe Barometer 1', *Studies in Public Policy*, no. 364. Glasgow: Centre for Public Policy, University of Strathclyde.

Rose, Richard and William Mishler (1996) 'Representation and Leadership in Post-Communist Political Systems,' *Journal of Communist Studies and Transition Politics*, vol. 12, no. 2 (June), pp. 224–46.

Rose, Richard, William Mishler and Christian Haerpfer (1998) *Democracy and its Alternatives: Understanding Post-Communist Societies*. Baltimore, MD: Johns Hopkins Press.

Rothschild, Joseph (1974) *East-Central Europe between the Two World Wars*. Seattle, WA: University of Washington Press.

Rothschild, Joseph and Nancy M. Wingfield (2000) *Return to Diversity*, 3rd edn. New York: Oxford University Press.

Rub, Friedbert W. (1994) ' "Schach dem Parlament". Über semi-präsidentielle Systeme Regierungssysteme in einigen postkommunistischen Gesellschaften', *Leviathan*, vol. 22, no. 2, pp. 260–92.

Rupnik, Jacques (1990) 'Central Europe or Mitteleuropa?', *Daedalus*, vol. 119, no. 1 (Winter), pp. 249–78.

Rush, Myron (1974) *How Communist States Change Their Rulers*. Ithaca, NY: Cornell University Press.

Rychard, A. (1992) 'Politics and Society after the Breakthrough: The Sources and Threats to Political Legitimacy in Post-Communist Poland', in George Sanford, ed., *Democratisation in Poland, 1988–90*. London: Macmillan; and New York: St. Martin's Press.

Sachs, Jeffrey (1993) *Poland's Jump to the Market Economy.* Cambridge, MA: MIT Press.

Sakwa, Richard (1999) *Postcommunism.* Buckingham: Open University Press.

Sanford, George (1999) *Poland: the Conquest of History.* Amsterdam: Harwood Academic Publishers.

Sanford, George (2002) *Democratic Government in Poland.* Basingstoke: Palgrave.

Saxonberg, Steven (2001) *The Fall: A Comparative Study of the End of Communism in Czechoslovakia, East Germany, Hungary and Poland.* Amsterdam: Harwood.

Schedler, Andreas (1998) 'What is Democratic Consolidation?', *Journal of Democracy*, vol. 9, no. 2 (April), pp. 91–107.

Schleifer, Andre (1997) *Government in Transition.* Cambridge, MA: Harvard Institute for International Development, Harvard University.

Schmitter, Philippe (1988) 'The Consolidation of Political Democracy in Southern Europe', unpublished manuscript.

Schmitter, Phillipe (1992) 'Interest Systems and the Consolidation of Democracy', in Gary Marks and Larry Diamond (eds), *Reexamining Democracy.* London: Sage, pp. 156–81.

Schöpflin, George and Nancy Wood (eds) (1989) *In Search of Central Europe.* Oxford: Polity Press.

Schumpeter, Joseph A. (1976) *Capitalism, Socialism and Democracy.* London: George Allen & Unwin.

Schwartz, Herman (2000) *The Struggle for Constitutional Justice in Post-Communist Europe.* Chicago: University of Chicago Press.

Schweissfurth, Theodor and Ralf Alleweldt (1997) 'Die neuen Verfassungsstrukturen in Osteuropa', in Georg Brunner (ed.), *Politische und ökonomische Transformation in Osteuropa*, 2nd edn. Berlin: Arno Spitz.

Sedelmeier, Ulrich and Helen Wallace (2000) 'Eastern Enlargement', in Helen Wallace and William Wallace (eds), *Policy-making in the European Union*, 4th edn. Oxford: Oxford University Press, pp. 427–60.

Seewann, Gerhard (ed.) (1995) *Minderheiten als Konfliktpotential in Ostmittel- und Südosteuropa.* Munich: Oldenbourg.

Shepherd, Robin H.E. (2000) *Czechoslovakia: The Velvet Revolution and Beyond.* Basingstoke: Macmillan.

Shlapentokh, Vladimir, Christopher Vanderpool and Boris Doktorov (eds) (1999) *The New Elites in Post-Communist Eastern Europe.* College Station, TX: A&M. University Press.

Shvetsova, Olga (1999) 'A Survey of Post-Communist Electoral Institutions, 1990–1998', *Electoral Studies*, vol. 18, no. 3 (September), pp. 397–409.

Skalnik Leff, Carol (1996) *The Czech and Slovak Republics: Nation versus State.* Boulder, CO: Westview Press.

Slosarcik, Ivo (2001) 'The Reform of the Constitutional Systems of Czechoslovakia and the Czech Republic in 1990–2000', *European Public Law*, vol. 7, no. 4 (December), pp. 529–47.

Spiewak, Pawel (1997) 'The Battle for a Constitution', *East European Constitutional Review* (Spring/Summer), pp. 89–96.

Staar, Richard (ed.) (1998) *Transition to Democracy in Poland*, 2nd edn. Basingstoke: Macmillan.

Staniszkis, Jadwiga (1991) *The Dynamics of Breakthrough*. Berkeley: University of California Press.

Stark David and Laszlo Bruszt (1998) *Postsocialist Pathways: Transforming Politics and Property in East Central Europe*. Cambridge and New York: Cambridge University Press.

Stein, Eric (1997) *Czecho/Slovakia: Ethnic Conflict, Constitutional Fissure, Negotiated Breakup*. Ann Arbor: University of Michigan Press.

Steinberg, R. (1995) 'Die neuen Verfassungen der baltischen Staaten', *Jahrbuch für öffentliches Recht*, vol. 43, pp. 55–67.

Stephens, Philip (1997) 'The Glass Wall', *Financial Times*, 14 November, p. 14.

Stiglitz, Joseph (2002) *Globalization and its Discontents*. London: Allen Lane.

Stokes, Gale (1997) *Three Eras of Political Change in Eastern Europe*. New York and Oxford: Oxford University Press.

Subtelny, Orest (2000) *Ukraine: A History*, 3rd edn. Toronto: University of Toronto Press.

Sunstein, Cass R. (1995) 'A Constitutional Anomaly in the Czech Republic?', *East European Constitutional Review* (Spring), pp. 50–1.

Sunstein, Cass R. *et al.* (1995) 'Rights After Communism', *East European Constitutional Review* (Winter), pp. 61–9.

Swain, Geoffrey and Nigel Swain (1998) *Eastern Europe since 1945*, 2nd edn. London: Macmillan.

Swain, Nigel (1985) *Collective Farms Which Work?*. Cambridge and New York: Cambridge University Press.

Swain, Nigel (1992) *Hungary: The Rise and Fall of Feasible Socialism*. London: Verso.

Szalai, E. (1999) *Post-Socialism and Globalization*. Budapest: Uj Mandatum.

Szalai, Julia (1996) 'Why the Poor are Poor', *The Hungarian Quarterly*, vol. 37, no. 144.

Szalai, Julia (1998), 'Women and Democratization: Some Notes on Recent Changes in Hungary', in Jane S. Jaquette and Sharon L. Wolchik (eds), *Women and Democracy: Latin America and Central and Eastern Europe*. Baltimore, MD: Johns Hopkins University Press, pp. 185–202.

Szczerbiak, Aleks (2000) 'Public Opinion and Eastward Enlargement. Explaining Declining Support for EU Membership in Poland', Working Papers on Contemporary European Studies No. 34, Sussex European Institute, University of Sussex.

Szczerbiak, Aleks (2001a) *Poles Together? Emergence and Development of Political Parties in Post-communist Poland*. Budapest: Central European University Press.

Szczerbiak, Aleks (2001b) 'Explaining Kwasniewski's Landslide: The October 2000 Polish Presidential Election', *Journal of Communist Studies and Transition Politics*, vol. 17, no. 4 (December), pp. 78–107.

Szelenyi, Ivan and Szonya Szelenyi (1991) 'The Vacuum in Hungarian Politics – Classes and Parties', *New Left Review*, no. 187 (May–June), pp. 121–37.

Szelenyi, Ivan, Eva Fodor and Eric Hanley (1997) 'Left Turn in Post-Communist Politics: Bringing the Class Back In?', *East European Politics and Society*, vol. 11, no. 1 (Winter), pp. 190–224.

Szoboszlai, Gyorgy (1990) *Parlamenti Valasztasok 1990. Politikai Szociologiai Korkep*. Budapest: MTA Politikatudomanyi Intezet.

Taras, Ray (ed.) (1989) *Leadership Change in Communist States*. Boston, MA: Unwin Hyman.

Taras, Raymond (1995) *Consolidating Democracy in Poland*. Boulder: Westview Press.

Taras, Ray (ed.) (1998) *Postcommunist Presidents*. Cambridge and New York: Cambridge University Press.

Ticktin, Hillel H. (1993) 'The Growth of an Impossible Capitalism', *Critique*, no. 25, pp. 119–32.

Tittenbrun, Jacek (1993) *The Collapse of 'Real Socialism' in Poland*. London: Janus.

Toka, Gabor (1997) 'Political Parties in East Central Europe', in L. Diamond, M.F. Plattner, Yun-han Chu and Hung-mao Tien (eds), *Consolidating the Third Wave Democracies*. Baltimore, MD: Johns Hopkins University Press.

Tokes, Rudolf L. (1990) 'Hungary's New Political Elites: Adaptation and Change, 1989–1990', *Problems of Communism*, vol. 39, no. 6 (November–December), pp. 44–65.

Tokes, Rudolf L. (1996) *Hungary's Negotiated Revolution: Economic Reform, Social Change and Political Succession*. Cambridge and New York: Cambridge University Press.

Tucker, Robert C. (1981) *Politics as Leadership*. Columbia, MO: University of Missouri Press.

Tworzecki, Hubert (1996) *Parties and Politics in Post-1989 Poland*. Boulder, CO: Westview Press.

Tworzecki, Hubert (2002) *Learning to Choose: Electoral Politics in East-Central Europe*. Stanford, CA: Stanford University Press.

Ulram, Peter and Fritz Plasser (2001) 'Mainly Sunny with Scattered Clouds: Political Culture in East-Central Europe', in Geoffrey Pridham and Attila Agh (eds), *Prospects for Democratic Consolidation in East-Central Europe*. Manchester: Manchester University Press, pp. 115–37.

UNECE (2002) *Economic Survey of Europe* No. 1.

Vachudova, Milada Anna (2001) 'The Czech Republic: The Unexpected Force of Institutional Constraints', in Jan Zielonka and Alex Pravda (eds), *Democratic Consolidation in Eastern Europe*. Volume 2: *International and Transnational Forces*. Oxford: Oxford University Press, pp. 325–62.

Van der Meer Krok-Paszkowska, Ania (2000) *Shaping the Democratic Order. The Institutionalisation of Parliament in Poland.* Leuven: Garant.

Van Zon, Hans (2001) 'Neo-Patrimonialism as an Impediment to Economic Development: The Case of Ukraine', *Journal of Communist Studies and Transition Politics*, vol. 17, no. 3 (September), pp. 71–95.

Varga, Zsuzsanna (2001) *Politika, paraszti erdekervenyesites es szovetkezetek Magyarorszagon 1956–1967.* Budapest: Napvilag Kiado.

Vickers, Miranda and James Pettifer (1997) *Albania: From Anarchy to a Balkan Identity.* London: Hurst.

von Beyme, Klaus (1968) *Die verfassunggebende Gewalt des Volkes.* Tübingen: Mohr.

von Beyme, Klaus (ed.) (1996) *Transition to Democracy in Eastern Europe.* Basingstoke: Macmillan.

von Beyme, Klaus (2001a) *Russland zwischen Anarchie und Autokratie.* Wiesbaden: Westdeutscher Verlag.

von Beyme, Klaus (2001b) 'Parties in the Process of Consolidation in East-Central Europe', in Geoffrey Pridham and Attila Agh (eds), *Prospects for Democratic Consolidation in East-Central Europe.* Manchester: Manchester University Press.

Waele, Jean-Michel de (ed.) (2002) *Partis politiques et démocratie en Europe centrale et orientale.* Brussels: Editions de l'Université de Bruxelles.

Wagstyl, Stefan (1999), 'Effects of Russian Storm Shrugged Off', *Financial Times: World Economy and Finance Supplement*, 24 September.

Wenzel, Michal (1998) 'Solidarity and Akcja Wyborcza Solidarnosc – An Attempt at Reviving the Legend', *Communist and Post-Communist Studies*, vol. 31, no. 2 (June), pp. 139–56.

Wesolowski, Wlodzimierz (2000) 'Democratic and National-Liberal Leadership in Times of Transformation', *Polish Sociological Review*, vol. 4 (132), pp. 367–86.

Wheaton, Bernard and Zdenek Kavan (1992) *The Velvet Revolution: Czechoslovakia, 1988–1991.* Boulder, CO: Westview Press.

White, Stephen and Daniel N. Nelson (eds) (2001) *The Politics of the Postcommunist World*, 2 vols. Aldershot and Burlington, VT: Ashgate.

White, Stephen, Elena Korosteleva and John Löwenhardt (eds) (forthcoming) *Postcommunist Belarus.*

Whitehead, Laurence (1997) 'East-Central Europe in Comparative Perspective', in Geoffrey Pridham, Eric Herring and George Sanford (eds), *Building Democracy? The International Dimension of Democratisation in Eastern Europe.* London: Cassell, pp. 30–55.

Wiener, Gyorgy (1998) 'Valasztas es rendszervaltas – 1990', in Gyorgy Foldes and Laszlo Hubai (eds), *Parlamenti Valasztasok Magyarorszagon 1920–1998.* Budapest: Napvilag Kiado, pp. 297–328.

Wightman, Gordon (1998) 'Parties and Politics', in Stephen White, Judy Batt and Paul G. Lewis (eds), *Developments in Central and East European Politics 2.* London: Macmillan; and Durham, NC: Duke University Press, pp. 147–65.

Wiles, Peter (1982) 'Zero Growth and the International Nature of the Polish Disease', in Jan Drewnowski (ed.), *Crisis in the East European Economy: The Spread of the Polish Disease*. London: Croom Helm.

Williams, Kieran (1997) 'National Myths in the New Czech Liberalism', in Geoffrey Hosking and George Schöpflin (eds), *Myths and Nationhood*. London: Hurst, pp. 132–40.

Williams, Kieran (2000) 'Introduction: What was Meciarism?', in Williams (ed.), *Slovakia after Communism and Meciarism*. London: SSEES.

Wilson, Andrew (2001) 'Ukraine's New Virtual Politics', *East European Constitutional Review*, vol. 10, no. 2/3 (Spring/Summer), pp. 60–6.

Wilson, Andrew (2002) *The Ukrainians: Unexpected Nation*, 2nd edn. New Haven and London: Yale University Press.

Winiecki, Jan (1988) *The Distorted World of Soviet-Type Economies*. London: Routledge.

Wojtaszczyk, K.A. (ed.) (1997) *Poland – Government and Politics*. Warsaw: Elipsa.

Wolczuk, Kataryna (2001) *The Moulding of Ukraine: The Constitutional Politics of State Formation*. Budapest: Central European University Press.

Wolczuk, Roman (2002) *Ukraine's Foreign and Security Policy, 1991–2000*. London and New York: RoutledgeCurzon.

Woldendorp, Jaap, Hans Keman and Ian Budge (2000) *Party Government in 48 Democracies (1945–1998). Composition-Duration-Personnel*. Dordrecht: Kluwer.

World Bank (1996) *World Development Report 1996: From Plan to Market*. Oxford: Oxford University Press.

World Bank (2000) *Making Transition Work for Everyone: Poverty and Inequality in Europe and Central Asia*. Washington: World Bank.

World Bank (2002) *Transition, the First Ten Years: Analysis and Lessons for Eastern Europe and the Former Soviet Union*. Washington: World Bank.

Wright, Mark [Peter Rutland] (1984) 'Ideology and Power in Czechoslovakia', in Paul Lewis (ed.), *Eastern Europe: Political Crisis and Legitimation*. London: Croom Helm, pp. 111–53.

Wyman, Matthew, Stephen White, Bill Miller and Paul Heywood (1995) 'The Place of "Party" in Post-Communist Europe', *Party Politics*, vol. 1, no. 4 (October), pp. 435–48.

Zatkuliak, Jozef (1996) *Federalizacia ceskoslovenskeho statu 1968–1970. Vznik cesko-slovenskej federacie roku 1968*. Prague and Brno: Ustav pro soudobe dejiny and Doplnek.

Zielonka, J. (ed.) (2001) *Democratic Consolidation in Eastern Europe. Volume I: Institutional Engineering*. Oxford: Oxford University Press.

Zielonka, Jan and Alex Pravda (eds) (2001) *Democratic Consolidation in Eastern Europe. Vol. 2: International and Transnational Factors*. Oxford: Oxford University Press.

Zubek, Voytek (1991) 'Walesa's Leadership and Poland's Transition', *Problems of Communism*, vol. 40, nos. 1–2 (January–April), pp. 69–83.

Index